God's Ultimate Purpose

God's Ultimate Purpose

An Exposition of Ephesians 1:1 to 23

D. M. LLOYD-JONES

THE BANNER OF TRUTH TRUST

THE BANNER OF TRUTH TRUST
3 Murrayfield Road, Edinburgh EH12 6EL
PO Box 621, Carlisle, Pennsylvania 17013, USA

© 1978 D. M. Lloyd-Jones
First published 1978
ISBN 0 85151 272 0

Printed and bound in Great Britain by
Morrison & Gibb Ltd., London and Edinburgh

Preface

This volume consists of sermons preached on Sunday mornings
in the course of my regular ministry at Westminster Chapel,
London, during 1954–1955. Some readers may be curious as to
why they did not appear in *The Westminster Record* and why they
have been preceded in book form by my sermons on Ephesians
chapter 2, under the title *God's Way of Reconciliation*, and on
chapter 5:18 to the end of this same Epistle, which have appeared
under the titles *Life in the Spirit*, *The Christian Warfare* and *The
Christian Soldier*.

The explanation is that I felt that the themes dealt with in those
volumes were of more immediate relevance. I yielded also to the
pressure that was brought upon me by those who felt that there
was an urgent need for guidance from Scripture on the general
questions of peace among nations, the problem of racism, and
the mounting problems in the realm of relationships between
husbands and wives, parents and children, masters and servants,
and also the problems raised by the cults, eastern religions and
the new interest in the occult.

I am ready to confess that in adopting this procedure I may
well have been guilty of allowing my pastoral heart to govern my
theological understanding, and especially my understanding of
the Apostle Paul's invariable method. My only defence is that in
those other volumes I have repeatedly stressed that the teaching
could only be understood in the light of the great doctrine which
the Apostle lays down in this first chapter. And now, I hope to

make full amends in this volume, and, 'God willing,' in further volumes on Chapters 3, 4 and 5 :1–18.

Our world is in a state of utter confusion, and, alas, the same is true of the Christian Church and of many individual Christians. It is idle to call people to listen to us if we are uncertain ourselves as to what we mean by the terms 'Christian' and 'Christian Church'. In this first chapter of his Epistle to the Ephesians, the Apostle deals with those very questions in a most sublime manner, reminding us at the very outset that we have been 'blessed with all spiritual blessings in heavenly places in Christ'. He goes on to tell us that this is true of Jewish and Gentile believers, that the power of the resurrection is working in each of us and in the Church which is His body. The epistle to the Ephesians is the most 'mystical' of Paul's epistles, and nowhere does his inspired mind soar to greater heights. There is no greater privilege in life than to be called to expound what Thomas Carlyle called such 'infinities and immensities'. I can but pray and trust that God will bless my unworthy efforts and use them to help many to rise to the height of 'our high calling in Christ Jesus' and deliver those whose lives have hitherto been 'bound in shallows and in miseries'.

I have to thank Miss Jane Ritchie who kindly did the original transcribing, and also as ever, Mrs E. Burney, Mr S. M. Houghton and my wife for their customary help and encouragement.

London August 1978   D. M. Lloyd-Jones

Contents

GOD'S ULTIMATE PURPOSE

Ephesians 1:1–23

1 *Paul, an apostle of Jesus Christ by the will of God, to the saints which are at Ephesus, and to the faithful in Christ Jesus:*

2 *Grace be to you, and peace, from God our Father, and from the Lord Jesus Christ.*

3 *Blessed be the God and Father of our Lord Jesus Christ, who hath blessed us with all spiritual blessings in heavenly places in Christ:*

4 *According as he hath chosen us in him before the foundation of the world, that we should be holy and without blame before him in love:*

5 *Having predestinated us unto the adoption of children by Jesus Christ to himself, according to the good pleasure of his will,*

6 *To the praise of the glory of his grace, wherein he hath made us accepted in the beloved.*

7 *In whom we have redemption through his blood, the forgiveness of sins, according to the riches of his grace;*

8 *Wherein he hath abounded toward us in all wisdom and prudence;*

9 *Having made known unto us the mystery of his will, according to his good pleasure which he hath purposed in himself:*

10 *That in the dispensation of the fulness of times he might gather together in one all things in Christ,*

both which are in heaven, and which are on earth;
even in him:

11 In whom also we have obtained an inheritance,
being predestinated according to the purpose of him
who worketh all things after the counsel of his own
will:

12 That we should be to the praise of his glory, who
first trusted in Christ.

13 In whom ye also trusted, after that ye heard the
word of truth, the gospel of your salvation: in
whom also after that ye believed, ye were sealed
with that holy Spirit of promise,

14 Which is the earnest of our inheritance until the
redemption of the purchased possession, unto the
praise of his glory.

15 Wherefore I also, after I heard of your faith in the
Lord Jesus, and love unto all the saints,

16 Cease not to give thanks for you, making mention
of you in my prayers;

17 That the God of our Lord Jesus Christ, the Father
of glory, may give unto you the spirit of wisdom
and revelation in the knowledge of him:

18 The eyes of your understanding being enlightened;
that ye may know what is the hope of his calling,
and what the riches of the glory of his inheritance
in the saints,

19 And what is the exceeding greatness of his power to
us-ward who believe, according to the working of
his mighty power,

20 Which he wrought in Christ, when he raised him
from the dead, and set him at his own right hand
in the heavenly places,

21 Far above all principality, and power, and might,
and dominion, and every name that is named, not
only in this world, but also in that which is to come:

22 And hath put all things under his feet, and gave
him to be the head over all things to the church,

23 Which is his body, the fulness of him that filleth
all in all.

I
Introduction

'Paul, an apostle of Jesus Christ by the will of God, to the saints which are at Ephesus, and to the faithful in Christ Jesus.'

Ephesians 1:1

As we approach this Epistle I confess freely that I do so with considerable temerity. It is very difficult to speak of it in a controlled manner because of its greatness and because of its sublimity. Many have tried to describe it. One writer has described it as 'the crown and climax of Pauline theology'. Another has said that it is 'the distilled essence of the Christian religion, the most authoritative and most consummate compendium of our holy Christian faith'. What language! And it is by no means exaggerated.

Far be it from me to try to compete with those who have thus described this Epistle, but it seems to me that any general description of it must take special note of certain words which are characteristic of it, and which the Apostle uses more frequently in it, perhaps, than in any other Epistle. The Apostle marvels at the mystery and the glories and the riches of God's way of redemption in Christ. These are the words, as I shall show, which he uses very frequently – the glory of it all, the mystery and the riches of God's way of redemption in Christ Jesus!

Another way in which the peculiar characteristic of this great Epistle can be stated is that it is a letter in which the Apostle looks at the Christian salvation from the vantage point of the 'heavenly places'. In all his Epistles he expounds and explains the way of salvation; he deals with particular doctrines, and with arguments or controversies that had arisen in the churches. But the peculiar feature and characteristic of the Epistle to the Ephesians is that here the Apostle seems to be, as he puts it himself, in 'the heavenly places', and he is looking down at the great panorama of salvation and redemption from that particular aspect. The result is that in this Epistle there is very little controversy; and that is so because his great concern here was to give to the Ephesians, and others to whom the letter is addressed, a panoramic view of this wondrous and glorious work of God in Jesus Christ our Lord.

Luther says of the Epistle to the Romans that it is 'the most important document in the New Testament, the gospel in its purest expression', and in many ways I agree that there is no purer, plainer statement of the gospel than in the Epistle to the Romans. Accepting that as true I would venture to add that if the Epistle to the Romans is the purest expression of the gospel, the Epistle to the Ephesians is the sublimest and the most majestic expression of it. Here the standpoint is a wider one, a larger one. There are statements and passages in this Epistle which really baffle description. The great Apostle piles epithet upon epithet, adjective upon adjective, and still he cannot express himself adequately. There are passages in this first chapter, and others in the third chapter, especially towards its end, where the Apostle is carried out above and beyond himself, and loses and abandons himself in a great outburst of worship and praise and thanksgiving. I repeat, therefore, that there is nothing more sublime in the whole range of Scripture than this Epistle to the Ephesians.

Let us begin by taking a general view of it, for we can only truly grasp and understand the particulars if we have taken a firm grasp of the whole and of the general statement. On the other hand those who imagine that, by giving a rough division of the message of this Epistle according to chapters, they have dealt with it adequately display their ignorance. It is when we come to the details that we discover the wealth; a summary of its message is most helpful as a beginning, but it is when we come to the particular statements and individual words that we find the real glory displayed to our wondering gaze.

The general theme of the Epistle is suggested at once in its first verse. This is characteristic of the Apostle; he could not restrain himself, but immediately proceeds to his theme. 'Paul, an apostle of Jesus Christ by the will of God' – there it is! The theme of the

Epistle, first and foremost, is God – God the Father. 'Grace be unto you and peace from God the Father and from the Lord Jesus Christ. Blessed be the God and Father of our Lord Jesus Christ.' The Apostle Paul always begins in this way, and this is how every Christian should begin. This is the theme that controls everything else. There was never any danger that the Apostle Paul might forget it, for he of all men knew that all is of God, and by God, and that to Him the glory must be given for ever and ever.

The Bible is God's book, it is a revelation of God, and our thinking must always start with God. Much of the trouble in the Church today is due to the fact that we are so subjective, so interested in ourselves, so egocentric. That is the peculiar error of this present century. Having forgotten God, and having become so interested in ourselves, we become miserable and wretched, and spend our time in 'shallows and in miseries'. The message of the Bible from beginning to end is designed to bring us back to God, to humble us before God, and to enable us to see our true relationship to Him. And that is the great theme of this Epistle; it holds us face to face with God, and what God is, and what God has done; it emphasizes throughout the glory and the greatness of God – God the Eternal One, God the everlasting, God over all – and the indescribable glory of God. This great theme appears constantly in the various phrases which the Apostle uses. Here are examples – 'Having predestinated us unto the adoption of children by Jesus Christ to himself, according to the good pleasure of his will'; 'having made known unto us the mystery of his will, according to his good pleasure which he hath purposed in himself'; 'in whom also we have obtained an inheritance, being predestinated according to the purpose of him who worketh all things after the counsel of his own will'. God, the eternal and everlasting God, self-sufficient in Himself, from eternity to eternity, needing the aid of no-one, living, dwelling in His own everlasting, absolute and eternal glory, is the great theme of this Epistle. We must not start by examining ourselves and our needs microscopically; we must start with God, and forget ourselves. In this Epistle we are taken as it were by the hand by the Apostle and are told that we are going to be given a view of the glory and the majesty of God. As we approach this study I seem to hear the voice that came of old to Moses from the burning bush saying,

'Take off thy shoes from off thy feet for the ground whereon thou standest is holy ground.' We are in the presence of God and His glory; so we must tread carefully and humbly.

But not only so, we are at once face to face with the sovereignty of God. Think of the terms which we find constantly running through the Scriptures, the great words and expressions of true Christian doctrine and theology. How little have we heard of them in this present century with our morbid, pre-occupied subjectivism! how little have we been told about the glory, the greatness, the majesty and the sovereignty of God! Our forefathers delighted in these terms; these were the terms of the Protestant Reformers, the terms of the Puritans and the Covenanters. They delighted to spend time contemplating the attributes of God.

Note how the Apostle comes to this point at once. 'Paul, an apostle of Jesus Christ by the will of God' – not by his own will! Paul did not call himself, and the Church did not call him; it was God who called him. He is an Apostle by the will of God. He states this very explicitly in the Epistle to the Galatians where he says, 'When it pleased God, who separated me from my mother's womb'. There is always emphasis on the sovereignty of God, and as we proceed in our study of this Epistle we shall find it standing out in all its glory everywhere. It is God who has chosen in Christ every one who is a Christian; it is God who has predestinated us. It is a part of God's purpose that we should be saved. There would never have been any salvation if God had not planned it and put it into execution. It is God who 'so loved the world', it is God who 'sent forth his Son, made of a woman, made under the law'. It is all of God and according to His purpose. It is 'according to the counsel of his own will' that all these things have happened.

This Epistle tells us throughout that we should always contemplate our salvation in this way. We must not start with ourselves and then ascend to God; we must start with the sovereignty of God, God over all, and then come down to ourselves. As we work our way through the Epistle we shall find that not only is salvation entirely of God in general; it is of God also in particular. Take, for instance, the great theme which Paul works out in the third chapter. The special task which had been committed to him as an Apostle is 'to make all men see what is the

[14]

fellowship of the mystery, which from the beginning of the world hath been hid in God, who created all things by Jesus Christ'. The mystery is that the Gentiles should be fellow heirs with Jesus. That was a 'mystery' which in other ages was not made known unto the sons of men as it is now revealed unto His holy apostles and prophets by the Spirit.

God controls everything, the time element in particular. As you read through your Old Testament have you ever wondered why it was that all those centuries had to pass before the Son of God actually came? Why was it that for so long only the Israelites, the Jews, had the oracles of God and the understanding that there is only one true and living God? The answer is that it is God who decides the time when everything is to happen, and so He reveals this truth which had hitherto been secret. This is but another illustration of the sovereignty of God. He determines the time for everything to happen. God is over all, controlling all, and timing everything in His infinite wisdom. At such a time as this I know of nothing which is more comforting and reassuring than to know that the Lord still reigns, that He is still the sovereign Lord of the universe, and that though 'the heathen rage, and the people imagine a vain thing', yet He has set his Son upon his holy mount of Zion (Psalm 2). A day will come when all His enemies shall lick the dust, and become His footstool and be humbled before Him, and Christ shall be 'all and in all'. Thus the sovereignty of God is emphasized in the introduction to this Epistle and repeated throughout because it is one of the cardinal doctrines without which we really do not understand our Christian faith.

Then, having said this, the Apostle proceeds to deal with the mystery of God, His greatness and the majesty of His sovereignty. The word 'mystery' is used six times in this Epistle to the Ephesians, thus more frequently than in his other Epistles. So I am justified in saying that this is one of the major themes of this Epistle, the mystery of God's ways with respect to us, the mystery of His will. We find it in this first chapter – 'Having made known unto us the mystery of his will, according to his good pleasure which he hath purposed in himself'. I wonder whether we always realize this as we should. Christian people, it is to be feared, sometimes approach these great truths and doctrines as if they could comprehend them with their understanding. We should never do so. If you start imagining that you can understand the mind and will of God you are doomed to failure, for these are mysteries with which no mind of man can ever cope. 'Great is the mystery of godliness'; no one can understand it. And if you try to understand God's ways with respect to man and the world I assure you that you will find yourself so overwhelmed that you will become miserable and unhappy. Indeed you may end by almost losing your faith and having a sense of grudge against God. 'The mystery of his will'! He is infinite and eternal, and we are finite and sinful, and cannot see and understand.

If ever you feel tempted to say that God is not fair, I advise you to put your hand, with Job, on your mouth, and to try to realize of whom you are speaking. Surely to object to the mystery is almost to deny that we are Christian at all. Is there anything more wonderful, more entrancing, more glorious for the Christian than to contemplate the mysteries of God? I trust that as we but approach these great themes you are already filled with a sense of divine expectancy, and long to go further and further into them. One of the most wonderful aspects of the Christian life is that in it you are ever going on. You think that you know it all, and then you turn a corner and suddenly see something you had not known before, and on and on you go. That is why the Apostle writes about 'the *riches* of his grace'; it is the glorious mystery which He has been pleased to reveal to us by His Holy Spirit. But God forbid that we should ever imagine that we shall be able to understand it all in the sense of fully comprehending it. My concern is not only to increase our intellectual knowledge of God, but to unfold 'the mystery' of His ways, in order that we may look at it, and worship Him, and confess our ignorance and smallness and frailty, and thank Him for the mystery of His holy will.

The next theme is the grace of God; and this word is used thirteen times in this Epistle. The Apostle keeps on repeating it. In the second verse he starts with it: 'Grace be to you, and peace, from God our Father, and from the Lord Jesus Christ'. This is the theme above everything else that is developed in this Epistle – God's amazing grace to sinful man in providing for man's salvation and redemption. 'The grace of God'; yes, and the abundance of it in particular – 'the riches of his grace'. That idea is found here more than anywhere else – 'the riches of his grace'!

'Blessed be the God and Father of our Lord Jesus Christ, who hath blessed us with all spiritual blessings in heavenly places in Christ.' In this Epistle we are given a glimpse into the riches, the abundance, the super-abundance of God's grace towards us; and if we do not look forward to an examination and investigation of this with the keenest possible anticipation, then it is doubtful as to whether we are Christian at all. Most people are interested in wealth and riches; we like to go to museums and other places where precious things are kept and stored; we like to look at gems and pearls; we stand in queues and pay a fee to see such wealth and riches. We boast of this as individuals and nations. I repeat, then, that the supreme object of this Epistle is to lead us in, and give us a view and a glimpse of the riches, the super-abundant riches of the grace of God. It all starts with God, God the Father who is over all.

But having said that, we move on to what invariably comes next in all the Epistles of this Apostle, indeed to what always comes second in the whole of the Bible – the Lord Jesus Christ. 'Grace be to you, and peace, from God our Father, and from the Lord Jesus Christ.' Have you noticed how frequently the Name occurs, the Name that was so dear and blessed to the Apostle? 'The Apostle of Jesus Christ', 'Grace be to you, and peace, from God our Father, and from the Lord Jesus Christ'; 'Blessed be the God and Father of our Lord Jesus Christ, who hath blessed us with all spiritual blessings in heavenly places in Christ', and so it continues. In the first verse Paul tells us at once that he is 'an apostle of Jesus Christ'. It sounds almost ridiculous to have to say it, and yet it is essential to emphasize that there is no gospel and no salvation apart from Jesus Christ. It is necessary because there are people who talk about Christianity without Christ. They talk about forgiveness but the Name of Christ is not mentioned, they preach about the love of God but in their view the Lord Jesus Christ is not essential. It is not so with the Apostle Paul; there is no gospel, there is no salvation apart from the Lord Jesus Christ. The gospel is especially about Him. All God's gracious purposes are carried out by Christ, in Christ, through Christ, from the beginning to the very end. Everything that God in His sovereign

[17]

will, and by His infinite grace, and according to the riches of His mercy and the mystery of His will – everything that God has purposed and carried out for our salvation He has done in Christ. In Christ 'dwelleth all the fulness of the Godhead bodily'; in Him God has treasured up all the riches of His grace and wisdom. Everything from the very beginning to the very end is in and through the Lord Jesus Christ. There is no Christian message apart from Him. We are called and chosen 'in Christ' before the foundation of the world, we are reconciled to God by 'the blood of Christ'. 'In whom we have redemption through his blood, the forgiveness of sins, according to the riches of his grace.'

We are all interested in forgiveness, but how am I forgiven? Is it because I have repented or lived a good life that God looks upon me and forgives me? I say with reverence that even the Almighty God could not forgive my sin simply on those terms. There is only one way whereby God forgives us; it is because He sent His only begotten Son from heaven to earth, and to the agony and the shame and the death on the Cross: 'In whom we have redemption through his blood.' There is no Christianity without 'the blood of Christ'. It is central, it is absolutely essential. There is nothing without it. Not only the Person of Christ but in particular, His death, His shed blood, His atoning substitutionary sacrifice! It is in that way, and that way alone, that we are redeemed. In this Epistle Christ is shown to be absolutely essential. We shall find it to be so as we come to the details. He is everywhere, He must be. We are chosen in Him, called by Him, saved by His blood. He is the Head of the Church as this first chapter reminds us. He is 'far above all principality and power, and might, and dominion, and every name that is named, not only in this world, but also in that which is to come'. He is 'the Head of the church, which is his body, the fulness of him that filleth all in all'; and He is at the right hand of God with all authority and power in heaven and on earth. Jesus, our Lord, is supreme; He is the Son of God, the Saviour of the world. That is going to be our theme. Are you beginning to look forward to it – to look at Him, to gaze upon Him in His Person, in His offices, in His work, in all that He is and can be to us?

Then in particular, as I have already been anticipating, the theme of God's great purpose in Christ is the practical theme of

this Epistle. We find it in the tenth verse: 'That in the dispensation of the fulness of times he might gather together in one all
things in Christ, both which are in heaven and which are on
earth; even in him.' Here we see God's purpose. The Apostle goes
on to tell us that this purpose has ever been necessary because of
sin. In the second chapter we shall find that he tells us about the
problems that harass the mind and the heart of man, and how they
are due to the fact that 'the prince of the power of the air, the
spirit that now worketh in the children of disobedience', is
controlling fallen man. He tells us that God's plan of redemption
is necessary because of the Fall of man, and how that was preceded
by the fall of that bright angelic spirit called the Devil, or Satan,
who has become 'the god of this world', 'the prince of the power
of the air'. This terrible power is the cause of the enmity and the
plight and the havoc that has been characteristic of the life of the
human race. The modern world is divided into rival factions, the
ancient world was in exactly the same case. There is nothing new
about this, it is all the result of sin and the devil's hatred of God.
It is the result of the loss of man's true relationship to God. Man
sets himself up as God and thereby causes all the disruption and
confusion in the world. But we are shown how at the very
beginning, even in Paradise, God announced His plan and began
to put it into practice.

The Old Testament is an account of how God began to work it
out. First of all He separated unto Himself a people called the
Hebrews, later known as the Jews. In their history we see the
beginning of His purpose of redemption. Out of the welter of
mankind God formed a people for Himself. He called a man
named Abraham and turned him into a nation. There we have the
beginning of something new. But then there was great rivalry
between the Jews and the Gentiles, so one of the major themes of
this Epistle is to show how God has dealt with this matter. The
great theme here is that He has revealed Himself not only to the
Jews but also to the Gentiles; 'the middle wall of partition' has
gone; God 'hath made both one'. There is a new creation; something new has come into being; it is called the Church; and this
work of God is to go on increasing, says the Apostle, until when
the fulness of the time shall have arrived God will have carried out
His entire plan, and all that is opposed to Him shall be destroyed.

Everything shall be united together and made one in Christ. That is one of the major themes of this Epistle. At first Jews only, then Jews and Gentiles, then all things. And all is to be done 'in and through Christ'.

That, in turn, leads to the other major theme, which is the Church. God's purpose is seen most plainly and clearly in and through the Christian Church, His great purpose of bringing together all nations in Christ. In her are found different people, different nationalities, coming from different parts of the world, with different experiences, different in appearance, different in psychology and in every conceivable respect; yet all are one 'in Christ Jesus'. This is what God is doing, until finally there shall be 'a new heaven and a new earth wherein dwelleth righteousness', and Jesus shall reign 'from shore to shore, till moons shall wax and wane no more'.

Nothing is more uplifting and wonderful than to see the Church in that light, and to see, therefore, the importance and the privilege and the responsibility of being a member of that Church. It is because of this that we must live the Christian life; and so in chapter 4 and to the end of the letter Paul emphasizes the ethical behaviour which is expected of Christians because they are what they are, and because that is the plan of God, and they must manifest His grace in their daily life and living.

There, then, we have taken a very brief view of the great themes of this Epistle. Let me summarize them in a simple, practical manner. Why am I calling your attention to all this? It is because I am profoundly convinced that our greatest need is to know these truths. We all need to look again at this glorious revelation, and to be delivered from our morbid pre-occupation with ourselves. If we but saw ourselves as we are depicted in this Epistle; if we but realized, as the Apostle expresses it in his prayer in verses 17–19, that we are to know 'what is the hope of our calling, and what the riches of the glory of his inheritance in the saints, and what is the exceeding greatness of his power to us-ward who believe, according to the working of his mighty power', what a difference it would make! Are you a miserable, unhappy Christian, feeling that the fight is too much for you? and are you on the point of giving up and giving in? What you need is to know the power that is working mightily for you, the same power that brought Christ from the dead. If we but know that we are meant to be 'filled with all the fulness of God' we should no longer be weak and ailing and complaining, we should no longer present such a sorry picture of the Christian life to those who live round and about us. What we need, primarily, is not an experience, but to realize what we are, and who we are, what God has done in Christ and the way He has blessed us. We fail to realize our privileges.

Our greatest need is still the need of understanding. Our prayer for ourselves should be the prayer of the Apostle for these people, that 'the eyes of (our) understanding may be enlightened'. That is what we need. In this Epistle 'the exceeding riches' of God's grace are displayed before us. Let us look at them, and let us take hold of them and enjoy them. Above all, and especially at a time such as this, how vital it is that we should have some new and fresh understanding of God's great plan and purpose for the world. With international conferences taking place almost on our doorstep, with the whole world wondering what its future is to be, and what the outcome of our present troubles is going to be, with men at the end of their wits, and at the end of their tether, how privileged we are to be able to stand and look at this revelation, and see God's plan and purpose behind it all and beyond it all. It is not to be brought to pass through statesmen but through people like ourselves. The world ignores it, and laughs and mocks at it; but we know for certain with the Apostle that 'all principality, and power, and might, and dominion, and every name that is named, not only in this world, but also in that which is to come', have been set beneath Christ's feet. The Lord Jesus Christ was rejected by this world when He came into it; they dismissed Him as 'this fellow', 'this carpenter'; but He was the Son of God and the Saviour of the world, the King of kings, the Lord of lords, the One to whom 'every knee shall bow, of things in heaven and things on earth, and things under the earth'. Thanks be to God for the glorious gospel of Jesus Christ, and for 'the riches of his grace'!

2

'Saints . . . and the faithful in Christ Jesus'

'Paul, an apostle of Jesus Christ by the will of God, to the saints which are at Ephesus, and to the faithful in Christ Jesus.'

Ephesians 1:1

As we have seen, the Apostle as he begins his letter plunges at once into the midst of great and profound truths. I suppose that all of us in varying degrees must plead guilty to the tendency to regard the introductions of these New Testament Epistles as being more or less formal. We tend to feel that introductions are more or less unnecessary, and that we can skip over them in order that we may hurry on to the great message that follows. In the readings of childhood we wanted to get to the heart of the story, and were often impatient with all the preliminaries; we wanted the excitement and the end of the story. That habit tends to persist, so that when we come even to the New Testament Epistles we feel that the preliminary verses and salutations are unimportant and have nothing to do with truth and doctrine. So we tend to read them very quickly and to rush on to what we regard as the essential teaching. But that is a profound error, not only with respect to Scripture, but also to anything that is worth reading. It is always good to pay attention to what an author at the outset deems to be necessary and important, for obviously he would not have introduced it if he had not had some object in mind. If that is true in general it is particularly true with regard to these New Testament Epistles, because in these preliminary salutations we find aspects of truth which are vital and essential.

Here, in the first verse of this Epistle, we have a notable example of that very thing, for the Apostle cannot even address the Ephesians without at the same time presenting them (and us) with an extraordinary description and definition of what it means to be a Christian. I call attention to this fact because people often misinterpret the teaching of the New Testament Epistles, for they fail to notice to whom the messages were addressed. The teaching of the New Testament Epistles is directed only and solely to Christians, to believers in the Lord Jesus Christ. It is utterly wrong and heretical to take the teaching of any New Testament Epistle and apply it to the world in general. The teaching is addressed to particular people, and here the Apostle leaves us in no doubt at all as to the persons to whom he is writing. He addresses them and immediately he describes them.

We must also be clear about the fact that the Apostle was writing what can be described as a general letter. The Revised Version does not say 'to the saints which are at Ephesus'. 'Ephesus' is omitted and that reminds us that in some of the ancient manuscripts the words 'at Ephesus' are not included. The oldest manuscripts of all do not contain the words 'at Ephesus', but they are found in other ancient manuscripts. The authorities however are agreed in saying that what really happened was that the Apostle wrote a kind of circular letter to a number of churches, and that his amanuensis probably left a gap so that the name of any one particular church could be inserted. This Letter to the church at Ephesus went to other churches also in the province of Asia, and it is probable that the traditional description 'The letter to the Ephesians' arose from the fact that the original copy did go to the church at Ephesus itself.

Let me emphasize also that this is not a letter addressed to some unusual and exceptional Christian people, it is not a letter addressed to some great scholar or theologian, it is not a letter addressed to teachers, it is not a letter addressed to so-called scholars who study the Scriptures. It is not a letter to specialists but a letter to ordinary church members. That is from every standpoint a most important observation, and for this reason, that everything the Apostle says here about Christians and members of churches must therefore be equally true of us. All the high doctrine which we have in this Epistle is something that you and I are meant to receive. The Epistle to the Ephesians – perhaps the crowning achievement of the Apostle's life and of his writings – is an Epistle that is addressed to people like ourselves. Ordinary members of the Church, of all churches, are meant to take hold of these doctrines, and understand and rejoice in them. They are not merely for certain special learned people; they are meant for each and every one of us.

Turning, then, to the Apostle's description of the Christian, of every Christian, we have here what we may call the irreducible minimum of what constitutes a Christian. In the body of this letter the Apostle says that he is anxious that these people should learn more and deeper and higher truths. Hence he prays that the eyes of their understanding may be enlightened: 'that the God of our Lord Jesus Christ, the Father of glory, may give unto you the spirit of wisdom and revelation in the knowledge of Him; the eyes of your understanding being enlightened.' That is the ultimate objective, but before he comes to that he reminds them of what they are already and of what they know already. This description of the Christian is a description of the Ephesian Christians at that time. They would never have been members of the Church at all, they would never have been recipients of this letter, were it not that these things were true of them. We find ourselves confronted here, then, by what the New Testament teaches is the basic irreducible minimum of what constitutes a Christian.

I am emphasizing this because it seems to me that it is the primary need of the Christian Church at the present time to realize exactly what it means to be a Christian. How was it that the early Christians, who were but a handful of people, had such a profound impact on the pagan world in which they lived? It was because they were what they were. It was not their organization, it was the quality of their life, it was the power they possessed because they were truly Christian. That is how Christianity conquered the ancient world, and I am more and more convinced that it is the only way in which Christianity can truly influence the modern world. The lack of influence of the Christian Church in the world at large today is in my opinion due to one thing only, namely, (God forgive us!) that we are so unlike the description of the Christians that we find in the New Testament. If therefore we are concerned about the state of the Church, if we have a burden for men and women who are outside the Church, and who in their misery and wretchedness are hurtling themselves to destruction, the first thing we have to do is to examine ourselves, and to discover how closely we conform to this pattern and description.

[24]

The Apostle describes the Christian in three main terms. The first term is 'saints'. 'Paul, an apostle of Jesus Christ by the will of God, to the saints . . .' – the saints at Ephesus, the saints at Laodicea, the saints in every other local church whether small or large. The first thing to say of a Christian is that he is a saint. I fear that may sound rather strange to some of us. We tend to say, 'Well, I am a Christian, but I am far from being a saint'. We are afraid of making such a claim; somehow we are afraid of this particular designation; and yet in the New Testament we are addressed as 'saints'. We must discover therefore why the Apostle uses this word, and what is meant by 'saint' in its New Testament sense.

The first thing it means is that we are people who are set apart. That is the root meaning of the word the Apostle uses here and as other biblical writers use it. Primarily it means separated, set apart. A good illustration of this meaning is found in the nine-teenth chapter of the Acts of the Apostles where we read that when certain difficulties and oppositions arose the Apostle separated the disciples and then began to meet with them in the school of Tyrannus (verse 9) and then taught and built them up in the faith; he separated them. That is the essential meaning of this word 'saint', and the Church is a collection of saints. The Church is not an institution, she is primarily a gathering, a meet-ing of saints. The perfect illustration is that of the children of Israel under the old dispensation. They were a people set apart by God, they were taken out of the world, they were given a certain uniqueness by God, they were 'God's own people'. They are described as 'a chosen generation, a royal priesthood, an holy nation, a peculiar people' – a people for God's particular posses-sion and interest. Such is the definition of the children of Israel in the Old Testament. In one sense they were a nation among many other nations and yet they were different; they had certain rights which other nations did not have, they had received from God certain revelations of the Word of God which Paul refers to as 'the oracles of God'. In other words they were a separate people, in the world but not of the world, set apart on their own by God; that is to say, they were 'saints'. So the Christian is a man primarily who is segregated from the world.

The Apostle says exactly the same thing at the beginning of his

Letter to the Galatians – 'Grace be to you and peace from God the Father, and from our Lord Jesus Christ, who gave himself for our sins, that he might deliver us from this present evil world, according to the will of God and our Father'. We are delivered out of the world, separated from the world. The Christian today, like the children of Israel of old, while he is in the world is not of the world; he is a man like other men, and yet he is very different. This is primary, basic truth. The Christian is not like anybody else, he is separate, he is apart, he is unique. He stands out, he has been called out by God, he has been separated from the world, separated to God. Is this obvious about us Christians today? The separation does not just mean that we attend a place of worship on Sunday morning whereas most people do not. That is a very important part of it; but it is not the vital part, because such attendance may be the result of mere custom and habit or a part of the social round. The question is, are we truly separated as persons, are we essentially different from the world?

This not only means that we are set apart in an outward sense, it means that we are set apart because we are cleansed inwardly. That is the real meaning of the word 'saint'. Instinctively we think of a saint as some holy person. That is right, and we must grasp this second element in the meaning of this word. A saint is someone who has been cleansed in many ways. He has been cleansed from the guilt of his sin, cleansed from that which excludes him from the presence of God. If to be a saint means that you are taken out of the world and brought into the presence of God, is it not clear that something must have happened which has made you fit to come into the presence of God? It is sin that separates man from God; hence, before anyone can be separated for God, he or she must be cleansed from the guilt of sin. So that is the first thing that is true of the Christian; he has been cleansed, as the Apostle reminds us, by the blood of Christ, 'In whom we have redemption through his blood, the forgiveness of sins, according to the riches of his grace'.

But the cleansing does not stop at this point. The saint is one who has been cleansed also from the pollution of sin. It is not merely outward cleansing; it is inward also, because sin affects the whole being. A saint is one who has been cleansed from that which pollutes his mind and heart, his actions, and everything

[26]

else. He is cleansed outwardly, he is cleansed inwardly; he has become, as the Bible calls him, a 'holy' person. Mount Sion is referred to as 'the holy mount', and the vessels that were used in the temple were called the 'holy vessels'. That means that they were cleansed and set apart and used for nothing else; they were 'holy unto the Lord'. That is what is meant by a 'saint'; a saint is someone who has been cleansed and set apart and is 'holy unto the Lord'. Before it was applied to the Christian this term originally applied to the children of Israel. 'Ye are a holy nation, a peculiar people,' a people for God's particular possession.

At this point I make two practical comments. The first is that these remarks apply to every Christian – to the saints at Ephesus, to all saints worldwide, to all the faithful everywhere. We must learn to shed once and for ever the false dichotomy which Roman Catholicism has introduced at this point. It picks out certain people and calls them 'Saints'. There is nothing wrong in paying tribute to a man who is outstanding; but that is not what Romanists do. They call these special people 'Saints', and only these. But that is wrong and unscriptural. Every Christian is a saint; you cannot be a Christian without being a saint; and you cannot be a saint and a Christian without being separated in some radical sense from the world. You do not belong to it any longer, you are in it but you are not of it; there is a separation which has taken place in your mind, in your outlook, in your heart, in your conversation, in your behaviour. You are essentially a different person; the Christian is not a worldly person, he is not governed by the world and its mind and outlook. We must examine ourselves, and discover whether we correspond to this description. Is it not true to say that the masses of men and women living round and about us (many of them are unhappy and disturbed about themselves and their lives) do not come to speak to us and ask us questions, do not fly to us in their trouble, because they do not feel that we are any different from themselves, that there is not that about us which suggests that we are essentially different? We have accepted the false idea that only certain Christians are saints, we have not realized that every Christian is meant to be separate from the world.

It is just here that we should see the whole marvel and miracle of the Christian faith and Christian redemption. Recall the kind of

[27]

city which Ephesus was. Read the nineteenth chapter of the Acts of the Apostles and you will find that it was a great city, prosperous, but thoroughly pagan. Its inhabitants worshipped a goddess called Diana and they cried 'Great is Diana of the Ephesians'. They were proud of themselves, and of their goddess. Not only so, there was much practice of sorcery and magic and things of that kind. The Apostle Paul visited the city and all he found was a group of twelve men who were disciples of John the Baptist, but they were very uncertain in their minds as to the truth. Can you imagine anything more hopeless? As the Apostle walked through Ephesus he found it almost completely pagan, filled with arroganre and pride, and abounding in cults and in everything that is opposed to God. What hope was there that Christianity should ever flourish in such a spot? But Paul preached and was used of the Spirit; the church was established, and these saints came into being, and later Ephesus became the seat of the labour of the Apostle John. We need to remind ourselves that the gospel is not human teaching; it is 'the power of God unto salvation, to every one that believeth', and when it enters a city, as it did in the person of the Apostle Paul filled with the Holy Spirit, nothing is impossible.

Are you a Christian who is feeling rather hopeless about a husband or wife or child or some other relative? Do you feel that because of their intellectualism, or their training, or their surroundings, their conversion to Christ is altogether hopeless and cannot be attempted? Remember the saints at Ephesus, yes, and at Corinth and in Galatia. The gospel is the power of God; it has accomplished mighty things and is still the same. It can take hold of the most hopeless individual and turn him into a saint. That is its primary function, that is the thing for which God has sent it forth.

But let us turn to the Apostle's second term – 'faithful'. We must be careful as to the meaning of this term 'faithful'. In a sense it is a somewhat unfortunate translation, because we tend to give, not a primary meaning to this term, but, once more, a secondary meaning. Essentially this word 'faithful' means 'exercising faith'. To illustrate this, consider the case of Thomas the Apostle and

how he refused to believe the testimony of his fellow disciples
when he came back to them after an absence and when they told
him that the Lord had appeared amongst them. Thomas said he
would not believe unless he saw the mark of the nails and put his
finger into the wounds. Then the Lord suddenly appeared and
showed Himself to Thomas and told him to do what he had said.
Thomas fell at His feet and said, 'My Lord and my God'. But
remember how our Lord gently rebuked him and said, 'Because
thou hast seen me thou hast believed: blessed are they that have
not seen and yet have believed'. And then He said, 'Be not
faithless but believing'. The word translated in John 20:27 as
'believing' is the same word as is translated 'faithful' in our text.
It means 'to be full of faith', to exercise faith. The Apostle
addresses these Christians at Ephesus as those who are believers,
people who exercise faith; they are Christians because they are
believers.

Here, again, is something that is fundamental and primary and
vital. You cannot be a Christian apart from a certain belief; what
makes us Christian is that we believe certain things. Go back
again to the nineteenth chapter of the Acts of the Apostles. What
we are told (vv. 1–2) is that Paul found certain disciples, but that
he was not happy about them, so he put his question to them:
'Did you receive the Holy Ghost when you believed?' And they
replied: 'We have not so much as heard whether there be any
Holy Ghost.' He then said to them, 'Unto what then were ye
baptized?', and they said, 'Unto John's baptism'. Then said Paul,
'John verily baptized with the baptism of repentance, saying unto
the people that they should believe on him which should come
after him, that is, on Christ Jesus'. When they heard this, they
were baptized in the name of the Lord Jesus.

In this incident we are told quite plainly what it is that makes us
Christians. A Christian is not merely a nice man, a good man, a
man who likes to be a member of a Christian Church, a man who
is vaguely interested in moral uplift and idealism. Certain men are
described today as outstanding Christians who only really believe
in what is called 'reverence for life'; but that is not according to
the New Testament teaching. A Christian is one who believes
certain specific truths; and the essence of his belief centres on the
Person of our Lord Jesus Christ. The Christian, the saint, is 'full

of faith'. In whom, in what? Faith in the Lord Jesus Christ! He believes that Jesus of Nazareth was the only begotten Son of God. He is full of faith in the Incarnation, he believes that the Eternal 'Word was made flesh and dwelt among us', that the Eternal Son came in human nature into this world; he believes in the Virgin Birth, and that Jesus manifested that He was the Son of God by His miracles.

The saints at Ephesus believed these truths; and Paul was enabled to work special miracles in Ephesus as a proof of them. They did not hold them lightly; they knew what they believed. But above all they believed that Christ Jesus came into this world 'to taste death for every man', they believed in the fact that it is by His blood that He saves us, that He bore the punishment of our sins, and died our death that we might be reconciled to God – 'In whom we have redemption through his blood, the forgiveness of sins'. They were full of faith in these things. They firmly believed that He had risen from the dead. They did not simply have some vague belief that Jesus still persists, but were fully assured that He rose from the dead and manifested Himself to many disciples, and last of all to this man Paul. They were full of faith also in the Person of the Holy Spirit. They believed that the Holy Spirit had been sent on the day of Pentecost, that 'the promise of the Father' had come, and that He could be received, and that believers knew that they had received Him. They were full of faith in these things. Are we 'faithful'? The vital question is not, are we members of churches, but are we full of faith in these things? Do we know whom we have believed? do we know Christian doctrine? do we understand the way of salvation as it is expounded in the Scriptures? We should be 'ready at all times to give a reason for the hope that is in us', says Peter, confirming Paul.

But there is a further meaning to this word 'faithful', the one that is generally given. It means that we keep the faith, that we hold to the faith, that we are constant in the faith, and loyal to the faith, and ready with Paul to defend the faith, and to contend earnestly for it. It means that we can be relied on, that we are dependable because we know the faith, and because we believe it and have trusted it. Let us not forget this secondary meaning, that we must be people upon whom others can rely and depend. We must not be people who are 'carried about by every wind of doctrine', and whose faith can be shaken by reading an article or a book by some church dignitary which denies the Deity of Christ or the Virgin Birth, and most other essential doctrines. We must be faithful, dependable, and reliable; we know what we believe, and stand with the Apostle and others in solid rank to defend the faith against all adversaries.

Even if terrible persecution should come we must not flinch. Many of these early Christians were told that if they persisted in saying that 'Jesus is Lord' and refused to say that 'Caesar is Lord', they would be put to death. However, they still said that 'Jesus is Lord'. Though you and I may not be tempted in that particular way, there are Christians in other parts of the world today who have to face the possibility of losing work or employment or their professional status, or being separated from their families, cast into prison, spat upon or shot or mutilated in some terrible way, simply because of their loyalty to this faith. They are standing, they are 'full of faith'; they can be depended upon and relied upon to stand to the last moment, and never to waver or flinch. You and I, at least at the present time, do not have to face open persecution, but we have to face sarcasm and derision, and are often made to feel that we are odd and strange people. You and I have to be faithful, whatever happens, no matter how much laughter and sniggering and jeering we encounter. Whatever the cost may be – financial, professional – we must be faithful, reliable, dependable, standing at all costs, come what may. Such is the Christian; he knows in whom he believes; and rather than deny Him he would sooner die.

Then, lastly, there is this great phrase, 'in Christ Jesus'. It is most important that we should understand what it means, and it is connected with 'saints' quite as much as with 'faithful'. They are saints in Christ Jesus, they are faithful in Christ Jesus. This phrase, as we shall see repeatedly as we go through this Epistle, is one of the great characteristic statements of the New Testament. It means that the Christian is one who not only believes in Christ, he is in a real sense 'in Christ'. He belongs to Him, he is united to Him, he is joined to Him. Take the New Testament illustration of the body. 'Ye are the body of Christ', says Paul to the Corinthians,

'and members in particular.' In the fourth chapter of this Epistle
to the Ephesians he uses the same analogy. He says that Christians,
who form the Church, are built up like a body. He says: 'Speaking
the truth in love' we are to 'grow up into him in all things, which
is the head, even Christ: from whom the whole body fitly joined
together and compacted by that which every joint supplieth,
according to the effectual working in the measure of every part,
maketh increase of the body unto the edifying of itself in love'
(chap. 4, 15–16). So to be a Christian means, not only that you are
a believer in Christ, outside Him; you are a believer because you
are joined to Him, you are 'in him'.

We find the same idea in the fifth chapter of Romans where
Paul works out a great analogy and contrast. He says that we were
all originally in Adam. Adam was not only the first man, he was
also the representative of the entire human race. Everyone who
has been born into this world was in Adam, a part of Adam,
joined to Adam, with the result that Adam's action has brought
its consequences upon all. But the Apostle goes on to argue that,
as we were all 'in Adam', so we are now – those of us who are
Christian – 'in Christ'. As 'in Adam', so 'in Christ'. The Christian
is one who is 'in Christ'. All that the Lord Jesus Christ has done
becomes true of us.

Again, in the sixth chapter of Romans Paul works it out and
says that when Christ was crucified we were crucified with Him;
when He died, we died with Him; when He was buried we were
buried with Him; when He rose again we rose with Him. He is
seated in the heavenly places. Paul says in the second chapter of
this Ephesian Epistle, 'God hath raised us up together, and made
us sit together in heavenly places in Christ'. We are seated in the
heavenly places with Christ at this moment because we are 'in
Christ'. What a tremendous, staggering, overwhelming truth – I
am a part of Christ, I belong to Him, I am a member of the body
of Christ! I am not my own, I have been 'bought (purchased) with
a price'. I am in Christ. He is the Head, I am one of the members.
There is a vital, organic, mystical union between us. All the
blessings we enjoy as Christians come to us because we are 'in
Christ'. It is 'of his fulness we have received, and grace upon
grace'. 'I am the true vine', says our Lord Himself, 'and ye are
the branches.'

[32]

All that is for you if you are a Christian. Do not talk about your weakness or helplessness; He is the Life, and you are joined to the Life, you are part of the Life, you are a branch in the Vine, 'in Christ'. We shall return to this, but let us take hold of it in principle now. Let us meditate upon it, and let me encourage you to do so by ending with two brief comments. Why do you think that the Apostle, in describing the Christian, puts these three things in the following order – 'saints', 'faithful', 'in Christ'? The answer is very simple. The first and the most obvious thing about the Christian always should be the fact that he is a 'saint'. The Apostle had the City of Ephesus in his mind's eye; he saw as it were an oasis in the desert of wealth, paganism, sorcery and loose living. Standing out in the desert is this green oasis – it is the Church, the saints. That is a very good way of looking at the Christian. Anyone looking at the world should at once be impressed by this fact that there are certain people in it who stand out and are quite different because they are 'saints'. That should be the first impression we make; everyone – neighbours, friends, colleagues and fellow-workers – should know that we are Christians. It should be obvious, it should stand out because we are what we are, because of these things that are true of us. We read of our blessed Lord that 'he could not be hid', and that should be true of us in this sense; it should be impossible to conceal the fact. But it does not mean that I preach and force my Christianity upon people, and make myself an awkward person. It is rather a quality of saintliness, something that is full of grace and charm, a faint likeness to the Lord Himself. It should be evident and obvious that we are a separate people, a different people, because we are a holy people.

Then let us note the importance of keeping intact the relationship between a saint and being faithful, the relationship between holiness and being a believer in the Lord Jesus Christ. These things should never be separated. However much we may delude ourselves, there is no such thing as a theoretical Christian. It is possible to hold the doctrine of the faith in the lecture room, to give an intellectual assent to these things, but that does not make us Christian. Hence Paul put 'saint' before 'faithful'. Dr William Temple has said, 'No one is a believer who is not holy, and no one is holy who is not a believer'. These two things must never be separated, you must never put a gap between justification and sanctification. If you are a Christian you are in Christ, and in Christ what happens is that 'He is made unto us wisdom and righteousness and sanctification and redemption'. You cannot, you must not try to divide Christ. It is a false doctrine which says that you can be justified without being sanctified. It is impossible; you are a 'saint' before you are 'faithful'. You have been separated. That is why you believe. These things are indissolubly linked together. God forbid that we should ever separate or divide them! Holiness is a characteristic of every Christian, and if we are not holy, our profession of Christ is valueless. You cannot be a believer without being holy, and you cannot be holy in this New Testament sense without being a believer. 'What God hath joined together let not man put asunder.'

3
Grace, Peace, Glory

'Grace *be* to you, and peace, from God our Father,
and *from* the Lord Jesus Christ.'

Ephesians 1:2

In this second verse, which is still a part of the salutation of the
Apostle to the Church at Ephesus and elsewhere, he proceeds to
tell us about the benefits we should be enjoying as the result of
being Christians. He does so in words which in some one form or
another are to be found at the commencement of most New
Testament Epistles – 'Grace be to you, and peace.' It was the
custom among ancient peoples to greet one another in this way
when they met, and the favourite salutation which one Jew
addressed to another was 'Peace, peace be with you.' 'Peace' was
their favourite term. The Apostle, however, does not merely say
that, he goes well beyond it. He takes the familiar term and lifts it
up into the new Christian realm. So the Christian greeting and
salutation is much greater, much wider, much more profound
than the more or less formal salutation with which men used to
greet one another.

I emphasize this matter because I think it is of great importance.
The Apostle does not use words such as this lightly and loosely
and thoughtlessly; it is not a mere formula which he uses automatically at the beginning of a letter; the words are charged with
profound meaning. As he uses these words and expresses this
desire for the Ephesians, he is desiring for them that they may
experience fully all the endless riches that are to be found in the
gospel of our Lord Jesus Christ. In other words, we shall see as
we analyse this verse that it contains some of the profoundest
truths of our faith, and that its terms are of the most vital
importance.

I digress for a moment to point out that when we read our Bibles nothing is more important than that we should look at every word, and question it as to its meaning. How easy it is to do a certain amount of Bible reading every day, followed perhaps by a brief prayer! If your main concern is simply to read a certain amount each day you may well skip over words such as these, these profundities of our faith. Here at the very beginning, in this preliminary salutation, the Apostle plunges at once into the very depths of the profoundest truth and doctrine that is to be found anywhere in the Scriptures. Or, to state it in a different way, this verse is a kind of overture to the entire Epistle. It is the characteristic of great pieces of music, certain types of music in particular, to have an overture. The musician starts by composing the main body of the work, which may have various movements or acts, each having its theme. Then, having finished the work, he goes back to the beginning and writes an overture in which he collects together the main motifs or themes that have emerged in the body of the work. He does so by throwing out a suggestion, perhaps in a few bars, to whet your appetite and in order that you may have some idea of what he is going to develop in the main body of the work.

This second verse, I suggest, is the overture to this entire Epistle; its major themes are all hinted at here. We shall go into them in greater detail later, but let us note them at the very beginning – 'grace' and 'peace'. 'Grace be to you, and peace, from God our Father, and from the Lord Jesus Christ.' No two words are more important in the whole of our faith than 'grace' and 'peace'. Yet how lightly we tend to drop them off our tongues without stopping to consider what they mean. Grace is the beginning of our faith; peace is the end of our faith. Grace is the fountain, the spring, the source. It is that particular place in the mountain from which the mighty river you see rolling into the sea starts its race; without it there would be nothing. Grace is the origin and source and fount of everything in the Christian life. But what does the Christian life mean, what is it meant to produce? The answer is 'peace'. So there we have the source and there the estuary leading to the sea, the beginning and the end, the initiation, and the purpose for which it is all meant and designed. It is essential for us, therefore, to carry these two words in our minds because within the ellipse formed by grace and peace everything is included.

What is grace? It is a term notoriously difficult to define. Grace essentially means 'unmerited favour', favour you do not deserve, favour you receive but to which you have no right or title in any shape or form, and of which you are entirely unworthy and undeserving. We may call it condescending love – love coming down, or stopping down. Or we may call it beneficent kindness. All these terms are descriptive of what is meant by this extraordinary term which is constantly put before us in the New Testament, by this amazing and wonderful word 'grace'. It is not surprising that Philip Doddridge lived to contemplate it as he tells us in the words –

> *Grace! 'tis a charming sound,*
> *Harmonious to the ear: . . .*

It is one of the most beautiful words in every language.

With regard to 'peace', the danger always present with this word is to give it a connotation, or attach a meaning to it, which falls short of its complete meaning. 'Peace' does not merely mean cessation of war, rest and quiet. Certainly it means rest and quiet but it means much more. The ever-present danger with regard to 'peace' is to think of it as merely an absence of such things as boisterousness or discord or fighting. It may well be that because the nations of the world think of peace in those terms we have never had a true peace. The peace dealt with in history books is merely a cessation of war; but 'peace' in the Bible does not merely mean that you stop fighting; it goes far beyond that. It is interesting to find that the actual root meaning of the Greek word that is translated 'peace', is 'union', 'union after separation', a bringing together, a reconciliation after a contest and quarrel.

The word finds a place in the expression 'a peace offering', as presented by a man making a proposal for peace. He is proposing a union, a bringing together, a reconciliation. In other words two persons who have quarrelled and have been fighting put down their weapons, and look at one another and shake hands. They are joined, there is a reconciliation; where there was contest and separation they have been brought together. This idea is brought out in the second chapter of our Epistle, where we read, 'He hath

made both one, and hath broken down the middle wall of partition between us' (v. 14). Two parties have been brought together,
the middle wall of partition has gone, and by one Spirit they come
together to the one Lord. That is the meaning of 'peace'.

'Grace be unto you, and peace, from God our Father, and from
the Lord Jesus Christ'. There we have grace at the beginning and
peace at the end; but we have not finished. The moment you
confront such a statement you are driven to ask a question. Why
does the Apostle wish this for these Ephesians? The answer to
that question, as I have already been saying, is the whole of
Christian doctrine. We must learn how to read the Scriptures;
and there is no one thing that is more important when we do so
than just this, to ask questions of it.

Why do we need grace and peace? Why does the Apostle wish us
to know them? Why does he use these terms rather than some
other terms? The answer leads us immediately into fundamental
Christian truths. By desiring grace and peace for us he is telling
us the truth about ourselves, he is telling us what we need. We
need the grace which will lead to peace because man is what he is
as the result of the Fall and of sin. What that means in detail is
expounded fully by the Apostle in his second chapter. Man in
sin is at enmity with God. Man by nature, as he is born into this
world, is a hater of God. He is not only separated from God, but
he fights God, he is an enemy, and alienated in his mind from God;
everything in him by nature is utterly opposed to God. Such is
the truth about man, and the result is that man in this condition
is fighting God, striving against Him, hating Him. Man in his
natural state is ready to believe any claim in a newspaper that
someone has proved that there is no God. Man jumps at such
statements and delights in them because he is a God-hater. He is
in a state of enmity against God.

Furthermore, because man is in this relationship to God he is
also in a state of enmity against himself. He is not only engaged
in this warfare against a God who is outside of him; but he is also
fighting a war within himself. Therein lies the real tragedy of
fallen man; he does not believe what I am saying but it is certainly
true of him. Man is in a state of internal conflict and he does not

[38]

know why it is so. He wants to do certain things, but something inside him tells him that it is wrong to do so. He has something in him which we call conscience. Though he thinks he can be perfectly happy whatever he does, and though he may silence other people, he cannot silence this inward monitor. Man is in a state of internal warfare; he does not know the reason for it, yet he knows that it is so.

But in the Scriptures we are told exactly why this is the case. Man was made by God in such a way that he can only be at peace within himself when he is at peace with God. Man was never meant to be a god, but he is for ever trying to deify himself. He sets up his own desires as the rules and laws of his life, yet he is ever characterized by confusion, and worse. Something in himself denies his claims; and so he is always quarrelling and fighting with himself. He knows nothing of real peace; he has no peace with God, he has no peace within himself. And still worse, because of all this, he is in a state of warfare with everyone else. Unfortunately for him everyone else wants to be a god as well. Because of sin we have all become self-centred, ego-centric, turning in upon this self which we put on a pedestal, and which we think is so wonderful and superior to all others. But everyone else is doing the same, and so there is war among the gods. We claim that we are right, and that everyone else is wrong. Inevitably the result is confusion and discord and unhappiness between man and man. Thus we begin to see why the Apostle prays that we may have peace. It is because of man's sad condition, man's life as the result of sin, and as the result of his falling away from God. He is in a state of dis-unity within and without, in a state of un-happiness, in a state of wretchedness.

But it does not even stop at that; man has brought all this upon himself by his disobedience to God. He cannot get away from this. He has tried to put forward every other conceivable ex-planation of his condition, but none is adequate. He has tried the theory of Evolution and on the basis of that outlook and teaching man should by now have been emancipated and there should be peace; but peace has not come. So man tries to explain his lot in other ways; but he cannot do so. Man has brought all this evil upon himself because of his desire to be a god. This is proved by the fact that he dislikes correction, and indeed the whole idea of law. He ridicules it, and regards law as an insult; he does not recognize the need to be kept right by law, and he resents its interference.

But the great message of the Bible is that though man has fallen into sin and has got himself into this wretched state, God has still been concerned about him, and God has both intervened and interfered. He has given laws and directions, but man has invariably rejected them. It is God who has appointed governments and magistrates in order to keep sin within bounds; but man is always fighting against order imposed from without. He dislikes it, and thereby shows his terrible hatred of God and his enmity against God. Man has always rejected what God has provided for him, and so there is only one inevitable conclusion to come to with respect to man. Man richly deserves the fate he has brought upon himself. Indeed we can go further and say that man deserves something much worse; he deserves to be punished. But man is not only a law breaker who deserves to be punished, he is also a fool. He rejects and will not listen to God's law, and therefore he deserves punishment, he deserves damnation. There is no excuse for man, he deliberately sinned and fell at the beginning, and he deliberately rejects God's guidance still. There is no plea that can be offered for such a person. Give him the Bible and he laughs at it. Though we find in the Bible that the men who have conformed to it have found happiness and peace, men reject it; though it is clear that if all people in the world were truly Christian most of the problems would disappear, man still rejects Christianity. Such creatures deserve nothing but punishment and hell. Such is man's condition as a result of his own fall into sin.

But it is just at this point that the marvellous message of the gospel comes in. The whole message of the gospel is introduced by this word 'grace'. Grace means that in spite of everything I have been saying about man, God still looks upon him with favour. You will not understand the meaning of this word 'grace' unless you accept fully what I have been saying about man in sin. It is failure to do the latter that explains why the modern conception of grace is so superficial and inadequate. It is because man has an inadequate conception of sin that he has an inadequate conception of the grace of God. If you want to measure grace you must measure the depths of sin. Grace is that which tells man that in spite of all that is so true of him God looks upon him with favour. It is utterly unmerited, it is entirely undeserved; but this is the message of 'Grace be unto you'. It is an unmerited and undeserved action by God, a condescending love. When man in sin deserved nothing but to be blotted out of existence God looked on him in grace and mercy and dealt with him accordingly. So this one word 'grace' at the beginning of the Epistle introduces the entire gospel.

This is the great theme of the Scripture in all its parts. For instance Paul write in Romans 5, 'While we were yet sinners, Christ died for us. Much more then, being now justified by his blood, we shall be saved from wrath through him. For if, when we were enemies, we were reconciled to God by the death of his Son, much more, being reconciled, we shall be saved by his life.' He says that we were not only sinners but enemies; not only had we fallen from God and disobeyed Him, and found ourselves in this wretchedness, but beyond that there is this enmity, this hatred, this antagonism in the spirit. The gospel asserts that, in spite of our enmity towards God, He has given His Son for us and our salvation. What He has done is to make peace. In the second chapter of this Epistle we read that He has reconciled us unto Himself and has brought us into a state of union with Himself. His looking upon us in grace has resulted in peace, and it is a perfect peace. God's grace in action undoes completely everything we have described as resulting from sin.

First and foremost it gives a man peace with God: 'Therefore being justified by faith, we have peace with God' (Romans 5:1). We have been reconciled to God; the enmity between us and God has gone because of what God has done in His grace. But the result of grace is not only peace with God, it gives a man peace within. It enables a man for the first time in his life to answer an accusing conscience; it enables a man for the first time in his life to have rest in mind and heart. For the first time a man is able truly to live with himself, and to know that all is well. The conflict has ended in this fundamental sense, and he understands for the first time the cause of all his troubles. He sees a way of overcoming all his difficulties, and glimpses the final victory that is awaiting him in Christ.

That, in turn, leads him to a state of peace with other people. We shall deal with this in detail later, but here it is in a nutshell at the very beginning. The moment a man becomes a Christian nothing remains the same, and nobody else remains the same to him. The person he formerly hated he now sees as a victim of sin and of Satan, and he begins to feel sorry for him. Knowing the grace of God, and experiencing this new peace which has been given to him, his former enemy has become someone for whom he prays. He begins to carry out his Lord's injunction to 'love your enemies, and pray for those who despitefully use you'. The enmity is abolished by the new view. He now desires to be reconciled, and to be at peace.

But to this peace *with* God, peace within, and peace with others, the Scripture goes on to tell us that something further is added which is called 'the peace *of* God'. This means that whatever may be happening round and about you, you have within you 'the peace of God which passeth all understanding' and it 'keeps your hearts and minds through Christ Jesus' (Philippians 4:7). God has not only given you peace, He has provided for the preservation of peace. You are garrisoned by a power and a Person which will keep you at peace. Many things may happen to you, you will be the victim of temptation to sin and you may not know what to do, but this peace of God which passeth all understanding will garrison your hearts and minds. Those are some of the elements in the peace to which the grace of God leads, but what I am anxious to emphasize above everything else is that all this comes to us as the result of the grace of God. 'Grace be to you, and peace from God.' We deserve nothing, we do not even desire it, we cannot achieve it; but God gives it. It is all by grace, it is entirely a free gift of God.

But we must ask a second question: How does all this happen to us? on what basis can all this happen to us? The answer is given immediately in the two words 'our Father'. 'Grace be unto you, and peace, from God our Father'. Grace at once changes our whole attitude towards God because it has changed our whole conception of God. To the Christian God is 'our Father'. To the Christian God is not just some philosophical X in the distance, whom he talks and argues about cleverly in his philosophical books; God is not some great force, some mighty power away in some distant heaven; He is the Father, my Father, our Father. The whole relationship between man and God has been entirely renewed and changed. God is no longer some terrible far-distant law-giver waiting to punish us; He is still the law-giver, but He is also 'my Father'.

But we must be careful for there are pitfalls all around us. In what sense is God my Father? 'God', says someone, 'is the Father of all men'. It is true that there is a sense in which God is the Father of all men. Paul in preaching to the Athenians says God is our Father in this sense, that we are all 'his offspring' (Acts 17:28). That refers to God in His relationship to us as Creator. The author of the Epistle to the Hebrews writes similarly when he describes God as 'the Father of spirits' (Hebrews 12:9). God is the Father of all spirits as He is their Maker and Creator, and in that sense He is the progenitor of the spirits of all men. But when the Apostle says 'our Father' here, he is not speaking in that sense. God is not Father in the general sense only, but 'our Father'. Every man, having sinned, has fallen from that initial relationship, and therefore our Lord was able to say to certain Jews, 'Ye are of your father the devil' (John 8:44). Clearly, they were not the children of God.

So the Apostle, here, is not simply describing God in general terms of Fatherhood, in terms of creation. There is a new element and that is introduced in the next word, 'Grace be unto you, and peace, from God our Father, and from the Lord Jesus Christ.' This is the differentia of Christianity, this is the element that changes everything. It is the Lord Jesus Christ. Lest there be any uncertainty or confusion let us note what Paul says in this very salutation: 'Grace be to you, and peace, from God our Father, and from the Lord Jesus Christ.' The grace and peace come equally from the Lord Jesus Christ and the Father. This is vital doctrine. There is no such thing as Christianity apart from the Lord Jesus Christ; there is no blessing from God to man in a Christian sense except in and through the Lord Jesus Christ. Anything which claims to be Christianity without having Christ at the beginning and the centre and the end is a denial of Christianity, call it what you will. There is no Christianity apart from Him; He is everything.

Who is this Person whom the Apostle links with God the

[43]

Father? Look at the terms employed. He is the Lord, that is to say, Jehovah. The word here translated by 'Lord' was the word used by the Jews in the old dispensation for 'God'. It was the greatest name of all, the Name that was so sacred that they did not even dare to use it. 'Jehovah' is the Name of God, the Covenant God. The Name Jehovah is used of God the Father; and it is also the Christian's claim for Jesus Christ. He is the One who is described in the Gospels as Jesus of Nazareth, but Paul does not hesitate to say that He is God. He puts Him by the side of God, He is co-equal with God, He is co-eternal. He can be put there without any irreverence, He can be put there without blasphemy. He can be put there by the side of our true and living God, the Father. He is the Eternal Son of God, one with God from eternity.

But He is also Jesus. That means that He is also truly a man. A babe was born in Bethlehem and the Name given to Him was 'Jesus'. He was later a boy in the temple – Jesus of Nazareth. He was a carpenter, the Son of Joseph and Mary, and we read of His brothers. He is the Man who started preaching at the age of thirty, Jesus, the miracle-worker.

But in the next verse we are told still more about Him, 'Blessed be the God and Father of our Lord Jesus Christ'. He is the Lord, He is Jehovah, He is God, but God is also His God, and God is His Father. This is a great mystery. He Himself said just before the end of His earthly life, 'I ascend unto my Father and your Father, and to my God and your God' (John 20:17). He had already said, 'The Father is greater than I'; yet He Himself is the Lord Jehovah. He is also 'the firstborn among many brethren'. He is Jehovah, but He is also Jesus – the God-man. The amazing doctrine of the Incarnation is here in the second verse. Christ is the second Person in the blessed Holy Trinity who has come down in condescending love to reconcile us to God. He is the Lord Jehovah become 'Jesus', taking upon Himself our nature, taking upon Himself our problems, and even our frailties, and eventually our sins. He went to the darkest depths, even to the extent of feeling deserted by God while He bore our punishment. That is 'grace', the condescending love of God. 'God so loved the world that he gave his only begotten Son.'

The next word is 'Christ' – the Lord Jesus Christ. He is the Saviour, the Anointed One, the Messiah, the One who is sent to redeem mankind. He has come down from the glory into this world, but He went even lower than that. He was not ashamed to put on 'the likeness of sinful flesh'. He bore our punishment on the Cross, His blood was shed for us, and we are reconciled to God and have 'peace with God'. But, yet more wonderful, having taken our nature upon Himself He then gives us His nature. For Christ does not merely give us forgiveness, He gives us a new birth, and we become 'children of God'. 'The Son of God became the Son of Man, that the sons of men might become the sons of God', as John Calvin once said. It means that not only have we this peace with God and with others, but we enjoy the favour of God, because we are the children of God in Christ. God who is His God and His Father has become our God and our Father. So the Apostle could say, including us, who are Christians, with himself, 'Grace be to you, and peace, from God our Father, and from the Lord Jesus Christ'. The highest honour of all, the greatest gift of God's grace to us is that we become 'children of God' and that as such we shall spend our eternity in the presence of our Father. 'Grace', all undeserved, leads to peace, sonship, and ultimately to eternal glory.

4
The Everlasting Covenant

'Blessed *be* the God and Father of our Lord Jesus
Christ, who hath blessed us with all spiritual
blessings in heavenly *places* in Christ.'

Ephesians 1:3

Here, once more, we have one of those glorious, staggering
statements which are to be found in such profusion in the
writings of the Apostle Paul. Nothing, perhaps, is more characteristic of his style as a writer than the frequency with which he
seems to state the whole gospel in a phrase or verse. He never
tires of doing this; he says the same thing in many different ways.
This surely is one of his, even his, most glorious statements.

We must approach it, therefore, carefully and prayerfully. The
danger when considering such a statement is to be so charmed
and enraptured by the very sound of the words, and the very
arrangement of the words, that we are content with some passing
general effect, and never take the trouble to analyse it and thereby
to discover exactly what it says. We may be content with a purely
general aesthetic effect, with the result that we shall miss the
tremendous richness of its content. We must be unusually careful,
therefore, to analyse it, to question it, and to discover exactly the
meaning and the content of every word. And we must do this in
the light of the teaching of the Scriptures as a whole.

The first thing we have to do is to observe the context. First of
all, in the first verse the Apostle has reminded the Ephesians of
who they are, and what they are. Then in the second verse he has
offered a prayer for them, and has reminded them of the things
they can enjoy, and should enjoy, and should seek to enjoy –
'Grace be to you, and peace, from God our Father, and from the
Lord Jesus Christ'. Having done that he is now concerned to
remind them of how it is that they have become what they are,

and of how it is possible for them to enjoy these priceless blessings of grace and peace. That is the connection; and again we must emphasize the fact that this preliminary salutation is not a mere formality; it is full of the logic that always characterizes Paul the Apostle.

Having reminded them that they are 'saints', are 'faithful', and 'in Christ', and as the result of that should be enjoying grace and peace from the Lord Jesus Christ, he now proceeds to show how all that is possible in this third verse. There is a sense in which we can say truthfully that this third verse is the centre of the entire Epistle. The Apostle is concerned to do this above all else. He desires these Christian people to come to an understanding and realization of who they are and what they are, and of the great blessings to which they are open. In other words the theme is the plan of salvation, and the way of salvation, this tremendous process that puts us where we are, and points us to God and the things that God has prepared for us. He does this because he desires these Ephesian Christians and others to enter into their heritage, that they may enjoy the Christian life as they should, and that they may live their lives to the praise and glory of God. And, of course, the same applies to us. Whether we know it or not our main trouble as Christians today is still a lack of understanding and of knowledge. Not a lack of superficial knowledge of the Scriptures, but a lack of knowledge of the doctrines of the Scriptures. It is our fatal lack at that point that accounts for so many failures in our Christian life. Our chief need, according to this Apostle, is that 'the eyes of our understanding' may be wide open, not simply that we may enjoy the Christian life and its experience, but in order that we may understand the privilege and possibilities of our high 'calling'. The more we understand the more we shall experience these riches.

A lack of knowledge has ever been the chief trouble with God's people. That was the message of the prophet Hosea in the Old Testament. He says that God's people at that time were dying from 'a lack of knowledge' (4:6). It was always their trouble. They would not realize who they were, and what they were, and why they were what they were. If they had but known these things they would never have wandered away from God, they would never have turned to idols, they would never have sought to be like the other nations. There was always this fatal lack of knowledge. The New Testament is full of the same teaching.

We must therefore consider this verse very carefully because here the Apostle introduces us to this knowledge, this doctrine which leads into an understanding of what we are. We can look at it in terms of the following principles, and in the order in which they are presented by the Apostle.

The first proposition is that the realization of the truth concerning our redemption always leads to praise. It bursts forth at once in the word 'Blessed'. The Apostle seems to be like a man who is conducting a great choir and orchestra. This truth is what Handel seems to have understood so well; it is the characteristic of some of his greatest choruses. Think of the opening note of 'Worthy is the Lamb'. The Apostle starts off with this same tremendous burst of praise and acclamation – 'Blessed be God', 'Praised be God'. He always does so. Examine all his epistles and you will find that this is so. The first thing, always, is praise and thanksgiving, and this is so because he understood the doctrine; it was the result of his contemplation of the doctrine that he praises God.

Surely praise and thanksgiving are ever to be the great characteristics of the Christian life. Take, for instance, the Book of the Acts of the Apostles. It has been said of that Book that it is the most lyrical book in the world. In spite of all the persecution which those early Christians had to endure, and all the hardship and difficulties, they were distinguished by a spirit of praise and thanksgiving. They were people who were thrilled with a sense of peace and happiness and joy they had never known before. The same note is found, too, throughout the New Testament epistles – 'Rejoice in the Lord', 'Rejoice in the Lord always'. Even in the Book of Revelation which portrays trials and tribulations that are certain to face God's people, this note of triumph and praise is to be found running through it all. This is the ultimate peculiar characteristic of God's people, of Christians.

Praise is quite inevitable in view of what we have already seen in this Epistle. If we realize truly what 'grace' and 'peace' mean we cannot help praising. I suggest therefore, before we go any further, that there is no more true test of our Christian profession than to discover how prominent this note of praise and thanksgiving is in our life. Is it to be found welling up out of our hearts and experience as it invariably did with the Apostle Paul? Is it constantly breaking forth in us and manifest in our lives? I am not referring to the glib use of certain words. Certain Christians, when you meet them, keep on using the phrase 'Praise the Lord' in order to give the impression of being joyful Christians. But there is nothing glib about the Apostle's language. It is nothing formal or superficial; it comes out of the depth of the heart; it is heart felt.

All must surely agree that it is impossible to read through the New Testament without seeing that this is to be the supreme thing in the Christian life. It must of necessity be so, because if this gospel is true, that God has sent His own Son into the world to do for us the things we have been considering, then you would expect Christians to be entirely different from unbelievers; you would expect them to live in a relationship to God that would be evident to all, and that should above everything else produce this quality of joy. Even the Roman Catholics whose doctrine and teaching in general tend to depress and to oppose assurance of salvation, before they will 'canonize' anyone, lay down as an absolute essential this quality of joy and of praise. At that point they are absolutely right – praise should be the characteristic of all 'saints', of all Christians. Hence we find this constant exhortation in the New Testament to praise God and offer up thanksgiving. This is what differentiates us from the world. The world is very miserable and unhappy; it is full of cursing and complaints. But praise, thanksgiving and contentment mark out the Christian and show that he is no longer 'of the world'.

Praise distinguishes the Christian particularly in his prayer and in his worship. The Manuals on the devotional life which have been written throughout the centuries, and irrespective of particular Communions, agree that the highest point of all worship and prayer is adoration and praise and thanksgiving. Are we not all guilty at this point? Are we not aware of a serious deficiency and lack as we consider this? When we pray in private or in public what part does adoration play? Do we delight simply to be in the presence of God 'in worship, in adoration'? Do we know what it is to be moved constantly to cry out, 'Blessed be our God and Father', and to ascribe unto God all praise and blessedness and glory? This is the highest point of our growth in grace, the measure of all true Christianity. It is when you and I become 'lost in wonder, love and praise' that we really are functioning as God means us to function in Christ.

Praise is really the chief object of all public acts of worship. We all need to examine ourselves at this point. We must remember that the primary purpose of worship is to give praise and thanksgiving to God. Worship should be of the mind and of the heart. It does not merely mean repeating certain phrases mechanically; it means the heart going out in fervent praise to God. We should not come to God's house simply to seek blessings and to desire various things for ourselves, or even simply to listen to sermons; we should come to worship and adore God. 'Blessed be the God and Father' is always to be the starting point, the highest point.

But let us note that the praise and the adoration and the worship are to be ascribed to the blessed Holy Trinity. 'Blessed be the God and Father of our Lord Jesus Christ, who hath blessed us with all spiritual blessings.' The blessings come through the Holy Spirit. The praise and worship and adoration, indeed all worship, must be offered and ascribed to the Three blessed Persons. The Apostle Paul never fails to do this. He delights in mentioning the Father and the Son and the Holy Spirit. The Christian position is always and inevitably Trinitarian. Christian worship must be Trinitarian if it is true worship; there is no question, no choice about this. If we have the correct biblical view of salvation, then the Three Persons of the blessed Holy Trinity must always and invariably be present.

So often people stop at one Person. Some stop at the Person of the Father; they talk about God and about worshipping God and about having forgiveness from God; and in all their talk and conversation even the Lord Jesus Christ is not mentioned. Certain others seem to stop only and entirely with the Lord Jesus Christ. They so concentrate upon Him that you hear little of the Father and little of the Holy Spirit. There are others whose entire conversation seems to be about the work of the Holy Spirit and they are interested in spiritual manifestations only. There is this constant danger of forgetting that as Christians we of necessity worship the Three Persons in the blessed Holy Trinity. Christianity is Trinitarian in its origin and in its continuance.

But not only must we be careful always that the Three Persons are in our minds and our worship, we must be equally careful about the order in which they are introduced to us in the Scriptures – the Father, the Son, the Holy Spirit. There is what our forefathers called a divine economy or order in the matter of our salvation among the blessed Persons themselves; and so we have always to preserve this order. We are to worship the Father through the Son, by the Holy Spirit. Many evangelical Christians in particular seem to offer all their prayers to the Son, there are others who forget the Son altogether, but the two wrongs do not make one right. So we notice here at the commencement of this Epistle that the Apostle not only praises, but praises the three blessed Persons, and ascribes unto them thanksgiving and glory in this invariable order.

The second principle is that God is to be praised. My first principle was that a true realization of the nature of salvation leads to praise. Now we turn to consider why the blessed Persons of the Holy Trinity should be thus praised. There are many answers to that question, but we must concentrate on the one which the Apostle emphasizes specially in this verse. God is to be praised because He is what He is. The ultimate characteristic or attribute of God is blessedness. It is indescribable, but if there is one quality, one attribute of God that makes God God; (I speak with reverence) if there is one thing that makes God God more than anything else, it is blessedness. And God is to be praised. We are to say 'Blessed be God' because of what God is and what He does.

God is also to be praised because He has blessed us: 'Blessed be the God and Father of our Lord Jesus Christ, who hath blessed us with all spiritual blessings.' Before we come to that, however, we note that the Apostle has gone on to something else. God is to be praised and to be blessed because of the way in which He blesses us. I have already been hinting at that in reminding you of the importance of our relationship to the Three Persons in the blessed Holy Trinity. In other words, the greatness emphasized in this verse is the planning of our salvation; and not only the planning but the way in which it has been planned, the way in which God has brought it about. Once more must we not plead guilty to a tendency to neglect and ignore this? How often have we sat down and tried to contemplate, as the result of reading the Scriptures, the planning of salvation, the way in which God worked out His plan, and how He put it into operation? Our salvation is entirely from God but because of our morbid preoccupation with ourselves and our states and moods and conditions, we tend to talk of salvation only in terms of ourselves and of what is happening to us. Of course that is of vital importance, for true Christianity is experimental. There is no such thing as a Christianity which is not experimental; but it is not only experience. Indeed it is the extent of our understanding that ultimately determines our experience. We spend so much of our time in feeling our spiritual pulses and talking about ourselves and our moods and conditions that we have but little understanding of the planning of what God has done. But the Apostle generally starts with this, as also does the Bible.

I call attention to this matter, not because I am animated by some academic or theoretical interest, but because we rob ourselves of so much of the glories and the riches of grace when we fail to take the trouble to understand these things and to face the teaching of Scripture. We tend to take a chapter at a time; we pass on; and we do not stop to analyse and to realize what it is saying to us. Some even try to excuse themselves by saying that they are not interested in theology and doctrine. Instead, they want to be 'practical' Christians and to enjoy Christianity. But how terribly wrong that is! The Scriptures give us this teaching, the Apostle Paul wrote these letters that people like ourselves might understand these things. Some of the people to whom Paul wrote were slaves who had not had a secondary or even a primary education. We often say that we have not the time to read – shame on us Christian people! – the truth being that we have not taken the trouble to read and to understand Christian doctrine. But it is essential that we should do so if we really desire to worship God. If there is no praise in a Christian's life it is because he is ignorant of these things. If we desire to praise God, we must look at the truth, and expand our souls as we come face to face with it. If we want to say 'Blessed be God' from the heart we must know something about how He has planned this great salvation.

God's great plan is suggested in this verse. There was a great eternal council held between the Father, the Son and the Holy Spirit. The next verse tells us when it was held: 'According as he hath chosen us in him before the foundation of the world, that we should be holy and without blame before him in love.' Do we realize that our salvation was planned before the world was planned or created? It is the realization of this fact that makes a man stand on tip-toe and shout out praise to God – 'chosen before the foundation of the world'. The three blessed Persons in the eternal council were concerned about us – Father, Son and Holy Spirit. In the first chapter of the Book of Genesis we read that God said, 'Let us make man in our image', but, thank God, that council not only considered the creation of man, it went on to consider also the salvation of man. The Three Persons met in conference (I speak with reverence, in terms of Scripture) and planned it. Let us get rid for ever of the idea that salvation was an afterthought in the mind of God. It was not a thought that came to God after man had fallen into sin – it was planned 'before the foundation of the world'. The Apostle tells us that the work was divided up between the three blessed Persons, each One agreeing to engage in particular tasks. This is what led the old theologians to talk about the 'economic Trinity'. The three blessed Persons in the Trinity divided up the work – the Father planned, the Son put it into operation, and the Holy Spirit applies it.

This is made clear in our chapter. In verses 4–6 we are told of the Father's part; in verses 7–12 we are told about the Son's part; and in verses 13 and 14 we are told about the part of the Holy Spirit; and note that in each case the description ends with the phrase, 'to the praise of the glory of his grace', or similar words. The divine council considered everything 'before the foundation of the world' and the work was divided up and planned in that manner. The Father has His purpose, the Son voluntarily says He is going to carry it out, and He came and did it, and the Holy Spirit said He was ready to apply it.

But before we leave it, I must add this, that what really happened in that eternal Council was that God drew up a great covenant called the covenant of grace or the covenant of redemption. Why did He do so? Let me ask a question by way of reply. Why does the Apostle say, 'Blessed be the God and Father of our Lord Jesus Christ'? There are those who say that the answer is that He wants us to know the kind of Father God is. I agree with that. I remember an old preacher saying once that if you told certain people that God is a Father they would be terrified and alarmed. There are some people, he said, to whom the term 'Father' means a drunkard who spends all the family's money and comes home drunk. That is their idea of a father; it is the only father they have ever known. So God in His kindness, and in order that we may know the kind of Father He is, says: I am the Father of the Lord Jesus Christ. The Son is like the Father; but even that does not go far enough, there is much more than that here.

This new description of God is one of the most important statements in the New Testament. Go back to the Old Testament and you will find God described as 'the God of Abraham, Isaac, and Jacob'. God also speaks of Himself as 'the God of Israel', but now we have 'the God and Father of our Lord Jesus Christ'. This is in order to teach us that all the blessings that come to us come in and through the Lord Jesus Christ, and as a part of that covenant that was made between the three blessed Persons before the foundation of the world. Even the blessings that came to the Old Testament saints all came to them through the Lord Jesus Christ. Before the foundation of the world God saw what would happen to man. He saw the Fall, and man's sin which would have to be dealt with, and there the Plan was made and an agreement was made between the Father and the Son. The Father gave a people to the Son, and the Son voluntarily made Himself responsible to God for them. He contracted to do certain things for them, and God the Father on His side contracted to do other things. God the Father said He would grant forgiveness and reconciliation and restoration and new life and a new nature to all who belonged to His Son. The condition was that the Son should come into the world and take human nature and the sin of mankind upon Himself and bear its punishment, stand for them, and suffer for them and represent them. That was the covenant, that was the agreement that was made, and it was made 'before the foundation of the world'. God was able to tell Adam about that in the Garden of Eden when He told him that 'the seed of the woman shall bruise the serpent's head'. This had been planned before creation, and God began to announce it even there.

Later certain subsidiary arrangements were made. A covenant was made with Noah, with Abraham, with Moses. These are not the original covenant, the covenant made with the Son. They were temporary, but all these subsidiary covenants point to this great covenant. The types and ceremonial offerings and sacrifices were all pointing to Christ. 'The law was our schoolmaster to lead us to Christ' and His great offering. The law given to Moses does not annul the covenant made with Abraham, but that, in turn, points back to the great covenant made with the Son Himself in eternity.

Thus we begin to see why Paul says, 'The God and Father of our Lord Jesus Christ'. God before time, and before the world, saw our predicament and entered into this agreement with His own Son. He has taken an oath, He has signed, He has pledged Himself in a covenant, He has committed Himself. Everything is in Christ. He is our Representative, He is our Mediator, He is our Guarantor – all blessing comes in and through Him. Who can realize what all this meant to the Father, what all this meant to the Son, what all this meant to the Holy Spirit? But that is the gospel and it is only as we understand something of these things that we shall begin to praise God.

Look at the matter in this way. Here are you and I, miserable worms in this world, miserable worms with our arrogance and our pride and our appalling ignorance. We deserve nothing but to be blotted off the face of the earth. But what has happened is that before the foundation of the world this blessed God, these three blessed Persons, considered us, considered our condition, considered what would happen to us, and the consequence was that these Three Persons, God, whom man hath never seen, stooped to consider us and planned a way whereby we might be forgiven and redeemed. The Son said, I will leave this glory for a while, I will dwell in the womb of a woman, I will be born as a babe, I will become a pauper, I will suffer insult in the world, I will even allow them to nail Me to a Cross and spit in My face. He volunteered to do all that for us, and at this very moment this blessed Second Person in the Trinity is seated at the right hand of God to represent you and me. He came down to earth and did all that, and rose again, and ascended to heaven; and it was all planned 'before the world' for you and for me.

Do you still say that you are not interested in theology? Do you still say that you have not time to be interested in doctrine? You will never begin to praise God or worship or adore Him until you begin to realize something of what He has done for you. 'Blessed be the God and Father of our Lord Jesus Christ.' We are in the covenant; and we shall now try to consider some of the consequences of that covenant.

5
'All Spiritual Blessings in Heavenly Places'

'Blessed *be* the God and Father of our Lord Jesus
Christ, who hath blessed us with all spiritual
blessings in heavenly *places* in Christ.'

Ephesians 1:3

As we turn again to this great verse we come to a consideration
of the character of the blessings which we enjoy as Christians.
The Apostle obviously took great delight in the very expressions
and words; they always seem to make him burst forth in adoration
and thanksgiving. Once more we must be careful to take these
blessings in the right order. The Apostle starts with praise of God,
then goes on to the covenant of the eternal purpose; and it is only
after doing so that he comes down as it were to our level and
begins to deal with the actual blessings we enjoy.

The order is of extreme importance. Because of our wretched
subjectivity our tendency always is to concentrate at once on the
blessings; we always want something for ourselves. The Apostle
insists, however, that we start with God, and with worship. We
are not to rush into the presence of God in prayer or in any other
respect; we must always start by realizing who God is. What
would be thought of a person who tried to rush into Buckingham
Palace to see the Queen of England and refused to consider
matters of etiquette? Such an approach would be regarded as
insulting, and yet we all tend to act in that manner with respect
to Almighty God on account of our great concern to obtain a
blessing. But the Apostle insists upon the right and appropriate
order; and we must only consider the nature of the blessings after
we have worshipped God and praised His Name, and after we
have realized what God has done in order that it might be possible
for us to be blessed at all. Indeed it is only as we adopt this
Apostolic order that we shall really begin to enjoy the blessings.

I can certainly testify after many years of pastoral experience that the people who give me the impression of being most miserable in their spiritual life are those who are always thinking of themselves and their blessings, their moods and states and conditions. The way to be blessed is to look to God; and the more we worship Him the more we shall enjoy His blessings. This is most practical. The practical man is not one who runs after the blessings, but the man who considers the Source of the blessings and is in touch with that Source.

The first thing to observe is the way in which these blessings come to us. They come 'in Christ'. Though this expression comes at the end of the verse it is vital: 'Blessed be the God and Father of our Lord Jesus Christ, who hath blessed us with all spiritual blessings in heavenly places in Christ.' If you leave out the 'in Christ' you will never have any blessings at all. This is, of course, pivotal and central in connection with the whole of our Christian faith. Every blessing we enjoy as Christian people comes to us through the Lord Jesus Christ. God has blessings for all sorts and conditions of men. For instance, the Sermon on the Mount gives our Lord's teaching that God 'maketh his sun to rise on the evil and on the good' (Matthew 5:45). There are certain common general blessings which are enjoyed by the whole of humanity. There is what is called 'common grace', but that is not what the Apostle is dealing with here. Here, he is dealing with particular grace, with special grace, the blessings that are enjoyed by Christian people only. The evil as well as the good, the unjust as well as the just, enjoy common blessings, but none but Christians enjoy these special blessings. People often stumble at this truth, but the distinction is drawn very clearly in the Scriptures. The ungodly may enjoy much good in this world, and their blessings come to them from God in a general way, but they know nothing of the blessings mentioned in this verse. Paul is writing here to Christian people and his concern is that they should understand and grasp the special blessings and privileges possible to them as Christians, and so he emphasizes that all those blessings come in and through the Lord Jesus Christ, and in and through Him alone. You cannot be a Christian without being 'in Christ';

Christ is the beginning as well as the end, He is Alpha as well as Omega; there are no blessings for Christians apart from Him.

We must also emphasize that the blessings come exclusively in and through the Lord Jesus Christ. He has no assistant – 'There is none other name under heaven given among men, whereby we must be saved', says Peter in Acts 4: 12. An alternative translation of that is, 'there is no second name'. The Lord Jesus Christ needs no assistant, no supplement. Every blessing is in Him, not a single blessing comes from anywhere else. He is the only channel; there is only 'one mediator between God and men, the man Christ Jesus' (1 Timothy 2:5). All talk therefore about a 'Congress of World Faiths' or the advocacy of an eclecticism in which you choose the best out of the various religions of the world, is a denial of Christianity. The moment you add any name to that of the Lord Jesus Christ you are detracting from Him. At the same time you are deluding yourself. This great message which was committed to Paul of all apostles, emphasized this particularity, this exclusiveness, this intolerance of any other suggestions or addition.

This emphasis is seen still more clearly, perhaps, in the Epistle to the Colossians: 'It pleased the Father that in him [the Lord Jesus Christ] should all fulness dwell' (Colossians 1:19). It is all in Him. At the end of this first chapter of the Epistle to the Ephesians we read again: 'He hath put all things under his feet, and gave him to be the head over all things to the church, which is his body, the fulness of him that filleth all in all' (vv. 22–23). Paul is not content with saying this once. He says it again in the second chapter of the Epistle to the Colossians: 'In whom are hid all the treasures of wisdom and knowledge' (v. 3). You cannot add to that; all the treasures of wisdom and knowledge are in Christ, all the fulness of the Godhead is in Him. 'In him dwelleth all the fulness of the Godhead bodily' (Colossians 2:9). Christ is the sole Mediator of all blessings, the sole, exclusive channel through which they come. I repeat and stress this because I know in my own heart and experience, as I know it in the experience of others, how prone we are to forget this, how liable we are to go into the presence of God in prayer without realizing the absolute necessity of going in and through Christ.

The Apostle John states precisely the same truth when, referring to himself and his fellow apostles, he says, 'We beheld his glory, the glory as of the only begotten of the Father, full of grace and truth; . . . and of his fulness have all we received and grace for (or 'upon') grace' (John 1:14–16). In other words the Christian is what he is because he is joined to the Lord Jesus Christ. That is to say, he is, as we saw in the first verse, 'in Christ Jesus'. All the life in every part of the body comes from the Head; it is our mystical union with Him, our mysterious relationship to Him, that accounts for what we are. The Christian is a sharer in the life of the Son of God. All life comes from Him, and we all simply draw from Him. 'We drink of Thee the Fountain-head'. Our hymns as well as the Scriptures often state this truth; the saints of the centuries have realized it. Nothing matters so much as our relationship to the Lord Jesus Christ. That is why Paul keeps on reminding us of it; and we must never forget it. Without Him we are 'yet in our sins'. Every blessing we enjoy, everything good that we have achieved or experienced, all comes from Him. 'Every thought of holiness is His alone'.

The second truth about these blessings, the Apostle goes on to emphasize, is that they are 'spiritual'. 'Blessed be the God and Father of our Lord Jesus Christ, who hath blessed us with all *spiritual* blessings.' This is an important addition, an essential qualification. These blessings come from Christ, but they also come through the Spirit; they are blessings which are mediated to us from God through Christ *via* the Holy Spirit. It is by the Holy Spirit they become ours. Once more we cannot but pause in wonder and amazement at the perfection of this glorious plan of salvation worked out by the 'economic Trinity', the Father, the Son and the Holy Spirit, for our redemption.

But the particular work of applying to us the salvation that is in Christ is done by the Holy Spirit. His purpose and function is to glorify the Lord Jesus Christ, and what He does is to make it possible for us to receive everything He has done for us and everything that He makes possible for us. Hence a good way of looking at the life of the Christian in this world is to look at the Lord Jesus Christ when He was here on earth. Although He was the eternal Son of God He came and took human nature unto Himself. Having decided to live His life in this world as a man,

He did not employ the prerogatives of His Godhead in order to save us, but He lived His life among men. It was therefore necessary that He should have received the Holy Spirit, and in the Gospel according to John we are told that 'The Spirit is not given by measure to him' (3:34). At His baptism, when our Lord was setting out upon His public ministry, the Holy Ghost descended upon Him to enable Him and to anoint Him for His great task. That was necessary because He was living His life in this world as a man.

Now the wondrous truth taught here is that, as the Holy Spirit filled His life and enabled Him to live as described in the Gospels, the same is possible for us through Him. The same Holy Spirit who dwelt in Him dwells in us as Christians, and not only so, He brings to us and fills us with the life of Christ Himself. Thus the blessings we enjoy as Christians are all blessings in and through the Holy Spirit. Such is the type of life, the quality of life, which we are meant to be living as Christians. The Apostle John in a very striking verse in his First Epistle says that 'as he is, so are we in this world' (4:17). We do not propose here and now to work this out in detail; but we know that the Holy Spirit comes and quickens us. Think of Christ in all His fulness, and think of the sinner in his sin – 'dead in trespasses and sins'. How can such a person ever become spiritual? The Holy Spirit comes and quickens us. 'You hath he quickened who were dead in trespasses and sins' (Ephesians 2:1). He starts this enlightening process, He begins to give us an insight into spiritual things.

Man by nature is not interested in spiritual matters at all; they seem strangely remote to him. He is interested in the life of this world, in things that can be seen and touched and felt and handled; but when you begin to talk to him about the soul and the things of the spirit he really does not know what you are talking about. This is so because he is dead, and his life is governed by 'the prince of the power of the air'. He is interested in houses and in horses, in dogs, in animals, in furniture, in pleasures of various kinds, and business and great affairs; but begin to talk to him about communion with God and the life of the Spirit, and he is at once in an utterly strange realm. And he will remain in that condition until the Holy Spirit begins to quicken him, and to put a spiritual principle in his life. He needs a spiritual mind, a spiritual

[61]

outlook and a spiritual understanding; and the Spirit gives these blessings in regeneration. These are the preliminary blessings that come to us through the Spirit to prepare us to receive the fulness that is in Christ. He then proceeds to convict us of sin, to make us see something of our utter emptiness and woe. He makes us see how appalling it is that God should be of no interest to us, the things of eternity utterly remote, and these great things of the Spirit boring and unattractive to us. He makes us see the enormity of our sin.

Next, the Holy Spirit gradually leads us on to contemplate the Lord Jesus Christ and His perfect work on our behalf. He gives us the gift of faith by grace. 'By grace are ye saved through faith' (Ephesians 2:8). The Spirit creates faith in us. 'The natural man receiveth not the things of the Spirit of God: for they are foolishness unto him: neither can he know them, because they are spiritually discerned' (1 Corinthians 2:14). So the Spirit enables us to exercise this gift of faith and thus we come to believe on the Lord Jesus Christ. These are parts of that mysterious process which leads to our union with Christ, and which are described as the new birth, the being joined to Christ as a branch in the vine. The Holy Spirit then leads and guides us and keeps us in this union, so that we are enabled progressively to receive Christ's fulness, and 'grace upon grace', 'grace after grace'. Thus we are 'changed from glory to glory', and on and on it goes. This is not theory; it is fact, it is truth. This is what happens to us as Christians; this is God's way of salvation. This is in operation in Christians in the world today. It all comes through Christ, and as the result of this work of the Holy Spirit. These are the 'spiritual' blessings, blessings of the Holy Spirit that come about because the Holy Spirit dwells within us. Our bodies are 'the temple of the Holy Ghost' who dwells in us (1 Corinthians 6:19).

We must next proceed to look at the actual character of these blessings. The first thing the Apostle tells us about them is that they are 'in heavenly places'. 'Blessed be the God and Father of our Lord Jesus Christ, who hath blessed us with all spiritual blessings *in heavenly places* in Christ'. When you have read this Epistle to the Ephesians have you stopped to consider that expression – 'in heavenly places'? Did you think it was Paul's eloquence carrying him away? If so, you failed to realize that these are solid definitions, words which must be analysed and examined point by point. Every single expression is full of meaning. The blessings we enjoy are 'in heavenly places'. There is no doubt but that in that expression the Apostle has in mind the contrast we have already seen in the way in which he describes God as 'The God and Father of our Lord Jesus Christ' rather than as 'The God of Abraham, and of Isaac, and of Jacob'. Paul reminds us that as the covenant and the representative are different so the blessings are also different.

In the Old Testament the blessings came very largely, indeed mainly, in a material and temporal sense. It was estimated then whether a man was blessed or not by the number of cattle he had, the number of sheep and goats, and the extent of the land he possessed. God's way with men in Old Testament times was more pictorial. He frequently acted in a visible manner. He was then teaching the people as infants, as it were, so He gave external, obvious blessings which, being mainly earthly, could be seen here on earth. But as we enter the New Testament, we come into an entirely different realm. Here the blessings are 'in heavenly places'. We must look for these blessings, not so much here on earth, but 'in the heavenly places' beyond sight.

Here, clearly, we are face to face with a very important New Testament principle. Let me state it quite categorically; the Christian faith is frankly and openly other-worldly. I state the matter boldly because I know that this principle is not popular today when the emphasis is on the 'here and now'. This accounts for the present apostasy in the Church as well as for the so-called social gospel that was preached so much in the early part of this century and towards the end of the last century. The teaching was that Christianity is something that puts social conditions right, and deals with political problems in the 'here and now'. The modern man, we were told, is not interested in an other-worldly view. But whether we like it or not, the fact is that the blessings we enjoy in Christ are 'in heavenly places'.

We must understand, however, that this does not mean something completely and exclusively other-worldly. It does not mean that we are automatically to become monks or hermits or

[63]

anchorites; but it does mean that we have a right view of this world and our relationship to this world. The Christian, according to the New Testament, is in a very strange and wonderful position; he is still in this world but he does not really belong to it. This same Apostle Paul, writing to the Philippians, says: 'Our conversation is in heaven', or as James Moffatt has translated it, 'we are a colony of heaven'. Our real citizenship is in heaven. The Apostle frequently employs this idea of citizenship and says that we do not really belong to an earthly city or state. We are simply resident here, away from home; our citizenship is not here but in heaven. A well-known hymn states it very well –

I'm but a stranger here,
Heaven is my home.

The Apostle Peter likewise expresses the same idea when he writes: 'Dearly beloved, I beseech you as strangers and pilgrims, abstain from fleshly lusts' (1 Peter 2:11). We are but 'strangers and pilgrims' in this world; we do not belong to it. Christians are like people away on holiday; and they should remember the country from which they have come, and the realm to which they belong. This is the teaching of the New Testament throughout. A Christian is a man who is passing through this world. That does not mean that he despises it, for it is God's world, and we should see the marks of God's handiwork in the world. We should enjoy the creation, we should enjoy all the beauty and everything that is a manifestation of God's handiwork. 'The heavens declare the glory of God' and Christians of all people should realize that and enjoy it. Nevertheless we as Christians know that, though this is God's world, it is a fallen world; we know that sin has entered into it, and therefore, though it is still God's world, it can be dangerous to us. We must never 'conform' to its outlook and mind and mentality. The mind and outlook of the world is controlled by 'the prince of the power of the air, the spirit that now worketh in the children of disobedience'. In other words the Christian looks at this world in an entirely different manner from the non-Christian. He sees it as his Father's world, a world of glory and wonder. It is not the world of the Sunday newspapers; it is God's world. The Christian does not conform to it, but becomes 'transformed by the renewing of his mind'.

It is very difficult to translate all this into language but this is what the New Testament writers keep on saying. The Apostle Paul at one time was having great trouble in this world, but he says: 'Our light affliction, which is but for a moment, worketh for us a far more exceeding and eternal weight of glory' (2 Corinthians 4:17). 'And if our earthly house of this tabernacle were dissolved we have a building of God, an house not made with hands, eternal in the heavens' (2 Corinthians 5:1). That is typical of his other-worldly view. Again, in his Epistle to the Colossians he says, 'Set your affection on things above, not on things on the earth' (3:2). The Christian's relationship to the world is, that he realizes that it is God's world, and he can enjoy it and all that God has given him in and through it; but he never sets his affection upon it. For this reason the attitude of the Christian towards the things of this world, and towards the discussions and the striving that go on between men and women, is always one of detachment.

I have heard two statements recently that illustrate my point. I heard one man say that he did not understand how any Christian could possibly be a Conservative. But I heard another say that he really did not understand how any Christian could possibly be a Socialist. The fact of the matter is that both were wrong; any attempt to equate the teaching of the New Testament with any one of the political parties, or any other party, is to do violence to the teaching of Christ. The Christian, by definition, does not get excited about these things; he rides very loosely to them because heaven is his home. He is a citizen of heaven, and his blessings are there, not on earth. Although he receives many temporal blessings while he is here on the earth, the real blessings are in the heavenly places in Christ Jesus. Whether you rejoice in such teaching, or are disappointed, and have a dislike of this other-worldly religion depends upon the view you take of yourself and your soul. If you have seen yourself for what you really are, namely, as a journeyman passing through this world, you will not only not complain about the other-worldly view, you will thank God for it, and you will know something about that inheritance which is 'incorruptible and undefiled, and that fadeth not away, reserved in heaven for you, who are kept by the power of God through faith unto salvation ready to be revealed in the last time' (1 Peter 1:4–6).

The next word that arrests us is the word 'all' – blessed with '*all* spiritual blessings'. What a little word, and yet what a mighty word! It includes everything that we can ever need. Peter, in the first chapter of his Second Epistle, says that 'all things that pertain unto life and godliness' are provided for us, and that we are given 'exceeding great and precious promises' by God. Nothing greater is conceivable. The blessings I am to enjoy in this life, all the conceivable blessings of God in Christ through the Spirit, are described in a very wonderful way by Paul in this Epistle to the Ephesians. They start with forgiveness and go on to 'all the fulness of God'. The forgiveness is mentioned in the seventh verse of the first chapter and 'all the fulness of God' in the third chapter, verse 19. What blessings! Forgiveness means that your past is blotted out and cast into the sea of God's forgetfulness – 'as far as the east is from the west'. God has reconciled us unto Himself. We are on speaking terms with Him, and approach Him, no longer with a craven fear, but with a holy boldness and yet godly fear. Then we come to the great term 'adoption'. 'Having predestinated us unto the adoption of children by Jesus Christ to himself'. We are not merely forgiven and then left in the same position; we have been taken into God's family. That is the great theme of the second chapter – '. . . ye who sometimes were far off are made nigh by the blood of Christ' (v. 13). We were strangers and aliens outside the commonwealth of Israel, but now we have become 'fellow citizens with the saints and of the household of God' (v. 19). It is as if a miserable urchin in rags and tatters and filth in the street is taken by the hand and led into a palace, and washed and adopted as a son, and made a member of the family. And resulting from all this, we enjoy fellowship with God, with the Father and with the Son through the Spirit. 'This is life eternal, that they might know thee the only true God, and Jesus Christ whom thou hast sent' (John 17:3). Add to this the theme of progressive sanctification, which means that you not only look clean, but that you are clean. Not only have you been clothed with the spotless robe of Christ's righteousness, but He is working within you, and making you conformed increasingly to Himself until finally you will become 'spotless and blameless'.

At the same time He will give you power to withstand sin and Satan. In the last chapter of this Epistle we are given spiritual instructions – 'Take unto you the whole armour of God' (6:13). The armour is provided for us freely, but in addition we are given the strength of Christ Himself to use it. 'Be strong in the Lord and in the power of his might' (6:10). At the same time we can enjoy peace with God – peace within, peace with others – and happiness and 'joy unspeakable and full of glory', comfort in affliction, support in trial. We cannot exhaust the list of these blessings 'in heavenly places, but we must end with this: 'that ye might be filled with all the fulness of God' (Ephesians 3:19).

Those are some of the blessings, the spiritual blessings that are in Christ for us. Someone may ask whether all this is true for us today, and wonder whether such things are only meant for very exceptional people. The answer is that they are meant for all Christians – for you and for me. Paul says, 'Blessed be the God and Father of our Lord Jesus Christ, who *hath blessed* us.' He does not say that God intends to bless us in the future; what was necessary to procure these blessings has been done once and for ever; it has taken place already.

When am I to enjoy all these great and rich and wondrous blessings? The answer is, Here and now! Obviously all this comes to us in a progressive manner, for if 'the fulness of the Godhead' came into us suddenly we would crack and break; so it comes in instalments progressively. 'In whom ye also trusted after that ye heard the word of truth, the gospel of your salvation: in whom also after that ye believed, ye were sealed with that Holy Spirit of promise, which is the earnest of our inheritance until the redemption of the purchased possession, unto the praise of his glory' (vv. 13 and 14). He gives us, here, a foretaste of something which is to come, the first instalment of a great inheritance. We receive much here and now, but the things we are enjoying now are but the beginning, the shadow. Our receiving will increase and develop until finally, and eventually, we shall receive all in its glorious and blessed fulness, and shall enjoy it for ever and ever. 'Beloved', I say with John in his First Epistle, 'now are we the sons of God, and it doth not yet appear what we shall be; but we know that, when he shall appear, we shall be like him, for we shall see him as he is' (3:2). Already we are the sons of God and should therefore be enjoying these things, eating something of the first-fruits. Are you enjoying them? God has already given us

[67]

many blessings; and they will go on increasing until the blessed day dawns when 'the purchased possession' shall be finally redeemed and we shall be ushered into His glorious presence. Then, to use the words of the hymn, we shall 'gaze and gaze' on Him and enjoy a glorious eternity face to face with God. There will be no sin there, nothing to detract; we shall enjoy the fulness of God for ever and ever. 'Blessed be the God and Father of our Lord Jesus Christ, who hath blessed us with all spiritual blessings in heavenly places in Christ.'

6

'In Heavenly Places'

'Blessed *be* the God and Father of our Lord Jesus
Christ, who hath blessed us with all spiritual
blessings in heavenly *places* in Christ.'

Ephesians 1:3

Many go wrong in their entire thinking of Christianity, as we have
seen, because they start with a wrong standpoint. They have a
materialistic conception of Christianity, and fail to realize that the
Christian faith is positively other-worldly. The result is that they
are constantly in difficulty. There are many people who say that
they cannot be Christians because of the state of the world and
the things that are happening in it. Their argument is that, if God
is a God of love, who promises to bless all who come to Him,
then Christians should not have to suffer – to be taken ill or suffer
adversity. There we have an example of one of those initial misunderstandings resulting from a failure to realize that the blessings
that come to the Christian are 'spiritual' and are 'in heavenly
places'.

But we must look into this subject in a more detailed manner.
The Apostle never rises to greater heights in this Epistle or
elsewhere than in this particular verse, where he lifts us up into
the 'heavenlies' and shows us the Christian standpoint in its
greatest glory and majesty. In many ways the expression 'in
heavenly places' is the key to this particular Epistle, where it
occurs no less than five times. It is found in this third verse, and
again in the twentieth verse in this first chapter where Paul writes
about Christ being set at God's right hand in the heavenly places.
Some commentators do not like the word 'places' as they feel that
it tends to localize the conception. Yet merely to say 'heavenly' is
not enough. The same expression is found again in chapter 2,
verse 6, and in the tenth verse of the third chapter. The last

reference is in the twelfth verse of the sixth chapter in the statement 'We wrestle not against flesh and blood, but against
principalities and powers, against the rulers of the darkness of
this world, against spiritual wickedness in high (or heavenly)
places'. Obviously the Apostle would not repeat this phrase
unless it possessed some deep and real significance; and it is, I
repeat, one of the most glorious representations of the Christian
truth. If we could but see ourselves as we are in Christ in the
heavenly places it would revolutionize our lives, and change our
whole outlook.

In using the expression 'heavenly places' the Apostle is employ-
ing a descriptive term which was very popular in the first century.
It was a characteristic Jewish conception. He uses the same idea
in the second Epistle to the Corinthians, chapter 12, where he
gives us a bit of autobiography, and in verse 2 says, 'I knew a
man in Christ above fourteen years ago, (whether in the body I
cannot tell; or whether out of the body, I cannot tell: God
knoweth;) such an one caught up to the third heaven'. The
expression 'the third heaven' is exactly the same as 'the heavenly
places' as used in this Epistle to the Ephesians. The first heaven,
according to this conception, is what may be described as the
atmospheric heaven where the clouds are. That is the heaven that
is nearest to us, it is atmospheric. The second heaven can be
described as the stellar heaven; it is that part of the upper regions
where the sun and moon and the stars are placed. This is very
much further away from us than the clouds or the atmospheric
heaven, and the astronomic figures used by the scientists remind
us that the stellar heavens are a tremendous distance from us.

But there is a 'third heaven' which is neither the atmospheric
heaven nor the stellar heaven. This is the realm in which God, in
a very special manner, manifests His presence and His glory. It is
also the place where the Lord Jesus Christ in His resurrected body
dwells. Furthermore it is the place in which the 'principalities and
powers' to which the Apostle refers in the third chapter have their
abode; indeed it is the place of which we read in the fifth chapter
of Revelation, where the glory of God is manifested. There we
read of Christ in His glorified body, 'The Lamb that once was
slain', and of the bright angelic spirits, the 'beasts' and the 'four
and twenty elders'. All those angelic dignitaries and powers have

their abode there. And, still more wonderful and glorious, there also are 'the spirits of just men made perfect'. Those who have died in the Lord, 'in Christ', are with Christ there at this moment. They are in 'the heavenly places', in 'the third heaven', in that realm where God manifests something of His eternal glory.

We can now proceed to consider the meaning of 'in the heavenly places' in the light of these five references to it in this Epistle to the Ephesians. The Lord Jesus Christ, risen from the dead, is already in that realm in His glorified body, as we are reminded in the 20th verse. What the Apostle is saying, therefore, is that all we have, and all we enjoy as Christians, comes from Him and through Him who is there in that realm. More than that, by the new birth, by our regeneration, we are joined to the Lord Jesus Christ, and we become sharers and participators in His life and in all the blessings that come from Him. The Apostle's teaching is that we are 'in Christ'. We are part of Christ; we are so bound to Him by this organic mystical union that whatever is true of Him is true of us spiritually. As He is in the heavenly places so are we in the heavenly places also. The blessings we enjoy as Christians are blessings 'in the heavenly places' because they all flow out of Christ who is there.

Here, I suggest, we see more clearly than anywhere else the profound change that one undergoes by becoming a Christian. It is not a mere superficial change, it is not merely that we don some robe of respectability or decency or morality, it is not some surface improvement or some temporal change. It is as profound as this, that we are taken from one realm and put into another. As God brought the Lord Jesus Christ out of the grave, and from the dead, and set Him at His own right hand in the heavenly places, so the Apostle teaches that the change we undergo in our rebirth and regeneration leads to this corresponding change in us. It is in order that the Ephesian Christians may come to understand this more fully that Paul prays for them: 'the eyes of your understanding being enlightened, that ye may know what is the hope of his calling and what the riches of the glory of his inheritance in the saints; and what is the exceeding greatness of his power to us-ward who believe, according to the working of his mighty power which he wrought in Christ, when he raised him from the dead, and set him at his own right hand in the heavenly places.' That, and nothing less than that, is the truth about the Christian. Because of our limited capacities as the result of our finite condition and of our sin, we find it very difficult to take hold of these things; but the whole business of this Epistle to the Ephesians is to urge us to strive to get hold of them, to pray for enlightenment in order that we may understand.

The difficulty arises because of the fact that the Christian, of necessity, is in a sense two men at one and the same time. It is obvious (is it not?) that those who are not Christian simply cannot understand these matters at all. The Apostle states this clearly in the second chapter of the First Epistle to the Corinthians where he describes the difference between the 'natural' and the 'spiritual' man. He writes: 'He that is spiritual judgeth all things, yet he himself is judged of no man.' 'Judge' means 'to discern', 'to understand'. The Christian, says Paul, understands all things but he himself is understood of no man. By definition he is a man whom the non-Christian cannot possibly understand. One of the best tests, therefore, which we can apply to ourselves is to discover whether people find it difficult to understand us because we are Christian – not because we are naturally difficult, but because we are Christian. If Paul's statement is true, then a Christian must be an enigma to everyone who is not a Christian. The non-Christian feels that there is something odd about the Christian; he is not like everyone else; he is different. This must be so by definition, because the Christian has this heavenly life and belongs to this heavenly realm. But he not only eludes the understanding of the non-Christian; in a sense it is true to say that he cannot even understand himself. He has become a problem to others, and he has become a problem to himself because of this new nature that is in him. 'I live, yet not I, but Christ liveth in me' (Galatians 2:20). I am myself, I am not myself.

Let us analyse this a little further. The Christian has two natures, and is conscious of having two natures. He is still in a sense a natural man. What he has inherited by his birth from his forefathers, he still possesses. He is still in this world and in this life like everyone else. He has to live, he has to earn his living, and do various things in the same way as other people. He is still

[72]

living the so-called soulish, secular life, the life that is lived in terms of intellect and understanding. He studies various subjects, and, like everyone else, he is interested in political and social conditions; he has to buy and sell like everyone else. He can study the arts, he may be interested in music. That is his 'soul' life, his secular life, his mentality, which he shares with those who are not Christian. Indeed we can go further and say that he still knows failure in various respects; he is conscious of sin. At times, as he looks at himself, he wonders whether he is different from other people; he seems to be identical with them. He fails, he does things he should not do, he still feels guilty of sin. He appears to be a natural man still. If you take only a superficial view of the Christian you may very well come to the conclusion that there is indeed no difference between him and anyone else. But that is not true, for it is not the whole truth about him. In addition to all that, there is another nature, there is something else which has come in; and it is this something else which makes a Christian an enigma to other people and to himself. In a sense he is a natural man, but at the same time he is a spiritual man. The Apostle contrasts the natural man and the spiritual man, because the great thing about the Christian is that he has this additional spiritual nature. This is his chief characteristic, and it is the dominating factor in his life. The Christian at his very worst knows that he is different from the non-Christian.

Stating it at its very lowest, the Christian is still guilty of sin, but the Christian does not enjoy sin as he once did, and as other people still do. There is something different even about his sin because of this spiritual principle which is in him, this spiritual nature, this consciousness of a new life, of a life which belongs to a different order and realm. It is very difficult to state this in words; there is something elusive about it all, yet it is something that the Christian knows. It is essentially subjective although it results from the belief of objective truth. In other words, unless you feel that you are a Christian there remains a doubt as to whether you are a Christian. Unless something has happened to you experimentally, experientially, unless something has happened to you in the realm of your sensibilities, you are not a Christian.

Many at the present time are in danger of regarding faith in such a purely objective manner as to become unscriptural. They put their entire emphasis upon subscription to certain creeds and the acceptance of certain formulations of truth. But that may be nothing but intellectual assent. To be a Christian means that God through the Spirit is working in your soul, and has given you a new birth, and has put a principle of heavenly life within you. And you must know this. You cannot but do so. You are, of necessity, conscious of this something else, this difference, this power that is working in you, this disturbing element as it may prove. You are, of necessity, conscious even of a new conflict in your life. The person who is not a Christian is only one person; the Christian is two persons. To use scriptural terminology, the non-Christian is nothing but the 'old man'. The Christian, however, has a 'new man' also. And the new man and the old man do not agree; there is tension between the old man and the new man, and there is conflict – 'the flesh lusteth against the Spirit and the Spirit against the flesh' (Galatians 5:17). The very lowest stage of true Christian experience is that stage in which you are conscious of just that conflict. You do not yet know what it is to be 'filled with the fulness of God'; you know little, if anything, of a direct personal communion with Christ; but you know that there is something in you that is disturbing you, that there is, as it were, another person in you, that there is a conflict, that there is almost this dual personality, as it were, this duality. I am trying to, convey the fact of the consciousness which the Christian has of two natures. He is conscious of the two natures because he is 'in Christ' and Christ is 'in the heavenly places'. He has received that life from Christ, and he draws everything he has from Christ; and that is so different from everything else, that the Christian is conscious of having two natures.

But it is not only true to say that the Christian has two natures; he also has two interests because he lives in two worlds. The Christian is a citizen, at one and the same time, of two worlds. He belongs to this world, he exists in it; and yet he is aware of the fact that he belongs to another world as definitely as to this world. This is the inevitable consequence of the fact that he has these two natures. Hence the Apostle says that the Christian is one who has been translated 'from the kingdom of darkness into the kingdom of God's dear Son' (Colossians 1:13) – he has been translated, moved, and given a new position. And this change is parallel in a sense to that which has happened to Christ Himself. God manifested His power when He raised Christ from the dead and set Him at His own right hand in the heavenly places. Now something similar has happened to every Christian. We do not stay where we were, we have been moved, we have been translated from one place, from one realm, to another, from one kingdom into another kingdom, from one world into another world. This is a vital element in the whole experience of the Christian.

This does not mean that the Christian retires out of the world. Historically many Christians have fallen into this error, and have said, Because I am a Christian I no longer belong to the State. There are Christians who say that you should not vote in parliamentary elections, and that you should not take any interest in this world's affairs at all. But that is not true to scriptural teaching for the Christian is still a citizen of this world and belongs to the secular realm. He knows that this is God's world, and that God has a purpose for him in it. He knows that he is a citizen of the country to which he belongs, and he is aware that he has his responsibilities. Indeed, because he is a Christian, he should be a better citizen than anyone else in the land. But he does not stop at that, he knows that he is also a citizen of another kingdom, a kingdom that cannot be seen, a kingdom that is not of this world. Yet he is in this world, and the other kingdom impinges upon it. The Christian knows that he belongs to both kingdoms. So this becomes a real test of our profession as Christians. We are aware of the claims that our native land has upon us, and we are also aware of the claims of the heavenly kingdom. We are anxious not to transgress the laws of the land, and we are still more anxious not to hurt the 'King eternal, immortal, invisible' who dwells in that other realm and who is the Lord.

The Apostle goes on to say, however, that not only do we belong to that heavenly realm; in the sixth verse of this second chapter he makes a statement which sounds so daring as to be impossible. He says that God 'hath raised us up together, and made us sit together in heavenly places in Christ Jesus'. That means nothing less than that you and I in Christ at this moment are seated in the heavenly places. We are there; he does not say

that we are going to be, but that we are there. But how can that
be reconciled with the fact that we are still in this world of time
with all its confusion and contradiction? How are both these
things true at one and the same time? At first it sounds para-
doxical; and yet it is gloriously true about the Christian. Spiritually, I am in heaven at this moment 'in Christ', in one sense as
much as I shall ever be; but my body is still living on earth, I am
still in this world of time. My spirit has been redeemed in Christ
as much as it will ever be redeemed; but my body is not yet
redeemed, and I am, with all other Christians, 'waiting for the
adoption, to wit, the redemption of our body' (Romans 8:23).
Or, as Paul expresses it in writing to the Philippians, our position
in this world of time is that 'our conversation is in heaven; from
whence also we look for the Saviour, the Lord Jesus Christ: who
shall change our vile body, that it may be fashioned like unto the
body of his glorification, according to the working whereby he is
able even to subdue all things unto himself' (3:21). In my spirit,
I am already there, but I am still on earth in the flesh and in
the body.

The glorious aspect of this truth is that, because I am 'in
Christ', my body is going to be emancipated; the adoption, the
redemption of our bodies is going to happen; a day is coming
when I shall be in the heavenly places not only in my spirit but in
my body also. This is absolutely certain. We shall be changed, our
bodies shall be glorified, and be without any sin or any blemish or
wrinkle or spot. In spirit and in the body we shall be with Him
and see Him as He is; in the totality of our being and personalities
we shall be in those heavenly places.

The deduction we can draw from the Apostle's teaching was
stated perfectly by Augustus Toplady when he wrote:

> *More happy, but not more secure*
> *The glorified spirits in heaven.*

'The glorified spirits in heaven', the Christian people who have
gone on and are with Christ, are happier than we are. That is so
because we who are still in this life are 'burdened', and therefore
are 'earnestly desiring to be clothed upon with our house which is
from heaven' (2 Corinthians 5:2). Departed Christians no longer
have to struggle with sin in the flesh, and in the world; from it

they are fully delivered; it has ended as far as they are concerned; but we are still in the flesh, in the body, still struggling, still groaning. Because of their departure they are 'more happy'; but they are not more secure. They are no more 'in Christ' than we are. They are there now because they were 'in Christ' when they were here; we even now are 'in Christ', and we are seated together spiritually in the heavenly places with them, and with Christ, at this very moment. As the author of the Epistle to the Hebrews reminds us, 'We have not come to the mount that might be touched; we are come unto mount Sion, and unto the city of the living God, the heavenly Jerusalem, and to an innumerable company of angels, to the general assembly and church of the firstborn, which are written in heaven, to God the Judge of all, to the spirits of just men made perfect, to Jesus the mediator of the new covenant, and to the blood of sprinkling, that speaketh better things than that of Abel' (Hebrews 12:18–24). We are there now in our spirits; we shall be there ultimately in our bodies also.

That brings us to the realization that the Christian not only has two natures, and two existences, but also of necessity has two outlooks. The Christian looks out upon life and the world, and in one sense he sees it as everyone else sees it, yet at the same time he sees it differently. As Christians we do not look at anything as the world does, but as people who belong to the heavenly realm; we see everything differently, we see everything from the spiritual standpoint. Non-Christian men and women are considering the state of the world, the wars and the turmoil, the cause of these things and the possibility of another world war. They are considering suggestions as to what can be done, and the rightness or wrongness of having armies and engaging in fighting. These things demand attention. The Christian, as a citizen of this visible realm, has to arrive at decisions, and to be able to give reasons for his decisions.

As for the Christian church, in a sense she has nothing to do with the world's problems, and must not spend too much time on them. The church's primary task is to present the spiritual outlook and standpoint. She sees the cause of all troubles in an entirely different way. The worldly view sees the cause of war as a matter of the 'balance of power' as between nations and in terms of how to deal with this most effectively. That is right as far as it goes; but that is not the fundamental problem which, as Paul tells us in the last chapter of this Epistle, is that 'We wrestle not against flesh and blood, but against principalities, against powers, against the rulers of the darkness of this world, against spiritual wickedness in high places' (6:12). The Christian knows that the world is as it is because of sin, because of the devil; he sees all these things with a new perspective and understanding. He knows that they are but the manifestation of Satanic power; and that the conflict in this world is finally a spiritual conflict, not a material conflict. The world's problems are not merely the result of a clash of material conceptions only; they are produced by the powers of hell and Satan fighting against the power of God. In contrast with the world's view, the Christian view is much more profound. The Christian does not see things merely on the horizontal level; he sees them perpendicularly as well. With him there is always this basic spiritual element also – 'sub specie aeternitatis'. For this reason he is not as absorbed in these matters as the man who takes the horizontal view only, for he sees the profound character of the whole problem.

He knows, furthermore, that the only way to deal with these problems must be spiritual. The Christian knows that God has two ways of dealing with these problems which have resulted from the activities of the devil, and the fall of man, and of sin. The first is that God has restrained evil, and does so in many ways. He did so partly by dividing up the world into countries and setting the bounds of each. He did so by ordaining that there should be kings and heads of State, magistrates and powers. Let us never forget that 'the powers that be are ordained of God' (Romans 13:1). It is God who ordained governments and systems of government. That is why the Christian is exhorted to honour the King, and masters, and all in authority. In this way God is keeping evil within bounds, restraining evil. He does so by means of governments, by using statesmen, international conferences, and various other means. But they are only negative, they simply restrain evil. The police force can prevent a man from doing certain things which are wrong, but no police force can ever make a man good. The same applies also to governments. This is true

[78]

also of culture, of education, and of everything that is designed to improve manners, and to make life orderly and harmonious and enjoyable. All these agencies are part of God's mechanism for restraining sin and its manifestations and consequences. But they are all negative. A highly cultured man will never do certain things; but that does not of necessity mean that he is a good man. Culture certainly does not make him a spiritual man.

But there is this other positive aspect; God deals with the problems of the world in a positive and curative manner, namely, in and through Christ and His great salvation. He takes a man out of 'this present evil world' in spirit, and puts him into the kingdom of Christ. He puts a new principle within a man which not only discourages him from sinning, but gives him a love for holiness. The man becomes positively good, and he 'hungers and thirsts after righteousness'. He becomes like the Lord Jesus Christ. There is a new kingdom within 'the kingdoms of this world'; it is God's kingdom. That is the only cure. Eventually the kingdom of God is going to be so great that sin will be destroyed and banished, and will be no more. The Christian, and he alone, sees God's plan and purpose. The statesmen of the world who are not Christian, at their best know nothing about it; they see the situation only in terms of the visible and that which is immediately before them.

These two views are entirely different also with respect to the future. The non-Christian pins his faith to conferences, and imagines that if only men could have a Round Table Conference, and agree never to use the atomic bomb or the hydrogen bomb again, the world would then become more or less perfect. But this never seems to come about. He cannot get beyond the horizontal view, he knows nothing about this higher spiritual element. He believes in the perfectibility of man, and in the evolution of the entire human race. He believes that man will get better as he becomes more educated and that eventually he will banish war.

But, alas, that will never happen because of this spiritual element in the conflict. While man has sin in his nature he will not only be guilty of sin individually but also on a national and a world scale. Why should the mind of the mass be different from the mind of the individual? But, thank God, there is another message; and the greatest tragedy in the world is that the Church, instead of preaching her own true message, is preaching an earthly, human, carnal message. Has the Church nothing better to preach than an appeal to statesmen to solve problems? That is really a denial of the Christian faith, and reveals an abysmal ignorance of 'the heavenly places'. As Christians we have another view, we have something entirely different. Lectures on temperance will never make people sober, or statistics of war casualties put an end to war. We know that the problem is spiritual, and that the solution must be likewise spiritual. As it is from Satan that evil lusts and passions and desires ultimately come; so it is from Christ and Him alone, through the Spirit, that power to overcome can come. And He will not only come to the individual; thank God, He will come to the whole world. The Christian knows that that Christ who is now in the heavenly places will come again to this world in a visible form, riding upon the clouds of heaven, surrounded by the holy angels and the saints who are already with Him; and those who remain on earth when He comes will be changed and will rise into the air to meet Him, and all will be 'for ever with the Lord'. He will rout His enemies, and banish sin and evil. His kingdom shall 'stretch from shore to shore' and He shall be acclaimed as Lord by 'things that are in heaven and on the earth and things that are under the earth' (Philippians 2:10). That is Christian optimism, and it means that we know that it is Christ alone who can and will conquer. Are you 'in the heavenly places', are you aware of the two natures within you, are you aware that you belong to two realms? Have you got this new spiritual view of war and peace and the troubles of the world? Do you see it all from the perspective of heaven, and of God, and of the Lord Jesus Christ seated together with Him in the heavenly places? Blessed be the Name of God!

7
'Chosen in Him'

'According as he hath chosen us in him before the
foundation of the world, that we should be holy and
without blame before him in love.'

Ephesians 1:4

This verse is obviously connected with the previous verse; the
'according as' tells us so. 'Blessed be the God and Father of our
Lord Jesus Christ, who hath blessed us with all spiritual blessings
in heavenly places in Christ: according as he hath chosen us in
him before the foundation of the world, that we should be holy
and without blame before him in love.'

Here, the Apostle begins to explain to us how all the 'spiritual
blessings in heavenly places in Christ' become ours. The previous
verse has done so in a more general manner. But someone may
say: 'That is a great statement, and marvellous and wonderful;
but we are here on earth and we are conscious of sin and of failure;
how are we to be connected with such vast treasures of grace?
How does any Christian ever enjoy a single blessing?' The
Apostle begins to answer that question in this verse, by showing
what has been done by God in order that we may be connected
to all these exceeding riches of His grace: 'according as'! He says
that these blessings come to us in the way he describes from the
beginning of this fourth verse to the end of the fourteenth verse.
The 'according as' is the introduction to the entire statement. I
have already indicated in a previous study how this can be conveniently divided into three main sections: from verse 4 to verse 6
we are told what the Father has done; from verse 7 to verse 12 we
have the work of the Son; and in verses 13 and 14 we have the
work of the Holy Spirit.

As we approach this great statement let us look at any Christian person, ourselves included, and ask: What is it that accounts for the fact that any person who was once not a Christian is now enjoying these astounding blessings? What is it that leads to anyone becoming a Christian and enjoying the riches of God's grace? Doubtless large numbers of people would say immediately that the Christian is a person who has received blessing by believing on the Lord Jesus Christ. But note that that is not the first thing the Apostle says; he does not say that we are enjoying these blessings because we have believed in the Lord, or taken a decision, or given ourselves to Him or accepted Him as our personal Saviour. That, of course, is involved; but Paul does not start in this way. Neither does he start even with the work of the Lord Jesus Christ Himself. Many would probably put that in the first place. They would say that all this has become possible for us because of what the Lord Jesus Christ did for us when He came into this world – in His life and death and resurrection – and what he is still doing. But the Apostle does not put even that first. Indeed we observe that he does not start with anything that has happened in time and in this world. He goes right back into eternity, before the foundation of the world; and he starts with that which has been done by God the Father.

This is a staggering thought but it is entirely consistent with the whole of biblical teaching. It is just here that we all tend to go astray. Although we have the open Bible before us we still tend to base our ideas of doctrine on our own thoughts instead of on the Bible. The Bible always starts with God the Father; and we must not start anywhere else, or with anyone else. The Bible is, ultimately, the revelation and the record and the explanation of what God has done for the salvation of man. The Bible is the revelation of God's gracious purpose towards a world of sinful man; it claims to be such, and the revelation is in its every book. This is what accounts for its extraordinary unity. Its controlling theme is what God has done, what God has promised to do, what God began to do, what God has actually done, what He is going to do, and the amazing outcome of it all. And that is precisely what the Apostle is doing in this section of our Epistle. He is not giving expression to his own theories or ideas, but writing about what God has revealed to him. The Apostle Peter in the third chapter of his Second Epistle places the writings of the Apostle Paul on the same level as the sacred Old Testament Scriptures (vv. 15–16). In other words, he believed that they were inspired in the same way as the ancient Scriptures had been – 'holy men of God spake as they were moved by the Holy Ghost' (2 Peter 1:21). So the Apostle's teaching here is in obvious conformity with the entire biblical teaching.

The teaching is that those who enjoy these spiritual blessings in heavenly places in Christ do so because they have been chosen by God to do so. It is 'according as he hath chosen us in him before the foundation of the world'. That is the explanation of everything, so the Apostle starts with it. All the blessings and benefits we enjoy come from this fount, this source. Man by nature rebels against God. He does so as the result of the Fall. Having listened to the suggestion of the devil and having fallen away from God, he is under 'the wrath of God'. How is it that any individual person has ever come out of that morass? The answer is that God has chosen such a person to be delivered from it unto salvation. Such is the Apostle's categorical statement.

Here we are face to face with a great and profoundly mysterious subject. In the last analysis there are only two possible explanations of such a staggering statement. The first is to believe that we are chosen by God simply as the result of His own good pleasure, or, to use scriptural phraseology, 'according to the good pleasure of his will', and entirely apart from anything we have ever done or said or thought. Indeed it goes further and says that we are chosen by God out of the good pleasure of His own will in spite of ourselves, in spite of the fact that we were enemies, aliens, and even haters of God. The alternative explanation is that the Apostle is saying that Christians – those who enjoy these blessings – were chosen by God before the foundation of the world because God with His perfect foreknowledge saw that they would exercise faith, and thereby differentiate themselves from those who do not exercise faith. In other words God chooses those who of themselves have already chosen to be Christians, those who have decided to believe on the Lord Jesus Christ and have sought salvation. There is no third possibility.

The question confronting us therefore is: How do we face this? I put the question in that way for the reason that so many

Christian people today do not face the question at all. Some, indeed, do not even believe in facing it, others avoid it because it is difficult and mysterious. There are many Christian people today, it seems to me, who claim to be believers in the inspiration of the Scriptures but who nevertheless quite deliberately avoid large portions of Scripture simply because they are difficult. But if you believe that the whole of Scripture is the Word of God, such an attitude is sinful; it is our business to face the Scriptures. One advantage in preaching through a book of the Bible, as we are proposing to do, is that it compels us to face every single statement, come what may, and stand before it, and look at it, and allow it to speak to us. Indeed it is interesting to observe that not infrequently certain well-known Bible teachers never face certain Epistles at all in their expositions because there are difficulties which they are resolved to avoid.

As we approach this great mystery, nothing is more important than that we adopt the right approach. This involves, first and foremost, the spirit in which we approach Scripture. This great declaration of the Apostle has been rejected by some simply because it has been approached in the wrong spirit. Let me grant, quite frankly, that the proponents of the two views I have put before you have been equally guilty in this respect. This question is not to be approached in an argumentative spirit, nor in a party spirit. It is never to be approached with heat or with dogmatism; it is a subject to be approached with reverence, and with a sense of worship. More and more do I agree with those who say that there is a sense in which the Scriptures should always be read by us on our knees. If we realize that it is God speaking to us, surely that must be the way to approach it. Yet how often are these great and glorious statements discussed and debated with heat and acrimony and anger. We are on holy ground here, and we should take off our shoes from off our feet. If we do not approach this mystery in that spirit it is certain that we shall never begin to understand it. This is God's Word, and not simply the opinion of the Apostle Paul. The so-called Higher Critics have evaded this difficulty by saying that it is simply Paul's theology. If you hold that view, and pick and choose what you believe in the Scriptures, you can very easily manufacture a little gospel for yourself. But it will not be the gospel of the New Testament, it will not be 'the gospel of God'. I start with the assumption that this entire Book is the Word of God, and that this particular statement carries divine authority.

It must therefore follow that it is a statement which is not to be approached primarily in terms of our understanding. We must say with George Rawson the hymn-writer –

> *I may not reach with earthly wings*
> *The height and depths of God.*

How appropriate those lines are as we come to this subject! If we imagine that we can rise on the pinions of our little human understanding to a truth of this nature, we are simply betraying an astounding ignorance of the character of the truth. We are face to face here with something in the heart and mind of God. Earthly wings can never bring us to this height. This is, beyond everything else, a great mystery; that is why such sublime truths are presented in the Scriptures to none but believers. This is not something to be considered by the unbeliever; he cannot possibly begin to understand it for his whole attitude towards God is wrong. The essential trouble with the unbeliever is that his heart is wrong with respect to God. 'The fool hath said in his heart, There is no God' (Psalms 14:1), and because his heart is wrong he cannot possibly understand. The Apostle Paul is writing here 'to the saints that are at Ephesus', to people of God who alone are in a condition to receive such truth; and the same applies to us.

Another preliminary remark that is called for as we approach our theme is that it is good to approach such a truth in terms of our experiences as Christians. Instead of approaching it from a theoretical standpoint, and regarding it as a very interesting academic problem on the border line between theology and philosophy, we should approach it by saying to ourselves something like this: 'Here am I in this house of God while there are thousands of people who are not, and who are in their beds reading the Sunday newspapers or perhaps listening to the radio. Why am I different, what has made me different, why am I interested in these things, why bother myself about them at all – why am I a Christian?' Seriously consider what it is that has separated you from those others, what has put you into a different category. And when you find yourself on your knees praying to God, search and examine yourself, and ask yourself what has brought you to pray. Ask yourself whether the desire to pray arises from yourself alone, or from something else. Approach this profound question intellectually, and by the understanding, as well as from the standpoint of experience.

Bearing these preliminary considerations in mind let us now observe what the Bible really does say about 'chosen in him'. My first observation is that it is a statement, not an argument. The Bible never argues about these doctrines, it simply sets them before us; it makes a statement and leaves it at that. This is most significant, because the Bible does argue and give reasons at many points; but when it makes such particular statements as are found in our text it never presents them in the form of an argument.

Indeed we must go further; we can say in the second place that not only does the Bible not argue with us about these doctrines; it reproves us and reprimands us when we begin to argue because we do not understand them. The Apostle states this plainly in his Epistle to the Romans: 'Thou wilt say then unto me, Why doth he yet find fault? For who hath resisted his will?' (9:19). Take note of the Apostle's answer: 'Nay but, O man, who art thou that repliest against God?' He does not try to lead a discussion and work it out and explain it, as he could have done; he simply says, 'Nay but, O man, who art thou that repliest against God'. In other words the Apostle is telling us that we must start by realizing who and what God is, that we must realize of whom we are speaking. And he goes on to remind us that our relationship to the God of whom we are speaking is really that of a lump of clay to a potter. Realize, he says, before you ask your questions and put forward your arguments based upon your failure to understand, that you are assuming that your little mind is capable of understanding what God does. Realize that you are really suggesting that you, simple creature such as you are, small and petty as you often are in your human relationships, you who listened to the devil and brought ruin upon yourself – realize that you are claiming that your pigmy mind is able to

[86]

understand the infinite and inscrutable mind of the eternal God. Not only does the Bible not argue; it reprimands us for our arrogance in bringing our difficulties and pitting them against what God has revealed.

In the third place we observe that the Bible does not answer our questions about this matter, it does not give us a full philosophical explanation. There are real difficulties about this question – of course there are! – because it is from God; and the Bible does not pretend to give a detailed answer or philosophical explanation. It makes its statement and leaves it at that, and we should respond in the same manner as the Apostle Paul and say, 'Great is the mystery of godliness' (1 Timothy 3:16). We cannot begin to understand the mystery of the two natures in one Person, we cannot understand the truth of the Three Persons in one Godhead. These things are in a realm beyond man's understanding; and so is the doctrine that tells us that God chooses us. Our minds are too small; and not only small, we are also sinful and perverted. Even as Christians we still cannot think clearly; that is why there have been heresies throughout the centuries.

A fourth principle that is helpful in this connection is to note that the Bible gives us a number of such statements, all of them parallel to the statement in the verse we are examining. One of the fullest statements on this subject is found in the sixth chapter of the Gospel according to John. John's Gospel, perhaps, presents this doctrine more clearly than any other book in the Scripture. Read through the sixth chapter, then read the fifteenth chapter, and then read the seventeenth chapter of John's Gospel with its record of our Lord's high priestly prayer, and you will find this selfsame truth stated in a most powerful manner. I emphasize this because many people repeat in parrot fashion what they have heard or read in books, to the effect that this doctrine only comes in the writings of the Apostle Paul. Paul, of course, states it frequently. Take, for instance, his Second Epistle to the Thessalonians chapter 2: 'God hath from the beginning chosen you to salvation through sanctification of the Spirit and belief of the truth: whereunto he called you by our gospel, to the obtaining of the glory of our Lord Jesus Christ' (vv. 13-14). What a significant statement! 'He hath chosen you to salvation through (by means of) sanctification of the Spirit.' He separated you by the

Spirit to believe the truth. You have been chosen, set apart, by the Spirit in order that you may believe the truth. You are not separated because you believe it, but in order that you may believe it.

We find the Apostle Peter saying the same thing in his First Epistle, chapter 1, verse 2: 'Elect according to the foreknowledge of God the Father, through sanctification of the Spirit, unto obedience and sprinkling of the blood of Jesus Christ.' Again, the separation comes before the obedience and the believing of the truth. There are countless other similar passages which support this statement directly.

There are other statements, moreover, which show the same thing indirectly. Take the first two verses of the second chapter of this Epistle: 'You hath he quickened who were dead in trespasses and sins; wherein in time past ye walked according to the course of this world, according to the prince of the power of the air, the spirit that now worketh in the children of disobedience'. Note the statements 'dead in trespasses and sins', and 'quickened you'. In the First Epistle to the Corinthians, chapter 2, verse 14, we read: 'But the natural man receiveth not the things of the Spirit of God: for they are foolishness unto him: neither can he know them, because they are spiritually discerned.' Paul's teaching is that we believe these things because 'we have received, not the spirit of the world, but the Spirit that is of God, that we might know the things that are freely given to us of God' (1 Corinthians 2: 12). The princes of this world did not recognize Christ, Paul tells us, because they were natural men. Many of them were great men, able men, but they did not recognize Him, 'For had they known him they would not have crucified the Lord of glory.' 'But,' says Paul, 'God hath revealed [certain things] unto us by his Spirit: for the Spirit searcheth all things, yea, the deep things of God' (1 Corinthians 2: 8–10). We believe for one reason only, namely, because of the work of the Holy Spirit in us.

In the fourth chapter of the Second Epistle to the Corinthians we find the same truth: 'If our gospel be hid, it is hid to them that are lost: in whom the god of this world hath blinded the minds of them which believe not, lest the light of the glorious gospel of Christ, who is the image of God, should shine unto them. For we preach not ourselves, but Christ Jesus the Lord; and

[88]

ourselves your servants for Jesus' sake. For God, who commanded the light to shine out of darkness, hath shined in our
hearts, to give the light of the knowledge of the glory of God in
the face of Jesus Christ' (vv. 3–6). This is the answer to the
question as to how faith originates. The god of this world blinds
and makes men incapable of believing; the only true and living
God shines into our hearts, and we believe.

The doctrine of regeneration is another way of saying the
same thing. We can state it thus. If we hold that we become
regenerate because we have already believed, then we have to
show why we need to be regenerated at all. The purpose and
object of regeneration is to enable us to receive this new faculty,
this ability to receive God's truth. The doctrine of regeneration
has a great deal to say about election and this doctrine of divine
choice. Indeed, I go so far as to say that this doctrine should always
be approached in terms of the doctrine of regeneration which
teaches that I need a new nature before I can begin to understand
these things.

Having reminded you of those statements of the Scriptures let
me put some further considerations for your study and contemplation. Is it not clear and obvious that no man would ever
have produced this doctrine from his own mind? It is the very
last thing that man would ever have thought of. Let us admit that
it is the simple truth to say that all of us by nature dislike this
truth because we feel it is insulting to us. The natural man hates
this doctrine more than any other. We have all known something
of that hatred. Man would never have thought of it; it would
never have come into the thought-life of the Church were it not
that it is found in the Scriptures. Another way of stating it is to
say that there is no doctrine that shows so clearly the real nature
of sin, and the consequences of sin, as this particular statement.
For in reality it asserts that we are in such a position in respect
of sin that we are utterly helpless, and totally incapable of doing
anything for ourselves in the matter of salvation. That is what sin
has done to man, that is the depth to which sin has taken man;
he is indeed far estranged from God! The Scripture says that 'the
carnal (natural) mind is enmity against God' (Romans 8:7), that
man left to himself is an alien, an enemy in his mind by wicked
works and totally opposed to God. Such is the real picture of sin.

But now take note that this aspect of truth has nothing to do with evangelism. People often argue that this doctrine of divine election and choice leaves no place for evangelism, for preaching the gospel, for urging people to repent and to believe, and for the use of arguments and persuasions in doing so. But there is no contradiction here any more than there is in saying that since it is God that gives us the crops of corn in the autumn, therefore the farmer need not plough and harrow and sow; the answer to which is that God has ordained both. God has chosen to call out His people by means of evangelism and the preaching of the Word. He ordains the means as well as the end.

Finally, it is a good rule whenever you are confronted by a statement in Scripture which you find to be difficult and perplexing, to consult authorities, to consult the history of the Church, to consult the experience and the interpretation of those who have gone before us. We should thank God that we are able to do this. The Christian Church has taught through the centuries what the Apostle is saying here, namely, that God has chosen those who are Christian in spite of what they were, not because of any merit that He has foreseen in them, but because He was moved solely by His own mercy and compassion. Before anyone is tempted to dismiss this doctrine with a wave of the hand, feeling that it is all so simple, let me remind you of the names of some of those who have accepted this interpretation.

There is the great St Augustine who stands out, perhaps, between Paul and the Reformation, as the brightest star in the Christian Church. Then there is Thomas Aquinas whom the Roman Catholics call Saint Thomas Aquinas, the author of a compendium on Christian theology, the Summa Theologica. The next name I come to is the name of Martin Luther, then John Calvin, then Ulrich Zwingli, then John Knox of Scotland. Then we come to the Thirty-Nine Articles of the Church of England, then The Westminster Confession of the seventeenth century, the Confession on which all Presbyterian Churches claim to base their teaching as their subsidiary standard. Then think of the great names that belong to the great Puritan tradition – John Owen, Thomas Goodwin and many others. When we come to the eighteenth century there is George Whitefield, perhaps the greatest evangelist the Christian Church has known since Paul.

In America there was Jonathan Edwards who is almost universally regarded as the greatest philosophical theologian the United States has produced. As for the nineteenth century, we must mention the name of the great Charles Haddon Spurgeon. All these men held to the Pauline doctrine.

Let us turn also to the history of the men who started the various Foreign Missionary Socities such as the Church Missionary Society, the London Missionary Society, and indeed the British and Foreign Bible Society. The simple truth is that the men who started these Missionary Societies took that same view. The greatest evangelists the world has ever known, the greatest promotors of evangelism the Church has ever known, have taken this particular view. Indeed it is true to say that with but few exceptions the universal view of the Christian Church until the beginning of the seventeenth century was this view.

While there was opposition to this view in the seventeenth century, it became well-known through John Wesley and his followers and their Arminian teaching in the eighteenth century. It is also significant that as the Higher Criticism of the Bible gained currency and popularity in the later nineteenth century the older view receded even further into the background. With the advent of what is known as liberalism or modernism the teaching of God's election and choosing of His people in eternity almost completely disappeared. Surely that is of great significance.

There, then, are some of the facts which we should bear in mind before we begin to argue and to make sweeping statements. However, let us be clear about the fact that we are not saved by the view we take on this question. As I have already explained, there are two possible views. One is that God has chosen us in spite of ourselves, the other is that God has chosen us because He has foreseen that we would exercise faith. But I repeat that the view you take on this question does not determine your salvation. We are not saved by our understanding of these things, but by a simple childlike trust, and absolute faith and confidence in the Lord Jesus Christ and His work on our behalf. The view we take does affect our understanding, our intellectual apprehension; but thank God, that is not what saves us. We can be as certain that John Wesley is in heaven as that Jonathan Edwards and George Whitefield are there.

But someone may say that if the doctrine we hold does not determine our salvation, therefore it does not matter. But that is a false deduction. This statement about God's choice of us is here in the Scriptures and therefore must be considered. Paul puts it first in order to show how we become Christians and enjoy the Christian blessings, and although, as I have said, our understanding of it does not determine our salvation, it is of very great importance. It has reference to the sovereignty of God, and the majesty of God, indeed it is all-important from the standpoint of our understanding of the love of God. It is here we see the love of God at its highest. Furthermore, it is in the light of this doctrine that we see the certainty of the plan of salvation most clearly. If God's plan of salvation were to be dependent upon man, and the choice of man, it would certainly fail; but if it is of God from beginning to end, then it is certain. Nothing else can give me a sense of security. There is no doctrine which is as comforting as this; my security depends upon this fact, that I am what I am solely and entirely because of the grace of God.

Whatever authority I may have as a preacher is not the result of any decision on my part. It was God's hand that laid hold of me, and drew me out, and separated me to this work. I am what I am because of God's grace; and I give to Him all the glory. Were I to believe that my future is dependent upon myself and my decisions I would tremble in fear; but I thank God that I know that I am in His hand, and that 'He who has begun a good work' in me will go on with the work. In spite of myself, and what I was and am, the Lord will not let me go; He will not 'His purpose forego'. It is because I know that before time began, before the foundation of the world, He looked at me and saw me and selected me, and in His mind gave me to Christ – it is because I know that, that with the Apostle Paul I am able to say, that neither death, nor life, nor angels, nor principalities, nor powers, nor things present, nor things to come, nor height, nor depth, nor any other creature, shall be able to separate us from the love of God which is in Christ Jesus our Lord' (Romans 8:38–39). That is why all this matters; my sense of security and my joy depend upon it. Although my understanding of it does not determine my salvation, it does determine my experience of the joy of salvation, and the sense of security and certainty. Face this glorious truth on your knees, put it into the context of the whole of Scripture, remember the names of the men I have mentioned, and ask God to give you enlightenment and understanding by the Spirit in order that this particular statement may bring to you, to your soul, to your mind and heart and experience, increasing instalments of the exceeding riches of His grace.

8
'Holy and without Blame before Him in love'

'According as he hath chosen us in him before the foundation of the world, that we should be holy and without blame before him in love.'

Ephesians 1:4

Before I proceed to deal with the remainder of verse 4 we must note that the Apostle is careful to tell us that it is 'in Christ' that we are chosen; not merely that we are chosen, but chosen in Christ. God has separated us, has chosen us out of the world of mankind to be the inheritors of great blessings; and it is all in and through the Lord Jesus Christ. There is no better exposition of this passage we are examining than that which is found in the seventeenth chapter of the Gospel according to John where we have what is commonly known as our Lord's high priestly prayer. There we find our Lord making statements concerning Himself, such as, 'Thou hast given him power over all flesh, that he should give eternal life to as many as thou hast given him' (v. 2). The teaching is that the Father has given these people to the Son. Or take verse 6: 'I have manifested thy name unto the men which thou gavest me out of the world: thine they were, and thou gavest them me; and they have kept thy word'. These people – Christian people including you and me – belonged to God before they became the Son's people. Our position does not depend upon anything we do, primarily; nor primarily even upon the action of the Son. The primary action is that of God the Father who chose unto Himself a people out of the whole of mankind before the foundation of the world, and then presented, gave these people whom He had chosen to the Son, in order that the Son might redeem them and do everything that was necessary for their reconciliation with Himself. That is the teaching of the Lord Jesus Christ Himself. He came into the world, and accomplished

His work, for these people who have been given to Him by the Father. So He goes on to say: 'I pray for them: I pray not for the world, but for them which thou hast given me; for they are thine' (v. 9). But it is of vital importance that we should remember that it is all done 'in him'. The Apostle continually repeats the truth that there is nothing whatsoever given to the Christian apart from the Lord Jesus Christ; there is no relationship to God which is true and saving except that which is in and through the Son of God. 'There is one God, and one mediator [only] between God and men, the man Christ Jesus' (1 Timothy 2:5).

Having established these truths, we can now proceed to the remainder of this great statement: 'According as he hath chosen us in him before the foundation of the world, that we should be holy and without blame before him in love'. Here we see that every single phrase, almost every word, demands the most careful and serious consideration. Every statement is full of truth, vital truth, all-important truth. Therefore to rush over these great momentous statements is folly; indeed it is actually sinful.

We are told that we have been chosen so that 'we should be holy and without blame before him in love'. Here, again, the Apostle gives us one of those extraordinary synopses of the entire gospel. He means that it is the purpose of God in Christ for His people, to undo, to remove and to rectify completely the effects of sin and of the Fall of man. It is God's object in salvation to rectify completely all the results and the consequences of that terrible and most disastrous event. This is made plain in the Scriptures. For instance, we read in the third chapter of the First Epistle of John: 'For this purpose the Son of God was manifested, that he might destroy the works of the devil' (v. 8). The Fall was the work of the devil. How foolish they are who think that you can pick and choose portions of the Bible and reject others at will. The Bible is a whole, and we have no hope of understanding the New Testament gospel unless we accept the first chapters of the Book of Genesis with their account of the Fall of man into sin. Here, in these verses in the first chapter of this Epistle to the Ephesians, the Apostle Paul proceeds to show that the work of the devil is being destroyed and undone, so that these people whom God the Father has given to the Son, shall be entirely free from all the effects and consequences of that most tragic event termed the Fall.

The Apostle says that the purpose of God in choosing in election, is that we should be 'holy and without blame'. He says three things: we are to be 'holy and without blame', 'before God', 'in love'. The first statement consists of two elements – 'holy and without blame' – and they are obviously counterparts of each other. The Apostle never throws in words heedlessly. He uses two words which describe the same thing but do so from different aspects. They both refer to sanctification. Some have thought that the Apostle was referring to justification; but obviously that is not so, the words refer to sanctification, not merely to our standing, but to our inward condition, our sanctification. I believe that the Apostle used the two terms because he desired to bring out the doctrine in all its fulness. In chapter 5 of the Epistle he uses the term 'without blemish' – 'holy and without blemish' (v. 27). We can show the difference between the two in this way. 'Holiness' denotes a state of inward or internal purity; 'without blame' means an outward or external condition of purity. Holiness is the greater and stronger term, because it is concerned about the inward condition; but the outward condition is also important. The picture conveyed is that of fruit which has no specks upon it, no little portions of incipient decay, no putrefaction; it is perfect, it is entire. The Apostle himself expounds this idea in the fifth chapter of this Epistle where he says that it is ultimately Christ's purpose for the Church that she should be not only holy but without 'spot or wrinkle, or any such thing' (v.27). The Church is to be without blemish as well as pure; it is to be perfect outside as well as inside.

Another way of stating the difference is to say that 'holiness' is positive whereas 'without blemish' or 'without blame' is negative. You are positively holy, but that means negatively that there is the absence of pollution. And it is good to look at the matter in both ways. In practice that which is here given second place is generally given first place. We take an external view, and there does not seem to be anything which is obviously wrong; but the fact that the subject on which we gaze may look unblemished on the outside, does not guarantee that it is the same

inside. Negatively it is without blemish but positively it fails to
stand the test.

The two terms, taken together, mean an essential purity or
state of health, or wholeness. They mean a true and real life and
being, without anything in any way detracting, a perfect harmony
with every part fulfilling the function for which it was designed.
In perfect harmony everything works together. Looked at negatively, it means that sin in all its effects and aspects is entirely
absent. Holiness is ultimately an essential attribute of God. God
Himself has said, 'Be ye holy for I am holy'. We cannot conceive
of that, but we are told that 'God is light, and in him is no
darkness at all' (1 John 1:5). We can say, positively, that holiness
is light, and negatively, that there is no darkness. Beyond that we
cannot go; it means essentially a perfect being, absolute perfection, 'The Father of lights with whom is no variableness, neither
shadow of turning' (James 1:17). God is absolute light and glory
and perfection; He is absolutely pure without any suspicion of
alloy or any admixture; and the astounding thing we are told here
is that God has chosen us in Christ to become like Himself. That
is His plan and purpose for us; that is our destiny, to be like God,
'holy and without blemish'.

But we must go on to the second term, 'holy and without blame
before him'. Here again is a phrase which we can so easily slide
over and regard as of little significance. But it means that we are
in God's presence, actually before Him; we appear before Him.
It is another way of saying that we are in communion with Him,
that we are in fellowship with Him. Again let the Apostle John
expound the Apostle Paul. It is not that he states the truth more
clearly but that they complement each other. John's object in
writing his First Epistle is described thus: 'That which we have
seen and heard declare we unto you, that ye also may have
fellowship with us: and truly our fellowship is with the Father,
and with his Son Jesus Christ'. Then he proceeds to say: 'These
things write we unto you, that your joy may be full. This then is
the message which we have heard of him, and declare unto you,
that God is light, and in him is no darkness at all' (vv. 3–5). In
other words, 'before him', as used by Paul, means that the object
and purpose of our calling and election is that we may walk with
God; not only that we may enter into a conscious fellowship with

God, but that we may walk and abide in that fellowship, or as John expresses it, walk in the light with God.

An interesting light is thrown on this in a statement which is made about Abraham in the seventeenth chapter of the Book of Genesis where we are told that when Abraham was ninety-nine years old the Lord appeared unto him and said to him, 'I am the Almighty God; walk before me, and be thou perfect.' That was an invitation to Abraham from God to go for a walk with Him. That is what is meant by salvation; it is really the end and object of it. Man at the beginning had been created by God, and put into a garden. There he lived a life of perfect correspondence with God. He lived with God, he talked with God, he 'walked' with God. This is a phrase found occasionally in the Old Testament. 'Enoch walked with God.' Of course, to do so a man must be perfect, because God is perfect. 'Can two walk together except they be agreed?' (Amos 3:3). You cannot mix light and darkness, right and wrong, evil and good. Walking before God and being perfect are inevitably joined together because of the nature of God.

The third expression is 'in love' – 'that we should be holy, and without blame before him *in love*'. Commentators have spent much time on this phrase and their chief interest is as to where it belongs exactly. This emerges in the American Revised Standard Version which places 'in love' with 'predestinated' which belongs to the next verse. Others maintain that it should be attached to the word 'chosen' – 'according as he hath chosen us in love, that we should be holy and without blame before him'. But here in the Authorized Version it is attached to 'holy and without blame before him' (in love). The decision as to which of these three positions is correct cannot be made on linguistic grounds. It is not a question of the precise meaning of words. It must be decided on theological or doctrinal grounds; and personally I have no hesitation in asserting that what is found in the Authorized Version is correct. It belongs precisely to this definition of holiness, even as 'before God' is a definition of holiness. They say the same thing from different standpoints.

Let me explain. There is no question but that the essence of holiness is love. Paul in the Epistle to the Romans says that 'love is the fulfilling of the law' (13:10). We only conceive of holiness truly when we conceive of it in terms of love. Love is the opposite of enmity, the opposite of hatred, the opposite of strife. The Apostle is saying that as the result of God's choice of us and the work of Christ and the Spirit in us, what happens is that sin is removed, the obstacle between us and God is removed, and so we can appear before Him. And not only so, but we appear before the presence of God 'in love'. To appear in the presence of God as our Judge is something terrible to contemplate; the great thing that has been done for us in our salvation is that we appear before God 'in love'.

This is the greatest result of the effects of the Fall being undone. Man's condition by nature as we have seen is the exact opposite of that holiness and love. It is enmity against God; his mind is not subject to the law of God, neither indeed can be. Many dispute this assertion and claim that they know people who are not Christians but who believe in God and worship God. But when we take the trouble to find out the kind of god they worship, we find that he is not the God of the Scriptures. He is the god of philosophy, a god they have conjured up in their own minds. They have removed from God as revealed in Scripture everything they do not like. They do not believe in wrath, they do not believe in judgment, they do not believe in righteousness, or the teaching about the shedding of the blood of Christ, and the death on the Cross. They reject the essence of the biblical revelation, and thereby they prove themselves to be haters of God. 'The carnal mind is enmity against God' (Romans 8:7). When man fell he began to hate God, and as the result of the Fall man is opposed to God and is at enmity against Him. But as the result of salvation in Christ he appears before God 'in love'.

It is wrong therefore to attach the words 'in love' to the next verse, or to attach them to the word 'chosen' as if they are a description of God. They are a description of ourselves. If we are Christian we are lovers of God, we delight in Him. The holiness of the man who is in Christ, the holiness of the Christian, is not some mechanical conformity to the law, neither is it mere morality. A man may be moral without loving holiness. Morality is a negative quality – it means not committing sin. But that is not holiness. Holiness is positive, it is essentially a matter of loving. The Christian is a man who loves holiness and he appears before God because he is 'holy in love'. He 'hungers and thirsts after

[99]

righteousness', he delights in the law of God. He does not obey it as a task; he says with John in his First Epistle, chapter 5 verse 3: 'His commandments are not grievous'. That constitutes one of the best tests as to whether we are Christian or not. Do we have to force ourselves to live the Christian life? Do we enjoy Christian living? do we wish to be more Christ-like day by day? These are the tests, and they are tests of love. The law of God really calls us to love. Our Lord Himself taught this on an occasion when certain men came to Him one day, trying to trap Him by putting questions to Him. They asked Him, 'Which is the first commandment of all?' His reply was that the first of all the commandments was, 'Thou shalt love the Lord thy God with all thy heart and with all thy soul and with all thy mind and with all thy strength. This is the first commandment, and the second is like, namely this. Thou shalt love thy neighbour as thyself. There is no other commandment greater than these' (Mark 12:28–31). The whole object of the law is love first, your relationship to God, then your relationship to your fellow man. It is all a matter of love.

So we are to be 'holy and without blame before him in love', loving God, loving our fellow man, loving the law of God, delighting in it, and not merely conforming mechanically to a moral pattern. The Apostle's teaching is that the ultimate end and object of God's choice of us, of our election, is that we should become people of that character. Of course we do not attain to that perfection in this life and world; that is the ultimate goal. The will of God for us is absolute perfection, and we who are Christians shall stand before Him ultimately, 'faultless and blameless', 'without spot or wrinkle or any such thing'. No one will be able to bring a charge against us. We shall be like our Lord. But let us not forget that while we only attain unto it in perfection in the next world, it has started in this world. The principle is in us here and now; the seed has been implanted in us already. That is what the Apostle John teaches in the third chapter of his First Epistle. It is already in us in embryo; in its essence 'His seed remaineth' in us. The author of the Epistle to the Hebrews expresses this in the third chapter of his Epistle where he writes: 'Wherefore, holy brethren, partakers of the heavenly calling . . .' (v. 1). The Christian is a partaker of the heavenly calling. We are saints, which means that we are holy, and even here and now this principle of holiness is in us. We are already 'partakers of the divine nature', and the divine nature is holy. This essential holiness is in us, and it will grow and develop until finally we shall be absolutely perfect in the presence of God. This, the Apostle tells us, is the ultimate object of our being chosen.

I ask a question at this point: Are we surprised that this is the first thing that the Apostle tells us? Did we expect something else, such as, God has chosen us in order that we may be forgiven? That is not what Paul puts first; instead he writes, 'that we should be holy and without blame before him in love'. In doing so the Apostle is being consistent with the entire biblical teaching. Why must this come first? The answer is that it is God's plan, God's purpose. 'This is the will of God, even your sanctification' (1 Thessalonians 4:3). God's desire for us that we be holy comes before His desire for our happiness or anything else. Because God is holy this must always be first.

Remember also that we are 'in Christ'. What makes us Christian is that we are in Christ; not forgiveness only, though that is essential. And if we are 'in Christ' we must be holy, because He is 'holy, harmless, undefiled, separate from sinners'.

In the light of all this there are certain essential deductions which are of the most supreme importance. Salvation means, primarily and essentially, being in the right relationship with God – nothing less than that! Salvation must not be thought of primarily in terms of happiness, or in terms of laws or morality. It must not be thought of in terms of forgiveness only or primarily. We must not think of it in terms of the help that Christ is going to give us, in guidance or anything else. First of all it means being in the right relationship to God. That must be so because the essence of sin is separation from God. That leads to misery and our becoming slaves of the devil; but the primary trouble is the loss of the relationship to God. This must therefore be the first thing in salvation; and if we have ever thought of our salvation in any terms save our reconciliation to God and being right with God, we have misinterpreted the biblical teaching of salvation.

Secondly, because salvation refers essentially to our relationship to God, it must of necessity, always, from beginning to end, be thought of in terms of holiness. Everything in salvation is destined to bring us to this end of holiness. Hence the Apostle puts it first; everything in it is destined to that end, and leads to that end. From that I deduce that there is nothing which is so wrong, and such a complete misinterpretation of Scripture, as to separate justification from sanctification. Scripture teaches that, primarily, salvation involves a right relationship to God; hence salvation must always be thought of from beginning to end in terms of holiness. It is completely wrong therefore for a man to say that he has justification but has not yet gone in for sanctification. You cannot be justified before God and decide later on to be sanctified. There is nothing more dangerous or unscriptural than the utterly illogical division or separation of these two things. Holiness is the beginning and the end of salvation; and the whole of salvation is destined to bring us to that end.

So we must always start with holiness, as the Scripture does; and therefore the preaching of holiness is an essential part of evangelism. I stress this matter because there are certain quite different ideas about evangelism, some indeed that say the exact opposite. They maintain that in evangelism the preacher does not deal with holiness. The one aim is 'to get people saved', then later you can lead them on to holiness. But what is salvation? To be saved is to be rightly related to God, and that is holiness. The whole purpose of evangelism is primarily to tell men what sin has done to them, to tell them why they are what they are, namely, separated from God. It is to tell them that what they need above everything else is not to be made to feel happy, but to be brought back into a right relationship with the God who is 'light and in him is no darkness at all'. But that means preaching holiness. To separate these two things, it seems to me, is to deny essential biblical teaching. We must start with holiness, and continue with it; because it is the end for which we are chosen and delivered. We must never think of holiness as something we may decide to go in for; if you are not holy you are not a Christian. These things belong together. Christ has 'been made unto us, wisdom and righteousness and sanctification and redemption'. You cannot divide Christ or select portions of Him; you are either in Christ, the whole Christ, or you are not 'in him'. And if you are 'in him' you are 'holy'.

Furthermore, because we have been chosen to holiness we must and will become holy. That is a startling statement; but it is of necessity true in the light of this statement of the Apostle. According to Paul we are not chosen with the possibility of holiness, but to the realization of holiness. God has not chosen us before the foundation of the world in order to create for us the possibility of holiness; He has chosen us to holiness. It is what He has purposed for us; not possibility, but realization. I therefore make this solemn asseveration, that those who do not appreciate this truth and show some signs of holiness in their lives, are not chosen, are not Christian. Being 'chosen' and being 'holy' are inseparable. However much doctrine a man may know, however much he may contend for election and predestination, if there is no element of holiness in him, he is not chosen. It is possible to be intellectually orthodox and yet not to be a Christian. The man who is chosen, is chosen to holiness; and if there is no evidence of holiness in his life it is proof that he has never been chosen. These are solemn thoughts, and yet they are inevitable in the light of this statement of Scripture.

My final comment is, that the teaching that God's choice of us is only 'in Christ' or because of Christ, far from leading to what is called Antinomianiam, that is to say, to slackness in life and living, is the greatest incentive of all to holiness. Many have tried to argue that the doctrine of 'being chosen' will lead men to say, 'If I am chosen all is well; it matters not what I do or fail to do.' But it does not work out in that way. Indeed the exact opposite is the case and for the following reason. Because it is God's purpose that we be holy, it will be carried out. I mean that if God has chosen you to salvation, God will make you holy. If, foolishly, you are not willing to be led by God, and to be drawn by His love, because He has chosen you He will employ another way of making you holy. This is indicated in what we read in the twelfth chapter of the Epistle to the Hebrews: 'Whom the Lord loveth he chasteneth' (v. 6). The man who is not being chastened is a bastard; he is not a child of God. What a momentous statement! God, who has chosen you to holiness, will make you holy; and if the preaching of the gospel does not do so, God has other means and methods. He may strike you down with illness, He may ruin your business. God will make you holy because He has chosen you unto holiness. Antinomianism is nonsense. If you are chosen of God unto holiness and to be without blemish, He will bring you to that condition; and if you defy Him, well then, terrible things may happen to you.

Paul explains this also in the eleventh chapter of the First Epistle to the Corinthians, where, dealing with the Communion Service, he says that, because certain Christians do not examine themselves, 'many are weak and sickly, and some even sleep', that is to say, some are even dead. Because they would not judge themselves God had corrected them. We are in the hands of God, and we are called to holiness. And He will have us to be holy men; He will make us holy. But it not only works in that manner; it works also in the following way. If you believe this teaching to be true, and if you realize its meaning, your own mind will be working with all its might in the direction of holiness. If I know that I am called to holiness it means that I have no time to lose. The Apostle John emphasizes this by saying that 'Every man that hath this hope in him purifieth himself, even as he is pure' (1 John 3:3). If you knew that you were to be presented to some great or august person you would prepare yourself for the occasion. The very realization of the privilege makes you do so; and the more you realize biblical truth and believe it and understand it, the more you will give yourself to striving after holiness. You will pursue it, as the author of the Epistle to the Hebrews urges us to do in the words, 'Follow peace with all men, and holiness, without which no man shall see the Lord' (12:14).

It is the appeal of love. We have been brought to love God in Christ. We believe that we have to stand in His presence. Does it not follow, then, that the one thing I do not want to happen when I stand before Him is that there should be the slightest suspicion of disappointment when He looks at me, because as His child I have failed Him, and have been unworthy of Him. 'Every man that hath this hope in him purifieth himself, even as he is pure' (1 John 3:3). There is nothing that so promotes holiness as this great doctrine, this precious truth, which tells us that because we are chosen of God we are going to be with Him, and are going to be like Him. There is no time to lose; we must be up and doing. I cannot possibly say, 'I am chosen and therefore I can do as I like, I shall be forgiven'. It works in the opposite direction. Our sense of honour is involved, love is involved, the desire to please is involved. Everything argues in favour of holiness. Whatever we may have expected, this comes first: 'According as he hath chosen us in him . . . that we should be holy and without blame before him in love'. Do you know that you are living in the presence of God, and walking with Him in the light? Do you love Him, do you know that you are going to be with Him? 'Blessed are the pure in heart for they shall see God.'

9
Adoption

'Having predestinated us unto the adoption of children by Jesus Christ to himself, according to the good pleasure of his will.'

Ephesians 1:5

The opening word of this verse reminds us of its intimate connection with what has gone before, where we have seen that the purpose of salvation is to destroy the work of the devil, and to restore us to a condition where we can stand again before God holy and without blame in love, and have communion with Him as Adam had before the Fall. But it does not stop at that. In this fifth verse the Apostle leads us on to something yet more glorious. It is as if we were climbing up a staircase to some wonderful high tower. We reach a kind of platform with a glorious view than which nothing greater seems to be possible. One would have thought that nothing could be added to the previous statement; but the Apostle does add to it, and he does so because he feels that he has not yet told us everything about 'the exceeding riches' of God's grace. So he goes on to tell us of a further truth, namely, that we have been 'predestinated unto the adoption of sons'. Not only do we stand before God, we stand before Him as His sons, as His adopted sons.

Here, again, is something which is truly staggering in its glory. How important it is that we should take these statements slowly, and not rush over them in a superficial manner as is so often done. Each statement here has its own individual message; and if we are to appreciate it fully and rejoice in it as we are meant to do, we must pause and analyse and look at each truth and gaze upon it, and allow its rich message to penetrate our minds and hearts. We must ever guard against the danger of being content with a mere knowledge of the letter of the Scriptures and of failing to discover its principles and doctrines. A superficial analysis of the books of the Bible is finally useless unless we realize the rich content of these individual statements. Indeed if we make a thorough analysis of any one of these New Testament Epistles we shall gain a good grasp of the main elements of Christian truth. Furthermore, to grasp the teaching of one Epistle helps us to go on to another and so we are able to understand the teaching of the entire Bible. It is truly astonishing to note how we encounter most of the primary essential doctrines of the Christian faith here in the very introduction to the Epistle to the Ephesians.

The particular statement with which we are about to deal is not merely a repetition of what the Apostle has been saying; it is something new, something additional. Let us note two points in connection with the translation. The Authorized (King James) Version reads thus: 'Having predestinated us unto the adoption of children by Jesus Christ.' This is one of those instances where the Authorized Version, unfortunately, is not as good as the English Revised Version translation which reads, 'Having foreordained us unto adoption as sons'. The word is 'sons', and not as the Authorized Version has it, 'children'. The American Revised Standard Version likewise has 'sons'; but most astonishingly we find that the Revised Standard Version, which is so popular at the present time, leaves out the term 'adoption' for no reason whatsoever. When it translates precisely the same word in chapter 8 of the Epistle to the Romans and chapter 4 of the Epistle to the Galatians, it uses the term 'adoption', but here it omits it. This reminds us of the importance of using and handling all these new modern translations most carefully and judiciously.

The next matter that must engage our attention is to note that the Apostle introduces a new term. In the previous verse he has said, 'According as he hath chosen us'; but now he writes about God 'having predestinated us'. Is this but a distinction without a difference? The answer is, that it is not so. The Apostle is not simply repeating himself by using a slight variation; he is really saying something new, something different. There is an important difference between 'chosen' and 'predestinated'. To 'predestinate' means to determine beforehand, to declare beforehand. The

Apostle means by this term that this was God's ultimate plan; it refers to the plan itself. 'Chosen' on the other hand emphasizes the way or the means or the method or the mode by which that plan has been put into operation and has been accomplished. The difference between the two terms is the difference between the plan, the thing pre-determined, thought out and purposed in the mind of God, and the execution of it. So we are confronted by the staggering statement that 'before the foundation of the world', it was God's plan and purpose that certain members of the fallen race of Adam – who had fallen right away from Him, and become aliens in their minds and who were under His wrath and deserved nothing but perdition – should become His sons. That is God's original purpose and plan in redemption. We have already seen that the Apostle states these things in a certain definite order, and whenever we think of salvation and redemption we should always keep in the forefront of our minds that God's original decision, or determination, was that certain members of that fallen race should stand before Him as His sons. In order to carry out that determination it was obviously essential that God should 'choose' and select certain people who should be brought to that glorious destiny. It is equally obvious that certain things had to be done to those people to fit and prepare them for their destiny. And that, as we have seen, was that they should become 'holy and without blame in love'. So we see the intimate and logical connection between these things. There is the original purpose, and in order to bring that purpose to pass certain people have to be taken hold of and made holy, because without being holy they could not possibly stand in the presence of God.

In other words we have a further insight through this additional statement in the fifth verse into why the Apostle says that we have been chosen unto holiness – 'that we should be holy and without blame before him in love'. Paul places holiness first because he is thinking of our sonship, our ultimate destiny. While it is most important that we should hold each of these truths in our minds separately and in orderly fashion, we must not think of them so much in terms of a time or chronological sequence, because all these things were in the mind of God at one and the same time. God sees the end from the beginning; and this is not a time arrangement but a logical arrangement – the original pre-determination, the original choosing to sonship.

But someone may ask, 'If that is the logical order, why does Paul put 'chosen' and 'holiness' before 'predestination'? The answer is that from the experiential standpoint 'chosen' and 'holiness' come before the adoption as sons. The Apostle was writing a pastoral letter to a number of Christian people, many of whom were slaves and servants, in order that he might establish their faith. So he writes in a manner which will be most helpful to them. A simple way therefore of testing yourself as to whether you are a child of God, and whether you have a spiritual mind, is to ask yourself whether all this seems to you to be a waste of time, or whether you see in it the most wonderful and glorious thing you have ever looked at in the whole of your life. Paul here brings us face to face with the most astounding thing that even Almighty God has planned and done for us. As you look into the scheme and plan do you delight in it? A child always delights in looking at his father's plan and purpose; and you and I have the privilege through the Scriptures of having a glimpse of the plan of God. If this means nothing to you, it means that you are a 'natural' man, not a 'spiritual' man. As the Apostle says, 'The natural man receiveth not the things of the Spirit of God, for they are foolishness unto him'; he sees nothing in them and is utterly bored by them. What do these things mean to you? They were written to very simple people, and we are meant to grasp and understand and rejoice in them.

In the next place we proceed to look at this central term 'adoption'. 'Having predestinated us unto the *adoption* of children'. This term 'adoption' is a most interesting one. The Apostle Paul is the only writer in the New Testament who uses it, and there is little doubt but that he borrowed it from Roman law. It is a term, an idea, of which Jews knew nothing. It was no part of their legal system; but it was a term used by the Romans. Now the Apostle Paul was a Roman citizen and he had lived in that atmosphere; so he naturally uses this term. Under Roman law adoption secured for the adopted child a right to the name and to the property of the person by whom he had been adopted. The moment a child was adopted by a person, that child had the legal right, an absolute legal right, to make such claims. On the other hand Roman law granted to the person who adopted the child all the rights and privileges of a father. It worked both ways.

The Apostle obviously uses the term in order to convey the particular idea of the place or status of a son. It is a purely forensic or legal term. It is important that we should grasp this because we cannot really enter into the privilege of our position as God's sons unless we understand what adoption means. It is a term that emphasizes relationship and standing, it also emphasizes rank and distinction. We are familiar with certain ranks of society, certain distinctions in society which confer privileges because of the position, or the rank or the status that one holds. This New Testament term embodies this meaning. It is a legal term which defines standing or status, rank, privilege, and position. Its emphasis is not upon the nature of the child so much as upon the rank of the child. Of course the nature is very important; but the term adoption does not emphasize that.

Let me illustrate. If you say of a person that he is an adopted child you are saying that he is not in a blood relationship to a certain man and woman. He has not a natural connection with them but he has been legally adopted by them; he stands as their child though he does not actually partake of their nature. It is this distinction which the Apostle employs here, and obviously it is an important one. The nature of the Christian as a new man in Christ, as a son, is determined not by adoption but by regeneration. We become children of God because we are born again, because we have become 'partakers of the divine nature', because the Holy Spirit enters into us, because we are born from above, because we are a new creation. Receiving this we become the children of God. But that is not conveyed by the term 'adoption' which does not place the emphasis upon the common nature which we have, but entirely upon the legal standing, upon the rank, upon the position; and upon the privileges that come from that position. In other words, adoption can be defined as the proclaiming of the new creature in his new relationship to God as a son. By adoption, then, we become sons of God and are introduced into and given the privileges that belong to membership of God's family.

Again, someone may ask: 'Why did the Apostle introduce this term and what exactly is the difference between it and regeneration; why did he differentiate and distinguish between them?' The answer is provided in the fourth chapter of the Epistle to the Galatians, verses 1–5. The Apostle's argument there runs thus: 'Now I say, That the heir, as long as he is a child, differeth nothing from a servant, though he be lord of all; but is under tutors and governors until the time appointed of the father. Even so we, when we were children, were in bondage under the elements of the world: but when the fulness of the time was come, God sent forth his Son, made of a woman, made under the law. . . that we might receive the adoption of sons.' Observe the distinction which Paul draws. A child is born of his parents and he has the nature of the parents in him; and because of that he is in a sense 'lord of all'. But while he is still a child he is little different from a servant. Indeed he is under tutors, servants, who can correct and can punish, and who can teach him. They seem to be superior to him and as a child he may be afraid of this tutor, or that particular servant. He is a true child; he is not adopted; but he is not of age. But 'adoption' means that when that child comes of age, a declaration is made concerning his status and position as heir. He is no more a son than he was before, but there is a difference all the same. He now has a certain standing, and his relationship to the governors and teachers has become different. They now address him as 'master'. His relationship to his parents in a fundamental sense has not been changed; as regards his blood and nature it remains exactly what it was. Yet from the standpoint of rank and legal position he is in a different position.

We can now see why the Apostle uses this particular term 'adoption'. It is as if he was not content with saying that we have become children of God by the second birth; he wants us to realize where we stand, and what our rank and privileges are. This is why it is so difficult to understand why those who were responsible for the translation given in the Revised Standard Version should leave out the term. Theological and spiritual understanding are clearly as important in the work of translation as linguistic proficiency, and arguably they are more important.

Let us then proceed to consider something of the privileges of our position as sons of God. That we may enjoy these is the final and the ultimate end of redemption. There is nothing higher than this. Our adoption is the highest expression even of God's love. I speak carefully, and with reverence when I assert that this statement and the parallel statements in the eighth chapter of Romans and the fourth chapter of the Epistle to the Galatians are the highest expression of the love of Almighty God. There is nothing higher than this, as is clear from the Apostle John's way of stating it: 'Behold, what manner of love the Father hath bestowed upon us, that we should be called the sons of God' (1 John 3:1). The world has nothing comparable to it. It is very much interested in greatness and in praise, interested in great men. It praises great men and showers its honours upon them. It talks about privileged positions and status and rank and honour. But all that the world knows in that respect is inevitably fading and transient. 'Change and decay in all around I see'. The world's honours are decaying honours; they only last while you are in this life and world. You cannot take them with you through death and the grave. The fashion of this world is passing away. What our Lord Himself said about such things and such people was, 'Verily I say unto you, they have their reward.' Let them make the most of it while they have it in this world.

Look at Dives and Lazarus; what a contrast! Dives has everything that the world can give – food and drink and honour and position. But he finds in death that he has nothing, while the poor man Lazarus, the beggar who was lying at his gate in this world full of sores, has everything in the next world. The world knows nothing about true honour and riches. It does not understand or appreciate them. Tell a man of the world that he can become a child, a son of God, and it means nothing to him. He is not interested in what he calls pie-in-the-sky, and he does not understand it. The world did not understand the Son of God when he was here; it dismissed Him as a carpenter; it saw no glory in Him. But His true disciples understood, and they said with John, 'We beheld His glory, the glory as of the only begotten of the Father, full of grace and truth.' They saw the glory shining forth though He assumed the form of a servant. This divine glory kept breaking through; and they saw it. Some of them saw it on the Mount of

Transfiguration, and they saw it elsewhere. And the glory which
is given by adoption to the children of God is similar to that
glory. As the hymn-writer says, it is

> *By this dark world unknown.*

The world does not know its truly great men, its real heroes. Our
history books indicate that the men who are given rewards by the
world, generally did not count in a spiritual sense, whereas the
men who are truly great were laughed at and ridiculed in their day
and generation.

The glory God gives is an unseen glory, but it is a real glory
because it is given by Him. Let me mention some of its manifestations in the privileges which we are given as adopted sons
of God. The first is that we bear the Name of God; we are
children of God, we are members of His family. Paul reminds us
of this at the end of the second chapter of this Epistle – we are 'of
the household of God'. Are you feeling dejected, are you feeling
ignored, are you discouraged by the fact that the world does not
know you? Do you feel that you do not matter, nor does it matter
what men may do to you? Let them despise and forsake you, and
ignore you and all you do; ignore them, and with Horatius Bonar
sing:

> *Men heed thee, love thee, praise thee not;*
> *The Master praises: – what are men?*

You are a child of God; God's Name is upon you, Christ's 'new
name', as the Book of Revelation puts it. His new name is written
upon you, and if you feel despised and dejected, join the hymn-
writer in praying:

> *Write Thy new Name upon my heart,*
> *Thy new best Name of Love.*

It is already there; God Himself has written it because He has
adopted you. You have a legal right to it, you can claim it. So
lift up your heart and obey the exhortation of John Cennick:

> *Children of the Heavenly King,*
> *As ye journey sweetly sing.*

Hold up your head, you have a glory the world knows nothing of,
a glory that will never fade away. It is indestructible and undefiled.

> *Behold the amazing gift of love*
> *The Father has bestowed*
> *On us, the sinful sons of men,*
> *To call us sons of God.*

The next thing we have to realize is that we are given the Spirit of the Son of God Himself, the only begotten Son. Paul states this again gloriously in Galatians 4, verses 4–6: 'When the fulness of the time was come, God sent forth his Son, made of a woman, made under the law, to redeem them that were under the law, that we might receive the adoption of sons. And because ye are sons, God hath sent forth the Spirit of his Son into your hearts, crying Abba, Father.' Because we are sons we have this privilege, that God has sent forth into our hearts the very selfsame Spirit that was in His only begotten Son. When the Lord Jesus Christ was here in this world as a man, He was given the Holy Spirit. We are told that 'God giveth not the Spirit by measure unto him' (John 3:34). He was enabled to do what He did by the Spirit, and we are told that because we are sons, God puts into us the same Spirit that was in His only begotten Son. What a privilege! We are in the same world and subject to the same contradiction of sinners. In His earthly life He was misunderstood by people, persecuted by people, tempted in all points like as we are, yet without sin. All that we have to endure He endured, and He went through it all triumphantly. It was the Spirit that enabled Him to do so, and the same Spirit is in us. He had to pray as we do; He was dependent upon this power as we are. He determined to live as a man, and He did so in that way.

But again, because we are sons, we are 'heirs of God and joint-heirs with Christ'. If you are interested in honours and possessions realize that because you are a child of God, you are an heir of God. Adoption confers the legal right to property. We are 'heirs of God, and joint-heirs with Christ'. 'Blessed are the poor in spirit: for theirs is the kingdom of heaven': 'Blessed are the meek, for they shall inherit the earth' (Matthew 5:3, 5).

Moreover we have a definite and certain hope of the completion of our final redemption. Paul assures us of this in Romans 8, verse 23: 'And not only they, but ourselves also, which have the firstfruits of the Spirit, even we ourselves groan within ourselves,

waiting for the adoption, to wit, the redemption of our body.'
In other words the argument is that because I am a son of God I
can be certain that a day is coming when even my body shall be
redeemed. My spirit, my soul, is redeemed but my body is still
a body of sin. It is not yet redeemed but it will be; and I am sure
of that because I am a son of God. My sonship is an absolute
guarantee of the blessing. That in turn guarantees the coming of
a day when we shall be enjoying what is called 'the glorious
liberty of the children of God', when we shall be free from sin and
'all that defileth' in 'new heavens and a new earth wherein
dwelleth righteousness' (2 Peter 3:13). It is all secure because God
is my Father and I am His child. And it is because He is my
Father and I am His child that I know that 'the very hairs of my
head are all numbered', that nothing can happen to me apart
from God. I know that neither hell nor any other power shall
ever be able to separate me from the love of Christ. I am His son
and He will never forsake me. He cannot do so. I have a
guarantee that though everything is opposed to me in this world
I shall go steadfastly on; He will lead me on because I am His
child, His son.

The Apostle goes even further in writing to the Corinthians,
and says: 'Know ye not that ye shall judge the world?' and then
adds that: 'Know ye not that ye shall judge angels?' (1 Corinthians
6:2–3). We are destined to judge angels because we are sons and
children of God. We are higher than the angels. They are but
'ministering spirits'. There is a day coming when we shall be
judging the angels of God in all their brightness and purity. We
shall be raised to that level because we are sons of God. That is
the great argument of the second chapter of the Epistle to the
Hebrews. The Christ was made for a time a little lower than the
angels; but God has raised us up to a level above the angels. Do
you realize these privileges? Were we all to do so we would never
be guilty of a spirit of bondage and of fear. Have we got this
'Spirit of adoption' in us? Do we cry 'Abba, Father'? Do we
realize these things and rejoice in them? That is to test whether
we are being led by the Spirit. 'For as many as are led by the
Spirit of God', says Paul in Romans 8:14, 'they are the sons of
God.'

Let us pause and contemplate these things. Let us arouse

ourselves to a realization through the Spirit of what adoption means and the things that follow from it. Let us spend less time with the newspapers and with all the talk about worldly honours. Let us face these things; they belong to us. We, as Christians, have been predestinated to the adoption of children by Jesus Christ unto God Himself. Praise be unto God for having looked upon us miserable, damned sinners, and for having raised us up to such an indescribable height of glory.

10

Higher than Adam

'Having predestinated us unto the adoption of
children by Jesus Christ to himself, according to the
good pleasure of his will,
'To the praise of the glory of his grace, wherein he
hath made us accepted in the beloved.'

Ephesians 1:5–6

We must remind ourselves that in verses 4, 5 and 6 the Apostle is
concerned to show us the part the Father plays in this great
redemption which we enjoy. He will go on to show the part
played by the Son, and subsequently the part played by the Holy
Spirit; but he starts with the Father, 'The God and Father of our
Lord Jesus Christ', and we have seen that that includes our
adoption as God's sons and all the privileges that come to us as
the result of it. But we cannot leave this great subject at this point,
because the moment we look at it carefully we find that certain
principles are implied in this statement which are vital to the
Christian position, and which, if we neglect or misunderstand
them, may very well militate against our well-being. As Christians
we are still in this world, and we are surrounded by enemies and
antagonists. The fact that we become Christian does not mean that
everything is going to be plain and clear, that we shall have no
difficulties, and that there will be no dangers and pitfalls along
our pathway.

One cannot read the New Testament without seeing that very
early in the history of the Church errors began to creep in,
heresies began to arise, and some went astray in their doctrine,
and misunderstood certain aspects of the truth. Indeed it can be
said that most of the New Testament Epistles were written
because of this. They were written to correct misunderstandings
and errors; and that is why we ourselves are considering these
things. We are still in the same position. Our interest in these
things is not merely theoretical. This same Apostle Paul reminds

[117]

us in his First Epistle to the Corinthians chapter 15, verse 33, that 'Evil communications corrupt good manners', by which he means that if we go astray in our doctrine, eventually our life will go astray as well. You cannot separate what a man believes from what he is. For this reason doctrine is vitally important. Certain people say ignorantly, 'I do not believe in doctrine; I believe in the Lord Jesus Christ; I am saved, I am a Christian, and nothing else matters'. To speak in that way is to court disaster, and for this reason, the New Testament itself warns us against this very danger. We are to guard ourselves against being 'tossed to and fro and carried about with every wind of doctrine', for if your doctrine goes astray your life will soon suffer as well. So it behoves us to study the doctrines in order that we may safeguard ourselves against certain erroneous and heretical teachings that are as rife and as common in the world today as they were in the days of the early Church.

Let us then proceed to consider further the Apostle's categorical statement, which is that God has 'predestinated us unto the adoption of children by Jesus Christ to himself, according to the good pleasure of his will'. Let us consider first the light which this statement throws upon the teaching so common today about the universal Brotherhood of man.

There is an idea current that God is the Father of all, that all therefore are the children of God, and that what the Christian Gospel emphasizes so much – especially in its evangelical presentation – about the necessity of the death of Christ upon the Cross is utterly unnecessary, and is nothing but a kind of Jewish legalism. This teaching asserts that the Jews, like many other primitive peoples, believed that the gods had to be placated by means of sufferings; but, of course, all that has nothing whatsoever to do with the only true and living God who is love. They maintain that if we but understand the teaching of the New Testament properly we would know that God is our Father and that He is the Father of all men. There is no need to talk about conversion and regeneration and rebirth and to say that the Cross is absolutely vital and central. All, they argue, are the children of God and God is a loving Father. To take sin too seriously is morbid and unhealthy, and is but a relic of Jewish legalism. If we have sinned, God as our Father will forgive us freely and immediately. We need not be worried about these things; for all men, being the children of God, are going to heaven. All warnings about hell and punishment and retribution, they say, should be banished out of our minds and our terminology. We should rid ourselves once and for ever of all the legalistic notions which the Apostle Paul especially has foisted upon the original primitive Gospel of Christ, which was nothing but a constant elaboration of the one theme that God is our Father and that God loves all men.

Those who hold such ideas do not merely make statements; they try to substantiate what they say from the Scriptures. They point out that the Apostle Paul himself, preaching to the Athenians about God, said, 'We are also his offspring'; and then they ask, 'Is not that enough?' Furthermore, they say, we read in the Epistle to the Hebrews, chapter 12, verse 9, 'Shall we not much rather be in subjection unto the Father of spirits, and live?' Here, they say, is a statement that God is the Father of all spirits, or the spirits of all men. Then we are told in the Epistle of James, chapter 1, that God is the 'Father of lights', which means the Father of the light that is in every man. They bring forward such statements and challenge us to reply.

We reply by saying that surely no one can read the Bible even superficially, without seeing clearly that it teaches that there is a fundamental and central division of mankind into two groups. There are those who belong to God, and there are those who do not belong to God; there are God's people, and there are those who are outside His covenant; there are the good and the bad, the saved and the lost, those who go to everlasting bliss, and those who go to everlasting perdition.

This division starts with Abel and Cain, it continues with those who were saved in the Ark and those who were lost – the family of Noah and all the rest of the world. Then we see it in Abraham and his descendants, as distinct from all the other nations. We find it in the teaching concerning the broad way and the narrow way, and in a variety of metaphors. As a clear-cut division it runs right through the Scriptures, until in the Book of Revelation we find those who are inside the heavenly city in contrast with those who are outside with the dogs and who are consigned to perdition. But how is this to be reconciled with the statements previously quoted from Acts 17 and elsewhere? The answer is, as we have seen earlier, that God is the Father of all men in the sense that He is the Creator of all men. He is the Originator of the whole of mankind; and when we are told that we are all 'his offspring' it means that we are all the result of His work, His activity; we are all the result of His creation. And it is in that sense that He is 'the Father of spirits'.

But we do not leave it at that; there are specific statements in the Scriptures that state the division still more strongly. God, in the Old Testament, says repeatedly of the children of Israel, 'Israel is my son' (e.g. Exodus 4:22). He does not describe the other nations as His sons. Then look at the statement we have in this very Epistle where Paul says: 'Among whom also we all had our conversation in times past in the lusts of our flesh, fulfilling the desires of the flesh and of the mind; and were by nature the children of wrath, even as others' (2:3). We were all children of wrath by nature, says the Apostle. Our Lord Himself gives the same teaching when in a disputation with the scribes and Pharisees, He refers to His antagonists as the children of the devil. He says, 'Ye are of your father the devil'. He even adds, 'If God were your Father, ye would love me' (John 8: 42, 44). You cannot say, He says in effect, that God is your Father, because you are proving that God is not your Father. As the children of the devil you are like your father, and belong to your father. If you were the children of God you would love me. But you do not love me, and therefore you are not the children of God. Then there is that specific statement in John's Gospel, chapter 1, verse 12: 'He came unto his own, and his own received him not. But as many as received him, to them gave he power to become the sons of God', the children of God. Clearly they were not the children of God as they were, but some are given the right and the authority to become the children of God as the result of receiving the Lord Jesus Christ. Obviously the argument is, that unless they receive Him they are not the children of God, and have neither right nor authority to call themselves such, and to regard themselves as such.

Again, there is the statement in Romans 8: 14: 'As many as are led by the Spirit of God, they are the sons of God.' Such statements, surely, are sufficient to deal with this question. And here it is very explicitly in the text we are now considering. The Father has predestinated us; it is essential to remember that the Apostle is writing to Christians only. He is writing to members of churches only, not a general letter to the world. His whole object is to show Christians that they no longer belong to the world. They are a 'holy people', the people who have been 'called unto holiness', without blame, 'to stand before him in love'. They are no longer 'dead in trespasses and sins', they are no longer 'the children of wrath, even as others'. These are the special people who have become Christians; and it is only of them that he says that they have been 'predestinated unto the adoption of children'.

We see clearly, therefore, that there is nothing which is more contradictory of the plain teaching of the Scripture from beginning to end than the idea that God is the universal Father of all, that all are His children, and that ultimately all are going to heaven. Indeed I do not hesitate to assert that there is no teaching which is finally so inimical to our souls and their salvation as this teaching about the universal Fatherhood of God. If God were the Father of all in that sense, then the Lord Jesus Christ need never have come into this world. So, as we value our own souls and the souls of others, let us reject with abhorrence such perverted notions, and let us do all we can to deliver others from the clutches of such teaching.

Positively, and in the second place, we can say that the whole emphasis of the teaching here is that we only become sons in and through the Lord Jesus Christ. He is essential: 'according as he hath chosen us *in him* before the foundation of the world, that we should be holy and without blame before him in love.' Again – 'having predestinated us unto the adoption of children *by Jesus Christ* to himself according to the good pleasure of his will, to the praise of the glory of his grace wherein he hath made us accepted in the beloved'. In the light of such words it is almost inconceivable that anyone should ever go astray with respect to this matter. There is only one explanation of the fact that many do go astray; it is the power of the devil! The Apostle keeps on repeating these statements about the Lord Jesus Christ. He keeps on emphasizing, 'in him', 'by him', 'through him', 'in the beloved'; and he does so because he is so eager to show that it is only in Christ that we can become the sons of God. The erroneous teaching does away with the necessity of Christ, because it claims that we are all, by our very creation and being, children of God.

We must realize that it is only to 'as many as receive him', that the Lord Jesus Christ gives the right, the authority, to become the children of God. The Lord said: 'I am the way, the truth, and the life; no man cometh unto the Father but by me' (John 14:6). He is absolutely essential. If He had not come from heaven to earth, none of us could ever have become children of God; we would have remained 'the children of wrath'. It is only as the result of everything that began in the Incarnation, in the Birth at Bethlehem, in all that He did and was, in all that He still is and does – it is only as the result of these happenings that we become the sons of God. Unless we see that the Incarnation is an absolute necessity, that Christ's obedience to the law had to take place, that He must needs suffer and die, that He had to bear our sins, to make the atonement and to reconcile us to God – unless we realize and see clearly that all this was absolutely essential before we could become the sons of God, we are yet in our sins, we are harbouring a delusion, and at the last day, when we go forward imagining that we are sons, we shall find ourselves confronted with the words 'I never knew you; depart from me, ye that work iniquity' (Matthew 7:23).

The Apostle uses his words carefully. Note that as regards our holiness he says that we are 'in Him', but with regard to the adoption he says 'by Jesus Christ'. It is as the result of my union with Christ I am made holy; it is by the work of Christ or through the work of Christ that I receive the adoption and become a son of God. In other words, the 'through' or 'by' emphasizes the work that Christ has done, the things that He had to do before I could ever become a son.

We must safeguard this doctrine by the following consideration. While we rejoice in the fact that we are the sons of God – the sons of God in Jesus Christ – we must be careful to draw a clear distinction between His Sonship and our sonship, lest we go astray in another fashion. We are 'the sons of God', but we are not sons of God in the same way as the Lord Jesus Christ is the Son of God. He is the Son of God by eternal generation; we are the sons of God by adoption. It was because of this distinction that our Lord at the end of His earthly life said to one of His disciples: 'I ascend to my Father and your Father, and to my God and your God.' He did not say, 'I ascend to our Father and our God'. Our sonship is derivative, we derive it from Him; it is because we have been adopted 'in him'.

To state this truth still more explicitly, we must be clear that we are not made gods; we do not become divine in that sense. While it is true that we are partakers of the divine nature, we are still human beings. The Lord Jesus Christ is 'Substance of the eternal Substance', 'Very God of Very God'. He is essentially different from us, and yet we are adopted into the family. It is impossible to comprehend this; but it is important for us to recognize it, because there have been people at times who have taught wrongly that Christians become gods, that we become divine. There is no teaching to that effect in the Scripture. Our standing, our position, our rank is that of adopted children. There is a sense in which we can call the Lord Jesus Christ our Brother, but we should be careful as we do so. He stands eternally the Son of God who took upon Him human nature. We are human, adopted into the family of God and given the privileges and the standing and the status of sonship.

Another matter which must receive our attention is the question, To whom does this sonship belong? The Apostle Paul says: 'Having predestinated *us* unto the adoption of sons by Jesus Christ to himself.' Does that apply to all Christians; or does it only apply to some Christians? I raise that question because there is a teaching to the effect that all Christians do not become sons of God, that it is only true of some. It says that all Christians are the 'children' of God, but that only certain special Christians become 'sons' of God. This teaching was given notoriety some years ago by certain people who claimed for themselves an unusual degree of sanctity, a peculiar depth of teaching. They claimed that they had advanced beyond others, and were therefore entitled to be separate from others because of the depth of their teaching. Their teaching was that whereas all Christians are children, not all Christians become sons. They went further and taught that it is only the sons who shall take part in 'the first resurrection'. It is only they who are entitled to be 'with Christ'. The children, they said, will not be with Christ, they will be left on the earth; but the sons will be with Christ always and enjoy His glory in an exceptional manner. It was a teaching that separated Christians into 'children' and 'sons'.

The grounds on which they based their teaching were as follows. They said that in the Revised Version's translation of Matthew 5 : 9 we read: 'Blessed are the peacemakers, for they shall be called *sons of God*.' Then in the forty-fifth verse of Matthew 5 Christians are told to love their enemies, 'that ye may be sons of your Father which is in heaven'. Likewise in Luke 20:36 we are told that Christians 'are the sons of God, being sons of the resurrection'. They also argued that in chapters 3 and 4 of Galatians there is a difference between the Old Testament saints and the New Testament sons, that it is only the latter who are called sons in the highest sense. In the light of the teaching of the Scripture itself such teaching is utterly false. We really need not go further than this fifth verse of this first chapter of the Epistle to the Ephesians: 'Having predestinated *us* unto the adoption of sons.' The Apostle is clearly referring to himself and to all the Christians to whom he was writing, to the members of the churches at Ephesus and Colosse and the various other churches to whom this circular letter was being sent. He does not say 'having predestinated "a certain number of us", a "certain select few of us", to the adoption of sons by Jesus Christ to himself'. 'Having predestinated *us*' – all Christians, without any division, without any distinction.

And not only so; in the Scriptures, and in the Epistles particularly, the terms 'children' and 'sons' are always used interchangeably. There is no more perfect example of this than in the eighth chapter of the Epistle to the Romans where the Apostle is dealing with the whole question of sonship. He says, 'Ye have not received the spirit of bondage again to fear; but ye have received the Spirit of adoption, whereby we cry Abba, Father' (verse 15). Then he continues: 'The Spirit itself beareth witness with our spirit that we are the children of God' (verse 16). Clearly he is writing about the people whom he has just described as 'sons'. But here he calls them 'children', 'and if children then heirs, heirs of God and joint-heirs with Christ'. In the same paragraph, as part of the one argument, he uses the term 'sons' and 'children' interchangeably.

But there is a yet more striking statement in the third chapter of the Epistle to the Galatians in verse 26, as translated in the Revised Version: 'For ye are all sons of God, through faith in Christ Jesus.' All sons of God through faith! And again in Galatians 4: 'Wherefore thou art no more a servant, but a son; and if a son, then an heir of God through Christ.' It is exactly the same argument as in the Epistle to the Romans where Paul uses the word 'child'.

But perhaps the final proof of the utter wrongness of this teaching is found in the writings of the Apostle John. In his Gospel and in his Epistles, he never uses the word 'sons' at all; he always uses the word 'children'. Sometimes in the Authorized Version it is given as 'sons', but that is a mistake. The word John uses in the original is always the word 'children'. Clearly the Apostle John was not aware of the distinction on which this false teaching lays so much emphasis.

How subtle the devil is! He comes as an angel of light and draws divisions and distinctions which are not found in the Scriptures. He confounds Christian people, and deludes them into imagining that they have something higher, something esoteric, something that is only understood by the special few, and which cannot be taught to the majority of Christians because they are not yet ready to receive it. How important it is that we should read our Scriptures carefully! 'Having predestinated *us* to the adoption of sons.' All Christians are sons of God; they share the same privileges on earth, and they shall enjoy the same privileges in heaven and throughout eternity. There are none of these artificial gradations. We are all, thank God, by the grace of God in Christ, the sons of God and in the same privileged position.

But, lastly, leaving these matters of heresy and false teaching, let me end on something which will gladden our hearts, I trust, and enable us to see how wonderful this statement is. I put it in the form of a proposition. Redemption does not stop at merely undoing the effects of the Fall and sin; it goes beyond that! I began by saying that what we are told here is that Christ and His work have been designed to undo the effects of the Fall and of sin. But Paul tells us here that God has gone beyond that by giving us in Christ this adoption of sons. Something of the meaning of this is brought out in his comparison in the fifth chapter of his Epistle to the Romans where the Apostle uses the terms 'in Adam' and 'in Christ'. We are all by nature the descendants of Adam. Adam was created perfect in a state of innocence. He was placed in Paradise in the Garden of Eden, and he was enabled to enjoy fellowship with God. Yet he was still but a creature. He was certainly the lord of creation, but at his height and in his perfection he was never more than that. But in Christ we are in a different position. As the Apostle tells us in chapter 15 of his First Epistle to the Corinthians: 'The first man is of the earth, earthy: the second man is the Lord from heaven.' Adam was perfect, Adam was innocent, Adam was made in the image and likeness of God, but he was never made a 'partaker of the divine nature'. As we have seen already, that privilege does not make us gods; but it does make a real difference to us. It puts us into a new relationship to God that even Adam did not enjoy.

Christians are 'in Christ'. As such we have been raised to a higher level than Adam. Though he was perfect Adam was subject to fall and failure; but – and I say it with reverence and to the glory of God – those who are 'in Christ' cannot finally fall away; they cannot become lost. 'No man shall pluck them out of my hand', says the Lord (John 10: 28–29). Not only has Christ in His work undone the tragic results of the Fall, not only has He blotted out our sins, He has advanced our position. 'Where sin abounded, grace did much more abound', says Paul in Romans 5:20. Isaac Watts in a great verse which is often, alas, left out of his hymn commencing 'Jesus shall reign where'er the sun', says:

> *Where He displays His healing power*
> *Death and the curse are known no more.*
> *In Him the tribes of Adam boast*
> *More blessings than their father lost.*

That is a statement of the truth concerning us. In Christ not only are the blessings which Adam lost restored to us, but we are

[126]

given even more; in this new relationship to God which we enjoy in Christ we stand in a higher position than Adam. The blessing, the promise of sonship, is not only to the peacemakers, it is not only to those who are unusually strenuous in their Christian life; God forbid that I should encourage anyone in sin, but let me say the following on the authority of God's Word. Though you may have fallen grievously into sin in your past life, now, as a believer in Christ, you are a child of God, a son of God adopted into this new relationship, given a new rank and status and position, raised to a level that is even higher than that of Adam before the Fall. And while it is true that in this life, and in this world we only enjoy some of the privileges and the honours and the blessings attached to it, we know that all these are but the 'first fruits', they are but the 'foretaste'. 'The crowning day is coming by and by' when we shall 'see him as he is' and, being 'like him' we shall enter into all the prerogatives and privileges of our heavenly sonship. This is, and will ever be true of all Christians, all who belong to Christ, all who are 'in him'.

11

The Glory of God

'To the praise of the glory of his grace, wherein he
hath made us accepted in the beloved.'

Ephesians 1:6

God has done for us all that we have been considering, and all
that the Apostle proceeds to tell us, 'according to the good
pleasure of his will' (v. 5). He has not been moved to do all this
by anything in us whatsoever; it is entirely of Himself. Salvation
is not according to man's desire or request. Man by nature, and
in sin, does not desire salvation. Salvation is not a response on
God's part to anything in man; it is entirely from God. He was
moved by His own grace, mercy, and compassion. The Apostle
has been emphasizing this truth; and he now proceeds to give us
the reason why God has acted in this way. Here we have the great
motive behind redemption, the ultimate purpose in the mind and
wisdom of God, which has led to all the blessings resulting
from this great purpose of salvation. The ultimate motive of it all
is, 'to the praise of the glory of his grace'. It is all for the glory
of God.

But the astonishing thing, indeed the almost incredible thing,
is that God purposed to reveal that glory in us and through us.
We have been chosen to be holy, and to the adoption of sons, in
order that we might be 'to the praise of the glory of his grace'.
Note how all these statements are connected and how all of them,
separately and together, are designed to 'the praise of the glory
of his grace'. The Apostle shows us how we should regard ourselves in the light of all this, and how we should react to it all.
There is no more thorough test of our profession of the Christian
faith than our attitude to these things. Does it correspond to the
terms which Scripture always uses when it makes reference to any

aspect of God's plan of redemption? The Bible always refers to the advent of the Son of God into this world in thrilling terms. The Old Testament prophets rise to their greatest heights when they are foretelling the coming of the Son of God into this world. Think, for instance, how Isaiah writes of it and rises to his greatest height in doing so in chapter 40 of his book.

The same thing is true of all the prophetic writers. The New Testament takes up the theme, and especially in those glorious passages dealing with Christ's coming into the world. 'Great is the mystery of godliness', says Paul. He always bursts forth into praise and thanksgiving as he contemplates the glory of God in our redemption. This is the most astonishing thing that has ever happened in this world, or will ever happen. The coming of the Son of God into this world from heaven is always in the Bible a theme for praise and glory and thanksgiving. I ask, therefore, whether that is our response to it. Is that the effect which it has upon us? As human beings we all tend to show our reactions, our enthusiasms. You have but to pass a football ground on a Saturday afternoon, and you will hear people expressing themselves very definitely. The same thing happens when they listen to a play or when they see anything that pleases them. When they read a book that pleases them they must tell someone about it and talk about it. Do we Christian people do the same with respect to the Advent of the Son of God into this world? I sometimes fear that the majority of people who are outside the church today refuse even to listen to the gospel mainly because we have failed to give them the impression that this is the most wonderful event that has happened. We are not singing His praises and magnifying the grace and glory of God as we should. The people are therefore indifferent. In this verse the Apostle reminds us that the entire atmosphere in the Church should be one of praise: 'To the praise of the glory of his grace, wherein he has made us accepted in the beloved.' So let us proceed to discover what it is that calls for this praise and adoration and thanksgiving.

The first and the greatest truth concerning salvation is that it is a revelation of the glory of God – 'to the praise of the glory of his grace', or if you like, 'to the praise of his glory as it is manifested by himself in and through his grace'. This is the chief reason for praise. It is almost impossible to say anything about 'the glory of God' because our language, our terminology, our words are quite inadequate to convey any true sense of it. But we can say that the 'glory of God' is the essential nature of God; it is that which makes God God. We are told in the first chapter of the Epistle to the Hebrews, verse 3, that the Lord Jesus Christ is not only the 'express image' of the Person of God, but is also the brightness and the effulgence of the glory of God. If there is one term which describes God more than another it is this term 'glory'. It includes beauty, majesty, or, better still, splendour. It also includes the idea of greatness and might and eternity. All these terms are included in this one term 'glory'. We cannot go beyond it. This resplendent radiance is suggested in the expression used by the Apostle John in his First Epistle: 'God is light, and in him is no darkness at all' (1:5). The first and greatest truth about salvation is that it reveals to us the glory of God, the majesty, the splendour of God. In the Old Testament we find that this is the term which is always used to convey the immediate presence of God. In the First Book of Kings, chapter 8, we read that the glory of the Lord filled the temple, and in many places we are told that the glory of God always dwelt in the innermost court of both tabernacle and temple. There were the cherubim above the mercy-seat and the ark of the covenant, and there was the Shekinah glory. We are told that even the high priest himself was only allowed to enter once a year into the Holiest, and then not without blood. This was because the glory of God dwelt there. That gives us some idea of the transcendent glory of God, and we note that it is generally associated with the conception of our salvation. The glory and the mercy-seat are found together in the same innermost sanctum, 'the Holiest of all'.

The glory of God is generally mentioned in connection with God's dealing with man in salvation in some manner. It is most interesting to trace this right through the Old Testament. Rather surprisingly the first time we meet it is immediately after man had sinned. Before that we are told God communed with man, and man with God, in Paradise. All was perfect, but alas, man listened to the devil and as punishment for his rebellion and sin he was turned out of the Garden. Then we are told that at the east end of the Garden God placed cherubim and a flaming sword to prevent man from returning to Paradise and having access to the Tree of Life. We are to understand that the flaming sword and the cherubim are a manifestation of the glory of God. The glory of God leads to the punishment of sinful man, and keeps him in his place before it reveals to him a way of pardon and reconciliation. We read of Abraham being given a glimpse of 'the way' in Genesis, chapter 15. Similarly we read that the children of Israel as they journeyed from Egypt to Canaan were led by a pillar of cloud by day and a pillar of fire by night. That was an example of God giving His people a manifestation of His glory in connection with their deliverance.

We recall also the description that Isaiah gives of what happened when he was called to his prophetic office. He was given a vision of a temple filled by 'the train' of the Lord, and says: 'And the posts of the door moved at the voice of him that cried, and the house was filled with smoke' (Isaiah 6:1–4). The glory of the Lord was manifested to him, and he said, 'I am a man of unclean lips'; he was utterly humbled by the experience.

But it is when we come to the New Testament that we find this element still more clearly. In the lyrical announcement of the Incarnation that was made to the shepherds as they watched their flocks by night we read that suddenly a multitude of the heavenly host was heard crying out and saying, 'Glory to God in the highest, and on earth peace, good will toward men'. Note the order. The Saviour has been born, the Child is in the manger in the stable in Bethlehem: but the response of the heavenly host is, 'Glory to God in the highest', and only after that, 'peace, good will toward men'. The moment salvation is mentioned it is the glory of God that is most prominent. Salvation is a revelation of that above everything else, and it is not surprising that Paul writes to Timothy and says that what has been committed to him is 'the gospel of the glory of the blessed God'. In writing to the Corinthians he says: 'God who commanded the light to shine out of darkness, hath shined in our hearts to give the light of the knowledge of the glory of God in the face of Jesus Christ' (2 Corinthians 4:6). When the Son of God came into this world, above all else He was revealing the glory of God. 'And we beheld his glory' (John 1:14).

This is the way in which we should be thinking of our salvation. Does it fill us with a sense of wonder and praise and amazement? Do we realize that we have been called to 'the praise of the glory of his grace'? As the chief element in sin is that we do not give to God the glory that is due to His Name, so the chief thing about salvation should be that it brings us to a realization of the glory of God. Our view of sin has gone astray. We tend to think of certain actions as being sinful, and when we say that we have sinned we mean only that we have done something wrong, and that we are bearing the consequences of that. All that is true about sin, but the real essence of sin is that we are not giving the glory to God that is due to Him. Man was originally made that he might glorify God. 'The chief end of man is to glorify God and to enjoy Him for ever', as the Shorter Catechism reminds us; and the heinous character of sin is that it is a failure to glorify God. In the same way, when we are thinking of salvation, we must not think of it in the first instance in terms of our deliverance from particular sins, or even from condemnation. It includes that, of course, but the chief thing about it is that the glory of God has been revealed to us through it, the glory of His love and grace that have embraced us where we were. Our thinking about salvation should always, primarily, be in terms of the glory of God. On scriptural grounds this must be our chief criticism of all evangelism that simply emphasizes the great benefits which we receive, and our deliverance in various respects, and which never mentions the glory of God which is revealed in all this.

We must emphasize that our salvation is the greatest and highest manifestation of the glory of God. The glory of God is displayed in everything that God does. It is to be seen in Nature – 'The heavens declare the glory of God' (Psalms 19:1). We fail to see this glory because we are so blinded by sin. We look into the skies and think of stars in terms of the scientists' view of distance. But the Psalmist sees the glory of God. God has made the stars, and set them in order; He set the planets in their courses. The seasons likewise witness to His glory. But man in sin does not see this; he 'worships the creature rather than the Creator'. The glory of God is manifested in flowers, indeed in all things in the creation; they are the work of 'his fingers' (Psalms 8); but man in sin is blinded to it.

The glory of God is seen likewise in History. Looked at deeply one sees that God is over-ruling it all. Men talk of their plans and ambitions, and their wars; but it is clear that God has been over-ruling it all. It is all under His almighty hand. This is seen particularly clearly in Old Testament history in such instances as the Flood, the deliverance from Egypt, the dividing of the Red Sea, the dividing of the river Jordan, and especially in the giving of God's law at Mount Sinai.

But what I am emphasizing is that it is in our redemption in the Lord Jesus Christ we see the glory of God at its greatest height. In the first place it is in redemption we see most fully the wisdom of God. This is seen, I repeat, in nature and history, but to see it in its true glory you must see it 'in the face of Jesus Christ'.

Nothing but the wisdom of God could have contrived our salvation. We have noted the condition of man in all his troubles as the result of sin. The history books tell us what the world has done about it. Man has planned his schemes designed to produce his utopias, he has trusted to education and politics and endless other remedies; but it has all ended in failure as is proved by the state of the modern world. Man's wisdom always 'comes to nought' as Paul reminds the Corinthian church (1 Corinthians 2:6). I repeat: nothing but the wisdom of God could have contrived our salvation. It can be seen in the judgment of the world by the Flood. If we saw things through Christian understanding, every time we hear a thunderclap we would praise God and hear in it a manifestation of His might. But all that is as nothing compared with His power in redemption. His power in defeating Satan and bringing all his work to nought on the one hand, and all the positive blessings we receive on the other, teach the same lesson. Hence Paul says in verse 18 of our chapter: 'The eyes of your understanding being enlightened; that ye may know what is the hope of his calling, and what the riches of the glory of his inheritance in the saints; and what the exceeding greatness of his power to us-ward who believe, according to the working of his mighty power, which he wrought in Christ when he raised him from the dead and set him at his own right hand in the heavenly places.' In order to redeem us God had to deal with the power of Satan and the power of death. He has done so and mastered and conquered them and everything else that was inimical to our well-being.

In the same way the glory of God is revealed in His holiness and His righteousness. The ancient law given through Moses had revealed the holiness and righteousness and justice of God, and His view of sin, and His condemnation of it; but for a full manifestation of the holiness and righteousness of God we must hasten to Calvary's hill. There is only one answer to the question as to why Christ had to die – the holiness of God! The holiness of God is such that He cannot deal savingly with a sinner unless sin has been dealt with; nothing less than the death of His Son can satisfy the holy demands of this righteous God. So on the Cross He has 'set him forth as a propitiation to declare his righteousness' (Romans 3: 25 and 26).

But above all else the glory of God has been revealed to us in His grace. The question must arise in our minds as to why in view of our rebellion and arrogance and sin God has done anything for our good. The answer is found in His grace; and you know nothing of this until you see it 'in the face of Jesus Christ' and the grace that streams from it. It was because of this that Samuel Davies cried out in his famous hymn:

> *Great God of wonders, all Thy ways*
> *Are matchless, godlike, and divine;*
> *But the fair glories of Thy grace*
> *More godlike and unrivalled shine.*

It is there that you see His love, and the glory of that love.

Still more astonishing, in a sense, is the fact at which I have already hinted that the glory of God is to be revealed finally in and through us. God has chosen us to holiness, predestinated us to the adoption of sons to this end. By making us children, by making us holy, God reveals the glory of His holiness. Notice how Paul states this in chapter 3, verse 10 of this Epistle: 'To the intent that now unto the principalities and powers in heavenly places might be known by the church the manifold wisdom of God.' The Apostle Peter in his way says, 'which things the angels desire to look into.' They do not understand the matter fully, but they 'look into' it. All mine are thine, and thine are mine', says our Lord to the Father in John's Gospel, chapter 17,

[134]

'and I am glorified in them' (v. 10). 'Let your light so shine before men', says our Lord again, 'that men may see your good works and glorify your Father which is in heaven' (Matthew 5:16). We have been called 'to the praise of the glory of his grace'. We should live and conduct ourselves in such a manner that as men and women see us they shall be compelled to say, 'What a glorious God! Nothing can explain these people save the glory of the almighty God'.

How should we view ourselves in the light of all these truths? Here is the Apostle's answer: We have been called. We know He has 'made us accepted in the beloved'. Unfortunately the English Revised Version and the Revised Standard Version have gone completely astray in their translation here. They have, 'to the praise of the glory of his grace (his glorious grace) which he freely bestowed on us in the Beloved'. The Authorized Version translation says, 'accepted in the beloved'. That comes nearer to what the Apostle wrote, but even that does not bring out the true meaning. The word the Apostle used here was the very word that is used in Luke's Gospel, chapter 1, verse 28: 'And the angel came in unto her, and said, Hail, thou that art highly favoured, the Lord is with thee: blessed art thou among women.' The word means 'highly favoured'. The Revised Standard Version has, 'Hail, O favoured one'. The English Revised Version has, 'Thou that art highly favoured'. So we should translate it in exactly the same way in this Epistle, and read, 'To the praise of the glory of his grace, we know that he has highly favoured us in the beloved'. Surely this is the meaning the Apostle was concerned to convey! He uses the same word with respect to us as the archangel used about the Virgin Mary, 'Hail, thou that art highly favoured'. That meant that God had chosen Mary of all women in the world to bear His Son. She had been created for this, that the Son of God should enter her womb and be born of her.

The Apostle speaks similarly about us. He has already told us that we have been predestinated unto the adoption of sons. But it is greater even than that! Not only are we made sons of God, but Christ comes into us – 'Christ in you, the hope of glory' (Colossians 1:27). As He had physically entered into Mary so spiritually He enters into everyone of us who are His children. 'That holy thing that shall be born of thee shall be called the Son of God' (Luke 1:35). Yes, and because we are partakers of the divine nature Christ is, as it were, born in us, and so with Mary we are 'highly favoured'. God has chosen us, we do not know why, but we do know that this means that we are 'highly favoured'. God in His infinite wisdom and in infinite love and grace and mercy, before the foundation of the world, decided that you and I were to be 'highly favoured', and that by His grace we should not only be redeemed from the ravages and the consequences of sin, and be adopted into His family, but that in us His very Son should come to dwell, and our bodies should become 'the temple of the Holy Ghost'. This is the Apostle's conception of the Christian; and this is how we should habitually think of ourselves as we walk through life in this world.

Why am I what I am as a Christian? There is only one answer, I have been 'highly favoured' by the grace of God. I give Him all the glory – 'He that glorieth, let him glory in the Lord' (1 Corinthians 1:31). Is this your view of salvation? Are you giving the entire glory to God, or are you reserving a little for yourself? Are you saying that it is your belief that saves you? If so you are detracting from the glory of God. The glory is entirely His – 'to the praise of the glory of his grace in which he has highly favoured us in the beloved'.

12

'In the Beloved'

'To the praise of the glory of his grace, wherein he
hath made us accepted in the beloved.'

Ephesians 1:6

We must now look at the last three words in this sixth verse –
'in the beloved'. They constitute one of these magnificent
summaries of the gospel. As we have seen, the Apostle emphasizes that we must always think of the gospel in terms of the
glory of God. It is all 'to the praise of the glory of his grace'. He
has also reminded us, and especially in this sixth verse, of the
extraordinary privileges that we enjoy as the result of being
accepted (highly favoured) 'in the beloved'. The Apostle then
proceeds to tell us how God has manifested His glory in our
salvation: it is 'in the beloved'. Every blessing that man ever
enjoys from God is always in and through the Lord Jesus Christ.
In other words we are entitled to say that God's glory is revealed
ultimately and finally and most completely in and through the
Lord Jesus Christ.

We note again the Apostle's reference to our Lord. We have
noted previously the way in which the Apostle keeps on repeating
the name of the Lord Jesus Christ. He mentions Him twice in the
first verse, calling himself 'an apostle of Jesus Christ', and
referring to the saints as 'the faithful which are in Christ Jesus'.
He mentions Him once in the second verse: 'Grace be to you, and
peace, from God our Father, and from the Lord Jesus Christ.'
It is obvious that nothing gave the Apostle greater pleasure than
to refer to the Name of the Lord. We find the Name twice in the
third verse: 'Blessed be the God and Father of our Lord Jesus
Christ, who hath blessed us with all spiritual blessings in Christ'.
Paul cannot leave Him alone, he constantly brings in the Name.

Then he mentions Him again in the fourth verse: 'According as he hath chosen us in him before the foundation of the world, that we should be holy and without blame before him in love.' He seems to fear that we shall forget Him or leave Him out of our thinking. Once more we find the Name in the fifth verse: 'Having predestinated us unto the adoption of children by Jesus Christ to himself, according to the good pleasure of his will.' And then suddenly, at the end of the sixth verse, instead of saying 'to the praise of the glory of his grace, wherein he hath made us accepted in the Lord Jesus Christ', he says, 'wherein he hath made us accepted in *the beloved*'.

We must ask why the Apostle varied his terms. We can be quite certain that it was not accidental. He is writing under the inspiration of the Holy Spirit, so nothing he does is accidental. He has been using the terms 'Jesus Christ', 'the Lord Jesus Christ' and 'Christ', but suddenly he speaks of 'the beloved'. Why does he do so? As we come to consider this let us remind ourselves that when we are reading the Scriptures we must never take anything for granted; we must always be alert and alive, and always ready to ask questions. How easily one can miss the great blessings found in the very introduction to an Epistle such as this by simply sliding over the terms as if they did not matter! The Apostle deliberately says 'in the beloved' and not 'in the Lord Jesus Christ' or 'in Jesus Christ' or 'in Christ'. He does so, I suggest, because he is concerned to bring out in its full force and intensity what is after all the most wonderful thing of all about this great salvation. It is a glorious and wonderful thing that you and I should be made holy; it is equally marvellous that we are made, by adoption, the sons of God. It is almost incredible, but nevertheless true, that it is through people like ourselves that God is eventually going to show to 'the principalities and powers in the heavenly places' His manifold wisdom; it is by the Church that He plans to manifest the glory of His wisdom. But the most wonderful thing of all about this salvation is the way in which God has done all this. He has done so, says the Apostle, reaching the topmost height of his climax, 'in the beloved'.

Let us observe its emphasis. This is the key that leads us into the whole mystery of the Incarnation, and all that God has done in His Son. It is 'in the beloved'. The first message that this phrase conveys to us is about the Person of the Lord Jesus Christ. It is Paul's way of reminding us that the Lord Jesus Christ is God's beloved Son, God's 'only begotten Son'. This is what makes Christianity and its salvation unique and separate and different from everything else. It is not the record of man trying to rise up to God and trying to find God; it is the record of what God has done, and especially through His only begotten Son. 'The beloved' is the term that is always used to emphasize this truth. For instance, we find it in connection with our Lord's baptism. A voice came from heaven which said: 'This is my beloved Son', or 'This is my Son, the beloved, in whom I am well pleased' (Matthew 3:17). Again we find it in the record of what happened on the Mount of Transfiguration. The voice again came from heaven, and said: 'This is my beloved Son, hear him' (Matthew 17:5). Each time when the veil of heaven is drawn back a little, as it were, and man is given some glimpse of the eternal glory through the Son, this is the term that is used.

Our Lord Himself also used the term 'beloved' in His parable of the wicked husbandman. He points out in His story how the master had sent various servants to his vineyard in order to plead with those husbandmen to do their work properly, and to warn them, and so on. But they took them and killed them all. Then the master says to himself, 'I will send my beloved son, him they will honour' (Matthew 21:37). Our Lord uses the term in describing Himself in that parable, knowing that it is the term His heavenly Father habitually and characteristically uses with respect to Him – 'the beloved'. All this emphasizes the fact that our redemption has been worked out and achieved through the only begotten Son of God. We have seen that we become sons by adoption, but that He is Son by eternal generation. He is one with the Father, one substance, indivisibly. The only begotten of the Father, coming eternally out of the Father – one with the Father, indivisibly, inseparably. The term 'beloved' conveys all that to us; and the Apostle clearly used it deliberately in order to bring out that aspect of the truth, and to emphasize it. 'The beloved' is none other than the Substance of the eternal Substance – God, the eternal Son.

We have seen also that, as the result of being made holy, and as the result of our adoption as sons, we are to live 'to the praise of the glory of God'. And the world is to see something of the glory of God in us and through us. But God's glory is manifested in its fulness and intensity in the Person of His Son, 'the beloved'. The author of the Epistle to the Hebrews expresses it in the words: 'God, who at sundry times and in divers manners spake in time past unto the fathers by the prophets, hath in these last days spoken unto us by his Son, whom he hath appointed heir of all things, by whom also he made the worlds; who being the brightness of his glory, and the express image of his person, and upholding all things by the word of his power, when he had by himself purged our sins, sat down on the right hand of the Majesty on high' (1:1-3). Our Lord is 'the brightness of God's glory', He is 'the express image of God's person'. So what we are told here is that our redemption has been achieved, and made possible, because God has sent into this world His beloved Son, the brightness of His own glory and the express image of His own Person, the outshining, the effulgence of the glory and the majesty and the brightness of God Himself.

The Apostle John in the same manner, in the Prologue of his Gospel, in the fourteenth verse says, 'We beheld his glory, the glory as of the only begotten of the Father, full of grace and truth'. John says, in effect, We have seen His glory. Though He came in the likeness of sinful flesh; though He humbled Himself and took upon Him the form of a servant, we saw something of the shining forth of the glory. He and others had seen it on the Mount of Transfiguration, and in other places, and they had seen it after the Lord's resurrection.

So when we consider the great statements in these verses, and as we think about the glory of God as it has manifested itself in the redemption of men, we must never forget that this is the highest point in the manifestation of that glory, that God Himself has come in the Person of the Son, the Beloved, the One in whom 'dwelleth all the fulness of the Godhead bodily'. In the man Jesus we see 'The Word made flesh'. All that is conveyed to us in this term 'the beloved'. The Son, however, is not only the 'only begotten' and not only the 'express image' of God's Person, and 'the brightness of his glory'; because of this relationship He is One whom the Father has loved from all eternity. God loves us, but not in that way. There was never a beginning of the Father's love for the Son. He is 'the beloved', the One apart, the One who has always enjoyed the whole of God's love, the One on whom the whole of God's love and affection are centred, and in whom they dwell. There is no term which expresses so perfectly, and so completely, the relationship between the Father and the Son as this expression 'the beloved'. So as we think of the Babe of Bethlehem, as we think of the meaning of the Incarnation, re-member who it is that God sent forth – His Son, 'the beloved'; the eternally loved One. It is He who has come into the world in order to save us.

But let us now go on to look at this term as it is a measure of the Father's love toward us. The Apostle has been emphasizing, as the whole Bible emphasizes, that our salvation is the result of the love and the grace and the mercy of God. But if we would really know the love of God we must grasp something of the truth about this Person. Those who claim to believe in the love of God without believing in the Lord Jesus Christ are simply displaying their ignorance of the love of God. There are people who are foolish enough to say that they cannot believe in the Virgin Birth and the Incarnation, that they cannot believe in the Atonement, and the punishment of sin, because of their belief in the love of God. But thereby they merely display a fundamental ignorance of the love of God. To know something of the love of God one must have some understanding of what has happened in and to the Son of God, 'the beloved'. It is in Him that we measure the love of God truly. The very fact that God ever sent Him into this world is astounding in and of itself. We cannot conceive of these things; our minds are too small, they boggle at the very conception. We cannot conceive of eternity, bound as we are by the idea of time. We ourselves, and our minds, are finite, so our very thinking is limited. It is difficult for us to grasp the idea that there was never any beginning to God the Father, God the Son, and God the Holy Spirit, that they exist from eternity to eternity.

The fact is that the Lord Jesus Christ, the Son, was in the

bosom of the Father from eternity. That is the term used by the Apostle John in his Prologue: 'the only begotten Son who is in the bosom of the Father, he hath declared him.' He was eternally in the bosom of the Father, enjoying the unmixed and perfect bliss and love and holiness and glory of heaven and of eternity; and the astounding thing we are told in connection with our salvation is that 'When the fulness of the time was come, God sent him forth' (Galatians 4:4), sent Him out from that glory, out from heaven and the radiance and the glory and the magnificence of it all, sent Him forth into the world.

It was the Father who sent Him. 'God so loved the world that he gave his only begotten Son' (John 3:16). It is only in the light of that fact that we begin to measure the eternal love of God. It was His own beloved, His only begotten Son that God sent forth upon this terrible errand, and for such terrible people! Like the father in our Lord's parable of the wicked husbandmen, God the eternal Father sends His own Son, His only Son. He had sent his prophets and other leaders, but they had been rejected and their message had been ignored; but now the time comes when the eternal Father says, I will send forth My Son, My beloved Son, I will send Him to them.

Further, if we are to have some conception of the love of God we must read the four Gospels, and in our minds and imaginations we must think of God the Father looking down upon all and observing and watching what was happening to His beloved Son. All parents, surely, know something of this experience. They send their children out on the voyage of life, and they watch them, they keep their eye upon them, they see the storms and trials coming, and they watch with concern, with love, at times trembling for them, fearful for them. Multiply that by infinity and we still have no conception of what it meant to the eternal Father to send His Son into the sea of sin and evil in this world. Such is the love of God. He sees men reviling His Son, He sees men laughing at Him, He sees men taking up stones to throw at Him, His Beloved. The God who made the world out of nothing, and who could bring it to an end in a moment, the God with whom nothing is impossible looks on and watches the world refusing His 'beloved', persecuting Him and wounding Him. There we have some measure of the love of God. As you read the story in the four Gospels remember that it is 'the beloved' you are reading about, and that the Father is ever looking at His Beloved and at the world's treatment of Him.

But let us hasten on to the most astounding thing of all. We see Him staggering up Golgotha, we see Him nailed to a tree. The Father is still looking down upon it all. The Beloved is finally rejected, despised of men, spat upon, scourged, hated, reviled, nailed to the tree. We cannot conceive the agony, the suffering, the shame that were involved. The Father looks at His Beloved as He endured the contradiction of sinners against Himself. That is the measure of God's love. As the Apostle Paul expresses it in chapter 8 of his Epistle to the Romans, 'He spared not his own Son, but delivered him up for us all'. He did not spare the Beloved, though He had loved Him with that eternal love from all eternity, and with all the intensity of His divine being; though He is 'the beloved', His Father did not spare Him. He spared Him no suffering. He 'laid upon him the iniquity of us all'; He struck Him, He smote Him with those stripes which we deserved. And the reason why He did not spare Him any suffering was that you and I might be forgiven.

> *Thou didst not spare Thine only Son*
> *But gav'st Him for a world undone,*
> *And freely with that blessèd One*
> *Thou givest all.*

If you would know anything about the love of God you must start with this term 'the beloved'. It was of this 'beloved' that Paul says that God has 'made him to be sin for us, who knew no sin, that we might be made the righteousness of God in him' (2 Corinthians 5:21). He made His Beloved a sin offering for us, that we might be made the righteousness of God in Him.

But let us look at this term for a moment as it is the measure of the Son's love. We have been looking at it as the measure of the Father's love; let us now look at it from the other side. We must not compare them, it would be wrong and it would be foolish to do so. And yet there is a difference between a father and a son, and the Lord Jesus Christ is the Son of God eternally, and

[143]

sonship is sonship for Him also. So we can look at the Son's love and what the procuring of our salvation meant to Him. Try for a moment to think of the self-emptying that took place at the Incarnation in terms of this expression 'the beloved'. He who had been in the bosom of the Father from all eternity, enjoying perfect unmixed bliss, decides to leave it for a while. He through whom all things were made, and by whom all things consist, the everlasting Word, the Word of God, the express image of God's person, humbles Himself, He divests Himself of the insignia, the signs of His eternal glory, and says 'Here am I, send me'. He volunteered to become a man, to take unto Himself human nature, to lay aside the prerogatives of His position and of His unique relationship to the Father. And He entered into the Virgin's womb. It is 'the beloved' who was there, going through the whole process of development as an embryo. It is inconceivable, it is baffling; but it is true. Then the time came when He was born in a stable and for want of a cradle they put Him in a manger.

Who is that helpless infant? It is 'the beloved' – the one on whom the love of God had been poured from all eternity. Now He knows something about weakness and helplessness. Follow the story through – the suffering, the misunderstanding, 'the contradiction of sinners'. He spent eighteen years apparently quite unknown, indeed until the age of thirty. He who had experienced all the fulness of God directly in love, has now humbled Himself and put Himself into such a position that He knows what it is to be lonely, to feel a sense of desertion, and to meet face to face the contradiction of sinners. He who made all things is suffering at the hands of the very people whom He had made. That is the measure of His love. Look at the despising and the persecution that followed. We cannot understand what it meant to Him except in the light of this term 'the beloved'. How glad we should be that the Apostle did not say 'the Lord Jesus Christ' here, but instead said 'in the beloved'!

The height of the paradox of this love, the thing that no human mind can encompass, is that when you stand at the foot of the Cross and listen, you hear these words being uttered: 'My God, my God, why hast thou forsaken me?' Everyone else had forsaken Him, His disciples had fled and had left Him, but now He cries, 'My God, my God, why hast *thou* forsaken me'? The one who utters that cry is 'the beloved', the one who had basked in the sunshine of the eternal love from eternity, without intermission. He reaches a point wherein even He has lost sight of the face and the smile of His Father. And He experienced that for you, for me. If He had shrunk from it we would not be saved, we would not be forgiven, we would not be Christians, we would not be children of the second birth. The 'beloved' descended even to that degree of ignominy and died. His body was buried in a grave and a stone was rolled against its door. He descended into hell – 'the beloved'. He went 'into the lowest parts of the earth' – He who had made everything out of nothing. And it was for us, and for our salvation. It is only as we realize who it is who is suffering in that manner that we realize the depth and the intensity of His love toward us.

Our final thought is that this term 'the beloved' tells us about our relationship to God. So far we have been dealing with *His* relationship to God; now let us look at the term as it expresses *our* relationship to God. Let us climb with the Apostle from rung to rung as he moves up this tremendous ladder. We are called, we are chosen to holiness, to sonship, to the praise of God's glory – yes, even higher, as this word reminds us. We are to be loved by God even as His Son was loved by Him. Have I gone too far? am I exaggerating? Have I suddenly given rein to my imagination? Am I going beyond the Scripture? I answer by quoting the words of the Son Himself, in His high priestly prayer in the Gospel of John, chapter 17, verse 23: 'I in them, and thou in me, that they may be made perfect in one; and that the world may know that thou hast sent me' – and then, and most astounding of all – 'and hast loved them as thou hast loved me'. I confess frankly that if it were not there in that verse I would not believe it; but it *is* there. The truth about the Christian, the truth about the one who is 'in Christ', is that because he is in Christ and is adopted as a son in the Beloved, God the Father loves him as he loved His own Son – 'as thou hast loved me'. That is even beyond sonship, but it means an intimacy of communion with God that we share with the Son Himself. It is not only a question of rank or of position, it is not merely that we have been adopted legally: the Father now loves us as He loved the Son Himself. It is staggering and stupendous.

The Apostle not only says it here but elsewhere also. In his Epistle to the Colossians he makes an appeal for ethical conduct and morality and behaviour, and this is how he states it: 'Put on therefore, as the elect of God, holy and beloved, bowels of mercies' (3:12). Note the way in which he describes us: 'Put on therefore, as the elect of God,' 'holy' – but still more marvellous, 'beloved'. We are the beloved of God. It is the ultimate height of our salvation and redemption, that the Christ who came down from the Glory to earth and went into Hades, has risen and has taken us up with Him. He has placed us in a position where we are loved as He is loved, 'holy and beloved'. Paul says the same thing in his Second Epistle to the Thessalonians: 'But we are bound to give thanks alway to God for you, brethren, beloved of the Lord' (2:13). We are not only brethren, we are beloved, 'beloved of the Lord', because God 'hath from the beginning chosen (us) to salvation through sanctification of the Spirit and belief of the truth'.

Are you convinced, are you satisfied? Do you realize that that is the ultimate height of salvation? It is because everything we have is 'in the beloved' that we ourselves become 'the beloved' of God. God loves the Christian as He loves the Son; we share that love, nothing less. Have you ever been tempted to think that God is not fair to you, that God is dealing rather harshly and unkindly with you? Never harbour such a thought again. Whether you understand what is happening to you, or not, this is the truth concerning you. In Christ, and because He is 'the beloved', you are the beloved of God also. We are 'brethren, beloved of God'.

'The Son of God became the Son of man,' said Calvin, 'that the sons of men might be made the sons of God'. Yes, and I add, 'beloved of God' because we are 'in the beloved'.

13
Redemption

'In whom we have redemption through his blood, the forgiveness of sins, according to the riches of his grace.'

Ephesians 1:7

Here we have another of the magnificent statements in which this first chapter of the Epistle to the Ephesians abounds; a statement which summarizes in itself the whole essence and content of the Christian Gospel and the Christian faith. There is a sense in which one feels that when such a verse as this is read, nothing further is needed. And yet the history of the Church shows clearly that all such statements need exposition. This is so because, although we are Christians, we are not yet perfect. We are liable and subject to error, we are prone to heresy; and the history of doctrine in the Church shows abundantly that it is with respect to such statements as this that there has often been the greatest confusion in the minds and hearts of Christian people. This is not at all surprising, for we are face to face here with the heart of the gospel, and we can therefore anticipate that the great adversary of our souls, 'the accuser of the brethren', and the enemy of God, the devil, will be more anxious to confuse us, and to becloud our minds and our understandings at this point than at any other. It is therefore most essential that we should look at Paul's statement and analyse it, and be certain that we grasp its meaning, because it brings us face to face with the very nerve and centre of the Christian faith.

We must start, of course, by looking at the context. The words 'in whom' insist upon our doing so. Obviously they refer to the One who has been described at the end of the previous verse as 'the beloved'. The Apostle has told us that we have been 'accepted in the beloved'. 'In whom', he now says, 'we have redemption'.

We note also that this word brings us to a point of transition in this preliminary statement in the introduction to the Epistle. We have reminded ourselves already that the work of salvation is divided up in the Scripture between the three blessed Persons in the Holy Trinity, the Father, the Son and the Holy Ghost. In verses 3–6 we have been considering the work of the Father, the great purpose of the Father, the eternal plan of God, that which God has purposed before the foundation of the world for us. His purpose is that we should 'be holy and without blame before him in love', that we 'receive the adoption of children', of sons, by Jesus Christ unto Himself, that we should be 'to the praise of the glory of God's grace', and that we should become 'beloved' in 'the beloved'.

But now we come to consider how that purpose has been carried out in and through the Son. So from the beginning of this seventh verse to the end of the twelfth verse we shall be considering the particular work of the Son in the economy of redemption. Then in verses 13 and 14 we shall look at the work of the Holy Spirit in this great plan and purpose. We have been given the great picture of God's ultimate objective for us; and we have glanced at our exalted position of sonship, and at its requirement that we should be holy, without blame, without blemish and without spot in the presence of God. But we are still on earth, still fallible and still sinful; and the question that arises in our hearts is: How can we ever be brought into such an exalted state and condition?

Obviously much needs to be done to us before we can ever be brought to such a position. The great obstacle to our ever getting there is the obstacle of sin; sin in general and sins in particular. It is our sins that have come between us and God, as the prophet Isaiah reminds us, saying, 'God's arm is not shortened that it cannot save, nor is his ear heavy that it cannot hear', but our sins have come between us and our God (59:1–2). So before we can ever arrive at the predestined position which God has purposed for us, something has to be done about this problem of our sin and our sins. It was to perform this special and peculiar work that the Son of God came into this world. God in His own eternal wisdom and foreknowledge, and according to His own purpose, devised a way whereby man could be reconciled to Himself. And the way is that which is outlined here. The obstacle has been removed, the problem has been solved.

> *There is a way for man to rise*
> *To that sublime abode;*
> *An offering and a sacrifice,*
> *A Holy Spirit's energies,*
> *An Advocate with God.*

As we turn to the Apostle's exposition, we note that the first thing he tells us is that this obstacle which stands between us and God, and which must be removed before we can ever be reconciled to God, has been dealt with in Christ. 'In whom' – this 'beloved' of whom he has been speaking, and whom he has mentioned so frequently! We must not assume that because it has been emphasized so often that there is no need to emphasize it again, because it is just at this point that so many people stumble with respect to the matter of salvation. Certainly, as far as my own pastoral experience is concerned, no problem has arisen so frequently as just this. You ask a person: 'Do you think you are a Christian?' and the reply one so frequently gets is: 'Well, I am trying to be one,' or 'I am trying to become one'. Such a statement is a clear indication that this first primary statement in connection with the way of salvation has never been understood.

So let me state it clearly once more. At the heart and centre of the gospel stands the truth that there is no salvation at all apart from the Lord Jesus Christ. 'Christianity is Christ.' Anything which may represent itself as Christianity but which does not insist upon the absolute necessity and cruciality of Christ is not Christianity at all. Unless He is the heart and soul and centre, the beginning and the end of what is offered as salvation, it is not Christian salvation, whatever else it may be.

Let us in the first place state negatively that we do not and cannot save ourselves. Or to put the matter in another form, we cannot make ourselves Christian. One would have thought that, after nearly two thousand years of Christianity in the world, it would be unnecessary to make that statement. Yet I assert that it is more essential than ever. If you are still thinking in terms of making yourself a Christian, or trying to be a Christian, it is a clear indication that you are on the wrong road; and as long as you are on that road you will never become a Christian. The first thing we have to realize, and to understand, is that no man has ever made himself a Christian; that no-one ever can make himself a Christian. All the efforts we may make – fasting, sweating, praying – will make no difference, indeed they may well be the greatest hindrance. That, of course, was the actual experience of the Apostle Paul himself. He had been trying to reconcile himself to God; and his grand discovery on the road to Damascus was that that was the very essence of error, and that all in which he had boasted was 'dung' and 'refuse'. That is the story of all the great saints. It was the realization of this that led to the Protestant Reformation. This is what revolutionized the life of Martin Luther, John Calvin, John Knox, and all the great leaders in the true Church, including John Wesley and all others to this present day. The nerve of this statement, 'In whom we have redemption' is to tell us that we can never make ourselves Christian, and that to try to make ourselves Christians is to display that we do not understand even the first step in the way of salvation.

But, further, the Lord Jesus Christ did not come to tell us what we have to do in order to make ourselves Christian. There are some who think they can put themselves right with God without mentioning Christ at all. But there are others who believe that His main purpose in coming into the world was to teach us, and to instruct us, and to give us a stimulus and an example as to what we have to do in order to save ourselves. But that is equally wrong. What He tells us to do is even more impossible than the law that was given through Moses. The Sermon on the Mount, which is our Lord's exposition of the Ten Commandments, shows how utterly impossible it is for anyone to keep the Ten Commandments in his own strength. Our Lord did not come to tell us what we have to do in order to save ourselves; He came to save us. He came to do something for us, to act on our behalf. That is the very essence of the gospel. 'In whom.' It is in Him that we have salvation. 'The Son of man has come to seek and to save that which was lost.' It is He Himself and what He has done on our behalf that constitutes our salvation.

There are others who think that our Lord came in order to tell us that God was ready to forgive us. They say: There are many

statements in the Old Testament which tell us that God is a
Father; that God is love and that God is ready to forgive. They
tell us that He is 'plenteous in mercy', and 'gracious, and full of
compassion', that 'like as a Father pitieth his children, so the
Lord . . .' and so on. They continue: Now all that was revealed in
the Old Testament. God had announced to the nation of Israel
and through them to the world that He was a God that was ready
to forgive sins. But mankind finds it difficult to accept that
teaching and to believe it. So, they continue, God decided to send
His own Son so that as people would see Him and listen to Him,
and behold His works, they would believe that God is love, and
that He is ready to forgive. They suggest therefore that our Lord
came in order to teach us about God's love and about God's
readiness to forgive. They argue that He did so in the parable of
the Prodigal Son, and so forth.

But they do not stop even there. They say that God went even
further than that; He sent His Son even to the Cross; and what
you really see on the Cross on Calvary's hill is a great and glorious
display of God's love and of God's readiness to forgive. They
maintain that it works in this way: God sent His Son into the
world but the world did not recognize Him, the world indeed
crucified Him, but God tells us even from the Cross, 'I am ready
to forgive you even that'. 'Such is My love', says God to the
world, 'that though you have crucified My only Son I will forgive
you for doing even that!' To such people our Lord's death on the
Cross is the supreme statement of God's readiness to forgive.

But that is not what the Apostle tells us here. His statement is
not to the effect that the Lord Jesus Christ has come to proclaim
God's readiness to forgive, or that God is a forgiving God. It is
that the Cross of Christ is God's way of making forgiveness
possible. The message is not that God is prepared to forgive
Calvary, but that God forgives us through Calvary. It is what God
did at Calvary that produces our forgiveness. Calvary is not
merely a proclamation or an announcement of God's love and
readiness to forgive; it is God, through what He did in and by His
Son on Calvary's Cross, making a way whereby He can reconcile
us unto Himself.

The Apostle states this many times. He does not say that God
was in Christ announcing or making a proclamation of reconcilia-

tion and forgiveness. What he says is that 'God was in Christ reconciling the world unto himself' (2 Corinthians 5:19). It is in Christ that God reconciles the world unto Himself. 'In whom we have redemption.' The redemption is in Christ Himself. He is not the mere announcement of it; He is it, He Himself is it. 'God was in Christ' – in and through Christ, by means of Christ, in what He did to Christ – 'reconciling the world unto himself'. The Apostle goes further and says, 'He hath made him to be sin for us, who knew no sin, that we might be made the righteousness of God in him' (v. 21). Christ has been 'made sin for us'. Our sins have been laid on Him. And it is as the result of that action that God has reconciled us to Himself.

This, of course, is vital. If the Lord Jesus Christ is merely a statement of God's readiness to forgive, then He is but one of a number of such statements; and if you had sufficient understanding you could be saved by the Old Testament teaching without the coming of Christ at all. He would simply be the elaboration of a statement already made. But that is not the Christian doctrine of salvation and of redemption. The Christian doctrine of salvation and redemption is this – that Christ Himself is the salvation. Our salvation is in Him: as we find Paul stating it in the second chapter, 'He is our peace, who hath made of twain one, and has reconciled us'. He! The Lord Jesus Christ Himself! This can never be repeated too frequently, it can never be emphasized too much. I can put it in the form of a question: Do you believe, do you know that your sins are forgiven? Do you know that God has forgiven you? If you do I ask this further question – How does God forgive you? Let me ask another question which is still more searching: Do you believe, do you see, and do you know, that it is because of what happened in Christ, and because of that alone, that God has forgiven you? When you think of yourself and of the forgiveness of your sins, do you think solely in terms of the fact that God is love, that God is piteous, and that God is merciful and compassionate? Is Christ merely the greatest statement of God's love and compassion that has ever been made, or did He merely make the greatest statement with respect to it? Or do you see, and know, and rely solely, upon the fact that what happened in Christ is God's way of forgiving? That is the question. 'In whom we have redemption through his blood.' He is not only a preacher or teacher; He is the salvation. Paul sums it all up again in a great statement in the Epistle to the Corinthians: 'But of him are ye in Christ Jesus, who of God is made unto us wisdom, and righteousness, and sanctification, and redemption' (1 Corinthians 1:30). To be saved is to be in Christ; not simply to believe His teaching, but to be in Him, and to be a sharer in His life, in His death, in His burial, in His resurrection, in His ascension. 'In whom we have redemption through his blood.'

We must not stop at saying that our salvation is in Christ, for we are told in particular that He has redeemed us. 'In whom we have redemption through his blood.' Here we meet a very important term, *redemption*. And as we look at it, and analyse it, we shall see still more clearly the all-importance of what I have been saying. This is the word that is used throughout the New Testament with regard to our salvation. I have already quoted one example of this – 'Who of God is made unto us wisdom, and righteousness, and sanctification, and *redemption*' (1 Corinthians 1.30). Again, it is found in Paul's First Epistle to Timothy: 'Who gave himself a ransom for all' (2:6); and again, in the Epistle to Titus: 'Who gave himself for us, that he might redeem us from all iniquity, and purify unto himself a peculiar people, zealous of good works' (2:14). The Apostle Peter uses precisely the same expression, 'Forasmuch as ye know that ye were not redeemed with corruptible things, as silver and gold, from your vain conversation received by tradition from your fathers; but with the precious blood of Christ, as of a lamb without blemish, and without spot' (1 Peter 1:18–19).

As this is a vital term we must be clear as to its meaning in the Old Testament and the New. It means 'deliverance by the payment of a ransom'. A thing is redeemed by the payment of a stipulated price. This is illustrated in many ways in the Old Testament. For instance, if a man had become a slave as the result of being captured or conquered by another, he could be 're-deemed' by his nearest kinsman if the kinsman was able to pay the required price. The same applied to a man who had been put into prison. He could come out of prison if his kinsman paid the adequate price. This is the way in which the term is used in the Old Testament. And it is used in the same way in the New Testament; it is the term used about setting a slave free. A slave could be set at liberty by someone paying a purchase price for him. A slave could be bought in the market or he could be bought out of slavery. That is the essence of the meaning of this term 'redemption'. And as it is the term that is used to explain the doctrine of salvation it must be interpreted according to its New Testament and Old Testament meaning.

Our Lord Jesus Christ Himself confirms this usage of the term. In a most important statement in the Gospel according to Matthew, we read that our Lord said, 'Even as the Son of man came not to be ministered unto, but to minister, and to give his life a ransom for many' (20:28). He told His followers that He had not come into the world in order that they might minister to Him, but that He might minister to them. He had come to do something for them that no-one else could do, namely, 'to give his life a ransom for many'.

The teaching therefore is that the whole of mankind is in a state of bondage as the result of sin. We are held as slaves and as serfs, and we cannot set ourselves at liberty. In a sense, the story of the Old Testament is the story of mankind, and especially of the chosen nation, trying to set itself free from bondage by keeping the law, but completely failing to do so, for 'There is none righteous, no not one'. 'The whole world lieth guilty before God' (Romans 3:10, 19). The whole world is in a state of slavery to sin and to Satan; it is under the dominion of Satan. That is the term used. We are in bondage to the law which condemns us, having told us that, if we could keep it and honour it, it would save us. Its demands, its penalties, are plain and clear, but there is no man or collection of men that can ever pay the price of its demands. That is the fundamental teaching of the whole Bible, we are all by nature 'under the law' and in a state of condemnation.

But in the Lord Jesus something new has happened. He came into this world in order to redeem us. He came in order to pay the ransom price that would set us free, to lay down that deposit that would secure our emancipation. The term 'redemption' cannot be explained in any other sense, for this is its characteristic meaning everywhere in the Scriptures. The result is that we are told about ourselves as Christians, 'Ye are not your own, for ye are bought with a price' (1 Corinthians 6:19-20). A Christian, says Paul, is therefore a 'bondservant', a 'bondslave' of the Lord Jesus Christ.

The Apostle always describes himself in this way. What he says about himself in effect is this: 'I am the bondslave of Christ; I was the slave of Satan, but Christ has bought me in the market. So I am now the bondslave of Christ, I am His property, I belong to Him.' As Christians we are not our own, for we have been redeemed, we have been bought, we have been purchased. Notice how the matter is expressed in the Book of Revelation: 'Thou [the Lamb of God] art worthy to take the book and to open the seals thereof,' cry the glorified saints. Why? 'For thou wast slain and hast redeemed us to God by thy blood' (Revelation 5:9). It is in Christ that we are saved; and what He has done to save us is that He has bought us, He has redeemed us.

The term 'redemption' is still occasionally used. People who get into financial difficulties sometimes go to a pawnbroker, and they leave something with him as a deposit in order that they may receive a certain amount of money on loan. Then when they desire to have their possession back they return and pay money to the pawnbroker to redeem it. Thus the Lord Jesus Christ saves us by redeeming us, by ransoming us, by paying the price that was necessary for our liberation.

Another matter we must consider is the exact price which was paid in order to redeem us, and the Apostle does not leave us in ignorance about it: 'In whom we have redemption through his blood.' 'His blood!' Here is the very centre, the heart of the doctrine of our salvation. Have you noticed when you have read this statement that the Apostle specifically says, 'In whom we have redemption by his *blood*'? Why did he not say 'by his death'? Many people object to this; they say they cannot abide this 'theology of blood'. If it were 'by his death' they would not object so much. They feel that the words of the Apostle are too material-istic and that they savour of the blood sacrifices of primitive people. Hence we must emphasize again the fact that the Apostle in his use of terms is always deliberate. I suggest that he deliber-ately emphasizes the blood because what happened in the death of our Lord can only be understood adequately in terms of the Old Testament sacrificial language.

There are many other examples and illustrations of this characteristic language in the New Testament with regard to our redemption. Take for instance Romans 3:25: 'Whom God hath

set forth to be a propitiation through faith in his blood.' The same
is found in the second chapter of this Epistle to the Ephesians:
'But now in Christ Jesus ye who sometimes were far off are made
nigh by the blood of Christ' (v. 13). And again, it is found several
times in the ninth chapter of the Epistle to the Hebrews. Verse 12
reads: 'Neither by the blood of goats and calves, but by his own
blood he entered in once into the holy place, having obtained
eternal redemption for us.' In the tenth chapter the same author
writes, 'Having therefore, brethren, boldness to enter into the
holiest by the blood of Jesus' (v. 19). Again, we recall that the
Apostle Peter writes: 'Forasmuch as ye know that ye were not
redeemed with corruptible things, as silver and gold . . . but with
the precious blood of Christ' (1 Peter 1:18). Similarly the Apostle
John writes, '. . . the blood of Jesus Christ his Son cleanseth us
from all sin' (1 John 1:7). It is the blood that cleanses. It is always
the 'blood'. Again, in the Book of Revelation, we find the same
emphasis: 'Unto him that loved us, and washed us from our sins
in his own blood' (1:5).

It is not simply the death of Christ, but in particular 'the blood
of Christ'. This is to show us that what the Lord Jesus Christ has
done for us by His death is in line with the entire Old Testament
doctrine as to the value of sacrifices. Our Lord Himself claimed:
'I am not come to destroy but to fulfil' (Matthew 5:17). He says
that heaven and earth shall not pass away until every jot and tittle
of the law has been fulfilled (v. 18). He came to fulfil the law. After
His resurrection He says, 'These are the words which I spake unto
you while I was yet with you, that all things must be fulfilled
which are written in the law of Moses and in the prophets and in
the psalms concerning me' (Luke 24:44). The Old Testament
sacrifices and offerings point to Christ; they have their meaning in
Christ; what they teach always has reference to Him. The
teaching is that the design and object of the sacrifices is to propitiate God. The blood of bulls and of goats and the blood of the
sacrificial Paschal lamb was shed in order that God might be
propitiated, that God might be reconciled. It was all done to
propitiate, to appease God.

But we note further, that the propitiation was always secured as
a result of the expiation of guilt. Sin had to be punished because it
carried guilt with it. In the Old Testament times the sins were

placed upon the animals by the laying on of the hands of the High Priest and then the animals were killed; and so the guilt was expiated. One proof of this was that, on the day of atonement, the blood was taken and sprinkled on the mercy seat. God accepted it and He forgave the sins. God is propitiated as the result of the expunging, the wiping out, the making atonement for the sin. What has been done satisfies God and He therefore forgives; He is propitiated as the result of expiation.

Observe that expiation was always achieved in a vicarious manner. I mean that the guilt was transferred to something else, to an animal, to a beast: the beast died vicariously. The result of such sin offerings was always to produce forgiveness and pardon for the offender who had thus suffered in and through his substitute. Such is the Old Testament teaching.

Now all the animal sacrifices and offerings in the Old Testament were but an adumbration, a foretelling of what Christ was able and willing to do once and for ever. In the ninth chapter of the Epistle to the Hebrews we are given a full explanation of it all. We are told that the blood of bulls and of goats, and the ashes of an heifer, were but figures, they merely covered sins for the time being; they could not cleanse the conscience, they could not purify the heart. But Christ has come, and He has offered Himself, and He has taken His own blood into the heavenly sanctuary, and He has laid it upon the heavenly altar. His is the blood that secures our forgiveness, once and for all; He has done this 'once and for ever'. It is the sprinkling of His blood that obtains this forgiveness, and for this good reason, that 'without the shedding of blood there is no remission' (of sins) (Hebrews 9:22).

Now we begin to see why the Apostle speaks about the blood of Christ and not simply about the death of Christ. The mere killing of the animal was not enough; the blood of the animal had to be taken and sprinkled upon the mercy seat before God was propitiated. The author of the Epistle to the Hebrews tells us that, in the same way, Christ took His own blood and sprinkled it in the heavenly sanctuary, the consequence being that we are forgiven by God. The specific teaching concerning our salvation can therefore be stated in this fashion. We are saved in Christ, and by Christ alone; not by His teaching, but by what He has done, by what He has achieved, and by what God has done in Him and through Him. He has ransomed us, He has paid the price of our redemption, and that price was His own precious blood. He gave Himself for us. The Apostle Paul sums it up thus: 'I delivered unto you first of all that which I also received, how that Christ died for our sins according to the scriptures' (1 Corinthians 15:4).

In a sense I have simply been expounding that statement. The teaching of the Bible everywhere is that God has taken your sins and mine and has laid them upon His beloved Son. In the Old Testament, as I have reminded you, the high priests placed their hands on the head of the animal that was to be killed. In so doing they were transferring the people's sins and guilt to that animal. The animal was killed, the blood was sprinkled, and God forgave. That is what has happened in Christ. He (God) 'hath laid on him (the Son) the iniquity of us all'. 'Behold the Lamb of God that taketh away the sin of the world,' said John the Baptist (John 1:29). He is the Paschal Lamb, 'the Lamb slain before the foundation of the world'. These are the biblical terms. Christ has died for our sins; He has died as our substitute. 'He gave his life a ransom for many.' 'By his stripes we are healed.'

If this is clear to you, you will never again talk about trying to become a Christian, or trying to make yourself a Christian, or that you are a Christian because you are living a good life and not committing certain sins. His death, His blood, alone saves you. It does and will save you. Though you may have sinned yourself almost into hell until this moment, if you believe this message you are forgiven. That is the way of salvation; you are to trust solely, utterly, only, entirely to the fact that Christ is the Lamb of God on whom your sins were laid. He has paid your ransom price. He has delivered you from the law and from hell and death and the grave, and has reconciled you to God. You are not your own any longer, 'you have been bought with a price'. You have been redeemed by 'the precious blood of Christ'. There is nothing in heaven or earth which is in any way comparable to this, that I can say 'The Son of God ... loved me and gave himself for me', gave His life a ransom for me. His blood was shed that I might be forgiven.

Oh, the riches of His grace! Oh, the abundance of His love! It is here, and here alone, we truly see and contemplate that 'love so amazing, so divine'. Go to the Cross; stand there and look at it. 'Survey' it with Isaac Watts:

> *See from His head, His hands, His feet,*
> *Sorrow and love flow mingled down.*

Stay there until you see that you never have had, or ever will have, a vestige of righteousness, that all your goodness is as 'filthy rags'. But see your sins laid upon Him, and see Him paying the price, the purchase price, of your redemption, your salvation. Fall at His feet, worship Him and praise Him, and give yourself to Him saying –

> *Love so amazing, so divine,*
> *Demands my soul, my life, my all.*

14
'Through His Blood'

'In whom we have redemption through his blood, the forgiveness of sins, according to the riches of his grace.'

Ephesians 1:7

We return to this crucial statement once more in order that we may discover in it, and extract from it, some further riches of the grace of God. As we do so, I would offer a general remark. As we look at a statement such as this we are reminded of the importance of particulars. Now the great danger always in reading such a statement is to look at it in general only, and to regard the particular words and the precise statements as being more or less unimportant. To do so is a very false way of interpreting this or any other scripture. The particulars are all-important, the details are full of meaning, as we have already seen in considering the term 'blood'. The Apostle says 'by his blood', not 'by his death'. Every word is important, and possesses significance and meaning; and it is our business to observe exactly what the Apostle says; not what we think he should say, but what he actually says, in order that thereby we may derive true benefit. There are people who imagine that they can deal with the Apostle's introduction to the Epistle in one discourse. But that is to abuse it and to miss the rich doctrine and truth it contains. Every particular must be given its due weight and emphasis.

We must come back once more to this word 'redemption', because the Apostle forces us to do so: 'In whom we have redemption through his blood, the forgiveness of sins.' As we looked at it in our previous study we were interested in it mainly as it taught us something about the method of redemption, and we discovered that it was by the paying of a ransom price. But now we must look at this term more from the standpoint of what it brings to us, what it gives to us, and what it does for us. It is as the result of the paying of the ransom price that certain consequences follow for us. Firstly, we are redeemed and receive 'the forgiveness of sins'. So we must consider this term, 'the forgiveness of sins', as it tells us something about the redemption. Now, here, we must be careful to apply the principle of interpretation that I have been laying down. If you read Paul's statement superficially you might very well come to the conclusion that he is saying that redemption consists in, and is equivalent to, the forgiveness of sins. That would virtually be to make the Apostle say 'In whom we have redemption through his blood (even) the forgiveness of sins'. But that is not what he says; and there are very good reasons why he does not do so. Many of us have probably found ourselves reading this verse in that way or quoting it in that manner. As I hope to show there is a sense in which that is right; but there is another sense in which it is wrong, because it is incomplete.

'Redemption' as it is used in Scripture is a bigger term than is often supposed, and it is wrong to confine it to the forgiveness of sins. Take, for instance, the way in which Paul uses it in the Epistle to the Romans, chapter 8, verse 23, where he says: '. . . even we ourselves groan within ourselves, waiting for the adoption, to wit, the redemption of our body'. Or look at it in the First Epistle to the Corinthians, chapter 1, verse 30: 'But of him are ye in Christ Jesus, who of God is made unto us wisdom, and righteousness, and sanctification, and redemption.' Clearly in both instances redemption cannot be equated with 'the forgiveness of sins' only. Note the sequence in the second quotation. The wisdom of God unto us is even righteousness, sanctification, and then redemption. But the 'forgiveness of sins' comes at the beginning in the term 'righteousness', and the term 'redemption' is added even after 'sanctification'. In other words, redemption, as used in this particular verse, must be regarded as encompassing the whole of our salvation; and the Apostle is clearly thinking in terms of our ultimate glorification. We are not finally 'redeemed' until our bodies have been redeemed. But our bodies are not yet redeemed. So we can say that we are redeemed, and that we are yet to be redeemed. I am not fully redeemed until my body has been changed, and sin has been taken entirely out of it. 'The law of sin that is in my members' must have been taken right out before my full redemption is complete. So we see that this term 'redemption' is not just equivalent to, or to be equated with, the 'forgiveness of sins'.

That being so, we are obviously confronted by the question, Why then does the Apostle introduce 'the forgiveness of sins' at this point if it is not a definition of redemption? It is just here that we see something which is of vital importance, not only for our experience of this salvation, but also for our understanding of it with our minds. The reason why the Apostle adds this phrase about the forgiveness of sins at this point must be the following. He has used the term 'redemption'; and then proceeds to say that the first element in redemption is 'the forgiveness of sins'. Redemption is ultimately going to end in the glorification of my body; but it begins with the forgiveness of sins. This is the essential preliminary to sanctification and also to glorification. We must therefore start with forgiveness and emphasize it. It is the first vital step, the key which opens the door to everything that follows.

It is essential to realize that the first problem in connection with man and his salvation is the problem of the guilt of our sin. But this aspect of truth is heartily disliked by many who are interested in the problem of sin, but only because of their desire to be delivered from the power of sin. This is not surprising, of course, because sin always leads to misery; and no one wants to be miserable. So naturally we all crave for deliverance from misery; we all want to be happy; and if we come to see that sin is the cause of unhappiness, then we see that deliverance from the power of sin, and the ability to overcome sin, are the direct road to happiness. The result is that to preach Christ as One who enables us to overcome the power of sin is always popular. People are ready to believe in, or to accept a Jesus, or a Christ, who is going to make them happy; who is going to solve the problem of temptation and misery and sins. So as long as He is offered as One who helps us to live our lives, and to be happy, there is no offence whatsoever in connection with Him.

The gospel, however, does not start at that point, though we might like it to do so. For the same reason most people prefer to listen to preaching on the subject of Resurrection rather than on the Cross; and such preaching is popular today. There is virtually no offence in preaching which emphasizes the Resurrection, and a living Christ who is offered as a friend, or as a healer of the body, or as one who can guide us and solve our problems for us in various ways. But none of that is possible if you do not start with the Cross of Christ, His death, and His 'blood'. But there, immediately, 'the offence of the Cross' comes in. The 'stumbling block' to the natural man is always this crucified Saviour; this Saviour whose 'blood' is essential. But whether we like it or dislike it, it is what always comes first in the Scriptures. And it is essential and vital that it should so do.

By nature we all dislike the idea of the forgiveness of sins because we do not like to think that we need forgiveness. We do not like to be told that we are sinners, and we do not like such terms as 'justification'. We say 'That is legalism'. We are not interested in righteousness; we want happiness, we want power in our lives, we want anything that will give us joy. But before we can ever experience such blessings we have to be humbled to the dust. We do not like repentance, because it is painful, and because it means that we have to face ourselves and examine ourselves and see ourselves as we really are. But here we are reminded at once by the Apostle that we can know no deliverance from the power of sin until we have first of all been delivered from the guilt of sin. Redemption is first, and it starts with the forgiveness of sins. I do not hesitate to assert that unless you have realized that your sins must be forgiven, you are not a Christian. But you may say, 'But I am conscious that Christ is helping us'. I reply that Christ cannot help you, will not help you, until the problem of your guilt has first been dealt with. There are many people today who are using the name of Christ psychologically; yet even if psychological experiences can be real and beneficial we must not deviate from the Scriptural teaching. The first thing in Scripture is the forgiveness of sins; and all experiences must be examined in the light of this truth.

I remember a friend, a medical doctor, once telling me of a difficulty he had had with a certain friend of his in the same profession. Unfortunately the married life of the latter had run into difficulties. He and his wife were not Christians; but in their trouble and distress, everything having gone wrong, they went to my friend, who was a Christian. He wrote to me about this, saying, 'I felt somehow that I could not help them'. His difficulty was, he said, that they could not realize that the question of guilt came into their trouble. They wanted help and they had come to him because they had the idea that in one way or another Christianity can help you when your life gets into trouble and into a tangle. They were ready to believe in a Christ who could help them at that particular point; but my friend, being a true Christian, had been talking to them about the need of forgiveness, and of guilt. 'But,' he said, 'they do not seem to understand my language'.

That is the position of many. Our reply can be stated thus. The fundamental need of man is his need of God. Everything that goes wrong in life in this world does so because we are not rightly related to God. What we all need above everything is the redemption that He alone can provide, and which will reconcile us to Him. We cannot be blessed by God unless we are rightly related to Him. The wrath of God is upon all 'the children of disobedience'. As all blessings come from God, the first thing I need is to be reconciled to Him, and I cannot be reconciled to Him until the question of my sins and their guilt has been dealt with. Hence, whenever the Scripture talks about redemption, it always starts with the forgiveness of sins.

An excellent example of this principle is found in Paul's Epistle to the Romans, chapter 5, verse 10, where he argues: 'For if, when we were enemies, we were reconciled to God by the death of his Son, much more, being reconciled, we shall be saved by his life.' The living Christ, thank God, does help us. He is our companion, He is our aid, He is our strength, He is our power; by the life of Christ we are being saved. But observe that before that happens we have been saved by His death. His life does not avail for us until we are first of all delivered and saved from the guilt of our sins by His death. Paul says again in the eighth chapter of that same Epistle to the Romans, verse 32: 'He that spared not his own Son, but delivered him up for us all, how shall he not with him also freely give us all things?' He does not 'with him freely give us all things' until we have first of all been

[164]

saved by His death. There is no more subtle error than that of by-passing the need of the forgiveness of sins and of being interested only in blessings that are given by the risen Christ.

I read in an evangelical magazine some years ago a front-page article on the theme: The message of the gospel. I was most interested to observe that the death of the Lord Jesus Christ was literally not mentioned at all. He was depicted as Saviour, but only as the risen, resurrected Lord. According to that message it is Christ's life that delivers us: the Cross was not mentioned. There was no mention of our Lord's death, still less of His blood. The Cross was by-passed. The writer went directly to the risen resurrected Lord. The atoning, sacrificial, substitutionary death was absent from the article. But that is not the truth taught in Scripture. I will go further; that is not salvation. We need first of all to be reconciled to God. The first step in redemption is the forgiveness of sins; and if you do not recognize your guilt you will never get the help you are looking for. The first need of every sinner is not help and power to overcome sin and temptation, but that his past sins should be dealt with, and that he should be delivered from condemnation and from the wrath of God that is upon him. So the Apostle, very deliberately, when he mentions the word 'redemption' and as he comes to give us some insight into it, puts the first thing first, namely, 'the forgiveness of sins'. We are doomed, damned, guilty sinners by nature; and the first thing we all need is to be delivered from the wrath of God. In other words the Apostle introduces at this point the Christian doctrine of forgiveness. He not only says that it must come first, but he is very much concerned that we should know exactly what it means.

The modern ideas about forgiveness are generally inadequate, because we always think about it in terms of ourselves, and what we think, and what we do. The first thing we have to emphasize, therefore, is that forgiveness is not a simple or an easy matter, but extremely difficult. That tends to come to us as a surprise because, in general, we have such loose, sentimental notions concerning it. For instance, someone has done us wrong. Very well, we forgive him, we overlook it, we pretend we have not seen it. All is well; there is no problem at all. But according to the Bible (I speak with reverence) the forgiveness of sins was a tremendous problem for Almighty God. I do not hesitate to assert that the forgiveness of our sins is the only problem with which God has ever been confronted. The idea of God as an indulgent Father who just says 'All right, my child, come back, all is well' is completely unscriptural. There are those who teach that the whole of the doctrine of salvation is found in the Parable of the Prodigal Son. But that is not so; and it was never meant to be so. That parable was meant to teach one thing only, namely, that God was ready to forgive publicans and sinners as well as Pharisees. It was never meant to be a complete exposition of the way of salvation, for the same Christ who spoke that parable also said that He had to go to Jerusalem in order that He might 'give his life a ransom for many'.

The forgiveness of sins constituted such a problem that nothing but the shedding of Christ's blood could deal with it. God could not forgive sins merely by speaking a word. It was for Him a simple thing to create the world by the fiat of His word: 'Let there be light'. We ask with reverence, why did not God say, 'Let men be forgiven'? The answer is that forgiveness did not come in that way. And that is so because – I say it again with reverence – He could not do so. 'God is light, and in him is no darkness at all' (1 John 1:5). God is eternally just and righteous and holy, and He cannot contradict Himself. There was only one way whereby God could forgive sin. 'There was no other good enough to pay the price of sin'. It is only 'by the blood of Christ' that forgiveness becomes possible. Think of the power and the might of God. We see it in the snow and in the frost, and we can read about it in many places of Scripture, for example, Psalm 147. By the power of His word God rules nature and creation, and the nations of the world are to Him but 'as the small dust of the balance'. But when the problem of forgiving the sins of mankind arose it was necessary that the Son of God should leave the courts of heaven and come to earth and be born as a babe, suffer the contradiction of sinners against Himself, be put to death and shed His blood. It was the only way. Such is the difficulty raised by the problem of the forgiveness of sins.

Another truth suggested here is that God's way of forgiving sins is a very thorough way. It is not simply a matter of overlooking our sins and our transgressions. Sins cannot be dealt with in that way. Before God could forgive our sins He must deal with them in a thorough manner. The verse we are considering could be translated thus: 'In whom we have redemption through his blood, the forgiveness of our trespasses.' The word 'trespass' suggests a violation of law, a transgression of law. Notice, then, that God's way of forgiveness is first of all something that exposes the sin. Our tendency is always to cover it up in order that we may be happy. But God, first of all, exposes it, He unmasks it, He defines it, He pinpoints it. That was the real function of the law. Sin was in existence, as Paul argues in the fifth chapter of the Epistle to the Romans, from the moment Adam fell. But, he argues further, 'sin is not imputed when there is no law' (v. 13). The law was designed to define sin and to bring it home to us by imputation. But nowhere is sin so brought home to us as at the Cross of Christ and by the blood of Christ. Before we are forgiven we must realize something of the enormity of sin, and it is at the Cross that we do so. We see it as something so terrible, so horrible, such an affront to God, that it necessitates the Cross. The Cross therefore condemns us before it sets us free. This is why it is an 'offence' to the natural man. The Cross makes us see ourselves as worms, as miserable guilty sinners. And when a man really sees himself face to face with God and God's holy law, he realizes what he truly is. 'Vile and full of sin I am', says Charles Wesley, and rightly so. 'In me, that is, in my flesh, dwelleth no good thing . . . O wretched man that I am!' (Romans 7:18,24). Such is the language of people who have seen the guilt of their sin in the light of the Cross of Christ. Sin is so terrible, so foul and so vile that nothing could deal with it but the blood of Christ. And that is what happened on the Cross. It is not a patching over, a covering over of sin; it is not God saying, 'Do not worry, all is well'. It is God showing us sin as it is, really bringing it out to the light, and then dealing with it.

We can also say that God's way of dealing with sin is absolutely just. How important is this truth! The Apostle gives it strong emphasis in his Epistle to the Romans chapter 3, verses 24, 25 and 26: 'Being justified freely by his grace through the redemption that is in Christ Jesus, whom God hath set forth to be a propitiation through faith in his blood, to declare his righteousness for the remission of sins that are past, through the forbearance of God; to declare, I say, at this time his righteousness: that he might be just, and the justifier of him which believeth in Jesus.' That is Paul's way of saying that God's method of dealing with sin is strictly just. To forgive a sin or sins may, at times, be unjust. We can do someone great harm and great injustice if we forgive his sin too lightly and too loosely; we may be encouraging him to continue in wrong-doing. But God does not forgive sin in a manner that allows a man to go on sinning and relying upon the love of God to put everything right. That would not be just. Everything that God does must be just, must be righteous, must be holy, must be consistent with His character. And His way of forgiving sins by the blood of Christ is just because God in Christ has punished sin. Sin merits punishment. God said that He would punish sin and that the punishment would mean death. So if God went back on that, He would no longer be righteous and just. God's way of forgiveness is to deal with sin, to strike it and to give it the punishment it deserves, the condign punishment. And that is what He did in Christ on the Cross. As God forgives my sins by the blood of Christ, He declares His own righteousness and justice. He is still just, and at the sametime the justifier of me as a believer in Christ. That is the biblical doctrine of the forgiveness of sins. It shows the difficulty of the problem, the thoroughness of God's dealing with it, and also that the solution is just and righteous. God forgives us, because, and only because, our sin has been punished, and our guilt has been expiated.

But, thank God, we can go on to say that the forgiveness of sins as purchased by and through the blood of Christ is so thorough that it leads to a complete restoration of the offender to the favour of God. Because God has dealt with sin in the way explained in Scripture, we are forgiven absolutely once and for all. The forgiveness is final. We are completely reconciled to God by the death of His Son. 'God was in Christ reconciling the world unto himself, not imputing their trespasses unto them'. 'He hath made him to be sin for us, who knew no sin, that we might be made the righteousness of God in him' (2 Corinthians 5:19-21). God has dealt with our sins in such a thorough manner in Christ, and by His blood, that He has put them away once and for ever, and will never see them again.

The teaching in the Old Testament about the scapegoat was a pre-figuring of this truth. As described in Leviticus chapter 16, the high priest took a goat and put his hands upon it, thus putting Israel's sins on it; and then the goat was driven away into the wilderness never to be seen again. That is how God puts away sin. We read in the one hundred-and-third Psalm: 'As far as the east is from the west, so far hath he removed our transgressions from us' (v. 12). He could not remove them any further. God gave a specific promise to that effect when He made through Jeremiah the promise of the new covenant: 'Their sins and iniquities will I remember no more' (Jeremiah 31:34; Hebrews 10:17). What an astonishing thing! God has so dealt with our sins that He has taken them and He has cast them into the sea of His forgetfulness. That is an eternal forgetfulness. Our sins, in Christ, are forgiven absolutely, finally and completely; they are never to be seen again.

It is only God who could do that. You and I claim that we forgive people; but we find it difficult to forget. The glory of the doctrine of the forgiveness of sins in Scripture is that God not only forgives, but also forgets. 'Their sins and their iniquities will I remember no more.'

Let us note, finally, that the Apostle says: 'In whom we have redemption through his blood, the forgiveness of sins.' He does not say that we might have it; he says that we have it; it is a present possession. It is something that we are to enjoy here and now. 'Being justified by faith, we have peace with God,' says Paul. To be truly Christian is to know that your sins are already forgiven. The doctrine can be stated thus: God laid upon the Lord Jesus Christ all our sins, all the sins we have ever committed, all the sins we shall ever commit. They were all laid upon Him, they were all punished and dealt with at the Cross. When we fall into sin God does not need to do anything new, He has already done all in Christ. What He does is to apply the remedy of the Cross to us now. When a man believes on the Lord Jesus Christ there is no need for a fresh action on the part of God; He simply applies to him what was done once and for all on Calvary; and should he fall into sin again it is 'the blood of Jesus Christ God's Son' that will still cleanse him from all sin and all unrighteousness. It is the one way, it is the only way. Our salvation is based on a completed transaction. That is why the Apostle

[169]

emphasizes 'the blood of Christ'. Christ died once and for all. There is no need, says the Epistle to the Hebrews, that He should repeat the sacrifice; it has happened once and for all.

Such is the position of every true Christian at this moment. If we still say that we are not good enough to call ourselves Christians it simply means that we do not understand the first principle of salvation. If we say that we are trying to make ourselves Christians we have never seen the truth. The Christian is a man who realizes that he has been reconciled to God by the blood of Jesus Christ. While he was yet a sinner, while he was yet an enemy, and an alien in his mind, while he was going directly to hell, even then the work of salvation was all accomplished by the death, by the 'blood' of Christ. The Christian is a man who believes this and who knows that his sins have been forgiven freely and entirely and utterly once and for ever in and by the blood of Christ. He rejoices in the fact, and he says, 'I have redemption through his blood'. The forgiveness of sins leads to justification and righteousness, sanctification and glorification to come, and every other blessing 'according to the riches of his grace'.

Do you know that you have redemption? Do you know that your sins are forgiven? Look unto Him; stay at the Cross until you know this blessed truth, and see it and rejoice in it and say, 'I am reconciled; I have peace with God through Jesus Christ his Son'.

15
The Riches of His Grace

'In whom we have redemption through his blood, the forgiveness of sins, according to the riches of his grace.'

Ephesians 1:7

We now come to deal with the last phrase in this verse – 'According to the riches of his grace'. There are many ways of considering and studying the Scripture; and it must be clear by now that I am a follower and an exponent of one particular method. I regard the Scripture and these great statements in it as being comparable to a great art gallery where there are famous paintings hanging on the walls. Certain people, when they visit such a place, buy a catalogue from the guide at the door, and then holding it in their hands walk round the gallery. They notice that Item number 1 is a painting by Van Dyck, let us say; and they say 'Ah, that is a Van Dyck'. Then they pass on hurriedly to Item number 2 which is perhaps a portrait by Rembrandt. 'Ah,' they say, 'that's a Rembrandt, a famous picture'. Then they move on to further Items in the same way. I grant that that is a possible way of viewing the treasures of an art gallery; and yet I have a feeling that when such a person has gone through every room of the gallery and has said, 'Well, we have "done" the National Gallery, let us now go to the Tate Gallery', the truth is that they have never really seen either of the galleries or their treasures. It is the same in regard to the Scriptures. There are people who walk through this first chapter of this Epistle to the Ephesians in some such manner as I have described, and they feel that they have 'done' it. It is surely better to stand, if necessary, for hours before this chapter which has been given to us by God Himself through His Spirit, and to gaze upon it, and to try to discover its riches both in general and in detail. The Scriptures are meant to feed our souls, to enrich our minds, and to move our hearts; and if we are to know such experiences we must tarry with these things, we must drink them in and take of their fulness.

Let us then stand and look at this particular statement: 'according to the riches of his grace.' Surely every true Christian must desire to stop here. Surely the Apostle as he wrote under the inspiration of the Spirit expected the people to whom he wrote to meditate upon, and to pray over, and to think about this phrase, until their hearts should be ravished by it, even as his undoubtedly was when he wrote it. Let us start by noting the way in which the Apostle comes to this particular statement. He has first of all reminded us that the method or mode of our salvation is by the payment of a ransom. Next he tells us that the first thing we realize and appreciate as a result of our deliverance is 'the forgiveness of sins'. But he cannot leave it there. What is it that makes all this possible? What is it that gives us this salvation by ransom, this forgiveness of sins, that we enjoy? The answer, as it always must be, is 'the riches of his grace'!

In a sense the Apostle has already been saying as much. He hints at it in the very first verse; he implies it throughout. He himself is an Apostle 'by the will of God', which is just another way of saying 'by the grace of God'; for if God had not been a God of grace He could never have willed such a thing for such a man. But as he refers to it once more we notice that there is one change. In verse 6, for instance, the Apostle has used the term 'grace' – 'to the praise of the glory of his grace'. But here he speaks of the 'riches of his grace'. 'Grace', as he thinks of it in verse 6, is one of the manifestations of the glory of God, it is one of the facets of that eternal brightness that flashes upon us. Everything in God is glorious. His glory is manifested in an infinite variety of ways; grace is one of them, and one of the most notable. So as we read of 'the glory of his grace' in verse 6, here there is this change to 'the riches of his grace'. Why the change? For this reason: in the sixth verse, as a part of the whole statement of verses 3–6, the Apostle was looking at salvation from the God-ward angle or standpoint. And there, naturally, the thing that strikes him above all else is the glory of God's grace. But here he has started thinking of us and the forgiveness of our sins; he is looking at salvation from the man-ward aspect. 'Grace' whenever it is looked at from the man-ward side must always convey to us this idea of riches. Hence the Apostle introduces 'riches' at this point.

This is one of the Apostle's most characteristic statements. Indeed it is his favourite statement. In the second chapter, verse 4, he says, 'But God, who is *rich* in mercy, for his great love wherewith he loved us. . . .' Then in the seventh verse of that chapter he says, 'That in the ages to come he might show the exceeding *riches* of his grace in his kindness toward us through Christ Jesus'. Again in the third chapter in the eighth verse he says, 'Unto me, who am less than the least of all saints, is this grace given, that I should preach among the Gentiles the unsearchable *riches* of Christ'. This theme obviously filled the mind and the heart of this great Apostle. It was something that ravished his heart. As Philip Doddridge assures us, grace was to him 'a charming sound, harmonious to the ear'. It ravished his heart and moved his entire being. He never mentions 'grace' without going into some kind of ecstasy. The word always calls forth his superlatives. It had so gripped him and amazed him and moved him that he could scarcely control himself.

Such jubilation is not surprising in view of the wonderful thing that had happened to Paul on the road to Damascus. He never ceased to wonder that he who had been a persecutor and a blasphemer and an injurious person, insulting the Person of Christ; he who had thought with himself that he ought to do many things contrary to the Name of Jesus of Nazareth; he who had been a self-satisfied, proud, contented Pharisee, boasting of and smug in the contemplation of his abounding self-righteousness – that he of all men should ever have been forgiven and, moreover, called to be an Apostle, made a preacher of the Gospel, and sent out as the Lord's special emissary to the Gentiles – that he, of all men, should be the subject of the grace of God was truly an amazing fact, and as he looked at himself he was ever amazed.

The Apostle seems to ask himself, 'Is it possible? Am I still Saul of Tarsus? Am I still the same man? And if I am, what accounts for my being what I am now'? And there was only one answer – 'I am what I am by the grace of God'. 'The *riches* of his grace!' His greatest desire in life was that all might know this, that everyone might experience the *riches* of God's grace. In the third chapter of this Epistle, verse 8, he describes his calling: 'Unto me, who am less than the least of all saints, is this grace given, that I should preach among the Gentiles the unsearchable *riches* of Christ.' The 'grace' that made him a preacher drove him across continents, and across seas; it made him preach day and night with tears and pleading; it was the most vital force in his life. This was the thing that 'constrained' him, and made him say, 'Woe is me if I preach not the gospel'! He was driven by the thought of these riches of God's grace, and the ignorance of men and women concerning them. It was his chief reason for writing this Epistle to the Ephesians.

Paul tells the Ephesians that he is writing to them because they are constantly in his mind, and that he is always praying for them – 'the eyes of your understanding being enlightened; that ye may know the *riches* of the glory . . .' A similar statement occurs in the third chapter where he says, 'For this cause I bow my knees unto the Father of our Lord Jesus Christ, of whom the whole family in heaven and earth is named, that he would grant you, according to the *riches* of his glory, to be strengthened with might by his Spirit in the inner man', the Apostle's purpose being that they might 'know the love of Christ, which passeth knowledge' in its height and depth and length and breadth. In other words, he wants them to know 'the *riches* of God's grace'.

I would ask a question at this point: Do we individually know the riches of God's grace? Have we any experience of them? Are we aware of them? I am not asking whether we have all read the Epistle to the Ephesians; I am asking whether we know individually the riches of God's grace? Let us put ourselves to the following tests. To know the riches of God's grace invariably leads to the same result, in some measure, as it did in the case of Paul. It makes us sing, it makes us praise God, it makes us rejoice 'with joy unspeakable and full of glory'. It was because he knew these riches that the Apostle writes about them, prays about them, goes into ecstasies about them, and produces his superlatives. 'What can I say?', he seems to ask, 'how can I express what it all means?'

Note Paul's verbs and adjectives. He says that God has caused grace to 'abound' towards us; he talks about the riches of His grace; he talks about the 'unsearchable riches of Christ'. Language seems to be inadequate, the thing itself is so enthralling. And this is not confined to the Apostle. The same exuberance is found in Christian hymns. John Wesley translated a hymn of Count Zinzendorf, and in it we find the expression, 'boundless mercy'. There is no limit, no end, to it. His brother Charles writes similarly –

> *'Tis mercy all, immense and free,*
> *For, O my God, it found out me!*

And Isaac Watts agrees when he writes, 'When I survey the wondrous Cross'. He does not merely say that he has looked at the Cross; he stands and 'surveys' it; he stops there transfixed by it. This is the characteristic response of all the saints in all ages, and irrespective of any natural differences which may be found in them.

I press the question as to whether we really know these 'riches' of grace and glory. I am increasingly convinced that it is our failure at this point that accounts for many of our troubles and problems and failures. Our lives as Christians are too often 'bound in shallows and in miseries'. How different we are from the New Testament people. Where is the note of triumph and of joy and of praise and of thanksgiving? Are our hearts moved and ravished? It is not that I am concerned about feelings or ecstasies as such, but I assert that no man can appreciate the wealth and riches of God's grace without responding to it in amazement. One of the most delicate and sensitive tests of our Christian profession is the extent to which we are amazed by the *riches* of God's grace – 'Love so amazing, so divine'. Have we appreciated these riches? It is because so many of us have not done so that we are constantly grumbling, and complaining that we cannot see this or understand that. It explains also why many are miserable and look miserable, and therefore never attract a soul to Christ.

As we come to investigate these riches I can only indicate certain aspects or items, trusting that the sight of them will lead us to thought and to meditation and to contemplation which will go on increasing until we find ourselves 'lost in wonder, love and praise'.

How can we attempt to estimate and compute this great

[175]

wealth? In a sense we are assaying an impossible task, because the Apostle himself has said, '. . . to know the love of Christ, which passeth knowledge'. But the fact that we can never span it and comprehend it fully does not mean that we should not look at it at all. Let us go as far as we can at the present time, and then go on from there as day follows day, until time is no more. I believe that our eternity will be spent in that way. That is heaven, it seems to me. The glory of eternity will be our discoveries of fresh aspects of these riches, and the entering into further wonderful appreciations of the glory of God's grace.

The first test, I suggest, is that we discover the worth and the value of anything by knowing the price that was paid for it. This is a good test of a painting, a picture, or any work of art. What is it valued at? What is the price that has to be paid before it can be possessed? We have already considered the matter, but God forbid that we should be so mechanical in our thinking as to say that, because we have considered it once, we need never mention it again. There should never be a service or a meeting of Christians without our mentioning the precious blood of Christ: 'In whom we have redemption through his blood.' I fail to understand Christians who stay at home on Sunday nights saying, 'Ah, we need not attend tonight's "service"; we know all about the evangelistic message'. Do you know 'all about' the blood of Christ? Do you feel that you really know so much about it, that you can learn nothing fresh about it? A Christian who does not receive something in an evangelistic service is, to put it at its very lowest, in a most unhealthy condition. If your heart is not made to beat faster every time you hear about 'the blood of Christ' you are not like the Apostle Paul. The riches of God's grace are seen in the price that was paid for our redemption – 'In whom we have redemption through his blood'. Not gold or silver, or platinum, not any of the world's most precious metals; but the blood of the Son of God, the poured-out life of Him 'by whom all things were made, and by whom all things consist'. That is one way of estimating 'the riches of God's grace'.

The second way of appreciating the riches is to note the munificent way in which God gives us these riches. That is, in itself, an expression of the greatness of the riches. We have 'redemption through his blood, according to the riches of his grace'. All we

[176]

have is not the result of our requests to God; it is freely given by God. If you go to a wealthy person and make a request for a gift, and he, having considered it, says, 'Very well, I will give it to you', you are very grateful, and rightly so. It proves that he is a generous person. But when we come to think of this great salvation, all lesser giving pales into significance. God does not forgive us because we ask Him to forgive us. God did not send His Son into the world because mankind kept on pleading with Him to do so. Nothing in salvation is given to us by God by way of response to a request from us, nothing whatsoever! It is all and entirely and absolutely from God. He has given without being asked; He has poured it out without any request. It is, indeed, in spite of us, in spite of our being enemies and aliens and rebels, in spite of our turning our backs upon Him. It is in spite of all we are, and all that we have done, that God has given us 'the riches of his grace'. The initiative as well as the giving is entirely His.

Then we must go on to realize that the Apostle is emphasizing here that God gives all this to us, not in a grudging manner, but with a liberality and largesse which baffles description. James conveys an idea of this to us in the first chapter of his Epistle when he tells us that if any of us lack wisdom we should ask God 'who giveth liberally and upbraideth not'. If I may say so with reverence, God cannot give in any other way. God does not give grudgingly; His nature makes that impossible. God must be liberal. Because He is God, He can only act in one manner, and that is, that He gives with fulness, with freedom, with super-abundance, 'without let or hindrance' or limit. As we have already seen, the Apostle Paul in his third chapter says that God's way of giving 'passeth knowledge'. He talks there about measurements, about height and depth and length and breadth. As we live in time we instinctively think of vastness in terms of measures. We measure it with the help of telescopes, theodolites and other instruments. So the Apostle, as it were, invites us to bring all our instruments and all our agencies, and with them try to measure God's love and goodness to us. But he assures us that it is all futile. Go as far as you can and still you have not even begun; 'it passeth knowledge'. God's love and grace are 'a never-ebbing sea'. You may think that you see across it, and you launch out into it only to discover that there is still another horizon, and then another, and another, and another; it is endless, it is a vast abyss, 'it passeth knowledge'. 'The riches of his grace' are as large and as great and as profound as God Himself, for when God prepared our salvation He gave Himself in His Son. So 'the riches of God's grace' are really God Himself. He has treasured up all His treasures of wisdom and of grace in the Son; all is in Christ. The measure of the riches of God's grace is the measure of the Person of God. So we can say, in our puny, inadequate language, that the riches of God's grace are unfathomable. As William Cowper reminds us in one of his hymns:

> *Deep in unfathomable mines*
> *Of never-failing skill,*
> *He treasures up His bright designs,*
> *And works His sovereign will.*

Whenever we explore the words and ways and works of God we find ourselves in a large and 'wealthy place', as the Psalmist reminds us (66:12). The riches of God's grace are inexhaustible and although the saints of the centuries have been drinking out of this fountain, it is as full as it was at the beginning. Millions yet will drink out of it, but it will be still bubbling up to the surface. It matters not what your need or problem may be; there is nothing that can ever afflict the human heart or the human life, for which provision has not already been made. Jesus 'does all things well' (Mark 7:37). If any man comes to Me, says Christ, he will never thirst again (John 4:14). Never, never thirst! He is the all-sufficient One, and all who come to Him are fully satisfied.

We must next look at some of the details of these riches of God's grace. First of all there is what the Apostle has already mentioned – free forgiveness; forgiveness without any payment whatsoever. He demands nothing. His invitation is, 'Ho, everyone that thirsteth, come ye to the waters, come, buy . . . without money and without price' (Isaiah 55:1). There are some who are unhappy in their spiritual lives because they have not realized that first truth. They are still trying to bring some kind of money, some kind of payment. They say, 'I am not good enough yet, I am trying to be'. There is only one thing to say to such a person –

salvation is 'without money and without price' – not a farthing, not a cent! Nothing is demanded as payment and nothing will be received as payment. It is all by 'the riches of his grace'. Is there anything more insulting to a person who is giving you a gift out of the largeness of his heart than to put your hand in your pocket and to say, 'I would like to give you something for that'. And we have all been insulting the Almighty God by trying to offer Him something. Realize that salvation is the result of 'the riches of his grace':

> *Just as I am, without one plea*
> *But that Thy blood was shed for me,*
> *And that Thou bid'st me come to Thee,*
> *O Lamb of God, I come.*

> *Nothing in my hand I bring;*
> *Simply to Thy cross I cling;*
> *Naked, come to Thee for dress;*
> *Helpless, look to Thee for grace;*
> *Foul, I to the fountain fly,*
> *Wash me, Saviour, or I die.*

That is the language of the Christian.

Again, God's forgiveness is always a full forgiveness. That is still more marvellous. When God forgives us our sins He keeps nothing at all back. There is no reservation, and there are no conditions. He does not say, 'Now I am going to forgive you on condition' – never! 'I forgive you', says God, 'because my Son bore the punishment of your sins'. He justifies us freely, fully; our past sins are forgiven, our present sins are forgiven, our future sins are already dealt with there. O 'the riches of his grace'! If we belong to His Son, God's book of the law is put on one side; that ledger will never be brought out again as far as we are concerned. We are justified once and for ever. It is a full forgiveness.

More than that, it is a complete reconciliation to God. If you believe on the Lord Jesus Christ, if you believe that He has died for your sins, and borne your punishment, if you are resting only upon Him, I proclaim authoritatively to you that you have a complete reconciliation to God. There is nothing now between you and God because Christ has died for you. You have been fully restored to the fellowship of God, and fitted to enjoy as much as Adam enjoyed before he fell. Yea, more, because you are 'in Christ'! Are you enjoying this full fellowship with God? When you go to God in prayer do you go with a craven spirit, hesitant and doubtful; or do you go realizing that the way to God is wide open by the blood of Jesus? Such is the teaching of the Scripture, and it is an aspect of 'the riches of his grace'.

I fear that many of us are like the Prodigal Son. In desperation we go back home, and we believe certain things. But how inadequate was the Prodigal's idea and conception of his father's love. He went in fear and trembling saying, 'Father, I am no more worthy to be called thy son; make me as one of thy hired servants'. 'What are you talking about?,' says the father in effect. 'Bring out the best robe, bring out the ring, go and kill the fatted calf.' That is God's way. It is full reconciliation; it is as if the Prodigal had never done any wrong, as if he had never insulted his father before he left home, as if he had never left home at all. Everything is forgotten and banished; the reconciliation is complete. That is now our relationship to God in Christ Jesus. If we are trusting to Christ we are fully reconciled.

But the riches of God's grace go even beyond that! Not only is all this true of us, we can also know it to be true. We can have knowledge of it and assurance of it, and certainty concerning it here and now. It would still be a marvellous and a wonderful thing if God had reconciled us in Christ and had not told us that He had done so. It would be a wonderful thing if all of us when we come to die should have a sudden surprise and find that although, all through our lives, we had felt that we had so sinned against God that He could not forgive us, and in consequence had been miserable and unhappy, yet God had already forgiven us ever since we first believed in His Son. That would be marvellous; but God does not deal with us in such a manner. In the riches of God's grace He not only forgives us but also tells us that He has done so. We can have 'full assurance of faith' and of hope, even in this world. We rejoice that 'being justified by faith, we have peace with God'. He is a poor Christian who does not know that his sins are forgiven. We have no right to be lacking in assurance of salvation; it is our birthright. God has given it; it is a part of

His purpose for us; it is an aspect of the superabundance that He gives us 'according to the riches of his grace'.

Then think of our sonship and the 'adoption' to which we have already referred. Consider them again and do not say foolishly, 'We have done with adoption'. Go back and contemplate that truth until you find yourself on your feet praising God. Then remind yourself once more of what it means to be 'in Christ'. And yet again, consider the gift of the Holy Spirit and our being 'sealed' by the Spirit of God until the time of 'the redemption of the purchased possession'. Make sure that you know something of the power of the Holy Spirit working in you. The Apostle prayed that these Ephesians might have that knowledge. He desired that they might know the 'exceeding greatness of his power to us-ward who believe' (1:19). God does not save us and forgive our sins, and then leave us to ourselves to fight the world, the flesh and the devil. He has given us the gift of the Spirit. By the Spirit Christ dwells in us, and He is 'able to do (for us) exceeding abundantly above all that we ask or think' (3:20). When you tend to feel oppressed by the devil and the world and the flesh, remember the power that brought Christ up again from the dead and which is working in you now 'according to the riches of his grace'.

Then go on to remind yourself of what the Apostle says in the second chapter about our having access into the presence of God as the result of 'the riches of his grace'. 'For through him (Christ) we both have access by one Spirit unto the Father' (v. 18). 'Heaven' means being in the presence of God and enjoying Him without let or hindrance or restraint; and the Apostle reminds us that according to the riches of God's grace we are given a foretaste of that blessing here in this world. We have access to the Father by Christ, through the Spirit. Do you know God? Are you enjoying God? Are you enjoying a life of fellowship with God? Do you know that God intends you to have that joy? You must not be content with anything less. You must believe these words, you must believe the message. Do not wait for a special feeling; take the Word of God as it is, and act upon it. God Himself has made this possible for us; and we are to receive of these riches.

The Apostle also writes about Christ 'dwelling in our hearts by faith'. Indeed, he goes on to say something still more astounding.

We are to 'know the love of Christ which passeth knowledge that (we) might be filled with all the fulness of God' (3:17–19). With Charles Wesley there is nothing we are able to say at this point except, 'Who can explore His strange design?', but we are to know, to experience and to enjoy it more and more. The fulness of God! Christ in our hearts by faith! Spiritual manifestations of the Son of God, times when He comes to you and you know that He is there! This does not mean that you see Him with the naked eye, but that you 'know and feel' that He is present. All this is offered us 'according to the riches of his grace'. It is not surprising that John Cennick in his hymn should exhort us, saying –

> *Children of the heavenly King,*
> *As ye journey, sweetly sing.*

Isaac Watts encourages us to do so by reminding us that 'Celestial fruit' can grow even on this earthly ground on which we live. This is how he expresses it:

> *The men of grace have found*
> *Glory begun below;*
> *Celestial fruit on earthly ground*
> *From faith and hope may grow.*
>
> *The hill of Zion yields*
> *A thousand sacred sweets,*
> *Before we reach the heavenly fields,*
> *Or walk the golden streets.*
>
> *There shall we see His face*
> *And never, never sin;*
> *There from the rivers of His grace*
> *Drink endless pleasures in.*
>
> *Then let our songs abound,*
> *And every tear be dry:*
> *We're marching through Immanuel's ground*
> *To fairer worlds on high.*

It is in this world, says the Apostle, that we are to taste the 'firstfruits' of the great harvest, and have a foretaste of the great feast which God has prepared for us in all its fulness in heaven.

Again, think of the armour which the Apostle speaks of in the last chapter of this Epistle. Everything necessary to enable us to stand in the evil day against the wiles of Satan is provided for us; every part of us is covered completely.

Such are some of 'the riches of God's grace'. And all this, of course, leads to joy and to peace and love. It also leads to a sense of security and of safety; and all, remember, is simply with reference to our life in this world and in time. Then lift up your eyes and see awaiting us, 'the hope of his calling' and 'the riches of the glory of his inheritance in the saints', the 'inheritance incorruptible and undefiled and that fadeth not away, reserved in heaven for us' who are in Christ. It is all prepared, and it is all a part of 'the riches of his grace'. We shall see Him as He is, and we shall be with Him, we shall reign with Him, we shall enjoy Him, we shall be like Him and lords of the universe with Him. When we return to God in repentance and faith we do not do so as servants for we are adopted sons! And we are to enjoy all that our Father's heart and love have prepared for us. That is what is offered us in Christ Jesus according to the riches of God's grace.

What is there for us to say as we contemplate all this but,

> *Just as I am, and waiting not*
> *To rid my soul of one dark blot,*
> *To Thee, whose blood can cleanse each spot,*
> *O Lamb of God, I come.*

> *Just as I am, poor, wretched, blind;*
> *Sight, riches, healing of the mind,*
> *Yea, all I need, in Thee to find,*
> *O Lamb of God, I come.*

Poor pauper! Rise up, and in your rags and penury go to Him and begin to receive the riches of His grace. Believe Him when He tells you that all this and infinitely more is available now. Hold out your hand and receive it, and you will soon be rejoicing and amazed at the 'riches of his grace'.

16

The Mystery of His Will

'Wherein he hath abounded toward us in all wisdom
and prudence; having made known unto us the
mystery of his will, according to his good pleasure
which he hath purposed in himself.'

Ephesians 1:8–9

The Apostle here continues the statement which he began at the
beginning of the third verse. From verse 3 to the end of verse 14
is but one great sentence, broken up into its component parts; it
therefore constitutes one great statement. We are reminded by
the word *Wherein*, as it is translated in the Authorized Version,
that what we have before us is a continuation of the same theme.
Each particular statement has something new and fresh to con-
tribute, yet each one is related to all the others and they together
add up to one great pronouncement concerning God's way of
salvation. In describing it the Apostle has used his superlatives
but now we find that even they fall short of his desires; he must
add to them. This is how he does so: 'In whom we have redemption through his blood, the forgiveness of sins, according to the
riches of his grace, wherein he hath abounded toward us.' The
riches have 'abounded'! So it is to that aspect of the riches of
God's grace that we now turn.

In order to understand these two verses we must get clearly
in our minds exactly what the Apostle is saying, and that involves
a consideration of the exact phraseology of the two statements.
The Authorized Version reads: 'Wherein he hath abounded
toward us', but it is generally agreed that that is not a very good
translation. It is better to translate it: 'Which he has caused to
abound toward us'. That is preferable because 'Wherein he hath
abounded toward us' directs attention to God Himself, whereas
it is clear that at this point the Apostle is anxious to concentrate
upon 'the riches of his grace'. So he writes: 'the riches of his

grace which he hath caused to abound toward us'. He is emphasizing the way in which God's grace in its riches has abounded
toward us.

Then there is the further problem of deciding the relationship
of the phrase, 'in all wisdom and prudence'. There has been
much disagreement about this. In the Authorized Version and in
the English Revised Version these words 'in all wisdom and
prudence' are in the eighth verse and linked to God causing His
grace to abound toward us. But in the Revised Standard Version
there is a difference. There, these words are placed in the ninth
verse, and the translation reads, 'Grace which He lavished upon
us. For He has made known to us in all wisdom and insight the
mystery of His will'. Ultimately, of course, it comes to very much
the same thing; but if this is a description of how the grace of God
abounds toward us, then we should place 'wisdom and prudence'
in the eighth verse, and not in the ninth, and take them in
connection with the grace of God.

There are three possible ways in which we can deal with this
matter. We could say that God, in the exercise of His wisdom and
prudence, has abounded toward us in grace. Or we could say
that God has made known to us in all wisdom and prudence the
mystery of His will. That is how the Revised Standard Version
takes it. But it seems to me that a much better way, and one that is
suggested by the Authorized and Revised Versions is simply to
change the first part of verse 8 and to read: 'Which, [referring to
the grace] together with all wisdom and prudence, he has caused
to abound toward us.' I argue that it should be taken in that way
because I do not think it right to attribute the 'all wisdom and
prudence' to God, for the reason that as God is absolute wisdom
we have no right to say that God does anything 'in all wisdom'.
We can speak of a man doing things 'in all wisdom', but God is
essential wisdom, and therefore we cannot apply such an expression to Him. It is lacking in reverence.

This is even more applicable to the word 'prudence'. Nowhere
in the whole range of Scripture is the term 'prudence' ascribed to
God. You can use it with reference to men, but it is inappropriate
to use it with respect to God, whose ways are perfect and who is
absolute and eternal wisdom. So I argue that we must regard the
'wisdom' and the 'prudence' as being applied to ourselves, and

that Paul is saying that they have come to us as the result of the working of God's grace.

What the Apostle is saying therefore is that the riches of God's grace toward us have not stopped at the matter of forgiveness, but have so abounded that they have brought to us something further, namely, the wisdom and prudence that are absolutely necessary to a knowledge of the mystery of God's will, and of His eternal purpose in our Lord and Saviour Jesus Christ.

This, then, is the third great statement which the Apostle makes concerning the things which God has done with respect to us – He has chosen us; He has predestinated us; He has made known unto us the mystery of His will. There is a definite sequence here, as we are told in verse 9: '(God) having made known unto us the mystery of his will, according to his good pleasure which he hath purposed in himself.' God purposed in Himself before the foundation of the world this great scheme of redemption and of salvation; it is something that originated entirely in the mind and in the heart of God: He purposed it in Himself. And what He has purposed is this 'good pleasure' of His toward men, this 'goodwill toward men' which the angels spoke of to the shepherds, 'Peace on earth, goodwill toward men'.

But, says the Apostle, God has not only purposed and planned salvation; He has revealed it also; it is a mystery that He has made known. And, still more wonderful – and this is the particular message of these two verses – God has also done something which makes it possible for us to know this and to apprehend it and to receive it. This is the way in which the 'riches of God's grace' have 'abounded toward us'. It has done so 'in all wisdom and prudence' in order that we might have this insight and understanding into the mystery of God's will and His gracious purpose.

This then is the theme, and it is a particularly important one at this present time because here the Apostle is handling and dealing with the whole question of our approach to Christian salvation. This matter is provoking much discussion at the present time, as it has done so frequently in the history of the Church. It is a particular cause of stumbling to the modern man who has much to say about the place of man's mind and reason and understanding in connection with the faith. There are many who reject the Christian faith because they cannot understand it; they say that it is unreasonable, that it does not fit into the usual categories of thought, and so on. That seems to them to be good and sufficient reason for rejecting it and claiming that it has nothing to say to modern man. This is therefore a crucial matter, and of vital importance in connection with the preaching of the Gospel and evangelism. It determines our whole approach towards these questions, and particularly with respect to our methods. The question is: How does a man come to a knowledge of the great salvation which is in Christ, and to an understanding of the mighty and eternal purpose of God? To answer that question we can do nothing better than examine with care the terms which the Apostle uses.

His first term is 'mystery' – 'Wherein he hath abounded toward us in all wisdom and prudence; having made known unto us the mystery of his will'. 'Mystery' is a very important term in Paul's Epistles. But it is not confined to his writings by any means; it is a vital term throughout the New Testament. Our Lord Himself used it in His discourse reported in the thirteenth chapter of Matthew's Gospel, and in parallel passages such as Mark, chapter 4. Our Lord was explaining to the disciples His method of teaching the mystery, or the truth, concerning God's kingdom by means of parables. The disciples could not understand this; but our Lord explained it to them: 'Unto you it is given to know the mysteries of the kingdom of heaven, but to them it is not given' (Matthew 13:11). The teaching concerning the kingdom of heaven is a mystery; and He makes it known to disciples only. Though the Pharisees and others were standing by and hearing the same words, as He uttered His parables, they did not understand them and went away with a wrong impression. This was because of the *mystery* of the kingdom, says our Lord.

The Apostle Paul uses the term in the sixteenth chapter of the Epistle to the Romans: 'Now to him that is of power to stablish you according to my gospel, and the preaching of Jesus Christ, according to the revelation of the mystery, which was kept secret since the world began, but now is made manifest, and by the scriptures of the prophets, according to the commandment of the everlasting God, made known to all nations for the obedience of faith' (vv. 25–26). We find it also in the First Epistle to the Corinthians, chapter 2: 'Howbeit we speak wisdom among them that are perfect; yet not the wisdom of this world, nor of the princes of this world, that come to nought: but we speak the wisdom of God in a mystery, even the hidden wisdom, which God ordained before the world unto our glory' (vv. 6–7).

The Apostle uses the word again in the third chapter of this Epistle to the Ephesians where he speaks of '. . . the dispensation of the grace of God which is given me to you-ward: how that by revelation he made known unto me the mystery; (as I wrote afore in few words, whereby, when ye read, ye may understand my knowledge in the mystery of Christ) which in other ages was not made known . . .' (vv. 2–5). The Apostle Paul repeats himself frequently, as every good teacher does, and especially a teacher of the gospel who has something that is worth repeating. We find the word again in the First Epistle to Timothy, chapter 3: 'Great is the mystery of godliness' (v. 16). It is patently a key term: and if we fail to understand its meaning we shall certainly go astray in this matter of how a man becomes a Christian, and in regard to the relationship of reason to faith, and of mind to salvation.

The term 'mystery' as used in the New Testament does not mean a kind of mystic secret which is only revealed to a few initiates and which is deliberately kept from and guarded from everyone else, as was characteristic of the 'mystery religions' so common in Paul's day. Men had to go to the temples and pass through certain cultic procedures before being initiated into the knowledge of the mystery. It was a closely-guarded secret that was confined to certain philosophers and exceptional people; it was never given to the common people. There are certain cults and secret societies at the present time which are clearly based upon such ideas. Their meetings are held behind closed doors, and the candidate has to pledge himself never to divulge the secret and is taught a secret sign by which he may recognize his fellow devotees. That is the very antithesis of Christianity, which proclaims, preaches, expounds, heralds its message and desires everyone to know it. So the term *mystery* as used in the New Testament does not denote some closely-guarded mystic secret into which the initiates alone are admitted.

But still more important is the fact that when this truth is

[188]

described as a *mystery* it does not mean that it is something which is vague and nebulous and indefinite. That is perhaps the more important point to emphasize today, for there is a popular school of thought which teaches that the Christian faith can never be stated in propositions. Christianity, they teach, is essentially an 'encounter' which takes place at an 'existential moment' when God speaks to man and addresses him; and something happens to the man which can never be put into print or stated in cold words. Hence they say that the Bible is a fallible book because it is only men's attempts to state and to explain the vital experience they had at the moment of encounter. This, they maintain, is very different from calling upon people to believe certain propositions. They say, 'Truth can never be stated propositionally', because it is a mystery. In other words they define a *mystery* as something that is incomprehensible, something that man cannot state or express, and they add that any attempt to do so derogates and detracts from it.

It is of great importance for us to realize that that is not the meaning of 'mystery', nor does that view of it always appear in an intellectual and theological guise; it has attained a certain popularity in a movement whose slogan tells us that 'Religion is caught, not taught'. Religion, it is claimed, is a thing of the spirit, something undefinable, something you cannot state in cold terms; you just 'catch' it from others. Religion must not be stated in a confession of faith or some credal statement. To attempt this is to be rationalistic. You meet people who have it, you cannot tell exactly what it is, but you know they have it, and you would like to have it; but you can have it, and you catch it, and thus it spreads from one to another.

Such assertions utterly violate what the New Testament means by the term 'mystery', and are entirely subversive of the Christian faith. But they certainly provide an excellent basis for a successful ecumenical movement. The only hope of having a successful ecumenical movement is to say that you must avoid coming down to particularities, and that you must not insist upon anything. As long as we all believe in Christ in any manner we are all one, and a world church, inclusive of all religious persons, is within sight. As a religious paper, now defunct, said at the time of a great evangelistic campaign a few years ago, 'Let us have a theological truce during the Campaign'! All such talk, however, is based upon the idea that Christian truth is mysterious in the sense that it is incomprehensible to the human intellect, and that it can never be understood or stated in propositions, and that the only thing that matters is that we should all vaguely believe in Christ.

Positively, the word *mystery* in the New Testament does not mean something that is incomprehensible to the human mind, but is rather something that is undiscoverable by the unaided human mind. That is the vital difference. The wrong definition says that it is always incomprehensible. The second definition says that the human mind by its own efforts and endeavours can never arrive at it, but that when it is enabled to do so it begins to comprehend it. It is a mystery in the sense that man with his unaided, fallen mind and intellect can never discover it and arrive at it; but when it is revealed to him he is able to understand it. The Apostle Paul refers to it as 'God's wisdom', and as a 'hidden wisdom'. He says that 'the princes of this world' did not know it because they were seeking to understand it with their unaided mind. 'But,' says the Apostle, 'God hath revealed it unto us by his Spirit, for the Spirit searcheth all things, yea, the deep things of God.' 'We have received,' he goes on to say, 'not the spirit of the world, but the Spirit that is of God, that we may know the things that are freely given to us of God' (1 Corinthians 2:7-12). We may know these things; they become comprehensible as the result of the operation of the Holy Spirit.

In speaking thus the Apostle is but repeating what our blessed Lord had said before him. In the eleventh chapter of Matthew's Gospel we read that our Lord turned to His Father and said: 'I thank Thee, O Father, Lord of heaven and earth, that thou hast hid these things from the wise and prudent, and hast revealed them unto babes. Even so, Father: for so it seemed good in thy sight' (vv. 25-26). God hides the truth from the 'wise and prudent'; and it remains a mystery to them; but not to the 'babes'. God reveals it to the 'babes' in order that they may enjoy it. In other words the term 'mystery' means that this great truth concerning God's will and purpose of salvation can only be received when God makes it known and reveals it. And the Apostle says that He has done so. 'Wherein he hath abounded

toward us in all wisdom and prudence; having made known
unto us the mystery of his will.'

So 'mystery' does not mean something inherently and essentially incomprehensible to the human mind, but rather something
which is a secret beyond the reach of the natural human mind
but which God has revealed and unfolded to those who believe.
The entire New Testament teaching turns upon this, that believers
in Christ have entered into the secret, have had the mystery
revealed to them. Saving truth is no longer a mystery to the
Christian, it is only a mystery to the non-Christian. To the
Christian it is an open secret, because God in His grace and
kindness has been pleased to unfold it and to reveal it to him.

This being so, we must in the second place go on to ask: Is it
therefore true to say that, because God has made this revelation
of the mystery of His will in Christ, anyone who chooses to do so
can receive it and understand it? Does it follow that, because God
has revealed it in Christ, any man can come to the New Testament
and read it and apply his mind and his intellect to it and then
discover the message? The answer to that question is the very
thing that the Apostle is emphasizing here, and it brings us to
the words 'wisdom and prudence'. We start with the propositions
in the First Epistle to the Corinthians, chapters 1 and 2: 'The
natural man receiveth not the things of the Spirit of God' and
'not many wise, not many noble are called'. The truth was being
presented to those intellectual Greeks but they could not see it.
Men come to the New Testament with all their ability and understanding and training but they do not see the truth. They can
never do so without the Holy Spirit. The Holy Spirit, and His
operation upon us, are absolutely essential before we can receive
the truth and begin to understand it. 'Wisdom' is necessary, and
wisdom means knowledge and understanding. In other words the
best exposition of the two verses we are examining is to be found
in the first two chapters of the First Epistle of Paul to the
Corinthians. The great quest of the Greeks was for wisdom; the
great quest of all philosophers is for knowledge and for understanding; they try to find God and to understand Him and the
world, but 'The world by wisdom knew not God'. The world's

wisdom is not enough. But, says Paul, 'we speak the wisdom of God'.

God must give the understanding also. The Apostle in writing to the Corinthians in that same First Epistle and the third chapter says something that is of crucial importance: 'If any man seemeth to be wise in this world, let him become a fool, that he may be made wise' (v. 18). In other words, if you want to understand and enter into this wisdom of God you have to 'become a little child'. You have to renounce earthly wisdom and reliance upon human powers and faculties; you have to become a fool; you have to say 'I know nothing, my abilities are of no value here; I become as a little child'. 'Verily I say unto you, Except ye be converted and become as little children, ye shall not enter into the kingdom of heaven' (Matthew 18:3). The glory of the gospel, says the Apostle, is that God in His grace has revealed it unto us. His grace has so abounded toward us that we can say, 'We have the mind of Christ' (1 Corinthians 2:16). So ends the Apostle's argument. But notice that he also says in that second chapter of his First Epistle to the Corinthians, 'He that is spiritual judgeth all things, yet he himself is judged of no man' (v. 15). The Christian understands but the non-Christian does not understand him. Then Paul asks a question, 'Who hath known the mind of the Lord, that he may instruct him'? (v. 16). His answer is that, while no one can instruct God, nevertheless 'We have the mind of Christ': and we have it because of the riches of God's grace which has 'abounded toward us in all wisdom'. He has given us the power to understand and to comprehend.

But we receive not only 'all wisdom' but also 'prudence'. This word 'prudence' as used here in the New Testament does not carry the meaning that we normally attach to the word 'prudence'. We shall be able to see this by looking at some other examples of the use of the same word in the New Testament. When Simon Peter had made his great confession of faith at Caesarea Philippi he was surprised when our Lord told him that He had to go to the death of the Cross. Peter said: 'That be far from thee, Lord; this shall not happen unto thee.' But our Lord turned to him and said, 'Get thee behind me, Satan, for thou *savourest not* the things which be of God'. That meant that Peter did not appreciate them, did not understand them.

Take a further illustration in the Epistle to the Romans, chapter 8, verse 5: 'They that are in the flesh do *mind* the things of the flesh, and they that are after the Spirit do *mind* the things of the Spirit.' In the Greek, *mind* is the same term, and it means that 'fleshly things' are the interest of 'men in the flesh'; that is the realm that attracts them, that is where they live in their minds, the things of this world form their enjoyment. Or take again Colossians, chapter 3, verse 2: '*Set your affection* on things above.' Here we find the same word – *to set the affection* – as the one translated 'prudence' in our text.

These illustrations help us to understand the meaning of the term 'prudence'. It means a state of mind which includes the affections as well as the understanding. Wisdom is a matter of the intellect and of the understanding; prudence includes the affections as well as the mind. So it can be translated by the word 'insight' – 'in all wisdom and insight'. It means 'spiritual discernment', the ability to discern the excellence of the things of God, and to have a corresponding affection toward them. So the riches of God's grace have abounded toward us not only in the wisdom that gives me understanding; it takes up the whole of my soul, the whole man. It includes my affections, my interest, my love; my whole being is called out to it; and I desire it with my whole being.

That being the doctrine, I draw the following conclusions. If this is true, then advances in knowledge and in science, the advances of the centuries, make not the slightest difference in the matter of spiritual truth, and are completely irrelevant where that truth is concerned.

I came across a statement recently which shows how necessary it is to call attention to this today. I was reading a review of a book in which the reviewer dealt with those who delight in praising the theology of the sixteenth and seventeenth centuries, and also certain older Roman Catholic writers. This is what he wrote: 'I am less sure than I was, however, that the categories of those great days are adequate for a discussion of the problems raised for our thought by our neo-physicists.' What he meant was that there is little point in reading and considering the great theologies of the past, for they cannot help us now. We face the great problems raised by such new sciences as atomic physics and by the current advances in knowledge and thought and in our understanding of the cosmos and the nature of the universe. The reviewer asserted that there is no point in going back to older writers for we obviously must have something new before we can understand spiritual truth and the way of God with respect to man and the way of salvation at the present time. There are new problems, he claimed, because of the advances made by men's minds. But this is simply a complete denial of what the Apostle teaches in these two verses which we are considering, and indeed of the whole of the New Testament. The mind of man at its best, whether in the first or the twentieth century, is never adequate. To the natural man spiritual truth remains a mystery always. It was a mystery nearly two thousand years ago; it is equally a mystery today. The new astro-physics makes not the slightest difference. We are concerned about God, man, sin; and the splitting of the atom is completely irrelevant in this realm. To say that the age of the neo-physicists demands some new kind of truth and understanding is a denial of the very basis of the Christian faith.

Secondly, the Scriptures alone must always be our sole and final authority with regard to all these matters. Modernity makes no difference at all. The revelation is found in the Bible and it remains there unchanged and unchangeable. There is nothing additional in the twentieth century and there never will be. God has revealed the mystery: therefore to talk about the modern mind and the modern man is to deny the Scriptures. There will not be, there never can be, any advance on what has already been revealed. We live upon the 'foundation of the apostles and prophets' and cannot go beyond them.

Thirdly, the work of the Holy Spirit is absolutely essential to an understanding of the Scriptures. Whatever a man may be, and however great his natural ability may be, if he is not enlightened by the Holy Spirit he will not and cannot understand the Scriptures. The truth which they reveal is 'spiritually discerned'.

Lastly – and I delight to say this – because this is God's way there is hope for all to understand. As it is something which is revealed by God, and which He enables us to understand by giving us 'wisdom' and 'prudence', intellect or the absence of intellect does not make a vital difference. The understanding which is given by God through the Holy Spirit is open to all. Again I remind you of what the Apostle says to the Corinthians: 'Not many wise men after the flesh, not many mighty, not many noble are called.' 'God has chosen the foolish things,' the ignorant, the hopeless, the vile, 'the things that are not, to bring to nothing things that are, that no flesh should glory in His presence' (1 Corinthians 1:26–29). It is not power of intellect that makes a Christian; salvation is spiritual; it is all given by God. He gives us the wisdom and the prudence, as well as the truth. We are all on the same level, and we must therefore glory in nothing and in no-one save in the Lord Himself.

Incidentally, this truth is the whole basis of missionary activity. It is because of this that you can go to the heart of Central Africa and visit a tribe of people who cannot read or write and who have no learning. You can preach the gospel to them with the same confidence as you preach it in Western society, because God can enlighten them through the Holy Spirit. Most of the early Christians were slaves; the gospel is 'preached to the poor'. Throughout the centuries it has been the same. Thank God for this. If it were otherwise, men of intellect would have a great advantage over others; but here we are all one. 'There is none righteous, no, not one.' 'The world by wisdom knew not God.' 'It pleased God by the foolishness of preaching to save them that believe' (1 Corinthians 1:21). How we should thank God that He has made the riches of His grace to abound toward us 'in all wisdom and prudence, having made known unto us the mystery of his will, according to His good pleasure which He hath purposed in himself'! Let us join the Apostle Paul in saying, 'O the depth of the riches both of the wisdom and the knowledge of God! how unsearchable are his judgments, and his ways past finding out'! (Romans 11:33). Who but God would ever have contrived such a way of salvation, such a perfect way of salvation? 'For of him and through him and to him are all things, to whom be glory for ever. Amen.'

17

All Things re-united in Christ

'That in the dispensation of the fulness of times he might gather together in one all things in Christ, both which are in heaven and which are on earth, even in him.'

Ephesians 1:10

This verse explains the nature of the mystery which God has been pleased to reveal to us. I do not hesitate to assert that we have in this verse the key to the understanding of the chief practical purpose of this Epistle to the Ephesians. This is the message which the Apostle is most concerned to expound. At the same time, of course, he was anxious to tell them all the things which we have already considered; but the peculiar feature of this Epistle is that it is meant to be an exposition of this particular theme. Indeed we can go further and say that this verse states what is the central theme of all Scripture. From the standpoint of conception of thought and of range of meaning there is nothing greater. I do not mean that it is greater from the standpoint of our experience; in that respect it is certainly no greater than verse 7 – 'We have redemption through his blood, the forgiveness of sins, according to the riches of his grace'. But looked at from the standpoint of intellect, as a mighty concept, then we must say that it is even superior to verse 7, because in verse 10 we are taken right up into the heavens and find ourselves looking at God's final purpose with respect to this world. There is nothing higher than this, nothing beyond God's final purpose. It is bigger and greater than our personal salvation. In this verse we are transported above the matter of our personal salvation into the realm of the ultimate things – God's grand, comprehensive, final, ultimate purpose. The human mind can never contemplate anything greater. God gives us no greater privilege than to be allowed to look into this.

How wonderful it is to be able to do so in the light of the present state and condition of the world! We see the nations torn and divided; we see turmoil; we are aware of certain dread possibilities. To all thinking people the great question is, What is wrong with the world, and what can be done about it? To me the greatest tragedy of all at the present time is that so many Christian 'leaders', when they try to deal with this world situation, concentrate on what they think statesmen should do to resolve the recurring crises and to avert certain dangers. They state their opinions and give their advice. But neither they nor I are in any position to advise statesmen. That is the special task of the statesmen; and the larger the number of Christian statesmen we have the better. As a Christian I have my own thoughts and ideas about such things, but they have no authority whatsoever above the thoughts of anyone else.

But if I am not qualified to advise statesmen, I am commissioned to expound the Scriptures. I do not know what is going to happen in the world; no one else does. I do not know whether there is to be peace or war, and it would be a waste of time to attempt to deal with such a subject. But I purpose to deal with a subject which I do know, something which belongs to a much wider realm, and I am about to do so with the authority that God gives. The immediate future may bring war, or it may bring peace; I do not know; but I do know about the ultimate future. This is one of those points at which the Christian and the non-Christian are clearly differentiated and separated from each other. The Christian is interested in the ultimate and in God's plan, and he knows that history will end in a certain given way. There are many who believe that it is possible to Christianize the world, and that the main business of preaching is to try to persuade people to apply Christian teaching to the affairs of the world. But to expect Christian behaviour from people who are not Christian betokens a colossal ignorance of sin and its ways as they are revealed in the Bible. That is not the message that is revealed here and indeed anywhere in the Bible. What we are told here is something which is going to happen whatever men and nations may do or not do, for it is God's plan and it is absolutely certain. If you understand these things it enables you to look at the present world crisis and remain calm, because you know that God's ultimate plan is certain.

[197]

The best way, perhaps, of approaching this crucial statement in this tenth verse is again to take the words the Apostle uses, because if we are not clear about the meaning of the words, our understanding of the teaching will of necessity be wrong. The first word is the word 'dispensation' – 'that in the dispensation of the fulness of times . . .' What a sadly overworked word this is! It has been so abused and misinterpreted that one is almost afraid to use it at all. There are people who divide up the Bible into so many dispensations that one is left in a state of confusion. The authorities are agreed that 'dispensation' has two main meanings, and it is used three times in this Epistle. It is used in the second verse of the third chapter where Paul says: 'If ye have heard of the dispensation of the grace of God that is given me to you-ward; how that by revelation he made known unto me the mystery.' Again it is found in the ninth verse of the same chapter: 'And to make all men see what is the fellowship of the mystery, which from the beginning of the world hath been hid in God, who created all things by Jesus Christ.' The word translated 'fellowship' is the same Greek word as that translated 'dispensation' here. Again, the same word is used by the Apostle in the First Epistle to the Corinthians in the ninth chapter, verse 17. Talking about himself as a preacher he says: 'If I do this thing willingly I have a reward; but if against my will, a dispensation of the gospel is given unto me.'

How do we know which of its two main meanings to adopt? It all depends upon whether you regard it from the standpoint of a person who is in authority or from the standpoint of a person who is under authority. If you regard the word from the former standpoint its meaning is a plan, a scheme, an economy; if from the latter, it means an office, a stewardship or an administration. It is certainly clear that the first meaning applies here in verse 10; whereas in the second verse of the third chapter it is obvious that the second meaning applies, the reference being to office – 'If ye have heard of the dispensation of the grace of God that is given me to you-ward'. That was his work, his office. A stewardship, an administration, he says, had been given to him. But in the ninth verse of the third chapter it is equally clear that the term 'dispensation' means a 'plan' – 'and to make all men see what is the dispensation of the mystery, which from the beginning of the

[198]

world hath been hid in God'. Here in the tenth verse of the first chapter the term is obviously applied to God, the One who is in authority, and therefore it means a plan, a scheme, an economy. The Apostle is saying that we have been given this knowledge, this insight, into God's great plan. The mystery that has been revealed is that God has a great scheme, an 'economy' with respect to this world and that He is bringing it into operation.

The second expression to be considered is 'the fulness of times' – 'in the dispensation of the fulness of times'. Here the Apostle tells us when this great plan of God is to be put into operation, when this great purpose which was in the mind of God from eternity is really going to be fulfilled. The Apostle uses the same expression in the Epistle to the Galatians in the fourth verse of the fourth chapter. Referring to our Lord's coming into the world he says: 'But when the fulness of the time was come, God sent forth his Son, made of a woman, made under the law, to redeem them that were under the law, that we might receive the adoption of sons.' The whole span of time has been divided by the coming of the Lord Jesus Christ into this world. That is the division which is emphasized in the New Testament. The times in which we live are called 'the last times', 'the last days'. Prophets in the Old Testament write about the 'last days', and 'the last times'; and they all refer to the time that follows the coming of the Lord Jesus Christ into this world. He came in 'the fulness of the times'. Everything had been leading up to this, now the 'fulness' has arrived, and everything beyond that is referred to as 'the last times'.

Let us consider some examples of this usage. In the First Epistle to the Corinthians, in the tenth chapter, the Apostle says: 'Now all these things happened unto them', – that is, to the Israelites – 'for ensamples: and they are written for our admonition, upon whom the ends of the world are come' (v. 11). The moment the Lord Jesus Christ came into this world the 'ends of the world' had started. 'The ends of the world', says the Apostle, are come upon us. The author of the Epistle to the Hebrews makes the same point. 'God, who at sundry times and in divers manners spake in time past unto the fathers by the prophets, hath in these last days spoken unto us by (in) his Son.'

These examples help us to understand the meaning of the term

[199]

'fulness of the times'. The climax of the ages happened at the Incarnation. Time has been divided once and for ever by that event. In the 'fulness of the times' Christ came. So the Apostle teaches us here that God's great plan began to come into operation at the birth of the Lord Jesus Christ. What is happening at this present time is that this great plan of God is being worked out – in 'the fulness of the times', in these 'last days', 'in the ends of the world' – and it will go on until it is finally completed. God has given us this knowledge by means of the 'wisdom' and the 'discrimination', the 'prudence' He has given us. We can see that this great original plan of God has been put into operation in this world by the coming of Christ, that it is being carried on, and that it will continue until it is finally completed by His return again to this world.

The next thing we are told is that this great plan is being carried out in and through the Lord Jesus Christ. Paul writes: 'That in the dispensation of the fulness of times he (God) might gather together all things in Christ, both which are in heaven and which are on earth, even in him.' The Apostle took the trouble to repeat it, and is not content with saying 'in Christ', but must add 'even in him'. We have had occasion to emphasize this already several times. It is Christ always; the Apostle keeps on mentioning His Name; and he does so because all is in Christ. The Apostle worshipped and adored Him, and he seems to be saying to us: I can never mention His Name too frequently for it is all in Him; so let us give Him all the glory and the credit – 'Even in him'. The same note occurs in Colossians chapter one, verse 20: 'by him, I say.' Christ is central, Christ is essential, and anything which calls itself Christianity which does not go on repeating the blessed Name is ultimately a denial of Christianity.

The plan is that 'he might gather together in one all things in Christ' and we now proceed to consider its nature. Here is the very nerve and centre of the message, as found in the Authorized Version. The Revised Version reads: 'to sum up all things in Christ.' The Revised Standard Version reads: 'to unite all things in Him.' It is remarkable that these three translations for some reason have left out a most important word, namely, the word 'again'. The word the Apostle uses here which is translated 'sum up', 'unite', and 'gather together', is a compound word in the

Greek, beginning with 'ana' which means 'again'. Yet these translations leave that out. The Grimm-Thayer Lexicon says correctly that it means, 'to bring together again', for Himself. A. S. Way's excellent translation of the epistles of Paul and the Epistle to the Hebrews brings this out and translates it thus: 'For His purpose was to re-unite all things, . . . all made one in Him.' To gather together 'again'; not merely to unite, but to re-unite! Not to sum up only, but to sum up again! This 'again' opens up the whole meaning. Doubtless these other translations take this for granted, but it is something that must be emphasized, for it is only as we take note of it that we really arrive at the Apostle's doctrine. The word that Paul used also carries the idea of 'heading up'. I do not like the expression; it is a slang expression which is coming increasingly into currency; but that idea is present in the root meaning of the word the Apostle used. He is saying that God is going to 'head up again' all things in Christ.

That brings us to consider what is meant by, and included in, the 'all things', for the dispensation, the plan, the purpose, which is being carried out at this present time and which began with the Incarnation, is that God might reconcile in Christ all things. At once that is amplified or explained by the phrase, 'both which are in heaven and which are on earth'. The 'all things' are to be re-united in Christ.

A number of views have been put forward to explain this term. Some people do not hesitate to say that it means absolutely everything everywhere. They say that there is to be a universal redemption of everyone and everything. A second group does not go quite as far as that; but it says that there is to be a universal redemption of all intelligent beings. They do not hesitate to say that both good and bad men, bad angels, and the devil himself, are going to be redeemed and saved – all are going to be restored to God. This is what is called Universalism; and, alas, it is becoming increasingly popular today. Another view says that the expression 'things in heaven and things on earth' refers to Jews and Gentiles. It teaches that the Jews belong to the kingdom of heaven and are in a special position; and that the Gentiles belong only to the earth. This is one of the extravagances that one finds in a certain school of interpretation which draws a distinction between the kingdom of heaven and the kingdom of God, in spite of the fact that the terms are used interchangeably in the Scriptures. This school of thought draws a sharp division between the Jew and the Gentile, and teaches that the Jews will have a special place in the kingdom of God. They will be higher than others, they belong to the heavens, whereas the remainder of the saved belong to the earth. They therefore explain 'heaven' and 'earth' in terms of 'Jews' and 'Gentiles'. Others have said that this term 'all things' is a reference to all the people of God, all the redeemed. 'Things in heaven and things on earth', they say, means those Christians who have already left this world and are in glory; they are already in heaven, so that they are 'in the heavens', while others will be living on earth at the return of Christ; they are the ones that are 'on earth'. So the expression, 'all things which are in heaven and which are on earth', means the redeemed who have gone to glory and the redeemed who remain, the totality of the redeemed.

Surely we cannot accept those two Universalistic ideas, because, if we do so, it means that we find ourselves contradicting the plain teaching of Scripture in those places where there is a clear division between the saved and the unsaved, the good and the bad, the redeemed and the lost. In spite of the arguments based upon a philosophic idea of the love of God, the Scripture draws the ultimate distinction between eternal salvation and eternal destruction. There is not a vestige of evidence in Scripture to show that the fallen angels are included in any way in the scheme of redemption. So we reject those first two views. As we have already seen, we must also reject the view that regards Paul's words as descriptive of the Jew and the Gentile, because the same Apostle teaches the Colossians that 'There is neither Greek nor Jew, Barbarian, Scythian, bond nor free' (3:11). All such distinctions in this matter of salvation have gone, the middle wall of partition has been broken down. All in the kingdom are one, and always will be. There is only one salvation – by the blood of Christ – and no-one can enter the kingdom except by belief in Christ. Such is the universal teaching of the Scripture. So we reject that exposition.

The same applies to the fourth possibility, namely, that Paul's language is descriptive of the totality of the redeemed. The term 'all things in heaven and in earth' certainly includes that totality, but it does not go far enough. This is made quite clear in the parallel passage in the first chapter of the Epistle to the Colossians (v. 20). I suggest then that 'the things which are in heaven' includes the good angels which kept their first estate, and that 'the things which are on earth' includes not only the redeemed who will be on earth when Christ returns, but in addition it refers to the created universe itself, including the earth, animals and beasts.

The key to all this is found in that little word 'again'. God's plan, according to Paul, is to re-unite all things in Christ, to gather them together again, to bring back, to head up once more all things in Christ. The expression immediately suggests that things have already been in a perfect condition once, but that they are no longer in that condition. But they will be so again. They are to be 're-united'.

Originally all things were in a perfect state of harmony under our Lord Jesus Christ, as we are told in the first chapter of the Epistle to the Colossians, verses 15–19: 'Who [referring to the Lord] is the image of the invisible God, the firstborn of every creature: for by him were all things created, that are in heaven, and that are in earth, visible and invisible, whether they be thrones, or dominions, or principalities, or powers: all things were created by him, and for him: and he is before all things, and by him all things consist. And he is the head of the body, the church: who is the beginning, the firstborn from the dead; that in all things he might have the pre-eminence. For it pleased the Father that in him should all fulness dwell.'

There we have an account of creation's original condition. In the tenth verse of the second chapter of Colossians we read: 'And ye are complete in him (in Christ), which is the head of all principality and power.' Such terms as 'principality' and 'power' and 'dominions' and 'thrones' always refer to the angelic beings, the angelic powers, the great powers in the heavens. So what we are told is that the Lord Jesus Christ was the head of all these powers as He was also the head of the universe. Everything that was made and created was made and created in Him and by Him and through and for Him; not only the world and animals, but angels and thrones and principalities and powers. Furthermore there was perfect harmony in all these realms. The Lord Jesus

Christ was over all – over the angels and all powers and authorities and dominions; then over the world, the animals and the fruit of the earth. Man was made the Lord of creation over all animals and inanimate nature. All was absolutely perfect and in a state of entire harmony and unity. Everything worked harmoniously downwards from the great Head, and everything worked upwards, back again towards the Supreme Head, the Lord Jesus Christ.

But, alas, the unity and harmony did not continue; and the present situation of the world is due to that fact. The harmony has been destroyed. First of all there was a revolt, a rebellion, in heaven itself. The devil rebelled and fell, and a large number of the holy angels followed him and fell with him. Immediately there was discord, even in heaven. There is a most significant statement in the Book of Revelation, chapter 12, which throws great light upon the subject we are considering. In verse 7 of that chapter we read: 'And there was war in heaven.' Discord in heaven! War in heaven! 'Michael and his angels fought against the dragon, and the dragon fought and his angels.' But the discord was not confined to heaven. The fallen angel, namely, the devil, Satan, came and tempted man, and man fell. The result was discord amongst men – dispute, quarrelling, misunderstanding, warfare, bloodshed, murder, jealousy, envy, and all that follow in their train.

But we must remember that even the creation itself suffered as the result of sin. Paul says in the eighth chapter of his Epistle to the Romans that 'the creature was made subject to vanity, not willingly, but by reason of him who hath subjected the same in hope' (v. 20). When man fell the earth was cursed, and the story of creation ever since has been 'Nature red in tooth and claw', briars and thorns, troubles, diseases and pestilences. The harmony has gone; the original perfection has vanished and disappeared. That is the position of the world as a result of the fall of the angels, and the fall of man has stemmed from it.

Now we are in a position to see the doctrine of this verse which we are studying. The mystic secret which we as Christians are allowed to share is that God will ultimately restore the original harmony, and re-unite again all things in Christ. Christ is over all and the old harmony will be restored. And we are told how it is going to happen. In regard to men we have already noted that it happens as the result of the redemption through the blood of Christ. Reconciliation to God, and reconciliation with one another is by His blood, by His grace. He has 'made peace', 'the middle wall of partition' is removed. The old enmity, together with all divisions, is abolished. That is, incidentally, a further reason for rejecting the idea of a perpetual distinction between Gentile and Jew in Christ.

Let us be careful to observe that these blessings only apply to those who believe on the Lord Jesus Christ. No harmony is promised to others; they are sent to 'everlasting destruction'; but they will be outside the cosmos, as it were; they will be out of harmony and will not disturb it eternally. As regards the fallen angels it is clear that there is no hope for them. They are 'reserved in chains' in the pit until their final damnation comes (2 Peter 2:4; Jude 6). Satan also is to be cast into 'the lake of fire' where he and all his followers are to be tormented for ever (Revelation 20:10). As for the good angels, the Scriptures teach us that they come into God's good purpose. In the Book of Revelation, chapter 5, we are told that not only the saints and the redeemed sing the praises of the Lamb that once was slain, but angels – 'ten thousand times ten thousand, and thousands of thousands' – and the beasts and the elders all join with the saints in the same chorus. This is part of the harmony that is to be restored.

The same idea appears in the Epistle to the Hebrews, chapter 12, where we are told that already as Christians we have come 'unto Mount Sion, and unto the city of the living God, the heavenly Jerusalem, and to an innumerable company of angels, to the general assembly and church of the firstborn, which are written in heaven, and to God the Judge of all, and to the spirits of just men made perfect. . . .' 'An innumerable company of angels'? They are a part of the harmony; not that they are redeemed (they have never fallen) but they are under Christ's headship and they adore Him and worship Him. They are with us now, and they will be with us sharing in the eternal glory.

The earth is also involved. The Apostle Peter tells us in his Second Epistle, chapter 3, that a day is coming when there shall

be a destruction of the present earth and of the world by fire:
'The elements shall melt with fervent heat.' Evil and sin will be
burned out of the universe, and there will be 'a new heavens and
a new earth wherein dwelleth righteousness' (vv. 12–13). The
Apostle Paul likewise, in the eighth chapter of the Epistle to the
Romans, tells us that 'the whole creation groaneth and travaileth
in pain together until now'. It is waiting for 'the manifestation of
the sons of God'. Creation will be involved in the restoration of
all things: it will be 'delivered from the bondage of corruption
into the glorious liberty of the children of God' (vv. 19–21). The
author of the Epistle to the Hebrews joins in, in his second
chapter, and says: 'For unto the angels hath he not put in subjection the world to come, whereof we speak. But one in a certain
place testified, saying, What is man, that thou art mindful of him?
or the son of man, that thou visitest him? Thou madest him a
little lower than the angels; thou crownedst him with glory and
honour, and didst set him over the works of thy hands. Thou hast
put all things in subjection under his feet. For in that he put all in
subjection under him, he left nothing that is not put under him.
But now we see not yet all things put under him. But we see
Jesus, who was made a little lower than the angels for the
suffering of death, crowned with glory and honour.'

Christ represents us and we are in Him, and so we are going to
be elevated to the position of 'lords of creation' again, and
everything will be placed under us. The old original harmony
will be restored. Isaiah speaks of it prophetically. He saw that a
day was coming when 'the wolf shall dwell with the lamb, and the
leopard shall lie down with the kid, and the calf and the young
lion and the fatling together, and a little child shall lead them.
And the cow and the bear shall feed, their young ones shall lie
down together; and the lion shall eat straw like the ox. And the
sucking child shall play on the hole of the asp, and the weaned child
shall put his hand on the cockatrice' den. They shall not hurt nor
destroy in all my holy mountain, for the earth shall be full of the
knowledge of the Lord as the waters cover the sea' (Isaiah 11: 6–9).

The perfect harmony that will be restored will be harmony in
man, and between men. Harmony on the earth and in the brute
creation! Harmony in heaven, and all under this blessed Lord
Jesus Christ, who will be the Head of all! Everything will again

be united in Him. And wonder of wonders, marvellous beyond compare, when all this happens it will never be undone again. All will be re-united in Him to all eternity. That is the message; that is God's plan. That is the mystery which has been revealed unto us.

Once more I must ask some questions. Do you know these things? Are you prepared to give time to these things – to listen to them or to read about them? Do you know that these things are so marvellous that you will never hear anything greater, either in this world or the world to come? Do you realize that you have a part in these things? As I said at the beginning, I do not know whether another world-war is coming or not; but whether it be war or no war, as Christians we are in this plan of God. No bomb can be invented, no bacteria can be cultivated and used, no chemicals or gases can be brought into use, that can ever make the slightest difference to these things. That is God's plan as revealed in Scripture, and God's plan will be carried out; and if you and I are in Christ we are involved in it. We are destined to be elevated and restored to what man was meant to be. We shall be 'lords of the creation'. 'Know ye not that the saints shall judge the world . . . (and) angels?' says Paul to the Corinthians (1 Corinthians 6: 2–3). Let us decide to spend less time in reading the newspapers and more time in reading the Bible.

God forbid that we should abuse the Scriptures by reducing them to the level of our ideas or contemporary events. Look at the ultimate, look at God's grand and glorious purpose. Do not be over-particular in your interpretation of contemporary history, do not waste your time in attempts to fix 'times and seasons'. What matters is God's plan, God's eternal scheme, this 'dispensation', this 'economy', this purpose of which we are a part, which is being worked out since the beginning of 'the fulness of times'. Think of, and live for the ultimate restoration of that glorious harmony which is coming, when we with our whole being shall praise 'the Lamb that was slain'. He has redeemed us. Let us sing, 'Blessing and honour and glory and power be unto him that sitteth upon the throne, and unto the Lamb for ever and ever' (Revelation 5:13). Let wars come, let pestilences come, let hell be let loose, 'nothing shall be able to separate us from the love of God which is in Christ Jesus our Lord'. That is the Christian message for today. Thank God for it, and rejoice in it.

18

'We . . . Ye also'

'In whom also we have obtained an inheritance, being predestinated according to the purpose of him who worketh all things after the counsel of his own will: that we should be to the praise of his glory, who first trusted in Christ. In whom ye also trusted, after that ye heard the word of truth, the gospel of your salvation: in whom also after that ye believed, ye were sealed with that holy Spirit of promise, which is the earnest of our inheritance until the redemption of the purchased possession, unto the praise of his glory.'

Ephesians 1:11–14

Clearly one cannot deal with the entire statement in these verses on one occasion; but before we consider the separate statements it is good to deal with the statement as a whole. It is only as we are clear about the general theme, and grasp it, that we can truly appreciate and enjoy the particulars. Here we are looking at the end of the great sentence which, as we have seen, starts at the beginning of verse 3 and runs on to the end of verse 14. That sentence is surely one of the greatest sentences in the entire Bible. Obviously it does not finish at verse 10, because the Apostle goes on to say 'In whom also'. The 'whom' refers to someone already mentioned and the 'also' tells us of something additional. It is important that we should be carrying in our minds the whole sentence as we consider any part of it.

The Apostle is unfolding, let us remember, God's great and eternal purpose. That is stated, in its essence, in the tenth verse. The world is interested in politics and in the headlines in the newspapers; but here we are looking at something beyond all that, something that is unfolding and will continue to unfold, whatever may be happening on the worldly level. We are not saying that what happens on the lower level has no importance whatsoever, but the plan of God is altogether bigger and grander. God's plan and its out-working is also certain, while the world's arrangements are very uncertain. The Apostle has told us that God by the Holy Spirit has given us the 'wisdom' and 'prudence' without which these things remain dark to us and seem utterly remote from life. But once we become enlightened everything becomes clear to us, for we see that God is working out His plan and that we and our whole eternal destiny are involved in it. Having told us that the plan is the restoration of harmony, the Apostle goes on to tell us something of the way in which God is working it out. That is the theme which he now takes up in verse 11. We have looked at the plan in general; and now he brings us on to the details.

The very fact that Paul was writing this letter to the Ephesian Christians was a proof in itself of the carrying out of the plan. It was an amazing fact that such a man as Saul of Tarsus, a 'Hebrew of the Hebrews', should be writing a letter to Gentile Ephesians. He is doing so because it is a part of the unfolding, the carrying out, of this great plan of God. The great illustration that the world has seen so far of the carrying out of God's plan to re-make all things is what is to be seen in the Christian Church, and that is the great theme of this particular Epistle. It is one of the so-called 'Church Epistles', and in it the Apostle gives us his richest teaching with regard to the nature and the character of the Christian Church. The Church is an illustration, the supreme illustration in many ways in time, of God's gigantic, cosmic plan to restore harmony in every realm and sphere.

We cannot but notice in passing the interesting way in which Paul states his themes. Nothing is so absorbingly interesting as to observe his mind in operation. Every writer has his own particular characteristics, his own particular style of writing. Any one at all familiar with the New Testament can tell at once whether a particular paragraph comes from Paul or Peter or John. And the characteristics of the Apostle Paul as a writer are seen very clearly in the verses we are examining. They are seen in the very terms he introduces. Paul is never content with saying anything once, he has to add to it. Here, we find him saying, 'In whom also we have obtained an inheritance'. But he is not content with saying that we have obtained an inheritance, he tells us how this has happened – 'being predestinated according to the purpose of him who woıketh all things after the counsel of his own will'. He has already used similar expressions, but is prepared to continue using them.

I advert to this matter, and emphasize it, for this good reason, that this elaboration is a very good test of our appreciation of the Christian faith. Paul cannot say these things without being astonished and amazed at them. He was not merely interested in these things intellectually; he was not a mere lecturer; he was a preacher, an evangelist, a pastor. He cannot regard these things in a merely detached objective manner. So when he says 'We have obtained an inheritance' he is so amazed at the fact that he seems to wonder how it has happened to us, and he gives us the only possible explanation, which is, that it is 'according to the counsel of God's own will'. A word seems to fire him and he sees the whole panorama of salvation in it.

The pedants, of course, regard this as bad style. The Apostle, we are told, was not a good literary stylist; he lacked a chaste, pruned style; he is ornate, he multiplies his adjectives, he repeats himself, he crowds epithet upon epithet. He is guilty, say the authorities, of 'anacolutha', which means that, having started a line of argument, he allows a word to set him off, and he becomes so carried away and fired by it that he interposes praises to God. He seems to forget what he set out to say, and then returns to it. Sometimes, however, he fails to do so and leaves a sentence unfinished. What I am suggesting is that the 'anacoluthia' are an indication of his spirituality. He was not a mere *littérateur*, not a hack writer; he was not a man who wrote to make his living. He was an evangelist, an Apostle of Christ, and he enjoys writing about Christ and the things of Christ. To him syntax and sentences are not his chief concern. He was interested in the truth; and in these verses he pours it forth upon us.

These fourteen verses, as I have reminded you earlier are the introduction to the whole Epistle, and can be compared to a kind of overture which in an opera or symphony introduces the various themes. The Apostle reminds us of the fact that God is working out this great plan to re-unite, to head up again in Christ the whole cosmos, and now he begins to tell us how God is doing so. Take note, first, of two phrases, one at the beginning of verse 11 and the other at the beginning of verse 13. 'In whom also we have obtained an inheritance', and 'In whom ye also'. In these two phrases Paul shows us the beginning of the carrying out of this great plan. We must be quite clear, of course, about the exact reference of the 'We' to whom he refers in verse 11, and the 'Ye' in verse 13. There are those who say that the 'We' is just a kind of editorial 'we'; that the Apostle is referring to himself, but that instead of saying 'I' he says 'We'. There are others who say that the 'We' includes Jews and Gentiles, all Christians, irrespective of their origins. But surely both ideas are quite untenable.

In my view the 'We' is in contrast to the 'Ye also' – We and You. It is quite clear that the 'You' in verse 13 is a reference to the Gentiles as represented here by the Ephesians and the various other churches to whom this letter was probably sent. So we must insist upon saying that the 'We' here is a reference to the Jews. There is a further argument which clinches this exposition. We note that he says concerning this 'We' in verse 12: 'That we should be to the praise of his glory who first trusted in Christ.' The English Revised Version reads: 'We who had before hoped in Christ'. This supplies proof that the 'We' here is a reference to the Jews. If you take it as we find it in the Authorized Version, where we have 'Who first trusted in Christ', it emphasizes the fact that chronologically Jews believed in Christ before Gentiles began to do so. They believed first, then the others followed. Our Lord told His apostles that they were to be His witnesses 'both in Jerusalem, and in all Judaea, and in Samaria, and unto the uttermost part of the earth' (Acts 1:8). Historically it is the case that the Jews were the first Christians. Or taking the Revised Version, which says, 'Who had before hoped in Christ', it is a reference to the fact that throughout the Old Testament dispensation the Jews were looking forward to the coming of Messiah. In any case it is still a reference to the Jews.

The Apostle emphasizes the 'We' and the 'You' – We Jews, You Gentiles – because of the astounding fact that they have been brought together, they have 'been made one' in Christ. 'In whom also we have obtained an inheritance . . . and Ye also' – we are together in it. This, as I have already suggested, is not only the great theme of this particular Epistle, it is the theme of the whole of the New Testament and particularly of the New Testament Epistles. In this particular Epistle it is pre-eminently the theme. This is seen most explicitly in the second chapter. Paul repeats it many times and is never tired of doing so. In the third chapter he says that the dispensation had been committed to him to reveal the truth 'which in other ages was not made known unto the sons of men, as it is now revealed'. God had now revealed 'unto his holy apostles and prophets by the Spirit, that the Gentiles should be fellow heirs and of the same body' (vv. 2-6).

The Apostle never ceased to be amazed at this, and to be thrilled by it. So in his fourth chapter he says the same thing again. We recall also the interesting phrase he uses in writing to the Romans, where he tells them that what he was proud of above everything else was that he was 'the Apostle of the Gentiles'. He says 'I magnify my office' (Romans 11:13). This had produced a revolution in his life. We know what a narrow, bigoted Jewish nationalist he had been, and how he prided himself on his nationality. It made him intolerant, and the Gentiles were to him but dogs, outsiders. But now he is 'the Apostle of the Gentiles'. And in this Epistle to the Ephesian Gentiles, he must emphasize this marvellous thing God has brought to pass. God's great plan is already in operation; he is a part of it, and they are a part of it!

Paul begins his Epistle to the Romans on the same note: 'by Christ we have received grace and apostleship, for obedience to the faith among all nations' (1:5). Again, 'The same Lord over all is rich unto all that call upon him' (Romans 10:12), wherever they may happen to have come from. Again, in the Epistle to the Galatians, 'There is neither Jew nor Greek, bond nor free, male nor female' (3:28). The old divisions have gone, and to perpetuate such distinctions is a denial of the gospel of Jesus Christ. Such is his teaching, and such is the glory of it. This is the astounding thing that has happened. In the same Epistle to the Galatians he says, 'If ye be Christ's [whether Jew or Gentile], then are ye Abraham's seed, and heirs according to the promise' (3:29). We must get rid of all carnal, materialistic, national ideas. All that is finished; it is the spiritual seed in Abraham and Christ that counts in God's sight. There is a new nation consisting of God's people;

we Christians are God's people. This is the new way, the great theme of the New Testament, the new dispensation; all else has been abolished. God's purpose was to use the Jews temporarily; but now He has something bigger and greater, including both Jews and Gentiles.

Such is the Apostle's argument. If we turn to his Epistle to the Colossians we find it there; we find it everywhere. Perhaps it is true to say that in that bit of autobiography in the third chapter of the Epistle to the Philippians the Apostle expresses the matter most clearly (vv. 4–14). He condemns himself for what he had been and ridicules all his former foolish pride and boasting. However the really important matter is to be clear as to how all this has been done, how God has brought it all to pass. The Apostle tells us in a particularly interesting and entrancing manner; and it becomes the more interesting to us as we remind ourselves of the world as it is, with all its clashes and conflicts and divisions and tensions. In the light of biblical truth and against a world background, how wonderful it is to look at this plan of God as it is unfolded by the Apostle! At the same time it is particularly interesting to observe that God's way in Christ is so very different from that which frequently passes as Christianity at the present time, with all its emphasis on the political and social application of the gospel.

God's way of restoring harmony and unity is to produce Christians, and therefore Paul tells us certain things about the Christian. He gives us a perfect picture of Christianity and, as I understand it, he tells us five things concerning it.

The first thing we are told is that what makes us Christians is that we are 'in Christ'. There is no hope of unity apart from Christianity. There will never be true unity amongst men until men are Christians. There is no conceivable lasting unity and harmony, no hope of restoration to that which God originally made, except as men are made Christians. And we are Christians only as we are 'in Christ'.

Secondly, there are certain things that are true of us as Christians because we are 'in Christ'. Paul tells us what they are.

Thirdly, in a statement which shows both God's side and man's side, Paul gives us an explanation of the way in which we enter into these blessings.

Fourthly, he shows us the guarantee of the fact that we have these blessings, and, still more important, the guarantee of the fact that we shall never lose them. The Holy Spirit is the Seal 'until the redemption of the purchased possession'. At one and the same time He seals it to us and tells us that we are already in the plan.

Fifthly and finally, the Apostle stresses that the ultimate object of all things is the glory of God – 'to the praise of his glory' – 'unto the praise of his glory' (vv. 12, 14).

The first thing, then, is that what reconciles Jew and Gentile – and the only thing that reconciles them – is that they should become Christians, 'in Christ'. To be a Christian means to be in a new relationship to Christ, it means to be 'in Christ'. It does not mean that you have been born in a particular country, or that your parents or grandparents were Christians. Christianity means being 'in Christ'. In other words, God reconciles men by bringing them into a new relationship; and it is purely a question of relationships. All troubles in the world, between nations, between individuals, stem from a failure at some point in the realm of relationships.

There never will be a more perfect illustration of all this than this extraordinary picture of Jew and Gentile. Between them was this middle wall of partition; the Jew looked at himself in a certain way and so did the Gentile. But their relationships were all wrong because each made a god of himself and his position, and there was a clash between these respective gods. The Jew prided himself on being one of God's people, and that he had the law. The divine law had been given to his nation. They did not stop to ask whether they kept the law, whether they honoured it; that did not matter, the important thing was to possess the law. The Gentiles had never had the law; they were not given the law. The Jews despised all others as dogs who were outside the commonwealth of Israel, 'without God in the world'.

But this kind of attitude was not confined to the Jews. It was equally true of Gentiles, for example, the Greeks. The Greeks had a great heritage of learning and of intellectual ability; and there had been an astounding flowering period in the history of the mind of man when the outstanding Greek philosophers – Plato, Socrates, and Aristotle and others – had looked into the problems of life and elaborated their theories and drawn up their plans for Utopia. No one else had done that; they were a race apart, they were unique. The Jews and all others were to them Barbarians. So the Greek prided himself on his superiority.

Thus Jews and Greeks clashed and fought, as they must always do, and as they are doing in the modern world. Such then was the position; there was this division of mankind, this 'middle wall of partition' between them. Today we talk about 'curtains' – iron curtain and bamboo curtain – but they are in reality walls which have been built carefully by both sides. Each one is repairing the wall on his side. This is true of the life of the world today with all its clashes and divisions and unhappiness.

The Christian way is only one way of dealing with such a situation. But this does not mean, as so many teach, that what is needed is the application of the teaching of Christ to modern problems, and that the Church's business is to tell people how to behave in a Christian manner and to apply Christian principles. That is not the teaching of Paul. There is no greater heresy, in a sense, than to expect Christian conduct from people who are not Christians. Why should they behave in a Christian manner? They do not agree with Christian teaching and do not accept it. No one can live the Christian life without first becoming a Christian. The Apostle makes that quite clear in the second chapter of our Epistle where he says '. . . not of works, lest any man should boast; for we are his workmanship, created in Christ Jesus unto good works' (vv. 9–10). We have to be 'created in Christ' before we can do good works; we have to be alive before we can act. A dead man cannot act, and all who are not in Christ are 'dead in trespasses and sins'. They cannot carry out Christian teaching and have never done so.

I emphasize this because it is sometimes a stumbling block to Christians of weak faith, and is certainly a stumbling-block to many outside the Church. The difficulty presents itself in the following way. A man says to us, I cannot possibly believe in your Christianity; it has been preached and taught for nearly two thousand years, yet look at the world! They say, 'If your message is right, well then, why is not the world better than it is?' The answer is that true Christianity has never claimed that the world would become better and better in that way, for it is not a teaching to be applied by men as they are. It only works when men are together 'in Christ', in a new relationship.

Let us see how this has happened. What was it that brought Paul and the Ephesians together? What was it that made Jew and Gentile bow together on their knees to God and pray in one spirit? Christ is the answer. Christ came and lived and taught and died, and rose again for Jew and Gentile alike, for the Jew had not kept the law any more than the Gentile, and was condemned by the very law of which he boasted. When Paul, the Jew, saw the true meaning of the law and its spiritual character, and especially the meaning of the Cross, he saw that 'the whole world was lying guilty before God', that 'there is none righteous, no, not one'. The Jew was no better than the Gentile. 'All have sinned and come short of the glory of God' (Romans 3:9–23). The Jew is not superior to the Greek, the Greek is not superior to the Jew. They are all together grovelling in the dust in utter failure, and sinners in the sight of a holy God. They are made one even in condemnation and in sin. The pride is taken out of both, they are crushed to the ground. There is nothing that one can boast of as against the other; they are all equally hopeless.

But then the Gospel goes on to tell them that both can be redeemed and reconciled to God and to one another by the blood of Christ. It is only because Christ has made Himself responsible for their guilt and failure, and has died for them, that they can have this reconciliation; and they both receive it in exactly the same way. It is not the law that brings anyone into it; it is not philosophy that does so; it is Christ who brings both in. They are equal at every point. Both alike also need strength and power to lead this new life into which they have been brought; so they are given the same Holy Spirit, they are given the same new nature. Christ is in them and they are in Christ. It is all 'in him', and it all comes out of Him, and they all enjoy it together. They are created anew, born again, 'in Christ'. 'In whom we. . . . in whom ye . . .' (Ephesians 1: 11, 13).

The Church is largely wasting her time in talking politics, and in imagining that, if you give people the Christian ethic and urge them to practise it, the problems of the world will be solved. It cannot be done: regeneration is essential. God produces this final harmony again by regeneration, a new creation, new men in a new world – 'new heavens and a new earth wherein dwelleth righteousness'. That is God's method. It is only as we are all 'in Christ' that we can be reconciled. We become members severally of His body. 'Ye are the body of Christ, and members in particular' and so the eye does not say to the foot 'I have no need of thee', nor does the hand speak thus to any other part. All the parts are essential (1 Corinthians 12:14–27). That is the picture. All one – not in Christ as a teacher, but vitally, spiritually, mystically, members of His body and united in Him by the Holy Spirit.

The second matter we have to consider is what becomes true of us as Christians because we are 'in Christ'. Paul states this in a most interesting manner by saying, 'in whom also we have obtained an inheritance'. That is how it is expressed in the Authorized Version but the English Revised Version reads, 'in whom also we were made a heritage'. So the two versions differ at this point. The Revised Standard Version is pitifully weak and simply has the word 'appointed' and so misses the rich meaning of the word the Apostle used. He actually used a very interesting and old word, and this is the only place where it is used in the New Testament. It is a word that carries the meaning and conveys the idea of an inheritance obtained by casting a lot, or the drawing of lots. The difference in the translations found in the Authorized and the Revised Versions is due to the fact that the word is used in the passive tense; and it was because they were impressed by this that the revisers used the word 'heritage' instead of 'inheritance'. Because the blessing described is not the result of something we have done – indeed we are passive – they translated it as 'made a heritage'. But surely they were quite wrong. If they had remembered the context instead of concentrating on the word only, they would never have fallen into that error. A better translation would be, 'We have been made, possessors, or inheritors, by lot'; or 'We have been endowed with an inheritance by lot'.

I insist upon this, and say that the Authorized Version is very much nearer the truth. And for the following reason: in the fourteenth verse the Apostle definitely and explicitly speaks about an inheritance – 'Which is the earnest of our inheritance until the redemption of the purchased possession'. It is true, of course, to say that Christians are God's heritage. Paul himself says so in verse 18 of this first chapter, but here he is not emphasizing that truth, but rather our inheritance. What he says here is that the Jew and the Gentile are made one, not only because they have their sins forgiven in the same way, but also because they are inheritors together of the same heritage. 'We' have obtained a stake in it, says Paul, and 'you' have obtained a stake in it: we are in it together, we are 'fellow-heirs'.

It seems quite clear that this is what the Apostle is saying here. As I have already reminded you, in the third chapter he says that the special message committed to him was that the Gentiles should be 'fellow-heirs and of the same body'. Indeed he says the same in the second chapter in verses 12 and 13 – 'That at that time ye were without Christ, being aliens from the commonwealth of Israel, and strangers from the covenants of promise, having no hope and without God in the world. But now in Christ Jesus ye who sometimes were far off are made nigh by the blood of Christ' and have become members of 'the household of God' (v. 19). They are now in the same family.

In Christ Jew and Gentile are not only fellow-heirs together; still more wonderful, they are joint-heirs with Christ. That is the statement of the Apostle in his Epistle to the Romans in chapter 8, verse 17 – 'If children, then heirs; heirs of God, and (therefore) joint-heirs with Christ'. We are 'in him', we belong to Him, and therefore we are joint-heirs with Him – joint-heirs with one another and joint-heirs with Him. Everything is in Christ.

Were we to grasp this as we should we would not only be the happiest people on the face of the earth, we would also 'rejoice with joy unspeakable, and full of glory'. We would do so because with Paul we would realize that we have an interest in all this, we have a stake in it; we belong to the people who are going to share it. The great day is coming when sin and evil will be destroyed, and the devil will be cast into the lake of perdition. This perfect harmony will then be restored in the entire cosmos.

Such is the blessing that comes to one who is 'in Christ', a Christian. He is an heir of all blessing; he is going to be an inheritor of it. And so are all his fellow Christians. So we look forward together.

Ultimately it means seeing God. It means being with Christ and enjoying His glory. It means reigning with Christ: if we suffer with Him we shall also reign with Him. The kingdom of God and of His Christ is coming; and nothing can stop it. And we who are 'in Christ' are certain to be there. We shall be on this new earth and under the new heavens, and we shall enjoy Paradise, and eat of its celestial fruits. We shall spend our eternity doing so. We shall 'judge men', we shall 'judge angels', because we are 'in Christ'. With Him we shall enjoy that eternally blessed state which shall never end.

Men and women who believe this truth, and who know that it is true of themselves, are not over-interested in this world and what happens in it. The nations fight because they want to spread their empires, or to take a piece of land. The same is true of individuals. It is so because of their sense of values. People fight over money, over position, over popularity, over anything. It results from their possessiveness, selfishness, greed. Those are the only things they care about and value; and as long as they look at things in that way they will continue to fight and quarrel about them, no matter how educated and 'advanced' they may be. If it will suit their purposes to adopt Christian principles they will do so; nations have often used Christianity to spread empires! But that is not Christianity. The essence of the Christian's position is that he has seen the inheritance 'incorruptible and undefiled and that fadeth not away, reserved in heaven' by God, for them who are in Christ Jesus. A man who has had no more than a glimpse of such things rides very lightly to this life and its affairs. He has 'set his affection on things above, not on things on the earth', and he knows that all others who have done so are fellow heirs with him. So the fight and the quarrel and the middle wall have gone. We are all one, we are looking for the same things. The only harmony that this world will ever know is the harmony that is produced in and through men and women who in Christ have set their affection on the things above. 'In whom also *we* have obtained an inheritance; in whom *ye* also . . .'.

As John Newton says –

> *Fading is the worldling's pleasure,*
> *All his boasted pomp and show;*
> *Solid joys and lasting treasure*
> *None but Zion's children know.*

Oh the joy of being among the redeemed, the joy of knowing that though we may be stripped of everything here, our final inheritance is guaranteed and safe and sure! Have you got a stake in it? Has a 'lot' been given to you? It has, says Paul, to all who are 'in Christ', who have hope in Him.

19
The Counsel of His own Will

'In whom also we have obtained an inheritance,
being predestinated according to the purpose of him
who worketh all things after the counsel of his own
will: that we should be to the praise of his glory,
who first trusted in Christ. In whom ye also trusted,
after that ye heard the word of truth, the gospel of
your salvation: in whom also after that ye believed,
ye were sealed with that holy Spirit of promise,
which is the earnest of our inheritance until the
redemption of the purchased possession, unto the
praise of his glory.'

Ephesians 1:11–14

We continue our discussion of the Apostle's great statement. He
has announced that the great secret which God has revealed
concerning His purpose is that in this present age, and in Christ,
He has reunited the discordant parts, the separate parts, into
which sin has divided the world and the whole cosmos. God is
restoring the original harmony, in heaven and on earth, and He is
doing so in and through our Lord Jesus Christ. In the dispensation of the fulness of times it is His purpose that He might
'gather together in one all things in Christ, both which are in
heaven and which are on earth, even in him'. In these verses we
are considering the ways in which God is doing this, and have
already given attention to the first, and indeed in many senses the
chief way, namely, the formation and the growth of the Christian
Church. The Church is the new Israel, the spiritual Israel, the true
seed of Abraham, and she consists of Jews and Gentiles. But the
unity is established, as we have seen, by making these different
people Christians, and the Apostle incidentally tells us a number
of things about the Christian. We have already considered two
of them.

Now we come to consider, in the third place, the way in which all this has happened to us, how this has ever become true of us, knowing ourselves as we do. How does anyone become a Christian? How does anyone enter into this position in which he is 'in Christ' and a 'joint-heir' with Christ? Fortunately the Apostle deals with that subject also. He is not content with saying that this is true of us, he tells us how it has become true. And he does so, of course, because this was something at which he never ceased to wonder. As we proceed we find Paul using a number of terms which we have already encountered. We met them in verses 4 and 5. They include certain great terms and phrases which are to be found throughout the New Testament, terms which are absolutely essential to a true and ultimate understanding of the Gospel: 'In whom also we have obtained an inheritance, being predestinated according to the purpose of him who worketh all things after the counsel of his own will.' In verses 4 and 5 we find: 'According as he hath chosen us in him before the foundation of the world, that we should be holy and without blame before him in love: having predestinated us unto the adoption of children by Jesus Christ to himself.' Such are the terms. We are here face to face with high doctrine, with some of the great profundities of the Christian faith and the Christian message. Someone may ask: Why does the Apostle repeat these terms here, having already used them in verses 4 and 5? The explanation is not only simple but very important. In verses 4 and 5 the Apostle was taking a general view of God's purpose, he was looking at it, as it were, from that eternal standpoint. Now he is not merely looking at it in general, but also in its particular application to us. There, it was the great scheme itself; here, it is the scheme as applied to us. But he still uses the same terms as he used there. They apply not only to the thought but also to the application.

Many Christian people never study these terms, never dwell on them, never turn them over in their minds. Let me prove that contention by asking a question. How often have you heard anyone going slowly, and term by term, through this great chapter? Or, how often have you read them yourself in this way? Are we not in danger of avoiding these great terms because of certain associations which they have? This is something of which we, as Christian people, need to be very wary at this present hour, for certain aspects of New Testament truth are just not being considered at all because of an element of controversy attached to them. Large numbers of Christian people are totally ignorant of prophetic truth, for instance, because their attitude to it is determined by the fact that it leads to argument and wrangling about various theories. They imagine that that is a wise and sound position to take up. But what they are actually doing is deliberately to ignore God's Word; they are deliberately by-passing certain aspects and elements of God's revealed Truth. God means us to study and to face everything in His word whether it is difficult or simple, whether involved in controversy or otherwise. To say 'peace at any price' at the expense of God's revealed truth is surely an insult to God. These matters have to be faced, whether it is the truth concerning prophecy or whether it be the truth concerning these high matters of doctrine which the Apostle puts before us in these verses, as he has already done in verses 4 and 5.

How, then, do we approach the truth? First of all without prejudice. We all start with prejudices; we take up positions, and having taken them up, we argue for them and we defend them. We say 'I have always said this; my parents said it before me; I have always been taught to believe this; therefore I stand . . .' So it often happens that we have never really considered the Scripture teaching concerning these matters. We may never have read a book on the subject, or considered what those whom God has called and appointed as leaders in the Church throughout the centuries have said and taught concerning it. We start with a prejudice and we hold on to it, and feel that it is a part of our personality. We must defend it! Our minds are so shut and closed that we do not even consider the question. It is surely unnecessary to point out that that is a totally un-Christian attitude. Nothing is further removed from the Christian position. This was the attitude of the Pharisees, and it was the reason why they hated our Lord and His teaching. It was the same attitude that opposed the Apostles wherever they went to preach. This new theory, this new idea and teaching offended people's prejudices. May God give us grace to rid ourselves of the prejudices to which we are all liable, and to which we are subject as the result of sin.

[223]

The second matter which I would emphasize is that we must submit ourselves and our minds entirely to the Scripture. We must make a positive effort to ensure that we come to the Scripture as if we knew nothing, and that we allow the Scripture to speak to us, instead of reading our thoughts into the Scripture. This is an extremely difficult matter for all of us, because we all have preconceived notions which tend to become spectacles through which we look at Scripture. But we must submit ourselves to the Scripture.

I emphasize this negatively by saying that we must not come to these matters in terms of philosophy. We all tend to start with original or inherited ideas as to what God should do, and what it is right for God to do, and if God does not behave in that way, then we may even impute unfairness to Him. This is philosophy; this is an example of a philosopher pitting his mind against God's revelation. Nothing is more dangerous. Because they behave in such a manner many people show themselves to be most un-Christian. They say, 'I cannot understand this idea of the Incarnation – two natures in one person' – and so they reject it. The insistence on understanding is a part of philosophy. They do not understand the Atonement, they say, and therefore do not believe it. Most people who reject the gospel of salvation do so simply because they say they cannot understand it. Technically they are not philosophers; nevertheless they are speaking philosophically.

I emphasize therefore that it is of vital importance that we submit our minds to the Scriptures and their revelation and that we cease to think philosophically. In other words we must realize that we are face to face with something which we cannot understand. I will go further, it is something that we are not meant to understand before we believe. We recall how the Apostle deals with the position of a man who puts up his objection in this way. The Apostle simply replies by saying, 'Nay but, O man, who art thou that repliest against God?' (Romans 9:20). This truth is not to be understood, says Paul in effect, it is to be received. This is what God Himself has told us, and if you imagine that you can understand and span the mind of the Lord you are simply betraying the fact that your whole idea of God is wrong. That is ultimately the real trouble with all unbelievers; their thinking about God is all wrong. 'Who hath known the mind of the Lord, or who hath been his counsellor?' This is the question asked by Isaiah (40:13) and quoted in the New Testament (Romans 11:34). We are face to face here with the mystery of God's eternal mind; and it is so high above us that we should not even begin to try to understand it. We must come humbly to it and look at it and receive it. If you try to have a final understanding of these matters, or hope to be able to reconcile certain things intellectually, you are not only doomed to failure, but you are guilty of trying to do something which the Apostle rebukes in the strongest and clearest manner in the ninth chapter of the Epistle to the Romans. Further rebukes are found in the second chapter of his First Epistle to the Corinthians, for example: 'The natural man receiveth not the things of the Spirit of God.'

We are now able to approach these great matters in the right manner. The words of our text convey a truth meant for Christian people only; it is not a truth to be preached in an evangelistic service. It is a truth for the children, it is a truth for those who have been let into the secret; for those who have been given the Holy Spirit, who enlightens the mind and who gives under-standing. It is not for the natural man who does not understand any part of salvation, and least of all this. But it is a truth which the children of God throughout the centuries have always found to be most consoling, most encouraging and most reassuring. The right way to approach it is by remembering that the control-ling element in these matters is always the glory of God. 'That we should be to the praise of his glory, who first trusted in Christ'; again, 'which is the earnest of our inheritance until the redemption of the purchased possession, unto the praise of his glory'. The paragraph started with the words, 'Blessed be the God and Father of our Lord Jesus Christ'. You must start there and end there. We found it again in verse 6: 'to the praise of the glory of his grace wherein he hath made us accepted in the beloved.'

In every view of salvation the place given in it to the glory of God provides the ultimate test. The proof that it is truly scriptural is that it gives *all* the glory to God. None must be reserved for ourselves or for anyone else. The Apostle keeps on repeating it – 'to the glory of God', 'the glory of his grace', 'to his glory'.

[225]

Elsewhere he writes, 'But of him are ye in Christ Jesus, who of God is made unto us wisdom and righteousness and sanctification and redemption; that, according as it is written, He that glorieth, let him glory in the Lord' (1 Corinthians 1:30–31). My view of the way in which I have become a Christian must satisfy the test that it promotes and ministers to the glory of God. Salvation comes to us in spite of ourselves; we are nothing. We are not Christians because of our particular character or because of anything that we have done. It is all of God. The Apostle emphasizes this in the second chapter of this Epistle when he writes: 'For by grace are ye saved through faith, and that not of yourselves, it is the gift of God; not of works lest any man should boast' (v. 8). There is to be no self-glorying; no man must glory in himself.

This teaching is not confined to the Epistle to the Ephesians; it is to be found everywhere in Scripture. It runs as a great theme throughout the New Testament, perhaps most clearly of all in the Gospel of John. This particular aspect of truth is found most clearly on the lips of our blessed Lord and Saviour Himself as seen in the sixth chapter and the tenth chapter of John's Gospel. It is found likewise in the high priestly prayer in the seventeenth chapter. But it is equally true to say that it is the outstanding doctrine of the Old Testament also. It alone explains why Israel was the chosen race, why the Jews were the chosen people. It was not because of anything in them. Indeed, someone has said – and I believe there is a great deal of justification for so saying – that God chose them in order to show that if He could make something of such people He could do so with anyone. Consider their story as found in the Old Testament; nothing could be more miserable or hopeless. Their salvation was of God, and God says so, and says so specifically to them. He tells them plainly and repeatedly that He had not chosen them because there was anything meritorious in them, but for His own Name's sake, and that His glory might be manifested. The entire story in the Old Testament from the call of Abraham onwards is of God. 'You only have I known of all the families of the earth,' He says through the prophet Amos (Amos 3:2).

That is the over-all aspect of the truth, but Paul breaks it up into its component parts. The first thing he tells us is that God has 'purposed' all this. 'In whom also we have obtained an inheritance, being predestinated according to the purpose of Him . . .' This word 'purpose' emphasizes the fact that the original idea, the thought in its very inception, was something that had God for its author. The eternal God devised the purpose of restoring this unity, this harmony, and of doing so in terms of certain people 'before the foundation of the world'. But then the Apostle adds to that by saying, '. . . according to the purpose of him who worketh all things after the counsel of his own will'. This most important phrase, 'the counsel of his own will', is added, it seems to me, to safeguard the previous idea that the purpose is entirely and only God's; for which reason the Apostle has already said the same thing before. He did so in verse 5: 'Having predestinated us unto the adoption of children by Jesus Christ to himself, according to the good pleasure of his will.' Again in verse 9: 'Having made known unto us the mystery of his will, according to his good pleasure which he hath purposed in himself.' The repetition is the Apostle's way of saying that this purpose which God has conceived was not suggested to God by anyone else. I quote again the question of the fortieth chapter of Isaiah: 'Who hath directed the Spirit of the Lord, or being his counsellor hath taught him?' (v. 13). All is 'according to the counsel of God's own will'.

No-one suggested to God that it might be good to do this or that. It was not only not suggested to Him by anyone else, it was not even suggested to God, as some have supposed, by reason of His foreknowledge whereby He saw that certain people were going to think and do certain things, in consequence of which His own thoughts were determined. Such an idea is a complete denial of what the Apostle teaches here. Everything is according to the counsel of His own will. He thought with Himself, He deliberated and meditated with Himself. The whole plan of salvation from beginning to end is exclusively of God, with nothing at all from the outside. Everything originates in God, everything comes out from God. I said at the beginning that we were considering high doctrine. There is nothing more glorious than this, that God should have been pleased to reveal these things to us. That is why we should constantly thank God for the Bible and its teachings, which emphasize the application of God's grand design to you and me.

We are not considering some abstract truth. Before time, before
the creation of the world, God purposed, according to the
counsel of His own will, to restore harmony to the whole of the
cosmos; and in particular He has purposed that you and I should
have a part and place in it – 'In whom also we have obtained an
inheritance'. We have this part and place because God predestinated us to it according to the purpose which He purposed
according to the counsel of His own will. The result is that you
and I are sharing in this, and have tasted of the heavenly gift. You
and I know something about the 'firstfruits' of everlasting bliss
and glory. You and I are what we are for the reason that God
purposed according to the counsel of His own will that we
should be in it and should be sharers of it.

'Predestinated' means 'pre-determined'. What can be greater or
more staggering than this, that God thought of me, thought of
you there in the counsel of His own will! He not only conceived
the plan, He saw us in it. 'We,' says Paul – 'we Jews, who first
trusted in Christ were predestinated, and you Gentiles also have a
part in this inheritance. God has pre-determined that we should
both be in it, Jews and Gentiles. We are not only in the mind
and the heart of God; we were always there. We are there
now because we were there before the foundation of the
world.'

It is God also who works out this purpose. This is the most
amazing and the most consoling and comforting truth we can
ever know. It is the whole basis of my assurance at this present
moment; it is also the guarantee of my future. It is God Himself
who put me where I am, and 'He which hath begun a good work
in you will perform it until the day of Jesus Christ' (Philippians
1:6). I am in this plan of God, and I am what I am in spite of my
sin, in spite of all that is so true of me, in spite of the fact that I
was, with others, 'dead in trespasses and sins'. 'Being predestinated according to the purpose of him who worketh all things
according to the counsel of his own will.'

But we must not only think of it in a personal sense. This
purpose conceived in the eternal mind of God, beyond the
particular reference to you and to me, has in mind also the 'fulness
of the Gentiles' and the 'fulness of the Jews'. That will constitute
the great kingdom, the people, the family of God, gathered in that

[228]

way, and being gathered throughout the centuries. Such is God's plan.

In describing how this plan actually finds fulfilment, how it actually comes to us, how it begins to operate, the Apostle uses the word 'worketh' – 'In whom also we have obtained an inheritance, being predestinated according to the purpose of him who *worketh* all things after the counsel of his own will'. This is the Apostle's way of saying that God is not only entirely responsible for the initiation and the conception of the purpose, He is equally responsible for carrying it out. This, again, is of the very essence of the teaching of the Bible. It is indeed, in many ways, the whole story of the Bible. When man fell God immediately revealed His purpose. Man had listened to the devil, had sinned, had fallen; and in doing so had dragged the whole of humanity down with him. The earth itself had been cursed, and the harmony of God's cosmos had given place to strife and trouble.

God announced His plan, His purpose, by saying that the seed of the woman would bruise the serpent's head. As we read through the Old Testament we see God working out that plan. He is the worker, the one who does all. 'We are his workmanship.' Nothing is of us – 'Not of works, lest any man should boast' (Ephesians 2:9). As we read the history we see God bringing about the Flood yet saving a remnant, just one family – eight souls, Noah and his family. It was He who told them what to do to save themselves; He put them into the ark. We come later to the call of Abraham. This is all a part of the working out of God's great purpose. He was preparing for the coming of His Son, the Messiah, in whom the plan centred. But the preparation was necessary; and the preparation was entirely the work of God. He looked at Abraham in his pagan surroundings and He called him out from them. That was another vital step in the working out of the plan. He turned that man into a nation. Then come the patriarchs and their descendants, the children of Israel. We soon see them as slaves in Egypt and in an apparently hopeless situation. But God delivers them out of Egypt and leads them into Canaan. Constantly they sin and go astray, and He sends them prophets to warn them. Eventually they are carried away into captivity in Babylon; but He brings a remnant back into Canaan. Had the plan of God been dependent upon the Jews it would have foundered. But it was God Himself who was working it out.

Then, 'when the fulness of the time was come, God sent forth his Son, made of a woman, made under the law, to redeem them that were under the law, that we might receive the adoption of sons' (Galatians 4:4–5). God is now working out His plan through His Son. The Son came to work out our salvation. He obeyed the law, gave manifestations of His glory, and bore the sins of His own people in His own body on the tree, thereby making an atonement for our sins. Then He rose from the grave and ascended to heaven and sent down the Holy Spirit. It is all God's work; it is God working out His own purpose in all things 'according to the counsel of his own will'. And it is being worked out in us as well. Were it not so, not one of us would be a Christian. He quickens us, He convicts us, He regenerates us, and gives us His Spirit to dwell within us.

But someone may ask, What of the injunction, 'Work out your own salvation with fear and trembling'? The answer is: 'It is God who worketh in you both to will and to do of his good pleasure' (Philippians 2:13). It is God who has given us 'the Spirit that searcheth all things, yea the deep things of God', otherwise we would never understand these things at all. From beginning to end God is working out His great scheme and purpose. In the eighth chapter of the Epistle to the Romans the Apostle says in verse 28: 'We know that all things work together for good to them that love God, to them that are the called according to his purpose.' We note there the same terms – 'purpose', 'called', 'work'. Then Paul continues: 'For whom he did foreknow he also did predestinate to be conformed to the image of his Son, that he might be the firstborn among many brethren. Moreover, whom he did predestinate, them he also called, and whom he called, them he also justified; and whom he justified, them he also glorified.' It is God who works it all, from the beginning to the very end – 'He'! 'He'! 'He'!

But that is not the end of the story: it is only the beginning. It explains to us why and how we have become Christians. It explains why we are interested in these things, and enjoy public worship, and why we are not still living a worldly life as so many others do. It is nothing special or exceptional in us; it is not that we are different from or better than others by nature. We are no better than the world, any more than Jacob was better than Esau. Indeed it might well be that the reverse was the case. As a natural man Esau seems to have been a much better and finer and nicer type than Jacob. Salvation is based upon nothing in us. It is the fruit of God's purpose, 'according to the counsel of his own will'. It is the out-working by Himself of what He has predestinated, pre-determined.

We shall go on to consider the means God uses in order to do this, the way in which God works it out, and what He asks of us in the working out of His own great and glorious purpose. But we have started, as we must, where the Apostle begins, because what must ever be most prominent is the glory of God. 'That we might be to the praise of his glory, who first trusted in Christ.'

20

'Heard, Believed, Trusted'

'In whom also we have obtained an inheritance,
being predestinated according to the purpose of him
who worketh all things after the counsel of his own
will: that we should be to the praise of his glory,
who first trusted in Christ. In whom ye also trusted,
after that ye heard the word of truth, the gospel of
your salvation: in whom also after that ye believed,
ye were sealed with that holy Spirit of promise,
which is the earnest of our inheritance until the
redemption of the purchased possession, unto the
praise of his glory.'

Ephesians 1:11–14

We have seen that we are Christians because God works out His
own plan, and that in doing so He uses means. Here, we are told
exactly what those means are which God uses in order to place
us 'in Christ', in order to make us inheritors of the inheritance
which God has prepared for us in our blessed Lord and Saviour.
In verse 13 Paul says: 'In whom ye also trusted, after that ye
heard the word of truth, the gospel of your salvation'. These
words describe the means which God always uses in order to
make Christians. In the Book of the Acts of the Apostles we see
it clearly in practice. The Lord Jesus Christ, the Head of the
Church, to whom this work has been entrusted left but a handful
of people on earth when He ascended to heaven. It seemed quite
impossible that this great scheme of God could be carried out by
a mere handful of people – and such people! But it happened!
The Apostles were told to wait in Jerusalem until the Holy Ghost
should come upon them, and then they were to go out and to be
witnesses to Christ. They were to preach the Word. And they
went, as recorded in the Book of the Acts of the Apostles. This is
God's way of making Christians out of us. It is by means of, and
through the instrumentality of the 'word of truth, the gospel of
our salvation'.

The Apostle calls it 'the word of truth'. But that does not simply mean that it is a true word. It *is* a true word, of course, but Paul does not mean truth indiscriminately. He means a particular truth through which, and by means of which, we all receive our salvation – 'the word of truth, the gospel of your salvation'. It is a word that conveys a given truth which, when we see it, comes to us as the greatest good news we have ever known. It is the good news concerning the Lord Jesus Christ, the news concerning His Person, and the news concerning His work – who He is and what He has done. That, and nothing else, is the good news; and no one can become a Christian apart from this 'word of truth'.

Stated negatively it means that you do not become a Christian simply by having an experience or by having a different feeling within you from what you had formerly. Many think that that is what makes us Christians. Because they are now living a new kind of life they think they are necessarily Christians. But that may not be so. You cannot be a Christian apart from the truth, 'the gospel of your salvation'. This is fundamental. We are constantly reading in the newspapers of people who are praised and acclaimed as 'the greatest Christians of the century', but who sometimes believe in nothing except what they call 'reverence for life'. They do not believe 'the word of truth', they do not believe the Word of God: their position is not dependent on the Person of Christ and His work. There are many who think of Christians as those who are 'living a good life', making a great sacrifice to help others and to do good works. But such thinking is mistaken; there is no such thing as being a Christian apart from this 'word of truth'. This is God's way of making Christians; it is through 'the word of truth', the gospel of our salvation.

There are many agencies in the world which can give us experiences and a good feeling, and make us feel happy, and lead us to do much good. There are many cults which can produce such results. Our Christian argument against the cults is not that they do not lead to results but that they are not based on truth, for they do not present the word of truth. They certainly produce results. It would be ridiculous to deny that many cults have done good. There are people who testify that since they have become followers of a certain cult their whole life has been changed. They are now happy whereas formerly they were miserable; they have

[233]

lost their worries; they have got rid of certain pains; they are feeling altogether better in every way, and life is full of joy and happiness. Hence we have to insist that it is 'the word of truth' which God uses. It is through the gospel of our salvation; it is through the message that was delivered to the Apostles and which they were empowered to deliver to us. It is that alone which makes us Christian.

We can and must state this matter dogmatically. Consider a person who hitherto has been quite godless and irreligious, utterly heedless about all religious matters, and living a life of sin. This person suddenly finds a new interest, he begins to feel that after all there is something in religion. He begins to think that religion will help him, and someone tells him that all he has to do is to believe in God. He takes this up, and begins to read the Bible and to pray, and to worship God as he thinks best. He feels better as the result of so doing. He is now a religious person and he has this high intent of worshipping God and pleasing Him, and living to the glory of God.

Now I do not hesitate to assert that if that man's experience stops at that point he is not a Christian in the true sense of the term. The Christian is one who realizes that his entire position depends alone upon the Person and work of our Lord and Saviour Jesus Christ. 'The word of truth', 'the gospel of our salvation' is essential. The man whom I have just been describing is in exactly the same position as Old Testament Jews. They believed in God, they tried to please God and to keep His commandments, and to worship Him. They often sacrificed much in order to do so. That was the position of the Pharisees. They fasted twice in the week, and gave a tenth of their goods to the poor; they worshipped and lived for God according to their own way of thought. But they were not Christians, and they were great opponents of the Lord Jesus Christ.

What differentiates us from those who are not Christian is that we depend entirely upon this 'word of truth', this 'gospel of our salvation'. It is not good news to be told that you should worship God and please God. The good news is to be told of what God has done for us in Christ. That is gospel; it is this salvation which is available as the result of what the Lord Jesus Christ has done. Hence we read of the Apostle Paul exhorting young Timothy to 'preach the Word'. He does not tell him simply to exhort people to worship God or to live better lives, or to seek a certain experience. His exhortation is 'Preach the word', do the work of an evangelist (2 Timothy 4: 2,5). We read of ordinary Christians in Acts who 'went everywhere preaching the word' (8:4).

But we must be careful to give the full content of this word 'truth', for Christianity can be mis-used as a psychological agency. Furthermore there are many who have never known certain aspects of this word of truth who seem to think that they are Christian. But it is quite clear in the New Testament that there was an irreducible minimum which was deemed to be essential. In the first chapter of the First Epistle to the Thessalonians we are given a striking synopsis of this 'word of truth'. The Apostle Paul did not stay long at Thessalonica, but he stayed long enough to give them the essential truth, and he reminded them of this saying: 'They themselves show of us what manner of entering in we had unto you, and how ye turned to God from idols to serve the living and true God; and to wait for his Son from heaven, whom he raised from the dead, even Jesus, which delivered us from the wrath to come' (vv. 9, 10). Before we begin to talk about living a happier and a better life we must be aware of the need of being delivered from 'the wrath to come'. We cannot be Christians without having a conviction of sin. To be a Christian means that we realize that we are guilty before God and under the wrath of God. The Apostle had preached this same message to the learned philosophers in Athens and had told them that God had 'appointed a day in the which he will judge the world in righteousness' by Jesus Christ (Acts 17:31).

By nature we are all under the wrath of God, we are all sinners; so before we begin to ask for a happy feeling or an 'experience' we have to realize our dangerous position. We are condemned by God's law, we are under His wrath, we are in danger of eternal perdition. We need to be delivered from 'the wrath to come'. The good news of salvation is that we can be delivered from the wrath to come because the Lord Jesus Christ has borne the wrath Himself on our behalf. The Apostle Paul in writing to the Corinthians makes it clear that his work as a preacher was to proclaim that 'All things are of God, who hath reconciled us to himself by Jesus Christ, and hath given to us the ministry of reconciliation, to wit, that God was in Christ, reconciling the world unto himself'. But lest there be any misunderstanding he works it out in detail for his readers and adds, 'not imputing their trespasses unto them; and hath committed unto us [the preachers] the word of reconciliation. Now then we are ambassadors for Christ, as though God did beseech you by us: we pray you in Christ's stead, be ye reconciled to God. For he hath made him to be sin for us who knew no sin, that we might be made the righteousness of God in him' (2 Corinthians 5: 18–21). The good news of salvation is that God has done all in Christ, He has delivered us from the wrath to come, He has reconciled us to Himself. He has prepared for us this inheritance, and has made us His children. It is all the result of the fact that God has taken our sins and put them on His own Son and punished and dealt with them there. Thus He forgives us and gives us all these benefits. That is the message of salvation. That is 'the word of truth'. It is not sufficient that we should ask ourselves whether we believe in God, and try to worship God and to please God and to live a good life. Do we realize what God has done for us in Christ? Has this 'word of truth' come to us? Do I realize that my whole position is based upon this word of truth, the gospel, the good news of salvation?

There is another statement of this truth by this same Apostle in his First Epistle to Timothy where he says, that God 'will have all men to be saved' (2:4). But note that he is very careful to add immediately that that means 'to come to a knowledge of the truth'. It is not sufficient to be able to say, 'I am living a changed life, I am a different man, I am a better man than I was'. The vital question is, Have you a knowledge of the truth? do you know what you believe? can you give a 'reason for the hope that is in you?' The Apostle Peter says that we must be ready at all times to give a reason for the hope that is in us 'with meekness and fear' (1 Peter 3:15). So the Christian is one who has a knowledge of the truth, and the Word of truth, and he knows that all has come to him through that Word. God does this work in us by means of and through the Word.

Yet even the proclamation of the Word alone is not enough. We cannot read the Book of the Acts of the Apostles without finding evidence of this. We see the Apostles preaching the gospel to a crowd of people. It may be Peter or it may be Paul who is preaching this 'word of truth', 'the gospel of salvation'. But the result varies; some believe and some do not believe. Some not only believe but begin to rejoice; others are furious and begin to persecute and say, 'These men who have turned the world upside down are come hither also' (17:6). The Apostles were sometimes stoned; and men tried to kill them. Both parties, believers and unbelievers, had listened to the same word; so obviously it is not just a question of presenting the message. That has to be done because the word of truth is essential; but the mere presentation of the word of truth does not in and of itself accomplish the work. The additional essential factor is the work of the Holy Spirit.

The application of the truth of the Word is made by the Spirit. This is seen clearly in a statement by the Apostle in the first chapter of the First Epistle to the Thessalonians. The Apostle says in verse 5: 'Our gospel came not unto you in word only, but also in power, and in the Holy Ghost, and in much assurance'. Obviously, this is a vital statement, and he emphasizes it in all his writings. In the second chapter of this Epistle to the Ephesians he states it thus, 'And you hath he quickened, who were dead in trespasses and sins' (v. 1). He repeats it in verse 4, 'But God, who is rich in mercy, for his great love wherewith he loved us, even when we were dead in sins, hath quickened us together with Christ'. That is the work of the Spirit.

The work of the Spirit is an essential part of Christian doctrine. The message, the gospel of salvation, is preached to all and sundry, and a general offer of salvation is made to all men, but all men do not receive it. What determines the difference is the work of the Holy Spirit who brings the Word with 'power' and with 'much assurance' to those who become believers. We have another classical statement of this vital truth in the second chapter of the First Epistle to the Corinthians, where Paul talks about the 'mystery' committed to him which he has to preach. He then says: 'Which none of the princes of this world knew: for had they known it they would not have crucified the Lord of glory' (v. 8). The princes of this world did not recognize the truth, did not recognize Christ. How then can anyone become Christian; how had these Corinthians become Christians? The answer is: 'God hath revealed them [his truths] unto us by his Spirit: for the Spirit searcheth all things, yea, the deep things of God'. 'We have received,' he goes on to say, 'not the spirit of the world, but the Spirit which is of God; that we might know the things that are freely given to us of God' (v. 12). No man can believe on the Lord Jesus Christ apart from the action of the Holy Spirit. In 1 Corinthians Paul states it categorically thus: 'No man can say that Jesus is the Lord but by the Holy Ghost' (12:3). Without the operation of the Holy Ghost no man can do so. To the natural man these things are foolishness. 'The natural man receiveth not the things of the Spirit of God for they are foolishness unto him: neither can he know them, because they are spiritually discerned' (1 Corinthians 2:14). No man as he is by nature, and as the result of sin, can possibly believe the gospel. The work of the Holy Spirit is absolutely essential. In this connection our Lord Himself uttered words which are recorded in the eleventh chapter of the Gospel of St Matthew: 'I thank Thee, O Father, Lord of heaven and earth, because thou hast hid these things from the wise and prudent, and hast revealed them unto babes.' And He proceeds to say that there is but one explanation of this action, namely, 'Even so, Father: for so it seemed good in thy sight' (vv. 25-26). There is no explanation save this, that the Father has purposed it 'according to the counsel of his own will'. We cannot understand this, but we know that it is the truth. We have not made ourselves Christians; it is not anything in us – 'I am what I am by the grace of God' – and this is true of all Christians. This is not to be understood, but to be believed, to be accepted, to be wondered at.

There is a particularly interesting illustration of this matter in the account given in the Book of Acts, chapter 16, of how the gospel first came to the Continent of Europe in a city called Philippi. The Apostle heard that a number of women were accustomed to meet in a prayer-meeting on Sabbath afternoons by the side of a river outside the city wall. So he and his companions went out, joined the little prayer-meeting, sat down among the women, and spoke to them. They spoke this 'word of truth'; and we are told that a woman called Lydia was converted. She believed the truth and became the first Christian convert in Europe. But how did Lydia come to believe the truth? The answer is given in the fourteenth verse in that chapter in the words, 'whose heart the Lord opened, that she attended unto the things that were spoken of Paul' (v. 14). The hearts of all of us by nature are shut and closed to the truth, to this message of the gospel. The Word alone cannot open them or soften them. For that to happen the operation of the Holy Spirit is absolutely vital and essential. William Cowper reminds us of this in a hymn:

> *The Spirit breathes upon the Word,*
> *And brings the truth to sight.*

This is a dual operation. The Spirit is in the Word, but the Spirit must be in my heart also, and open it, before I can receive the Word. It is the Spirit who quickens us; it is the Spirit who enlivens us from the death of sin in which we all are by nature; it is the Spirit who gives us the faculty of belief; it is the Spirit who gives us a new principle of life which makes all these things possible. It is all summed up in the second chapter of this Epistle to the Ephesians in verse 8: 'For by grace are ye saved through faith; and that not of yourselves: it is the gift of God.' Faith is the gift of God. God enables us to believe by the Spirit. Apart from this operation of the Spirit we remain dead to the Word and we do not 'see' it. But when the Spirit breathes upon the Word He brings the truth to sight. We see it and so we believe it.

That brings us to the third and last step in regard to what you and I have to do. Without our knowing it, the Spirit has been working, and as the result of that three things happen. We hear it, we believe it, and we trust it or hope in it. The three words which the Apostle uses here in this Epistle are, 'In whom ye also *trusted* (or *hoped*) after that ye *heard* the word of truth, the gospel of your salvation; in whom also after that ye *believed*, ye were sealed with that holy Spirit of promise'. We must understand clearly that God through the Holy Spirit does not work or act upon us mechanically. God does not force our wills; God does not compel anyone against his will to believe the Gospel. That is not His way of working. We are not treated as automata. What happens is that God persuades the will; He makes the truth attractive to us. So no man has ever believed the gospel against

[239]

his will; he has been given to see it in such a way that he desires it, he admires it, he likes it.

This is true to our experience. There was a time when we saw nothing in these things, but now they have become everything to us. The difference is explained by the fact that there is a change in us as the result of God's operation by the Holy Spirit upon us. A truth which had appeared to us to be boring, uninteresting and unattractive suddenly becomes the most wonderful thing we have ever heard of. It is the same truth and we may have heard it from the same preacher. The fact is that we are different, we now have a new principle or disposition in us which enables us to exercise faith and gives us the ability to comprehend and to understand. We have been given the ability to comprehend and to understand. We have been given an 'anointing', an 'unction' by the Holy Spirit, as the Apostle John says (1 John 2: 20, 27). This working of God upon us and in us must never be thought of as if God bludgeoned our wills, forcing us or compelling us. He *leads* us to repentance, He leads us to belief by the operation of the Holy Spirit in revealing the Word and opening our hearts to receive it; and the result is that, as new-born babes, there is nothing we so much desire as 'the sincere milk of the word'. This new faculty, this new principle of life, makes all the difference.

Having made it possible for us to act, God calls upon us to act. The word is preached and we *hear* it. But hearing is not enough. We must not only hear this Word; we must believe it. And the man who truly hears it believes it. He has come to see himself as a sinner, he has come to see the law of God condemning him; he has some conception now of the holiness of God; and he realizes that he has to stand before God in the Judgment. So he is concerned, he is alarmed at his whole position. What can he do? He hears this message about Christ dying for sins and he says: 'That is the very thing I need; I want it; I believe it; although I do not understand it fully.' So having heard he believes; and he realizes that it is his duty to believe, because all are called upon to repent and to believe.

The last term used by the Apostle is translated in the Authorized Version as 'trusted'. In the Revised Version and certain other Versions it is translated as 'hoped'. That is equally good because the two words mean very much the same thing, namely, that we place our hope, our confidence, our trust, in every respect in the Lord Jesus Christ. That is what makes us Christians. So the Apostle says here about the Jews, 'that we should be to the praise of his glory, who first hoped in Christ'; or in other words, Jews who first realized that Christ is our only hope and our only source of confidence, our only ground of assurance. The Apostle proceeds to say: 'In whom ye also *trusted*'. The word *trusted* is added, and neither it nor the word *hoped* is in the original. 'In whom ye also [have obtained an inheritance] after that ye heard the word of truth, the gospel of your salvation'. They likewise had reposed their trust, their confidence and their hope in the Lord Jesus Christ alone. This is the best definition of a Christian that we can ever encounter.

The Christian is one who centres his every hope on the Lord Jesus Christ. When he thinks about his past, and looks back at it, he is given peace with respect to it, not simply because he believes that God is a God of love who is ready to forgive; no, he is given peace about his past because he knows that his past sins were laid upon the Lord Jesus Christ dying upon the Cross on Calvary's hill. He knows that Christ has borne them and carried them away. It is this alone which gives him confidence and hope and trust as he reviews his past; nothing less. Without that he has no sure hope, and is not a Christian. As regards the present, he is aware of his weakness, he is aware of his unworthiness, he is aware of the terrible power of sin and temptation within him; but he still has this hope and confidence and trust. And it is ever based on the truth, namely, the Lord Jesus Christ and His work –

I need Thee every hour, stay Thou near by,
Temptations lose their power when Thou art nigh.

and 'With Thee at hand to bless, I fear no foe'. Such are the expressions of his confidence in the present. And as he looks to the future that confidence remains unshaken. He does not know what is going to happen, he is in the same world as everyone else; wars may come, pestilences may come, the devil will certainly be there, temptation and sin will not change, the world will not change, nothing will change, and he is still weak; so how can he face it and meet it? He knows that the One who is with him 'will never leave him nor forsake him'. And then beyond all – death! It

[241]

is bound to come, it has to be faced. But still he is happy, he is full of hope and confidence and assurance. The One who has been with him in life will be with him in death. 'I will never leave thee, nor forsake thee' (Hebrews 13:5). So he can say with Paul, 'I am persuaded that neither death, nor life, nor angels, nor principalities, nor powers, nor things present, nor things to come, nor height nor depth nor any other creature shall be able to separate us from the love of God which is in Christ Jesus our Lord' (Romans 8:38-39). Is Christ the basis of all your hope and confidence and faith? If it is not so, you have no right to call yourself a Christian. But if you can say:

> *My hope is built on nothing less*
> *Than Jesus' blood and righteousness,*
> *I dare not trust the sweetest frame*
> *But wholly lean on Jesus' Name:*
> *On Christ the solid Rock I stand,*
> *All other ground is sinking sand,*

in that case you are a Christian indeed, and God will bless you.

21

Sealed with the Spirit

'In whom ye also *trusted*, after that ye heard the
word of truth, the gospel of your salvation: in whom
also after that ye believed, ye were sealed with that
holy Spirit of promise.'

Ephesians 1:13

In these words we are face to face with yet another addition to
this series of extraordinary statements which the Apostle has been
making concerning our position and our inheritance in our Lord
and Saviour Jesus Christ. We have observed already how his
formula for introducing some additional blessing is the expression, 'In whom ye also . . .' He had said in verse 7, 'In whom we
have redemption', then in verse 11 he proceeds to say, 'In whom
also we have obtained an inheritance'. But now we have something
that takes us yet further: 'In whom *also* after that ye believed, ye
were sealed with that holy Spirit of promise.' It is astonishing to
note the way in which, in this great statement which runs, as we
have seen, from the beginning of verse 3 to the end of verse 14,
the Apostle seems to be piling one glory upon another as he
unfolds to us the blessings which are ours as the result of the
riches of God's grace. God has indeed caused them to 'abound'
toward us.

The something further to which the Apostle is now about to
introduce us is 'after that ye believed ye were sealed with that holy
Spirit of promise'. Here he introduces to us in an explicit manner
for the first time in this chapter the Holy Spirit Himself. Clearly,
as we have noted, the Holy Spirit has been involved in everything
we have met hitherto. We cannot be aware of our need of redemption, we cannot receive our redemption, apart from the Holy
Spirit; indeed we cannot believe apart from the operation of the
Holy Spirit. But here He is mentioned explicitly, His actual Name
is introduced, and we are brought face to face with certain vital

aspects of the New Testament teaching concerning the Holy Spirit and His work. It is therefore a most important addition, and it is regrettable that, when this letter was divided into verses, a fresh verse was not commenced at this point; for this is a new subject and it should have been emphasized in that way.

This additional statement is particularly important from the experimental standpoint. The Apostle has been reminding us of all that is true concerning the gospel, and all that is provided for us in it. But here he brings the truth right home to us and reminds us of the way in which we can become certain of these things and enjoy something of their glory and their greatness even while we are in this world of time.

I am increasingly persuaded that it is our failure to understand this precise statement that accounts for so much lethargy and failure among us as Christian people at the present time. At least I will go so far as to assert that any Christian who is not experiencing the joy of salvation is in that state very largely because of a failure to realize the truth taught in this particular verse of Scripture, for in it we are brought face to face with the way in which we can enter into the fulness which we should be experiencing in Christ. To 'rejoice in the Lord', and to rejoice in Him always, is an essential part of God's purpose for us in Christ. Our Lord Himself, at the end of His life on earth, said not only, 'My peace I give unto you', but also 'My joy' (John 15:11). That is the heritage of a Christian. Christian people should be full of joy and of peace and of happiness. Not only so, but if we feel that we are ineffective as Christians and that our usefulness is not very evident, then I suggest that it is again due to this selfsame thing, namely, our failure to realize what is meant by God's sealing of His children by 'that holy Spirit of Promise'. Furthermore, it is one of the most vital of all the New Testament doctrines with respect to revival and reawakening in the Christian Church.

Sealing is a subject that has caused much controversy. It is not an easy subject, therefore; nevertheless we must face it. And the best way of doing so is to adopt our former method, and look at the terms which the Apostle uses: 'In whom also after that ye believed, ye were sealed with that holy Spirit of promise.'

Let us first take 'sealing' in its ordinary meaning, its customary usage among men. It has three main meanings. First, a seal is that which authenticates or conveys authority. Two men may draw up an agreement; it may be to sell a house or arrange a business, or something else in that realm. They have agreed about the terms, which have been written or printed; but as we know, that document is not really valid and neither man is going to be content with it, unless and until it is 'signed and sealed'. You need the seal in addition even to a signature. It makes it more authentic, it makes it more absolute – 'signed and sealed'. A seal therefore is that which conveys authority, or establishes the authenticity, the validity, the truth of a document or statement.

Another meaning which attaches to 'sealing' is that it is a mark of ownership. This is often used in the case of animals; the owner or the man who buys the animals puts his mark or his seal upon them to indicate that they belong to him. The same is done with property, or again on documents. It is to indicate that something, whatever it is, belongs to and is the property of the person who has used that particular seal. The seal has a particular image on it which belongs to one man only, and therefore, when you see that seal or image on anything, you know that it is the property or possession of one particular person.

Furthermore, a seal is also used for the purpose of security. If you desire a parcel to go carefully by post or by train you not only tie it up, but you melt sealing-wax on to the knots and then stamp the wax with a seal. If that seal has in any way been broken or marred it is an indication that someone has been tampering with the parcel. There is an instance of this in the New Testament. When our Lord was buried the Roman authorities and the Jews were concerned as to what His followers might do with His body, so they rolled a stone over the mouth of the grave and then sealed it to make it secure.

Thus we find that there are three main meanings to this term 'sealing' – authenticity and authority, ownership, and security and safety – and these will help us to understand what is meant by our being 'sealed by that holy Spirit of promise'.

We do well to pay attention to the scriptural usage of 'sealing', for terms of this kind generally carry the same meaning and connotation in all parts of the Word. Let us take note of two very important examples of 'sealing'. In the third chapter of the Gospel according to St John we read: 'He that hath received his testimony hath set to his seal that God is true' (v. 33). This is just another way of saying that when a man believes the gospel and accepts it, he is, as it were, expressing his agreement and authenticating that this is indeed the truth of God, and that what God says is true. It is a very bold statement, a very bold image to use, but there it is! Its opposite (though the word 'sealed' is not actually used) is found in the First Epistle of John: 'He that believeth not hath made God a liar; because he believeth not the record that God gave of his Son' (5:10). To believe the gospel is to put your seal to it and to say it is true; not to believe is virtually to say that God is a liar.

But there is a still more important use of 'sealing', and this is found in the sixth chapter of John's Gospel where we are given an account of our Lord feeding the five thousand. Having done so He put His disciples into a boat and told them to cross the sea; and He Himself went up into a mountain to pray. Later in the night He joined them and they arrived at the other side of the lake. A number of other people had taken to boats and had crossed over also, and they came crowding after our Lord, who turned to them and said: 'Labour not for the meat which perisheth, but for that meat which endureth unto everlasting life, which the Son of man shall give unto you: for him hath God the Father sealed' (v. 27). Here our Lord was telling the people that they should listen to Him because God the Father had sealed Him. They could not understand this saying and asked the Lord what were the works of God which they had to do. Our Lord replied saying, 'This is the work of God, that ye believe on him whom he hath sent'. They reply, 'If you say that God has sent you, what sign do you give us? what proof have you of the fact that you are indeed the Son of God, the Saviour and the Messiah?' They added: 'Moses, when he was leading our nation, gave our fore-fathers manna from heaven as a sign; what do you give?' Our Lord, in a sense, had already answered their questions by telling them that He had been 'sealed', that is, authenticated, by God. He says in effect, God has made it clear that I am His Son, that I, the Son of man, am the Son of God in that He has sealed me, has given me authority, has authenticated my claims, has established my ministry, and has anointed me as the Messiah.

The way in which God had sealed the Lord Jesus is to be found everywhere in the Gospels. God had sealed Him at His baptism by sending the Holy Ghost upon Him in the form of a dove. John's Gospel tells us that 'God giveth not the Spirit by measure unto him' (3:34). The Holy Ghost was sent upon Him in all His fulness. Although He was still the Son of God, eternal and co-equal with the Father, He had limited Himself, He had come in the form of a servant; and before He could do His work as the Son of man and as the Saviour, He needed the power of the Holy Spirit. So the Spirit was given to Him, not in measure, but in all His fulness. Thereby God set His seal upon Him.

Furthermore, 'a voice came from heaven saying, This is my beloved Son in whom I am well pleased' (Matthew 3:17). That voice spoke on three occasions, authenticating Him, sealing Him, pronouncing Him to be God's Son, the Messiah, the deliverer. It was because He was thus empowered by God through the Holy Spirit that our blessed Lord was able to speak and do His mighty works. He said: 'The words that I speak unto you I speak not of myself: but the Father that dwelleth in me he doeth the works' (John 14:10). Concerning the works, therefore, He claims that He is doing the works which the Father had given Him to do. That was His authentication, and it was manifested in His ability to expound the Scriptures though He had never received any training to do so. People listening to Him said: 'Never man spake like this man' (John 7:46), for He was speaking in all the fulness of the power of the Spirit. The same applies to His works. He was able to say: 'Though ye believe not me, believe the works' (John 10:38). The works were His authentication. That was the argument He used in the case of John the Baptist who had become uncertain concerning Him: 'The blind see, the lame walk, the lepers are cleansed, the deaf hear, the dead are raised, to the poor the gospel is preached' (Luke 7:22). These are the things the prophets had said the Messiah would do; so the fact that He was doing them is the seal that He was the Messiah.

Bishop Westcott sums up very well the meaning of 'him hath God the Father sealed' by saying that it means 'solemnly set apart for the fulfilment of (a) charge, and authenticated by intelligible signs'. The Father had authenticated the Son by intelligible signs – the miracles, the works, the words, everything about Him.

[247]

Having been given the Spirit in all His fulness He had been 'sealed', had been authenticated.

We have seen, then, the meaning of the term as it is found in common usage and also in Scripture; and we find that they coincide. In the case of our Lord we are told that a declaration was made saying 'This is my beloved Son', and that that was confirmed by His works and His words. Whatever men may do to Him He is authenticated as the Son of God and the Saviour, and though hell be let loose against Him, God's purpose is to be carried out in Him and through Him. 'Him hath God the Father sealed.'

This is surely most helpful as we come to consider the meaning of this term with respect to ourselves. It obviously must mean for us what it meant for the Lord Himself. It means that we can be authenticated, that it can be established by intelligible signs that we are indeed the children of God, heirs of God, and joint-heirs with our blessed Lord and Saviour Jesus Christ.

Now in order to get at the meaning of this term 'sealing' still more clearly let us consider when it takes place. Where exactly does the sealing come in the life and experience of the Christian? This has proved to be an interesting question, and indeed, to some, a problem. The Authorized Version reads as follows: 'In whom also after that ye believed ye were sealed with that holy Spirit of promise.' The English Revised Version reads: 'In whom having also believed . . .'; and the Revised Standard Version: 'You also, who have believed in Him . . .' The question therefore arises as to which translation is correct. When does this sealing with the Holy Spirit take place? Does it take place at the same moment as one believes, or is it subsequent to belief? The Authorized Version, which is not only a translation but also an exposition, clearly indicates that it is something which follows believing, that it is different from, separated from, distinct from believing, and not a part of believing. So we are faced with the question, Is this sealing of the Holy Spirit a distinct and separate experience in the Christian life, or is it something that happens inevitably to all who are Christians, so that you cannot be a Christian at all apart from this sealing?

The prevailing common teaching at the present time, and

[248]

especially in evangelical circles, is that the second alternative is the correct one. It is a teaching which says that the sealing with the Spirit is something that happens immediately, inevitably, inexorably to all who believe. But I cannot accept this, and to substantiate my opinion I mention the teaching of the seventeenth-century Puritan, Thomas Goodwin, and to a lesser extent that of his contemporary John Owen; also the teaching of Charles Simeon of Cambridge two centuries ago, and of Charles Hodge of Princeton, U.S.A., in his commentary on this Epistle in the later nineteenth century. These teachers draw a sharp distinction between believing (the act of faith) and the sealing of the Spirit. They assert that the Scripture teaches that, while it is true to say that no man can believe without the influence of the Holy Spirit, nevertheless this is not the same thing as the sealing with the Spirit, and that sealing with the Spirit does not always happen immediately when a man believes. They teach that there may be a great interval, that it is possible for a person to be a believer and therefore to have the Holy Spirit, and still not know the sealing of the Spirit. It is surely obvious that the godly men who gave us the Authorized Version held that view, because they deliberately introduced the word 'after'.

It is generally agreed that the Epistle does not say: 'In whom also believing ye *are* sealed with the Holy Spirit.' The word is in the past tense; it is not 'as you believed' or 'when you believed', it is at the very least, 'having believed'. The Revised Version suggests the past, 'having also believed, ye were sealed with the holy Spirit of promise'; and I suggest that even the phrase 'having believed' suggests that these two things are not identical, and that the sealing does not immediately follow the act of belief. What makes this so important is that it is assumed that the sealing with the Spirit, or the baptism with the Spirit, is something which every Christian must of necessity have experienced. It is maintained therefore that this is not something that happens in the realm of consciousness or in the realm of experience, it happens to all believers unconsciously. Therefore they are not to seek it. And the result of not seeking it is that they do not experience it; and the result of that is that they live in a state of believe-ism, saying to themselves that they must have had it, and therefore do have it. Thus they continue to live without ever experiencing

what was experienced by New Testament Christians and also by
many other Christians in the subsequent history of the Christian
Church.

So I assert that this 'sealing with the Spirit' is something
subsequent to believing, something additional to believing, and I
support my contention by reminding you of certain statements in
the Scriptures. For the first I go to the fourteenth chapter of
John's Gospel. There our Lord is addressing His believing
disciples. He is drawing a sharp distinction between them and the
world, and He tells them that the Holy Spirit is to be given to
them as another Comforter because they are God's people. He
says that the world cannot receive Him but they are about to
receive Him. The distinction is between believers and unbelievers. In the sixteenth chapter He further says: 'It is expedient
for you that I go away, for if I go not away, the Comforter will not
come unto you.' His coming is a great blessing to which they
must look forward. They should be glad, He says, that He is
going to the Father because this blessing will then come to them.
He is talking to believers; but He tells them that they are going to
receive this additional something. Turning to the first two
chapters of the Book of the Acts of the Apostles we find that the
teaching is still clearer. Our Lord is addressing men on whom He
has already 'breathed' the Holy Spirit, and to whom He has said,
'Receive ye the Holy Ghost' (John 20:22), yet we read in Acts
chapter 1, 'And being assembled together with them, he commanded them that they should not depart from Jerusalem, but
wait for the promise of the Father, which, saith he, ye have heard
of me. For John truly baptized with water; but ye shall be
baptized with the Holy Ghost not many days hence' (vv. 4–5).
They have already believed in Him fully; He has even breathed
the Spirit upon them; yet He says, 'Wait'. Something further is
needed by them. And in the second chapter of Acts we have an
account of how the blessing came; the very thing our Lord had
promised happened ten days later. Clearly the disciples were
believers in Him before then. It is monstrous to suggest that they
were not believers before the day of Pentecost. They were full
believers in the Lord Jesus Christ. He had expounded the
doctrine of the Atonement to them and they had understood it
after His resurrection. He had breathed the Spirit upon them.

They knew that He was the Son of God. Thomas had made his confession, 'My Lord and my God'. Yet still they had not received the Holy Spirit. It was at Pentecost they were 'sealed'; it was there that the authentication was given to them; and it is from there that their glorious ministry begins.

In the eighth chapter of the Book of the Acts of the Apostles we find that Philip evangelized the Samaritans, as the result of which many Samaritans believed the gospel. We are told quite explicitly that, having heard this message, they believed: 'But when they believed Philip preaching the things concerning the kingdom of God, and the name of Jesus Christ, they were baptized, both men and women' (v. 12). They believed on the Lord Jesus Christ, and Philip was satisfied that they had done so, and therefore baptized them. But in the sixteenth verse we read: 'for as yet he [the Holy Ghost] was fallen upon none of them, only they were baptized in the name of the Lord Jesus.' Then Peter and John went down from Jerusalem to Samaria and 'when they were come down they prayed for them that they might receive the Holy Ghost, for as yet he was fallen upon none of them, only they were baptized in the name of the Lord Jesus. Then laid they their hands on them, and they received the Holy Ghost'. They were already believers, they had believed on the Lord Jesus Christ. They could not have done so apart from the Holy Spirit working within them and opening their hearts and minds. But still the 'seal' had not been given. There was an interval. How wrong it is to say that immediately a man believes he is sealed by the Spirit! It certainly did not happen to these Samaritans, even as it had not happened to the apostles themselves.

In the ninth chapter of the Book of Acts we have the account of the conversion of Saul of Tarsus. He believed on the Lord Jesus Christ as the result of what happened to him on the road to Damascus; but it was not until three days later that he received, and was filled with the Holy Ghost, as the result of the ministry of Ananias.

In chapter fifteen of the Book of Acts we find a similar happening. The Apostle Peter is defending himself for having received Cornelius and his family into the Christian Church and for baptizing Gentiles. The report reads: 'And when there had been much disputing, Peter rose up, and said unto them, Men and brethren, ye know how that a good while ago God made choice among us, that the Gentiles by my mouth should hear the word of the gospel, and believe. And God, which knoweth the hearts, bare them witness [authenticated them], giving them the Holy Ghost, even as he did unto us.' God bare them witness, God established the fact that they had believed and were truly His by giving them the Holy Ghost. He 'sealed them'.

Another example of this sealing is found in the nineteenth chapter of the Book of Acts. Paul arrived at Ephesus, 'and finding certain disciples he said unto them' – according to the Authorized Version – 'Have ye received the Holy Ghost since ye believed?' (v. 2). But the Revised Version and the Revised Standard Version give a translation which reads, 'Did ye receive the Holy Ghost when ye believed?'. There can be no doubt that this latter translation is the correct one. Many feel that that settles the matter and proves that believing and receiving the Holy Spirit are synchronous. They regret that the Authorized Version has led so many into thinking that it is possible for one to believe and not receive the Holy Spirit until afterwards.

But this does not solve our problem; indeed I claim that, far from supporting the idea that receiving the Holy Ghost always follows immediately upon believing, this correct translation of Acts 19:2 does the exact opposite. I confess that at one time I myself fell into error on the matter. A little booklet bearing my name, entitled 'Christ our sanctification', includes the argument that if we but follow the Revised Version instead of the Authorized Version we shall see that there is no time interval between the believing and the sealing. I confess my former error. Actually I fell into it because I was concerned to show that sanctification is not an experience which is to be received after justification. This I still assert. But I was mistaken at that time with regard to the 'sealing', as I proceed to show.

When the Apostle put his question to these 'disciples', 'Did you receive the Holy Ghost when you believed?', the implication surely is obvious. It is that men may believe without receiving the Holy Ghost. If the two things happen together inevitably, it is an unnecessary question, and the Apostle would simply be asking them whether they were believers. But that is not what the Apostle asks them. His question is, 'Did you receive the Holy

Ghost when you believed?'. In other words, when he spoke to
these men he saw at once that they had not had the seal of the
Spirit, they had not received the Holy Ghost. So he says to them
in effect: Now look, you call yourselves believers, but did you
receive the Holy Ghost when you believed? Have you received
Him at all, you who claim to be believers? I suggest, therefore,
that the correct translation actually indicates quite clearly that
there is a distinction between these two things. We believe, and
of course we can only believe as the result of the operation of the
Spirit, but still we may not have received the seal of the Spirit.

The subsequent events in this story about Paul and the
'disciples' in Ephesus makes this yet clearer. The Apostle begins
to examine them and he asks: 'Unto what then were ye baptized?'
They say, 'Unto John's baptism'. 'Then said Paul, John verily
baptized with the baptism of repentance, saying unto the people,
that they should believe on him which should come after him,
that is, on Christ Jesus. When they heard this, they were baptized
in the Name of the Lord Jesus' (v. 4). Paul would never have
baptized them unless they had believed. They believed and
accepted what the Apostle said and so were baptized. Whatever
they were before, they were now clearly believers. But then we
read: 'And when Paul had laid his hands upon them, the Holy
Ghost came upon them, and they spake with tongues and
prophesied' (v. 6). They had believed but they still lacked the
'sealing of the Spirit'. The sealing only happened to them when
Paul laid his hands upon them. Surely this incident proves that
the men who gave us the Authorized Version were interpreting
Ephesians 1:13 correctly! They were theologically correct in
saying, 'In whom also after that ye believed, ye were sealed with
that holy Spirit of promise'. There was an interval between their
believing and their sealing, as there was in the case of Paul
himself and all the apostles, as there was in the case of the
Samaritans, as there was in the case of the 'disciples' in Ephesus.

However, let us make it clear that, though I am emphasizing
that there is a distinction between these two things, and that there
is always an interval – that sealing does not immediately and
automatically happen at believing – I would not be understood as
saying that there must always be a long interval between the two.
It may be a very short interval, so short as to suggest that the

believing and the sealing are simultaneous; but there is always an interval. Believing first, then sealing. It is only believers who are sealed; and you can be a believer without being sealed; the two things are not identical. It is believing that makes us children of God, that joins us to Christ; it is the sealing with the Holy Ghost that authenticates that fact. Sealing does not make us Christians, but it authenticates the fact, as a seal always does.

22

The Nature of Sealing [1]

'In whom also after that ye believed, ye were sealed
with that holy Spirit of promise.'

Ephesians 1:13

We must come to yet closer grips with this important statement
because, as I have already suggested, this is one of the most
vital statements for us as Christian people at the present time. If I
were asked to give a diagnosis as to what is wrong with the
Christian Church today, and as to what has been her chief trouble
for a number of years, I would suggest that it is her failure to
understand this statement. Because, for various reasons, we have
misinterpreted the Apostle's teaching the Church has been
lacking in vital power in her capacity of witness, and has resorted
to means and methods that have not always been consistent with
the teaching of the Scriptures. It is because Christian people have
not been manifesting the Christian life as it should be lived that
the world has ceased to be interested in Christianity. The story
of the Church through the centuries shows that every revival has
come as the result of a quickening in the Church among God's
people. Revival starts in the Church and spreads outwards. A
lifeless and moribund church never achieves anything of lasting
value, but when something happens in the Church the world
hears about it; its curiosity is aroused, and as on the Day of
Pentecost, it begins to ask what certain phenomena signify. Such
is the history of every revival; it is God's way of working. He
quickens His Church and His people first.

To be certain about these things we must first establish our
doctrine, for unless we are satisfied with regard to the doctrine

we are never likely to experience it. And it is because so many hold a wrong doctrine with regard to this question of the sealing of the Spirit that they lack the experience of it. Firstly, I remark that the Apostle himself gave us a very fruitful suggestion when he says that the Ephesian believers were sealed with 'that holy Spirit of promise'. He does not simply say, 'You were sealed with the Holy Spirit' but specifically refers to 'that Holy Spirit of promise'. Actually what the Apostle said was: 'You were sealed with that Spirit of that promise that holy.' Such is the exact translation. He repeats the word 'that' – 'that Spirit of that promise that holy'. Clearly this focuses our attention upon 'that promise', the Holy Spirit of that promise; which means, 'You were sealed with that Spirit which had been promised', the Spirit in connection with whom certain promises had been made. It is a simple matter to prove that throughout the Scriptures there has been this promise concerning the coming and the giving of the Holy Spirit in the particular manner in which it happened at Jerusalem on the day of Pentecost. Let us consider some of the Scriptures which indicate this.

In the prophecy of Isaiah there are many references to the day when the Holy Spirit would be poured forth. This is especially true from chapter forty to the end. The people were taught to look forward to this event. In the prophecy of Ezekiel it is found also in a striking manner, especially in chapters 36, and 37, with promises of the life-giving Spirit. God will take the 'stony' heart out of 'the house of Israel' and give them 'hearts of flesh'; He will pour His Spirit upon them. But perhaps the most striking example is that which is given in the second chapter of the prophet Joel. This is the passage which the Apostle Peter quoted and expounded on the day of Pentecost immediately after he and his fellow apostles had been baptized with the Holy Ghost. On being questioned, and on hearing the suggestion that he and his companions were drunk, Peter heard the people saying: 'These men are full of new wine.' He then began to speak and to say: 'These are not drunken as ye suppose, seeing it is but the third hour of the day: but this is that which was spoken by the prophet Joel.' Then he expounded the teaching of Joel to the people. The prophecy ran: 'It shall come to pass in the last days, saith God, I will pour out of my Spirit upon all flesh, and your sons and your daughters shall prophesy, and your young men shall see visions and your old men shall dream dreams', and so on. 'This is that', says the Apostle; God has done that which He promised through the prophets in those ancient times. Such is the meaning of the expression, 'Spirit of promise'.

Turning to the New Testament from the Old we find the same evidence. This was the very essence of John the Baptist's preaching. John's message was this: 'I indeed baptize you with water, but one mightier than I cometh, the latchet of whose shoes I am not worthy to unloose: he shall baptize you with the Holy Ghost and with fire: whose fan is in his hand, and he will throughly purge his floor, and will gather the wheat into his garner, but the chaff he will burn with fire unquenchable' (Luke 3: 16–17). He contrasts 'I indeed baptize you with water' with 'He shall baptize you with the Holy Ghost and with fire'. Such is the promise. The forerunner of the Messiah Himself calls attention to the difference between his ministry and our Lord's in terms of the coming of the Spirit: 'He shall baptize you with the Holy Ghost and with fire.'

Our Lord taught the same message. Take, for instance, the statement found in the eleventh chapter of Luke's Gospel, and especially in verse 13, which reads: 'If ye, being evil, know how to give good gifts unto your children, how much more shall your heavenly Father give the Holy Spirit to them that ask him.' That is our Lord's own teaching concerning a giving of the Holy Spirit by the Father; and note that it is in the context of importunity in prayer. There are those who teach that, on dispensational grounds, this no longer applies to us. They exclude from us altogether most of the teaching of our Lord as it is recorded in the Gospels. The Sermon on the Mount does not apply to us, much in the Gospels does not. They were for the Jews at that time, and will apply again in some coming age. But surely that is quite unacceptable. The teaching of our Lord is for all of us. He told His apostles as He was about to leave them that they were to teach and preach all the things that He had said; 'And lo', He said, 'I shall be with you even unto the end'. He gave them the Spirit to enable them to obey His commands. And among the teachings He gave them is, 'How much more shall your heavenly Father give the Holy Spirit to them that ask him!' (Luke 11:13).

There is a further significant statement in the seventh chapter of John's Gospel, which deals directly with this matter, and especially John's own comment upon it in verses 37 to 39. 'In the last day, that great day of the feast, Jesus stood and cried saying, If any man thirst let him come unto me and drink. He that believeth on me, as the Scripture hath said, out of his belly shall flow rivers of living water.' Then comes John's comment on it in brackets: 'But this spake he of the Spirit, which they that believe on him should receive, for the Holy Ghost was not yet given, because that Jesus was not yet glorified.' There, once more, we have clear teaching with regard to this 'holy Spirit of promise'. 'They who believe on me' – and no others – says Christ, are going to receive this. And John reminds us that this is a prophecy concerning something that would happen in the future.

Then, turning to the fourteenth chapter of John's Gospel, we have already seen that it is a part of the evidence on this matter. Our Lord was about to meet His death and to leave the disciples. They were downcast, and their hearts were troubled, feeling that life would be impossible without Him. But He says to them, 'Let not your heart be troubled; ye believe in God, believe also in me' (v. 1), and then He goes on to tell them 'I will pray the Father, and he shall give you another Comforter' (v. 16). In other words He promises them that the Holy Spirit will come. Chapters 14, 15 and 16 of John's Gospel are full of promises concerning the coming of the Holy Spirit, and what He is going to do to and for true believers.

Then finally comes the crucial statement in the first chapter of the Book of the Acts to which we have already referred (vv.4–8). The Lord commanded them not to depart from Jerusalem but to wait for the promise of the Father, 'the Holy Spirit of promise', this blessing of which John the Baptist and He, the Lord Himself, had taught. Here, after His resurrection, He is promising it once more, and again He contrasts it with the baptism of John. Then to cap it all, in the second chapter of Acts in verse 33 we find the important statement made by the Apostle Peter after this great thing had happened to him and the other apostles: 'Therefore, being by the right hand of God exalted, and having received of the Father the promise of the Holy Ghost, he hath shed forth this which ye now see and hear.' Peter says that the

Holy Spirit, so long promised, had been given at last to the Son in the light of His perfect work, and the Son had shed Him forth. The Holy Spirit that had been promised had actually been given. My last quotation is Galatians 3:14: 'That the blessing of Abraham might come on the Gentiles through Jesus Christ, that we might receive the promise of the Spirit through faith.' All these Scriptures indicate that this undoubtedly is the explanation of what the Apostle means by 'the Holy Spirit of promise'.

In what sense then can it be said that the Holy Spirit was not given until the day of Pentecost? Clearly it does not mean that the Holy Spirit had not been given at all, or in any sense, until the day of Pentecost. That cannot be the case because we find that even the men of the Old Testament dispensation had the Spirit. The one thing that David most feared after he had committed the terrible sins of adultery and murder is seen in his prayer, 'Take not thy Holy Spirit from me' (Psalm 51:11). The Holy Spirit was in David; he was the man he was because the Holy Spirit was in him. To lose the Spirit was the one thing he dreaded above everything else. Whatever God might do to him by way of punishment, he pleads that God might not remove His Spirit. The Holy Spirit was in all the saints of the Old Testament – in Abraham, Isaac, Jacob, and in all the elect of God. It was the Spirit in them that made them what they were. They were the children of faith; and as we are told by Paul, we as Christians are all the children of Abraham because we are the children of faith. Abraham, Isaac, Jacob, David and the rest were in the Kingdom of God. A man cannot be in the kingdom of God unless he is a child of God; and he cannot be a child of God without the Spirit. The Spirit was in all these men. Our position is that we are sharing with them, are made fellow-heirs with them of these blessings of God.

The disciples of our Lord had already received the Spirit in that sense long before the day of Pentecost. They were believers; and in a certain room our Lord had breathed upon them saying, 'Receive ye the Holy Ghost'. This was before the day of Pentecost (John 20:22). They had not only believed already, they had been enabled to do certain great works, and yet He still promises them the Holy Ghost. To these same men upon whom He had breathed the Spirit on that occasion He says, You shall receive this, 'you shall be baptised with the Holy Ghost not many days hence' (Acts 1:5). And it happened at Pentecost.

So the interpretation of the statement in John 7:39, 'The Holy Ghost was not yet given because that Jesus was not yet glorified', is that the Holy Ghost was not yet given in this particular manner. He had been given already in the other ways, but not in this way. This is a peculiar blessing that had not yet arrived; they had had other blessings, they were believers and it was as believers that they would receive this further blessing. So, clearly, this 'promise of the Father' is some special giving of the Holy Spirit which had been promised through the centuries, and finally by the Lord Himself, even by the resurrected Lord. And Pentecost saw its fulfilment.

In defining that fulfilment we must start with a number of negatives. We are driven to do so by the misunderstanding concerning this matter. To make positive statements is not enough; one has to be negative first so as to correct what one regards as false teaching. Clearly then this sealing with the promised Spirit does not mean the work of the Holy Spirit in regeneration, or repentance, or faith. That the Apostles were not regenerated until the day of Pentecost is an impossible suggestion. As we have seen, they were clearly born again well before that day, and had received the Holy Spirit. They believed in the Lord, they had repented, they had received new life.

But it may be argued that that was before Pentecost and that ever since Pentecost these two things happen together. The answer to that contention is supplied by the case of the Samaritans in the eighth chapter of the Book of Acts who had believed the Gospel as the result of Philip's preaching. They had believed on the Lord Jesus Christ – which cannot be done without the Holy Spirit – they had exercised faith, they were born again, they had repented and believed and had been baptized; but still they had not yet received the Spirit in the sense of 'sealing'. And this applies not only to the Samaritans, but also to Paul himself, and also to the Ephesian disciples mentioned in the nineteenth chapter of Acts.

Secondly, the fulfilment has no reference to the unction that is given to us by the Holy Spirit for our spiritual understanding. That the unction is from the Holy Spirit Paul makes abundantly plain in his First Epistle to the Corinthians, chapter two. The princes of this world did not recognize our Lord and did not believe in Him. But we do both because the Spirit who reveals all things, even the deep things of God, has enabled us, believers, to do so. 'Ye have an unction', an anointing, says John in his First Epistle (2:20, 27). Clearly this sealing with the Spirit does not apply here, because you can have this unction and spiritual understanding and still not know this sealing, as is proved in the last chapter of Luke's Gospel where we read that our blessed Lord and Saviour, having risen from the dead, took His disciples through the Scriptures – the Psalms and the Prophets and Moses – and showed them the truth concerning Himself. They received it; and they could not have received it without enlightenment by the Holy Spirit; but still they had not received the special blessing which came to them on the day of Pentecost.

Thirdly, and particularly important, the sealing with the Spirit is not sanctification. To believe that it is has been the chief error in connection with the subject. That sealing of the Spirit does not mean sanctification can be proved by the fact that there is no gap or interval between justification and sanctification, as there is no gap between regeneration and sanctification. The teaching of the Scripture is that the moment a man is 'born again' his sanctification has and must have started. The process of making him holy and separating him unto God has already begun. There is no greater error than to teach that you can receive your justification by faith and then later on your receive your sanctification by faith. Sanctification is not an experience, not a gift to be received: it is a work of the Holy Spirit in the heart which starts from the moment of regeneration. This sealing with the Spirit therefore cannot be sanctification; indeed it has nothing to do with it in a direct sense. It is something quite distinct and separate.

What helps to make this yet clearer is the fact that the Apostle in describing this sealing refers to it as something which has happened in the past – 'In whom, after that ye believed, ye were sealed'. But sanctification is not something that happens once and for all; it is a process that goes on and on increasingly and develops more and more. The Galatians were in a very poor state as regards sanctification, yet Paul says that they had received the Spirit in this sense of 'sealing'. The same applies to the Church in Corinth even more strikingly. Sealing is an experience, something that God does to us, and we know it when it happens. You cannot say that about your sanctification which is a work of God down in the depths of the soul, convicting of sin, leading to better desires. It is a work which goes on steadily and progressively, starting from the moment of our re-birth. But it is clear that there may be, and generally is, a gap between belief and sealing. Therefore sealing with the Spirit and sanctification are not one and the same thing.

I would go further still and say that sealing with the Spirit is not even a manifestation of the fruit of the Spirit. 'The fruit of the Spirit is love, joy, peace, longsuffering, meekness.' I hold that you can manifest such fruit without of necessity knowing 'the sealing of the Spirit', for the bringing forth of that fruit is a part of the work of the Spirit within us which goes on steadily and constantly in the process of sanctification. Fruit does not suddenly appear; it is the result of a process, it is a gradual development, a maturing. There are people who develop and show the fruit of the Spirit but who cannot say that they know 'the sealing of the Spirit'.

Once more, negatively, the sealing of the Spirit does not mean 'assurance' of salvation as the result of our believing the Word or as the result of arguments worked out from the Word. The common teaching concerning assurance of salvation is that the way to give people assurance is to take them to the Scriptures and then ask them, 'Do you believe this to be the Word of God?' If they say that they do, it is then pointed out to them that the Scripture says, 'He that believeth hath everlasting life', with many other such passages, for example, 'He that believeth shall not come into condemnation'; 'God so loved the world that he gave his only begotten Son, that whosoever believeth in him should not perish, but have everlasting life' (John 3:16). They are then asked, 'Do you believe in Him?'. If they do, they are again told: 'The Word says that if you believe in Him you have everlasting life.' So if they believe they must have everlasting life, and that becomes the basis of their assurance of salvation. It is deduced in that way from the Scriptures. But that is not the sealing of the Spirit, though it is quite right as far as it goes.

Another type of assurance is that which is obtained by reasoning from the First Epistle of John, an Epistle which is mainly concerned with the question of assurance of salvation. According to John there are a number of tests which we can apply in this respect. For instance, 'We know that we have passed from death to life because we love the brethren' (3:14). Another is that we know that we are Christians if we 'keep his commandments', and if we believe on the Lord Jesus Christ, and so on. If we can say honestly that we love God's people and prefer their company to any other we must be Christians. And if we arrive at a similar satisfactory answer to the other questions we can be assured that we are true Christians whatever doubts may arise in our hearts. These tests of the First Epistle of John are more thorough and better tests than those which are objectively based on the Bible. But the two taken together give strong grounds for assurance. And yet I am suggesting that the sealing of the Spirit is more than we have so far considered. It is a yet stronger and higher form of assurance. It includes the blessings mentioned, but goes beyond them. It is the Spirit in us that enables us to do what I have already described; but the sealing with the Spirit is something additional to that, and is something done by the Spirit to us.

My last negative is to say that the sealing is not the fulness of the Spirit, for later on in this Epistle to the Ephesians we shall find that the Apostle gives a commandment, an exhortation, in which he says, 'Be filled with the Spirit', which means 'Go on being filled with the Spirit' (5:18). That is something, therefore, which you and I can control. If we grieve the Spirit or quench the Spirit we shall not be filled with the Spirit. In any case it is something that is to be a perpetual state and condition, we are to 'go on being filled' with the Spirit. But here, in describing this 'sealing', the Apostle refers to something that has happened in the past. 'You were sealed', he says, you know that it has happened; and, furthermore, it was something that was done to you, not something that you do. So I suggest that we must draw a distinction between the sealing of the Spirit and 'the fulness of the Spirit' or 'being filled with the Spirit'.

It is not surprising that we tend to become confused about these matters; it is all due to the limitation of our human language; and sometimes the terms seem to be used interchangeably. Let me illustrate my meaning. In the first chapter of Acts the Lord promised the disciples that they should be 'baptized with the Holy Ghost not many days hence', but when we turn on to chapter 2 and to the great events on the day of Pentecost, we find that the fulfilment of the promise is described, not as 'baptized with the Spirit', but as being 'filled' with the Holy Ghost. What happened there is the fulfilment of what our Lord prophesied as 'You shall be baptized with the Holy Ghost'. But the word 'baptized' is not used in Acts chapter 2; the word used is 'filled'. Clearly the terms are used interchangeably.

The explanation seems to be that the baptism with the Spirit is the first experience of the fulness of the Spirit; it is the Spirit poured upon us in this exceptional fulness. The first time something outstanding happens is always unique. It happened to the Apostles, it happened to Paul, it happened to Cornelius, it happened to the Samaritans, it happened to the Ephesians, it happened to the Galatians, and it has gone on happening to Christians throughout the centuries as I shall show.

I am suggesting therefore that the 'baptism with the Spirit' is the same as the 'sealing with the Spirit'. But someone may well ask, 'Why use two different terms then?' If baptism is meant why does it not say baptism? Indeed why did not Luke use the word 'baptism' in the second chapter of Acts? The answer, it seems to me, is that in the first and second chapters of Acts, we are being taught the doctrine of the Spirit directly. The object there was to emphasize the giving of the Spirit, the fulfilment of God's promise; and it is called a baptism because the Spirit was poured out upon men and women. But here in Ephesians, Paul is talking about inheritance. He desires us as Christians to realize that we are inheritors, that we are about to enter into the possession of a great inheritance. And his concern is that we should be absolutely sure of the fact that we are inheritors. So his teaching is that the baptism of the Spirit is the 'sealing' that God gives to His promise that we are going to enter into this inheritance. Here, of course, the term 'sealing' is the more appropriate term. When we are talking about buying or selling property, or giving someone the promise of an inheritance, we produce a document and we put our seal upon the document, as we have seen. So it is obviously the appropriate term to use here. It is right to regard the blessing as a sealing because it seals the promise. But what seals the promise is the baptism of the Spirit, by which 'the promise of the Father' receives practical expression. It is that giving, that special giving, of the Holy Ghost that our Lord spoke about on the 'last day, the great day of the feast' (John 7:38–39). So let us not be confused by the terms, but realize that we are dealing with two different ways of looking at the same phenomenon and describing it in an appropriate manner in each particular given setting.

Having thus established the doctrine we are in a position to go on to deal with the thing itself, to consider what the Scripture tells us about this wonderful, this glorious 'sealing' that made such a difference to the Apostles and others. Acts 15:8 will help to lead us into it: 'And God, which knoweth the hearts, bare them witness, giving them the Holy Ghost even as he did unto us'. It is God's action, in which He bears witness that we are His children, that He is our Father, and that we are 'heirs of God and joint-heirs with Christ'. It is God's authentication of the fact that we really belong to Him.

23

The Nature of Sealing [2]

'In whom ye also trusted, after that ye heard the
word of truth, the gospel of your salvation: in whom
also after that ye believed, ye were sealed with that
holy Spirit of promise.'

Ephesians 1:13

Summing up what we have already found, we can say that one
can be a Christian without the sealing of the Spirit. You cannot
be a Christian without receiving the Holy Spirit. No man can be a
Christian unless the Holy Spirit is in him, for 'No man can say
that Jesus is the Lord but by the Holy Ghost' (1 Corinthians 12:3).
It is the Holy Spirit who convicts us of sin; it is only as we have
Him in us, and new life, that we can believe at all. And 'If any
man have not the Spirit of Christ he is none of his' (Romans 8:9).
Such statements do not refer to the sealing with the Spirit which
is something quite separate and distinct. We have suggested that
the sealing means that which authenticates us as sons of God. It
does not make us sons of God. Our Lord did not become the
Son of God at His baptism for He always was the Son of God.
The sealing of the Spirit during His baptism was the authentication, the stamp, the seal that Jesus of Nazareth is the Son of God
and the Messiah. And we are suggesting that the same applies to
Christians. The sealing does not refer to our possession of the
Spirit; it goes beyond that, it is additional, and authenticates to us
the fact that we are the sons of God, truly His people, and heirs,
joint-heirs with Christ, of a glorious inheritance. It is God's
action: 'In whom also after that ye believed ye were sealed.' It is
something that is done to the believer.

We can now take a further step in our definition of what the
sealing means and can go on to consider it positively. Our first

[266]

statement is to say that it is an experience; it is something experimental. I emphasize that for the reason that most of the books which have been written on the Holy Spirit during this present century go out of their way to emphasize that the sealing of the Holy Spirit is not experimental, and has nothing to do with experience as such. They state this quite categorically. A volume on the doctrine of the Holy Spirit, bearing the title 'Pneumatology', which is one of a series on biblical theology and which is excellent in many respects, when it comes to deal with the doctrine of the sealing of the Holy Spirit has the bold heading, 'The Sealing of the Spirit not experimental'. That is characteristic of the teaching on this matter during this present century, and indeed since about the middle of the last century. Great emphasis also is laid upon the fact that the baptism of the Holy Ghost or the baptism with the Holy Ghost is not at all experimental.

This is very germane to our discussion of this subject. The book to which I have referred states categorically, 'There is no experience or feeling related to the Spirit's baptism'. The explanation of why such an author says such a thing is quite simple. He feels that he has to say this because of what is found in the First Epistle to the Corinthians, chapter 12 verse 13, where Paul says, 'For by one Spirit have we all been baptized into one body'. That, they claim, is obviously a reference to the baptism of the Holy Spirit; and therefore they conclude that the baptism of the Holy Spirit clearly refers to the action of God in which He incorporates us into the body of Christ. It is therefore an action of God which applies to all believers in which they are quite unconsciously incorporated into the body of Christ. The argument is based upon the fact that the word 'baptism' happens to be used in this particular verse.

A real difficulty arises in this matter in connection with the word 'baptism'. It is assumed that wherever the words 'Spirit' and 'baptism' are found in the same statement the meaning must always be the same, and so it is concluded that the baptism of the Spirit means our incorporation into Christ, which is an event entirely outside one's consciousness and the realm of experience. The fallacy here is surely due to the failure to realize that the word 'to baptize' is used in many different ways in the Scripture. In one way or another this word *baptism* seems to have an almost hypnotic effect upon us and upon our minds and thinking. Take for example a statement made by our blessed Lord Himself: 'But I have a baptism to be baptized with; and how am I straitened until it be accomplished!' (Luke 12:50). Obviously our Lord was not referring to a water baptism; that had already happened to Him. He was not saying that He was going to be re-baptized in that sense. He was referring to His approaching trial and His death. It is comparable to what is often said of a soldier who for the first time in his life is actually in a battle. It is said that thereby he receives his baptism of fire. There are many different particular usages with regard to this word 'baptism', and the statement in 1 Corinthians 12:13 is but one of them. We are all placed into the realm of Christ by the Holy Spirit and into His body which is the Church. All Christians are in that way made members in particular of the body of Christ. But it does not follow that that is the only possible meaning of the expression 'baptized with the Holy Ghost'.

This is a vital point, for the reason that if it is right to say that this sealing with the Spirit is something outside the realm of our consciousness, and that it is entirely non-experimental, then in a sense it is something about which we should not be very much concerned, and it certainly in no way serves the purpose of the Apostle here in Ephesians 1:13, where he is concerned to give us assurance concerning our inheritance.

One way of demonstrating that that cannot possibly be the meaning of sealing here in Ephesians 1:13 is that the Apostle has already dealt with the matter of our being in Christ and in the Church in this very chapter. He started by saying 'Blessed be the God and Father of our Lord Jesus Christ, who hath blessed us with all spiritual blessings in Christ: according as he hath chosen us in him before the foundation of the world'. The term 'pre-destination', which we have considered in verse 5 and again in verse 11 – 'In whom also we have obtained an inheritance, being predestinated according to the purpose of him . . .' – again empha-sizes that same aspect. But here the Apostle has turned to the experimental aspect, telling us that we, Jews and Gentiles, are inheritors together. He certainly returns here to something he has said already, for he is telling us of a further blessing above and beyond what he has previously mentioned. But the teaching I am here opposing not only makes the Apostle guilty of tautology but

I suggest that it is an entirely unscriptural interpretation of the sealing with the Spirit.

It is common ground to say that the sealing with the Spirit and the baptism with the Spirit are the same. We are told in the first chapter of the Book of Acts: 'And being assembled together with them he commanded them that they should not depart from Jerusalem but wait for the promise of the Father, which, saith he, ye have heard of me; for John truly baptized with water, but ye shall be baptized with the Holy Ghost not many days hence.' That is a categorical statement. What our Lord promised happened at Jerusalem on the day of Pentecost as we are told in the second chapter of the Book of Acts. Yet in spite of the account of the event given there I am asked to believe that it is non-experimental, that it did not lead to any feelings or to anything whatsoever in the sphere of consciousness. Such a suggestion is almost unthinkable. Baptism, I am told, is something that God does to me of which I am unconscious. I am a member of the body of Christ but it has nothing to do with feelings at all; it is non-experimental. I am not aware of anything happening, it is an action that God takes. Does that tally with the account of what happened on the day of Pentecost at Jerusalem? Would something which is non-experimental and outside the realm of consciousness so affect people as to make onlookers say, 'These men are full of new wine'? Would it explain the way in which the Apostles spoke in other tongues, when Peter preached with power and authority and boldness? How slavish we can become in our use of terms! and how we rob ourselves of the blessings of God as a result! We are so afraid of excesses, we are so afraid of being labelled in a certain way, that we claim the baptism of the Spirit to be something unconscious, non-experimental, a happening that does not affect a man's feelings.

Such an argument is utterly unscriptural. Not conscious! The Apostles were as men who appeared to be filled with new wine; they were in a state of ecstasy. They were rejoicing, they were praising God; they were moved, their hearts were ravished; they experienced things which they had never felt or known before. They were transformed, and were so different that you can scarcely recognize them as the same Peter and James and John and the rest as they once were. Not experimental! Nothing can be more experimental; it is the height of Christian experience. This is not only true of what we read in the second chapter of the Acts; the same is found in Samaritans in Acts chapter 8, and also in the case of the Apostle Paul himself. He had believed on the road to Damascus but it was three days later when he was visited by Ananias that his baptism with the Spirit took place. It is equally plain and clear that what happened to Cornelius and his household is highly experimental, as is explained in a forcible manner in the fifteenth chapter of the Acts. And because of its crucial importance we find it recorded thus: 'And God, which knoweth the hearts, bare them witness, giving them the Holy Ghost as he did unto us' (v. 8). How did Peter know all this if the baptism of the Holy Ghost is something outside the realm of consciousness and merely the action whereby God incorporates us as members severally into the body of Christ? How could Peter tell that these Gentiles had become Christians? Peter was a Jew, and a very rigid Jew; it needed a vision from heaven on a housetop at Joppa to convince him that he must receive Gentiles into the Christian Church. And we know that even after that vision he was uncertain about the position of Gentiles in the Church and Paul had to withstand him to the face at Antioch. Yet Peter says: (How could I refuse them, after) 'God which knoweth the hearts bare them witness, giving them the Holy Ghost even as he did unto us'? It is obvious that there was tangible external evidence, sufficient to persuade the doubting Apostle. Yet this is described as 'non-experimental'. Peter could see that these men were filled with the Holy Ghost, baptized with the Holy Ghost, even as he and the others had been baptized on the day of Pentecost. When we have this 'seal of the Spirit' we know it, and others know it. It is the highest, the greatest experience which a Christian can have in this world. 'God bare them witness.' He set His seal upon them, says Peter in effect, so I received them into the Church. Who was I to refuse to baptize them with water when God had already baptized them with the Holy Ghost in a manner that was obvious to everyone? Nothing but some clear external manifestations could possibly have convinced the Apostle.

The same truth is found in the nineteenth chapter of Acts. Paul realized that the 'disciples' there mentioned were lacking in their experience and that they had not received the Holy Ghost; hence his question to them, 'Did you receive the Holy Ghost when you believed?'. Paul could not have discovered this if it is not something experimental. And similarly right through the Acts of the Apostles.

One of the most convincing proofs of my contention is found in the question put by Paul to the Galatians in chapter 3 of his Epistle to them: 'Received ye the Holy Ghost by the works of the law or by the hearing of faith?' (v. 2). Had they received this baptism with the Holy Ghost by the works of the law or by the hearing of faith? How can anyone answer that question if this is something outside the realm of experience? How can I know whether I have or have not received the Spirit if it is not something experimental? All these quotations from Scripture clearly contradict the unfortunate interpretation which appeared somewhere towards the end of the last century, and which seems to have been a kind of incubus upon interpretation ever since.

But if we go back into the history of the Church before that time we find a great richness in the exposition of our present theme. I have already quoted the names of Thomas Goodwin and John Owen, the Puritans; also those of Charles Hodge and Charles Simeon. I can also claim the support of John Wesley and George Whitefield. The sealing with the Spirit, or the baptism with the Spirit, is clearly experimental and experiential.

When we come now to consider what exactly this experience is, we find the best answer in Paul's Epistle to the Romans chapter 8, where we read, 'The Spirit himself beareth witness with our spirit that we are the children of God' (v. 16), or the parallel statement in the fourth chapter of the Epistle to the Galatians already quoted, 'And because ye are sons, God hath sent forth the Spirit of his Son into your hearts, crying, Abba, Father' (v. 6). Let us remind ourselves of the argument in the fourth chapter of the Epistle to the Galatians. 'The heir' – a young boy who is an heir to an estate – 'as long as he is a child differeth nothing from a servant, though he be lord of all, but is under tutors and under governors until the time appointed of the father' (vv. 1-2). That is a statement about which there can be no disagreement. Though that little boy is actually the heir of a great estate, because he is still only a boy he does not manage the estate, and he is not conscious of his own importance and dignity and of all that belongs to him. He must spend most of his time with tutors and servants. Indeed it often happens that such a boy who is the heir to so much may even be maltreated by tutors and servants, and punished by them. They keep him in his place, and he may even be afraid of them. He is virtually like a servant; indeed he may sometimes think that he would prefer to be a servant because they seem to be lording it over him.

All this does not affect his actual position, does not affect his relationship at all; but so far that is his experience. It is purely a matter of experience, not of status. 'Even so,' says Paul, 'when we were children we were in bondage under the elements of the world, but when the fulness of the time was come God sent forth his Son, made of a woman, made under the law, to redeem them that were under the law, that we might receive the adoption of sons' (vv. 3–5). We were sons even then, but we were kept under the law. But now Christ has come and we receive the adoption of sons; 'and because ye are sons God hath sent forth the Spirit of his Son into your hearts, crying, Abba, Father'. You now begin to 'experience' what you were before, in fact without realizing it.

Looking at the argument in the Epistle to the Galatians chapter 4 in greater detail, we find that the word which is translated '*crying*, Abba, Father' is most interesting. The Greek word for 'crying' is extremely old. Its original meaning is the 'croaking of a raven'. It was used to express any kind of elemental cry that came up out of the heart, something that is not always characterized by dignity or felicity of expression; it goes much deeper than that! It is the heart cry of a child, a cry that results from a relationship, the cry of a child who is pleading with his father.

It is most interesting and helpful to note that this selfsame word is used with regard to our blessed Lord Himself. In the fourteenth chapter of Mark's Gospel we find that our Lord used this same expression when he was in the garden of Gethsemane, and prayed saying, 'Abba, Father, all things are possible unto thee; take away this cup from me: nevertheless not what I will, but what thou wilt' (v. 36). Our Lord in His terrible agony, sweating great drops of blood, shows His realization of His filial relationship to His Father in a striking manner. He does not say 'Father' only; He says 'Abba, Father', a term of endearment in which Aramaic and Greek are brought together. This cry was the instinctive cry of a child who knows the relationship to the Father; He is appealing, 'Abba, Father, if it be possible . . .' So the Apostle tells us in the fourth chapter of Galatians that as the result of the work of Christ and this baptism of the Spirit we also are given the Spirit that was in Christ, and He makes us also cry 'Abba, Father'. We have become certain of God as Father, we know Him as Father. We no longer believe in God as Father theoretically, it is the cry of the heart, an elemental, instinctive cry that comes welling up from the depths. That is the result of the sealing of the Spirit.

We can explain it further by saying that the peculiar blessing given to the Christian differentiates him from the Old Testament saints. That is the real argument of the fourth chapter of Galatians. The Old Testament saints, Abraham, Isaac, Jacob, David – all of them – were children of God as much as we are. If we are not clear about that, we shall be confused everywhere. But Paul in his Epistle to the Galatians argues thus: 'If ye are Christ's then are ye Abraham's seed and heirs according to the promise' (3:29). When these Gentiles became Christians they became Abraham's seed, and joint-heirs with Abraham and with all believing Jews of the promises of God.

Similarly in the Epistle to the Ephesians the Apostle says that the special message given to him was to announce that the Gentiles should be 'fellow-heirs' with those Jews who already belonged to the kingdom of God. We can therefore look at the difference which the sealing of the Spirit makes in the following way. The saints under the Old Testament dispensation, and also the Apostles as believers and children of God before the day of Pentecost, were not only believers but also children of God. But, so far, they were like servants, they were under tutors, they lacked a true realization of their position, they were not able to cry, 'Abba, Father'. They believed that God was their Father, but they did not cry out from the depths of their beings, 'Abba, Father'. But once they were baptized with the Spirit, when the 'sealing' came, they cried 'Abba, Father' because God had poured into their hearts this Spirit of adoption, the Spirit of His own Son.

This experience is what is meant by the sealing with the Spirit, or the baptism with the Spirit. It happened to the Apostles on the day of Pentecost in Jerusalem. They had believed in our Lord and His salvation before, but now they were bubbling over with it and rejoicing in it with 'a joy unspeakable and full of glory'. Yet we are told by many evangelical teachers that it is not experimental! Thus, in our fear of the excesses that some who claim this experience may be guilty of, we often become guilty of 'quenching the Spirit', and robbing ourselves of the richest blessings.

This, then, is what is meant by the promise of the Spirit by the Father. It is 'the Spirit of adoption', 'the Spirit of sonship'; not the fact that we are sons, but our realization of it. In other words this sealing is that direct assurance which the Holy Spirit gives us of our relationship to God in Jesus Christ. We have already seen that there are two other types of assurance which are good and excellent as far as they go – the assurance obtained from the objective argument based on statements in Scripture and also the more subjective ground of assurance deduced from the so-called tests of life found in the First Epistle of John. But it is possible for us to know and to have an assurance beyond that, namely, that which is given by the sealing of the Spirit. 'The Spirit himself testifieth with our spirit that we are the children of God' (Romans 8:16). This is a direct and immediate testimony borne by the Holy Spirit to us. It is no longer something which I reason out of the Scriptures; it is not the result of spiritual logic or deduction; it is direct and immediate. It does not mean that we hear any audible voice, or that we see some vision. Generally it comes as the result of the Spirit illuminating certain statements of Scripture, certain promises, certain assurances. He brings them to me with power and they speak to me, and I am certain of them. These things become luminously clear to me and I am as certain that I am a child of God as that I am alive. This is something which happens to us in such a manner that we not only believe in general that all who are Christians are children of God, but the Holy Spirit tells me in particular that I am a child of God.

Now let me supply certain quotations which state this truth in a most moving manner. Let us start with Thomas Goodwin who writes, 'There is a light that cometh and overpowereth a man's soul and assureth him that God is his and he is God's, and that

God loveth him from everlasting'. 'It is a light', he says again, 'beyond the light of ordinary faith'. It is more than your belief of the Scripture and all the arguments you can deduce. He goes on to say, 'It is the next thing to heaven; you have no more, you can have no more, until you come thither'. It is, in other words, the biggest and the greatest experience which a Christian can have in this world. There is only one thing beyond that, namely, heaven itself. It is faith elevated and raised up above its ordinary note and its ordinary reach. It is the electing love of God brought home to the soul.

Now listen to John Wesley: 'It is something immediate and direct, not the result of reflection or argumentation'. Note that he emphasizes the same elements of immediacy and directness as Goodwin. The blessing is not the result of reflection or argumentation. Wesley then goes on to make this striking statement, 'There may be foretastes of joy, of peace, of love, and those not delusive, but really from God, long before we have the witness in ourselves'. In other words you can experience the general work of the Spirit long before this happens to you, before the Spirit of God 'witnessed with our spirits' that we have redemption in the blood of Jesus. According to Wesley's teaching you can be a good Christian, and you can have experienced the operations of the Spirit in many ways even including foretastes of joy and peace and of love from God Himself, long before you have this direct witness of the Spirit, this overwhelming experience.

Have you been 'sealed' with the Spirit? I am not asking you if you are a believer in the Lord Jesus Christ; I am not even asking if you have that type of assurance which is based on the first or second grounds; I am asking whether you know anything about the experience of being overpowered in your soul by the direct witness and testimony of the Spirit?

In order to help in that self-examination let me quote the experiences of certain great men of God in the past. Here is an experience described by John Flavel, a Puritan of some three hundred years ago – 'Thus going on his way his thoughts began to swell and rise higher and higher like the waters in Ezekiel's vision till at last they became an overflowing flood. Such was the intention of his mind, such the ravishing tastes of heavenly joys, and such the full assurance of his interest therein, that he utterly lost a sight and sense of this world and all the concerns thereof, and for some hours he knew no more where he was than if he had been in a deep sleep upon his bed'. Arriving in great exhaustion at a certain spring 'he sat down and washed, earnestly desiring, if it were God's pleasure, that it might be his parting place from this world. Death had the most amiable face in his eye that ever he beheld, except the face of Jesus Christ which made it so, and he could not remember, though he believed himself dying, that he had one thought of his dear wife or children or any other earthly concernment. On reaching his Inn the influence still continued, banishing sleep. Still, still the joy of the Lord overflowed him, and he seemed to be an inhabitant of the other world. He many years after called that day one of the days of heaven, and said that he understood more of the light of heaven by it than by all the books he ever read or discoveries he ever had entertained about it'.

That is an excellent account of the sealing with the Spirit, this foretaste of heaven.

Jonathan Edwards describes the same experience as follows – 'Once, as I rode out into the woods for my health in 1737, having alighted from my horse in a retired place, as my manner commonly has been, to walk for divine contemplation and prayer, I had a view that for me was extraordinary, of the glory of the Son of God as Mediator between God and man, and His wonderful, great, full, pure and sweet grace and love, and meek and gentle condescension. This grace that appeared so calm and sweet appeared also great above the heavens. The Person of Christ appeared ineffably excellent, with an excellency great enough to swallow up all thought and conception, which continued, as near as I can judge, about an hour, which kept me the greater part of the time in a flood of tears and weeping aloud'.

What a contrast to the teaching so popular today which says that sealing is not experimental; that it is all by faith. Jonathan Edwards continues his account: 'I felt an ardency of soul to be, what I know not otherwise how to express, emptied and annihilated; to lie in the dust and to be full of Christ alone; to love Him with a holy and pure love; to trust in Him; to live upon Him; to serve and follow Him and to be perfectly sanctified and made pure with a divine and heavenly purity.'

Let us bear in mind that Jonathan Edwards was one of

the greatest philosophers since Socrates, Plato and Aristotle.

Let us turn now to a very different man, D. L. Moody, who was not a philosopher nor in any way a great intellect. He writes: 'I began to cry as never before. The hunger for this increased. I really felt that I did not want to live any longer if I could not have the power for service. I kept on crying all the time that God would fill me with the Spirit. Well, one day in the City of New York, oh, what a day, I cannot describe it. I seldom refer to it, it is almost too sacred an experience to name. I can only say that God revealed Himself to me, and I had such an experience of His love that I had to ask Him to stay His hand.'

Or take the words of the great Welsh Baptist preacher Christmas Evans as he describes an experience which he had while travelling over a mountain-pass one day. He had been in a dry and lifeless state for a number of years as the result of believing the teaching known as Sandemanianism – similar to the 'Take it by faith' teaching – but now, having begun to pray to God to have mercy upon him, he says:

'Having begun in the Name of Jesus, I felt as it were my shackles loosening, the old hardness softening, and as I thought the mountains of frost and snow dissolving and melting within me. This engendered confidence in my soul in the promise of the Holy Ghost. I felt my whole mind relieved from some great bondage. Tears flowed copiously, and I was constrained to cry out aloud for the gracious visits of God by restoring to my soul the joy of His salvation and that he would visit the churches in Anglesey again that were under my care.'

The following are the words of the eloquent George Whitefield, perhaps England's greatest preacher:

'Soon after this I found and felt in myself that I was delivered from the burden that had so heavily oppressed me; the spirit of mourning was taken from me and I knew what it was truly to rejoice in God my Saviour, and for some time could not avoid singing psalms wherever I was. But my joy gradually became more settled and, blessed be God, has abode and increased in my soul, saving a few casual intermissions, ever since. Thus were the days of my mourning ended. After a long night of desertion and temptation, the Star, which I had seen at a distance before, began to appear again, and the Day Star arose in my heart. Now did the

Spirit of God take possession of my soul and, as I humbly hope, seal me unto the day of redemption.'

He had been a believer for some time before this, but now he was sealed with the Spirit. He goes on to say: 'My friends were surprised to see me look and behave so cheerfully, after the many reports they had heard concerning me.'

Again, hear the words of his friend John Wesley describing the famous experience in Aldersgate Street, London, on May 24th, 1738. Remember, again, that he had become a true believer in justification by faith since the previous March. He writes:

'I felt my heart strangely warmed, I felt that I did trust Christ, Christ alone, for salvation, and an assurance was given me that He had taken away *my* sins, even *mine*, and saved *me* from the law of sin and death.'

He had believed before, but now he had an assurance, he was given this direct, immediate, overwhelming experience and testimony by the Spirit, the sealing of the Spirit, and he felt these things. After this experience his ministry was transformed.

It is almost incredible that any should say that 'the sealing with the Spirit' is non-experimental, and so rob themselves of such experiences. Has your heart been ravished? Have you known this overwhelming experience of the love of God? Let every man examine himself.

24

True and Counterfeit Experiences

'In whom also after that ye believed ye were sealed
with that holy Spirit of promise.'

Ephesians 1:13

There is a sense in which I, for my part, am not concerned about
the terminology with regard to 'sealing' with the Spirit or
'baptism' with the Spirit. To me it is very regrettable that many
are so much concerned about the terminology, and especially
about the word 'baptism', that they fail to face the real question.
That question is, Do we know that we have been sealed with the
Holy Spirit? The question that should be uppermost in our
minds is not the question of terminology but the question of
whether we have the 'Spirit of adoption', whether we really are
crying 'Abba, Father' from the depths of our hearts. Terminology
has its place and it is important that we should have ideas clearly
in our minds; but it is the experience itself that matters most.
So we continue with our description of this blessing in order to
bring truth out yet more clearly.

The first result of the sealing with the Spirit is the immediate,
direct, blessed assurance that we are the children of God, 'heirs of
God and joint-heirs with Christ'. That is what the Apostle is
concerned about chiefly here. He is writing about an inheritance
which Jews and Gentiles have received together in Christ; and he
says that that is sealed to us by the holy Spirit of promise. But
there are certain other results that follow at the same time. One is
mentioned by the Apostle in his Epistle to the Romans, chapter 5,
where he says, 'Experience worketh hope, and hope maketh not
ashamed; because the love of God is shed abroad in our hearts by
the Holy Ghost which is given unto us' (v. 5). Note the expression,
'the love of God is *shed abroad* in our hearts'. It is comparable to the

[279]

term used in the second chapter of Acts about the Holy Ghost being 'poured forth'. It is the same idea exactly; not something vague and indefinite, but the love of God is 'shed abroad' in our hearts so that we are filled to overflowing with this love of God. The sealing of the Spirit leads to that shedding abroad of God's love in our hearts. So we have to ask ourselves whether we know and have experienced it. The question is not whether we believe in the love of God but whether that love has been 'poured' into us by the Holy Spirit. We must be careful not to reduce these terms to the measure of our experiences.

Another result of this sealing is described by the Apostle Peter when in writing to Christian people in his First Epistle, in chapter 1, he addresses them as 'strangers scattered abroad'. But although he does not know them he is able to say to them, 'Whom having not seen, ye love; in whom, though now ye see him not, yet believing, ye rejoice with joy unspeakable and full of glory' (v. 8). The relationship of these people to the Lord Jesus Christ is that they love Him and rejoice in Him with 'joy unspeakable and full of glory'. That is another result of this sealing. Is it right to assume, as so many do, that this is the normal, customary experience of all Christians?

At this stage someone may well ask about spiritual gifts, for it is clear from the second chapter of the Book of Acts that those who were at that time baptized by the Spirit received certain gifts; they spoke with other tongues, and there were clearly other manifestations. It is clear that on the day of Pentecost and subsequently, this sealing with the Spirit was accompanied by gifts. This has emerged in the various Scriptures which we have examined. So it is right that the question should be asked as to whether it therefore follows that, every time a person is sealed with the Spirit, of necessity he has some of these particular gifts. Fortunately we are given an answer to that question in the twelfth chapter of Paul's First Epistle to the Corinthians, where the teaching is that the Holy Spirit is the Lord of these gifts, and that He dispenses them and distributes them as He sees fit. To this man He gives one gift, to that man another gift. They do not all have the same gifts, they do not all have any one particular gift. Paul asks the question 'Do all speak in tongues'? 'Do all interpret'? 'Do all work miracles'? And clearly they do not. There are many gifts, and the Apostle gives a list of them – 'wisdom', 'helps', 'understanding' and so on.

There was trouble in the church of Corinth because of this, for the whole church of Corinth had become divided into groups and factions over the possession of particular gifts. Some were more spectacular than others, and the men who had the spectacular gifts despised those with the lesser ones. So Paul gives his teaching concerning the church as a 'body'; but his main emphasis is that the bestowal of gifts is the prerogative of the Holy Ghost. He can give gifts, He can withhold gifts, as He chooses and as He pleases.

It is interesting to observe that when we read the history of the Christian Church, and especially in terms of this doctrine of the sealing with the Holy Ghost, we find that many of these gifts given at the beginning do not seem to have been given in subsequent ages of the Christian Church. This becomes quite clear as we recall the experiences of the great men to whom we have referred, and who lived in different centuries and places and who were so varied in their natural gifts. Not one of them ever 'spoke with tongues'; but they had other striking gifts. Some had the gift of understanding, others the gift of teaching. Wesley had his amazing gift of 'administration', and organization. But none of them seems to have had the gift of miracles. But they clearly had the sealing with the Spirit.

So it is important that we should differentiate between the sealing itself and the gifts that may or may not accompany it. The central truth concerning the sealing with the Spirit is that it seals the inheritance to us, that it gives the assurance of sonship, and the 'Spirit of adoption' whereby we cry 'Abba, Father'. Unfortunately many have become confused over this question of the sealing because of their confusion about the whole question of gifts. Many are even afraid to consider it merely because they know people who claim to have had this sealing with the Spirit but who insist upon some particular gift as evidence. But Scripture itself, as we have seen, does not give us the right to postulate any particular gifts in connection with the sealing of the Spirit. There may be gifts, there may not be gifts. There is generally some gift, but the vital element is the assurance – immediate and direct – that we are the children of God. Therefore I do not ask whether you have spoken in tongues or not; what I ask once more is whether the love of God has been shed abroad in your heart? Are you rejoicing in Jesus Christ 'with a joy unspeakable and full of glory'? Have you been given a direct witness by the Spirit that you are a child of God, an heir of eternal bliss?

It is surely only in the light of this that we can understand the meaning of a phrase that was used by our Lord when speaking to the disciples shortly before His death. He said 'It is expedient for you that I go away, for if I go not away, the Comforter will not come unto you; but if I depart, I will send him unto you' (John 16:7). The Son of God was standing among the disciples and telling them not to allow their hearts to be troubled because He was about to leave them, indeed actually telling them that it was a good thing for them that He should be going. It is almost incredible that this could possibly be the case. He was the Son of God with all knowledge; He had been teaching them, and had always been there to advise them as to what to do and what not to do, and able to give them power to preach and to cast out devils. But now He is going away, and yet He says, 'It is good for you that I should go away'.

There is only one adequate explanation of that astonishing statement, and it is the truth concerning the sealing with the Spirit. The fact is that after Pentecost these disciples were more certain of Him than they had been when they were able to see Him with their naked eyes. They were more certain of Him, and of the truth of His doctrine. Not only had they a fuller understanding but they were now filled with His own Spirit and with His love. And we are meant to be in the same position, in a better position than if we had been actually alive when our Lord was here in the days of His flesh. So the question we ask ourselves is, Have we that understanding, have we that certain knowledge of our sonship, have we God's love shed abroad in our hearts?

To be yet more explicit and clear, let us consider a number of questions which are always raised when this doctrine is preached.

I would remind you that this is no new doctrine. It is a measure of the ignorance of modern evangelicalism to regard this as having originated in the present century. We have seen it in the teaching of the Puritans of the seventeenth century. John Wesley said many times that he believed that God had raised up the Methodists very largely to preach this special doctrine of assurance. He believed this truth so intensely that he tended at first to say that if you lacked this assurance you were not a Christian at all. He modified that later, saying of himself that prior to his experience in Aldersgate Street in May 1938 he had had the faith of a servant, not that of a son.

The first question often asked is, What is the relationship of the conversion experience to this sealing with the Spirit? It is argued that when a man is converted he is given a rest of soul: 'Being justified by faith we have peace with God' (Romans 5:1). Now what is the difference, someone may ask, between that and the sealing with the Spirit? When a man has this rest of justification he knows that his sins are forgiven, and he is given a sense of peace and of quiet. Is that therefore not the same thing? The answer is that the 'sealing with the Spirit' goes well beyond what is experienced at conversion. The man who is justified by faith believes the Word and believes the teaching of the Word, and as a result he has this sense of rest and of satisfaction. That may often be tested and shaken, however, and he will be driven back to the Word and will have to work out the scriptural arguments to silence his doubts. But as we have seen, when the sealing with the Spirit comes there is no longer any argument. That is so because this is a direct assurance, it is the Spirit Himself bearing witness with our spirit in an unmistakable manner.

There is a very beautiful illustration of this aspect of the truth in the works of the saintly, the 'heavenly' Dr Richard Sibbes, another of the great Puritans of 300 years ago. Dr Sibbes says that the difference between the conversion experience and the 'sealing' can be stated thus. It is like a child who has been a little mischievous and disobedient, who has a sense of guilt and is unhappy, and who keeps on running back to his father. The father receives him but he does not smile much at him. This is the father's way of reprimanding him and of punishing him for his disobedience; but the child by running back gets a certain satisfaction when he is with his father. This may go on for some time. Then one day as they are walking along a road together the child presses near to his father and touches him. The father continues just to look at him; but then after a while the father takes hold of the child, lifts him up and fondles him in his arms and showers his love upon him. That is the difference! Without the sealing of the Spirit you can know that your sins are forgiven; but not in this special and certain manner. This goes beyond the initial experience of forgiveness; this is God, if I may so express it, endearing us and showering His love upon us, overwhelming us. We observed that element in the case of those experiences which I quoted. There was always an overwhelming element. Even a man who had the powerful physique of a D. L. Moody felt that his body was cracking under the greatness of the experience of God's love, and he cried out to God to stop. He was afraid that the glory of the experience would actually kill him. Such is the difference between the two experiences.

Another question which is almost invariably asked is the relationship of sealing to sanctification. There are many who have become confused about the sealing of the Spirit because of this unfortunate confusion of it with sanctification. Some have tended to avoid this whole doctrine of the sealing with the Spirit because the only people they know who mention it also believe in the doctrine of the complete eradication of sin in this life. It is true that even John Wesley himself was guilty of that confusion in his teaching concerning 'perfect love' and what he called 'scriptural holiness'. The answer to the question is that there is no direct connection between the sealing with the Spirit and sanctification.

The Apostle Paul in this section of the Epistle to the Ephesians is not teaching the doctrine of sanctification at all; he has not yet come to it. All the Apostle is doing from verse 1 to verse 14 is to tell us what God has done to us in Christ. He is showing us our position in Christ as sons and heirs. Later he will deal with sanctification. So to bring in sanctification at this point is to confuse terms and to confuse the issue. Sealing has no direct connection with sanctification. Paul says that the sealing has happened to the Ephesians; therefore it cannot be something which is continuous. But sanctification is continuous.

I venture to compare the relationship between this experience of sealing and sanctification to the relationship of showers of rain and sunshine to seed that has been planted in the earth. Think of a farmer who has ploughed his land, harrowed it, sown seed into it, and then rolled it over, and left it. Weeks of cold, dull, dry weather go by, and he sees nothing at all. He wonders whether there is any life in that seed because he does not see any evidence of growth. After a while, however, a little evidence of growth begins to appear above ground. He looks at it day after day and begins to doubt whether he is going to have a crop. But then suddenly there is a shower of rain and a burst of warm sunshine; and he sees the grain almost visibly sprouting up. Then another shower comes and it is still more marvellous. That seems to me to be the connection between the sealing and sanctification. From the moment that the farmer sowed the seed the life was there and the process of growth had begun. In the same way, the moment a man is born again sanctification has already started.

Sanctification is not an experience to be received, it is the working out of the life of God in the soul, and it starts from the moment of re-birth. This must be so, because you cannot have the life of God in you without the activity of that life. But while that is true the process may appear to be quiescent for some time. But then this blessed experience of sealing is given, and like the shower and the sunshine on the earth it has a marked effect upon one's sanctification. It is not sanctification, but it has an inevitable effect upon it. The rain and the shower do not contain life; the life is in the seed; but the rain and sunshine greatly promote and stimulate the growth of the seed; similarly with this experience.

We can say that sealing with the Spirit promotes sanctification, but it does not necessarily guarantee it. It is not the same thing. It thus follows that it is possible for a man who has had this amazing experience of sealing with the Spirit to become a back-slider. It has often happened. He still remembers what has happened to him; he cannot get away from it. There are men who will tell you, in relating their experience, that it was that know-ledge alone that kept them sometimes even from suicide. They had that knowledge although all arguments seemed to be against it. The sealing does not guarantee a continuance in a sanctified life. The poet William Cowper helps us at this point. He asks –

> *Where is the blessedness I knew*
> *When first I saw the Lord?*
> *Where is the soul-refreshing view*
> *Of Jesus and His word?*

This is something to which a man can look back; it is an experience.

A further question which is often asked arises in the following manner. In the statement which has been quoted from John Flavel he says that during the greater part of a day he did not know where he was; he was so enjoying a visitation of God that he even forgot his wife and children in his ecstasy. Is it therefore correct to say that we have not been sealed with the Spirit until we have had some such overwhelming experience? The answer is that the intensity of the experience may vary considerably. The experience itself is unmistakable but the intensity varies even as the intensity of any experience varies. Our appreciation of music varies. Many people have an appreciation of music but it is not always with the same degree of intensity. Our appreciation of beauty and of flowers is not always the same. I may like flowers but I may not be able to say, 'To me the meanest flower that blows can give thoughts that do often lie too deep for tears'. I am not a Wordsworth; but I can appreciate beauty and flowers. The intensity may vary but that must not be understood as meaning that the experience may sometimes be uncertain. It is always certain and unmistakable; there is no question about that! If you have to persuade yourself concerning it, you do not know it. It is of the essence of sealing that it is unmistakable when it is given, for it is God's action.

That, in turn, raises the question of the place of emotion in this experience. Many are troubled about this. Modern Christians seem to be more frightened of emotion than of anything else. This is due to their failure to draw the distinction between emotion and emotionalism. Because they are afraid of emotionalism they are afraid of emotion. There are some who go so far as to boast that there is no emotion in Christian experience. They are pleased when people show no emotion at their conversion. Thus we can be led astray by confused thinking. There is a real difference between emotion and emotionalism. Is it conceivable that anyone can be told directly by God that he is God's child, and yet feel nothing, feel no emotion? There was never a more stolid, unemotional man by nature that John Wesley. He was a typical logician, somewhat prim and pedantic, who distrusted any tendency to excess, yet in the meeting in Aldersgate Street his heart was 'strangely warmed'.

'But', says someone, 'what about the excesses, the fanaticism, and the various phenomena that are sometimes reported? Are you not tending to encourage disorder? In the accounts of revivals strange phenomena are often reported; is all that a part of this sealing'? In reply we must emphasize that for God to visit a soul is the most overwhelming experience one can ever know; and it is not surprising therefore that sometimes the physical frame cannot stand it. We have been reminding ourselves of the case of Moody, who felt that he was on the verge of collapsing physically; and it is not surprising if, sometimes, when the Spirit of God enters into people with great power, they should lose their self-control for a while. This should not trouble us. But should it still do so, the best course to adopt is to read a great book by Jonathan Edwards entitled *On the Nature of the Religious Affections*. Jonathan Edwards passed through the great revival in Northampton in New England in 1735 and afterwards. There were many strange phenomena connected with it; some people were troubled about this, and asked, 'Is this a real work of the Spirit, or is it a counterfeit?' Jonathan Edwards answered such questions in that mighty volume. The essence of his argument is to demonstrate that it is not at all surprising if when the Spirit of God enters into a man's soul in power, unusual things should happen, and that his normal balance should be upset temporarily. This does not justify excesses but helps to explain them. So we need not be afraid of that element. We must remember also that at such a time of revival the devil is anxious to produce counterfeits and cause confusion. He turns people's attention to the phenomena, to the experiences, to the excitement; and there are always people who look only for such things.

So the question arises as to how we can tell the difference between the true and the counterfeit. There are certain tests which can always be applied. True emotion produced by the Holy Ghost always leads to humility, to reverence, to a holy love of God. A man may sing, or may dance for a while; but that does not persist. It is temporary and due to the weakness of the body; but what is permanent, and what proves genuineness, is that the man is filled with a sense of awe. He has been near the Majesty of God and is of necessity humbled. This emerged clearly in the accounts of the experiences of several of the great men of God which I have quoted. They very rarely spoke about it; there was no boastfulness. What had happened to them was almost too sacred to be mentioned. It leads to humility, and to a love of God, and a rejoicing in Christ with 'a joy unspeakable and full of glory'. It must do so because it is a revelation of something of 'the breadth and length and depth and height; and to know the love of Christ which passeth knowledge' (Ephesians 3:18-19). It is impossible to have even a glimpse of such an experience without being moved to the very depths of one's being. Yet one is humbled and at the same time is filled with a sense of awe and of reverence and amazement.

No man ever knew more about these matters than the Apostle Paul himself. As Christians we cannot read his letters without being moved. The emotion seems to come through and to grip us also. It therefore becomes a test of our knowledge of these things. The very Name of the Lord Jesus Christ always moved the great Apostle and seems at times to make him forget his argument and his logic for a while. He bursts out repeatedly into a hymn of praise and of thanksgiving; yet we note his great humility, his self-depreciation, his self-abasement. With all his burning, passionate love there is always reverence. The two elements are always present in the same man. He knew what it was to be lifted up into the third heaven, and yet he gives us this incomparable teaching, characterized by balance and wisdom and understanding. Let us then be careful lest in our fear of excitability and emotionalism and strange enthusiasm and some odd phenomena, we may become guilty of 'quenching' the Spirit, and thereby robbing ourselves and others of these wonderful blessings that God has for all His people. The question for each of us is: Is the love of God shed abroad in my heart? Do I know, beyond argument, beyond having to convince myself, that I am a child of God, and a joint-heir with Jesus Christ? Such is the result to which the sealing of the Spirit leads.

[288]

25

Problems and Difficulties concerning the Sealing

'In whom also after that ye believed, ye were sealed with that holy Spirit of promise.'

Ephesians 1:13

All who have ever written about this experience of the sealing of the Spirit are agreed in saying that it is very difficult to describe it in words. There is something about it which baffles description, as can be illustrated from the Book of Revelation: 'He that hath an ear let him hear what the Spirit saith to the churches; to him that overcometh will I give to eat of the hidden manna, and will give him a white stone, and in the stone a new name written which no man knoweth saving he that receiveth it' (2:17). There is almost a secret in it. But any man who has ever known it, even to the slightest and the faintest extent, will agree that there is nothing which he has ever known that is in any way comparable to it. Truths which he has believed before and which he has accepted and relied on, suddenly become luminous and plain with a clarity which is heavenly and divine. In love, even human love, there is always an element which cannot be put into words. It is much more so with this, because it is an experience of God's love, and in turn of our love going out to Him! We love Him because He first loved us, and there is something almost inexpressible about the experience. Yet it is the most real thing that can ever happen to us.

We have dealt with this subject at this length because it seems abundantly clear from the New Testament, and from the long history of the Christian Church, that there is nothing which is so essential from the standpoint of Christian witness and testimony as this experience of sealing. It is possible to witness in a mechanical manner, but that has very little value; only those who know this sealing are really effective witnesses. That is why our Lord told His disciples to stay at Jerusalem until they had received it. It is not only the highest experience a Christian can ever have; it is the way to make us effective as Christians, to make us alive and radiant. This is proved in every period of revival and of re-awakening.

But there are certain further difficulties with regard to this matter which we must consider. A most important question is: did all the first Christians have this experience? Paul seems to be saying that every member of the Church at Ephesus, and the other churches to which this circular-letter was sent, had been sealed by the Spirit: 'In whom also after that ye believed ye were sealed with that holy Spirit of promise.' If that is the case, it is argued, does not the same apply now? How therefore can it be said that one may be a Christian without knowing this sealing of the Spirit?

In many ways this is the most important question of all with respect to this teaching. I would add that it is also an extremely difficult question: and I can but suggest what for myself, at any rate, is an adequate and sufficient answer. The statement here is one of many similar and comparable statements which we find in the New Testament Epistles. Take for instance the statement in the fifth chapter of Paul's Epistle to the Romans where we read, that 'hope maketh not ashamed because the love of God is shed abroad in our hearts by the Holy Ghost which is given to us' (v. 5). Here Paul seems to be saying that the love of God has been shed abroad in all its profusion in the heart of every Christian. So we might well ask whether this happened to every one of the first Christians? And if so, why does it not happen to every Christian now? Or is it maintained that it does happen to all? The question is not as to whether we feel some occasional glimmerings of the love of God, but whether that love has been poured into our hearts until our hearts are overflowing? This verse, then, is a comparable statement. Again, in the First Epistle of Peter we have a statement which we have already quoted: 'Whom having not seen, ye love; in whom though now ye see him not, yet believing, ye rejoice with joy unspeakable and full of glory' (1:8). Is that true of us? Peter makes what appears to be a universal statement about all Christian people. There are other similar statements which we could quote. The statements seem to be universal, and to apply to all Christians to whom the letters were sent.

What then is the explanation, and how do we reconcile such statements with our contention that the sealing does not apply to all Christians? Now it is obvious that the Apostle Paul did not know every single member of the Church at Ephesus and of other churches, including the church of Rome. The Apostle Peter, as it is made clear, did not know the people to whom he was writing; he writes to them as 'the strangers that are scattered throughout Pontus, Galatia, Cappadocia, Asia and Bithynia'. But he had heard that there were certain Christians in certain places; and he writes a general circular-letter to them. He certainly did not have a detailed knowledge of every individual member as he writes this general letter to them. We can therefore draw the conclusion that in all these universal and general statements the writers are dealing with what they regard as the norm or the standard. They are not saying that this is true of necessity of every particular individual Christian. When they write a general letter to a church they write on the assumption that its members are what every Christian should be; and they address them as such. Peter is obviously doing so, and in spite of being aware that there were variations in the experiences of members of churches Peter writes to them in general saying: 'Whom having not seen, ye love; in whom, though now ye see him not, yet believing, ye rejoice with joy unspeakable and full of glory.' He is clearly stating what is the norm and the standard for every true Christian. That is one part of the answer.

But we can go further, and suggest that it is conceivable, indeed it is even likely, that most of these first Christians were given this experience. Take the event which is described in the second chapter of the Acts of the Apostles. Clearly that was unique not only in being a first occasion, it was also exceptional in its extent and in its intensity. I do not mean that it happened once and for ever, and that it was never to be repeated. To say that is a great error. I am suggesting only that at the beginning it was more intense than it has been subsequently. Now not only do we find repetitions of what happened on the day of Pentecost in later chapters of the Acts of the Apostles, but the story of every great revival in the history of the Church is more or less an exact repetition of what happened at the beginning. Whenever we have a great revival we find large numbers of people, perhaps hundreds of people at a time, having this remarkable experience which only seems to come to an occasional person here and there, now and again, in times when the Church is in periods of decline and lethargy. When there is a revival the blessing is poured out in a lavish manner, sometimes covering a wide area, and large numbers of people testify to the experience. Indeed it has often been pointed out that more can happen in a single day in a revival than might happen in a hundred years without revival. Not that in the more ordinary times the Church was not Christian. At such times the Holy Spirit is doing His more regular work, and those receiving this experience are more or less exceptional; but at a time of revival the vivid experience becomes more widespread.

This was still more obviously the case at the inauguration of the Christian Church. God was setting the standard, as it were, that which was meant to be the norm, or the pattern for the whole Church. It is as if God said, 'This is what I promise to do, this is an example of what is possible for you. I do it in order to encourage you to seek it'. So it is possible that in all those early churches, when they were founded, this sealing with the Spirit was given to all. We certainly see it happening to a large number on the day of Pentecost; we see it happening to certain Samaritans as the result of the visit of Peter and John; we see it happening to the Apostle Paul; and in the house of Cornelius; we see Paul giving the same blessing to the twelve disciples whom he found at Ephesus. That seems to be the norm and the standard in New Testament times.

To explain, therefore, why Paul here writes in this manner to the Ephesians, we are entitled to give one or the other of these two explanations – either that all Christians had actually received this blessing because they belonged to the early Church at the beginning, or that the Apostle was speaking generally concerning the norm and the standard rather than in terms of every individual member of the Church.

Our next question is still more relevant to us, and still more practical: Is the experience which I have been describing meant for every Christian? 'I have noticed,' someone may say, 'that you have emphasized what happened in the time of the Apostles and what happens in times of revivals; and also that the individuals whose experiences have been quoted were outstanding men such as Whitefield and Wesley and Jonathan Edwards and D. L. Moody.' Many have deduced from this that the experience is only meant for outstanding people and not for 'ordinary' Christians. But that is an entirely false conclusion to draw, as can readily be shown from Scripture. When the Apostle Peter preached on the day of Pentecost in the power of the Spirit, men cried out saying, 'Men and brethren, what shall we do?' Peter replied: 'Repent, and be baptized every one of you in the name of (the Lord) Jesus Christ, and ye shall receive the gift of the Holy Ghost; for the promise is unto you, and to your children, and to all that are afar off, even as many as the Lord our God shall call' (vv. 38–39). There is no limit, there is no distinction; it is not only meant for apostles or outstanding servants of God; it is meant for all Christian people. God is the Father of every Christian in exactly the same way. He is the Father of the humblest Christian in precisely the same manner as He is of the most exalted servant in the Church. The subsequent history of the Church confirms this abundantly. We have already seen that this seems to have been the case in the New Testament Church: 'The strangers scattered abroad' to whom Peter wrote rejoiced in Him with a 'joy unspeakable and full of glory'.

In the subsequent history of the Church you will find that people whose names have never been heard of have experienced the sealing of the Spirit. It was the case in the days of the evangelical awakening of two hundred years ago. Some of the early Methodist churches would not receive a man into church membership unless he had full assurance. That may have been excessive as a condition, it certainly erred on the right side, and proved the spirituality of the leaders in those churches. However, as I repeat, this is meant for all of us; and let us always bear in mind that it is not always present in the same intensity.

The analogy of the seal pressed on to melted wax helps here. Sometimes when a person uses a seal he finds that the impress on the wax is very plainly and clearly seen; but sometimes it is so faint and indistinct that it can only just be made out. But whether distinct or faint it is there; and it should be there. We must not insist that we all should have the profound and moving experience of a man like Jonathan Edwards, who tells us that his sense of the glory and love of God came upon him in waves and with such intensity that he was sweating, though the physical temperature was low. And you will find that such a man as Charles G. Finney, though so different theologically, describes the same experience in almost exactly the same terminology. While it need not happen in such great intensity I repeat that it is the birthright of every Christian to be absolutely certain and sure of his salvation—'because ye are sons, God hath sent forth the Spirit of his Son into your hearts, crying, Abba, Father' (Galatians 4:6). To use a human analogy: there may be a little child in a family who is not quite normal, or not fully developed, but it is as much a child of the father and mother as the highly intelligent members of the family. It is sonship that matters; therefore every Christian should know this sealing with the Spirit.

The remaining question which many ask is: Are we to seek this sealing? My answer, without any hesitation, is that we should most certainly do so. As we must be careful about the way in which we should seek it, it is wise to start with a negative. There is nothing in contemporary Christianity which is so dangerous and so unscriptural as the teaching that, with regard to each and every blessing in the Christian life, all that we have to do is 'to take it by faith', and not worry about feelings. This is taught with regard to conversion, sanctification, assurance and physical healing. Dreadful tragedies have happened in every one of these realms as the result of such teaching. Let me give certain examples.

The late gifted Andrew Murray of South Africa at one time was a great believer in what is called faith healing; and he taught it in the manner which we are criticizing. If a Christian were taken ill he should read the Scriptures and believe their teaching to be that it is God's will for a Christian to be always healthy. He should then go to God and tell Him that he believed the Scriptures and this particular teaching, and then ask Him for healing. But the vital point was that he should get up from his knees believing that he had already been healed. The fact that he did not feel better made no difference; he must take his healing by faith and proceed to live his life as if he were perfectly well. But there came a time when Andrew Murray ceased to believe after this fashion, and his biography explains how this happened. He had a favourite nephew who was suffering from a certain chest complaint, probably tuberculosis. Andrew Murray was due to go on a series of preaching meetings in a certain part of South Africa and the nephew was anxious to go with him; but in his ill condition he was not fit to go. The two men believed the same teaching about healing by faith and they both went on their knees together and asked God for healing. They rose to their feet both believing that the young man was healed. They packed their bags and went off together. But they had only been away for a short time when the young man died.

Let us be clear in our minds, then, that we do not receive this blessing in that way and apart from feelings; when we are sealed with the Holy Spirit of God we shall know it. It is not to be accepted by faith, apart from feelings. You must go on asking for it until you have it, until you know that you have it. The teaching of 'Take it by faith' is responsible, I believe, for much of the present undesirable state of the Christian Church. Many seem to go through the entire course of the Christian life in that way, saying, 'We do not worry about our feelings, we take it by faith', with the result that they never seem to have any experience at all. They live on what they suggest to themselves, it is a kind of auto-suggestion or Couéism. But when *God* blesses the soul, the soul *knows* it. When God reveals His heart of love to you, your own heart is melted by the experience. The Apostles and others who were filled with the Holy Spirit on the day of Pentecost were radiant, taken up above and beyond themselves, and they spoke with an amazing authority and assurance; and all who saw and heard them were amazed and asked 'What meaneth this?' (Acts 2:12). Let us be careful lest we rob ourselves of some of God's richest blessings. When God seals you with the Spirit you will know it. You will not have to 'take it by faith' irrespective of your feelings and your condition, and simply keep on saying,

'I must have had it, because I believe, I have taken God's word for it'. You will not have to persuade yourself; the persuasion will be done by the Holy Ghost and you will know something of this rejoicing 'with a joy unspeakable and full of glory'.

I am not suggesting, however, that we should indulge in what have been sometimes called 'tarrying meetings'. There was a sense in which those who started such meetings were right; at any rate they realized that such a policy was something experimental. But they were wrong when they went on to say, 'Let us meet together and let us wait until we have had the blessing we seek'. They would wait for days and sometimes weeks, with the result that, time and again, certain unfortunate results tended to follow. This was more or less inevitable as they were creating certain psychological conditions. If people wait in that manner without food and drink, and in a tense atmosphere, there is always an enemy on hand who is ready to produce a counterfeit. And there is always our own psychology, the power of persuasion, and the danger that people may work themselves into a false ecstasy. This danger became especially real when they said, 'I will not go out of the building until I have the blessing'.

Furthermore, there is the very real danger of forgetting the Lordship of the Spirit, and the sovereignty of God. It is He who decides when to give this blessing. It is He who decides to whom to give it. We cannot command it, and we must never adopt the attitude of saying, 'I am going to fulfil the conditions and wait until it has happened'. That is unscriptural; it is not God's method. He certainly told the disciples to tarry at Jerusalem until the day of Pentecost, for He had determined on that particular day, as He had revealed already to the Old Testament saints; but it supplies no precedent for 'tarrying meetings'.

What then should we do? Let me summarize the answer. Search the Scriptures, search the Scriptures for the promises, those 'exceeding great and precious promises' of which the Apostle Peter speaks (2 Peter 1:4). Realize what God means you to have, and what He offers you. In the third chapter of our Ephesian Epistle Paul says that he is praying for his friends: 'That he would grant you, according to the riches of his glory, to be strengthened with might by his Spirit in the inner man: that Christ may dwell in your hearts by faith; that ye, being rooted and grounded in love, may be able to comprehend with all saints what is the breadth, and length, and depth, and height; and to know the love of Christ, which passeth knowledge' (vv. 16–19). You and I are meant to know something about this love of Christ which passes knowledge. Do you know it? You are meant to know it; so I say, Read the Scriptures. And as you read the Scriptures say: 'That is meant for me, I am meant to know that Christ loves me in that manner. I believe it, but I have never known it, I have never experienced it; but I am meant to do so'. Then go on to say, 'I should have this; I ought to know this'. That will stimulate you to pray.

The next principle is to make sure that we are seeking the right thing. We are not to seek experiences and phenomena as such. We are to seek the Lord, to seek to know Him and His love. It is almost insulting to Him to seek His blessings and not to seek Him. He has done all this for us in order that we might know Him, the only true God, and Jesus Christ whom He has sent. Seek Him; seek the knowledge of Him, seek His righteousness, seek His holiness. Seek all these and you will never go astray. But if you seek ecstasies and visions and feelings, you will probably have them; but they will be counterfeit. Seek Him, and you cannot go wrong.

The next step is to do all that we can to prepare the way. 'Mortify, therefore, your members which are upon the earth' (Colossians 3:5). We must be cleansed, and must cleanse ourselves, if this loving Guest is to enter in. 'Mortify, therefore, your members.' Get rid of sin, purify your hearts; get rid, says Paul, of 'all filthiness of the flesh and of the spirit' (2 Corinthians 7:1). 'Purify your hearts, ye double minded,' says James (4:8). Then take Peter's advice in the first chapter of his Second Epistle: 'Add to your faith virtue', and so on (vv. 5–8). The man who fails to do this is short-sighted, says Peter; he does not 'see afar off', he does not realize 'that he was purged from his old sins' (v. 9). But if you do these things 'you will make your calling and election sure', and 'an entrance shall be ministered unto you abundantly into the everlasting kingdom of our Lord and Saviour Jesus Christ' (vv. 10–11). We must concentrate on making our 'calling and election sure'.

Then, positively, as we have seen, we are to put into practice he virtues which the Apostle Peter mentions in detail: 'Add to your faith virtue, and to virtue knowledge, and to knowledge temperance, and to temperance patience, and to patience godliness, and to godliness brotherly kindness, and to brotherly kindness charity (love).' Peter exhorts us to do these things. He does not merely say, 'Go to a meeting and wait for it, or receive it by faith'. We have to 'furnish out our faith', to fill it out with these other things. We are to labour at it – 'Work out your own salvation with fear and trembling' (Philippians 2:12).

If you read the lives of the great men of God whose experiences I have quoted, you will find that they all followed these injunctions. They were all men who laboured in reading the Scriptures and trying to understand them; they purified their lives by self-examination and mortification of the flesh. As you read the biographies of Whitefield and Wesley and Jonathan Edwards and John Fletcher of Madeley, and others, you will find that all these men gave themselves to spiritual exercises. They did not 'take it by faith' and persuade themselves that they must have received it; they gave themselves to seeking God. All this, of course, leads invariably to prayer. You must pray for this blessing. I like Thomas Goodwin's word here: 'Sue Him for it,' he says, 'Sue Him for it', 'Give him no rest', as Isaiah says (62:7).

I know of no better prayer to offer than that found in one of the hymns of William Williams, the Welsh hymn-writer, which has been translated thus:

Speak, I pray Thee, gentle Jesus,
Oh, how passing sweet Thy words,
Breathing o'er my troubled spirit
Peace which never earth affords;
All the world's distracting voices,
All enticing tones of ill,
At Thine accents mild, melodious,
Are subdued and all is still.

Tell me Thou art mine, O Saviour,
Grant me an assurance clear;
Banish all my dark misgivings,
Still my doubtings, calm my fear,

> *Oh, my soul within me yearneth*
> *Now to hear Thy voice divine,*
> *So shall grief be gone for ever,*
> *And despair no more be mine.*

That is the way! Offer up that prayer to Him until He has answered it. 'Tell me Thou art mine, O Saviour, grant me an assurance clear.' Has He granted you that request? Has He whispered to you, has He spoken to you? Pray for His blessing, seek it, be desperate for it, hunger and thirst for it. Keep on praying until your prayer is answered. Take time, in other words. Take time! Not only 'take time to be holy' but take time to seek this sealing with the Spirit. Keep on, never cease; and your experience one day will be:

> *Sometimes a light surprises*
> *The Christian while he sings;*
> *It is the Lord who rises*
> *With healing in His wings.*

This may well happen when you least expect it. The lives and the testimonies of the saints throughout the centuries are agreed in saying that God tends to do this for us at certain special times. Sometimes when a man has to go through a very great trial God gives him this blessing just before the trial comes. How kind is our God! What a loving Father! When He knows that something is about to happen to you that will test you to the very depth of your being, He grants you this blessed assurance, so that you can go through the trial triumphantly. It may happen after a period of apparent desertion. Sometimes, after a time when the fig tree was not blossoming and all the trees were bare, when all had gone wrong, suddenly the light breaks, and He speaks and He whispers His love to us, and gives us 'the white stone' with the 'new name', and feeds us on 'the hidden manna'.

Many Christian people have only known this just before their death; and they have agreed in saying that it was their own ignorance that prevented their receiving it earlier. They had not sought it as they should have done. They were good men, they had lived the Christian life, they had even been used of God; but they had never heard His 'accents mild, melodious'; He had never whispered in their hearts. Their desire for the blessing had been too spasmodic; they had not longed for it and sought it as they should have done. But face to face with the end, they have sought it with a new intensity, and He has heard them and has spoken to them. There are many such Christians. God has granted them this blessed direct assurance just before He took them to Himself for ever.

So I say again, Seek it. Be satisfied with nothing less. Has God ever told you that you are His child? Has He spoken to you, not with an audible voice, but, in a sense, in a more real way? Have you known this illumination, this melting quality? Have you known what it is to be lifted up above and beyond yourself? If not, Seek it; cry out to Him, saying, 'Speak, I pray Thee, gentle Jesus', and 'Sue Him for it', and keep on until He speaks to you.

26

'The Earnest of our Inheritance'

'Which is the earnest of our inheritance until the redemption of the purchased possession, unto the praise of his glory.'

Ephesians 1:14

This statement is obviously a continuation of what the Apostle has been saying in verse 13 and especially concerning the sealing with the Holy Spirit of promise. It is not only a continuation of, but also an addition to that statement and to the entire statement which the Apostle has been making from the beginning of this Epistle.

We have seen that the sealing with the Spirit is the exceptional assurance which God gives to His people; it is 'the Spirit testifying with our spirits that we are the children of God'. But the Apostle, in his desire to strengthen and to comfort and to build up the Ephesians, feels that he cannot leave the matter there, because there is another aspect of the truth which, from the experimental and experiential standpoint, is in a sense still more precious. He deals with this in verse 14. The connection is as follows: '... after that ye believed ye were sealed with that Holy Spirit of promise, which is the earnest of our inheritance until the redemption of the purchased possession.'

It is unfortunate that the Authorized Version and certain other translations have *which* instead of *who*, because it is the Spirit Himself to whom the Apostle is making reference.

I emphasize that the Apostle is not repeating himself here or saying the same thing again in a different way. This is not a case of tautology, he is really adding to the truth, he is taking us a step further, and still with the object and purpose of helping us to see something more of the glory of our position in Christ Jesus. It is all 'to the praise of his glory'. This is another facet, another

[301]

glimpse, another angle of vision of that eternal glory which resides in our blessed Lord and Saviour.

It is interesting to observe how the Apostle almost invariably links together these two things – the sealing and the earnest. He does so in the Second Epistle to the Corinthians, where he says: 'Now he which stablisheth us with you in Christ, and hath anointed us, is God, who hath also sealed us and given the earnest of the Spirit in our hearts' (1: 21–22). Paul also does very much the same thing – although he does not actually use the term for sealing – in the fifth chapter of that same Second Epistle to the Corinthians, where he says: 'Now he who hath wrought us for the selfsame thing is God, who also hath given unto us the earnest of the Spirit' (v. 5). It is only as we understand this type of doctrine that we can be truly established. The whole purpose of doctrine is not merely to give us intellectual understanding or satisfaction, but to establish us, to make us firm, to make us solid Christians, to make us unmovable, to give us such a foundation that nothing can shake us. And surely this is our greatest need at the present time. As Christian people we need to be stablished, and to learn to think of ourselves not so much in terms of particular experiences as in terms of our whole position and the greatness of that which God has planned and intended for us.

We start then by looking at the meaning of this term *earnest* – 'which is the *earnest* of our inheritance'. It is a term which is used frequently in connection with business transactions, although it is not used as commonly today as was once the case. At one time it was a very common term in all transactions of buying and selling, and there is general agreement that it then had two meanings. One was that it was a kind of pledge that is given, a guarantee. A man buying a piece of land, for example, had not sufficient money to pay for it all; so the custom was that, as he promised to pay it all at a later date, for the time being he gave the other person something as a pledge and a guarantee that he would eventually pay the full price.

But there is a richer meaning to this term, namely, that it is not only a pledge but also an instalment, actually a small part of the full price to be paid. There is a subtle but a real difference at this point. You can give something as a pledge which is not of the same nature as the thing itself. For instance, in buying a piece of land you can give a pledge of money; it is a pledge, it is a guarantee, but it is not an earnest. What is peculiar to an earnest is that it is a pledge or a guarantee which is also of the same kind and of the same nature as the thing itself. For instance, in the case of the transference of money, if you give a portion of the money it is an earnest in addition to being a pledge; whereas if you gave an article of clothing or an article of furniture as a pledge it would be a pledge, but it would not be an earnest. The characteristic of an earnest is that it is an instalment, the first payment in kind of the very thing itself. It is vital to the true understanding of this doctrine that we should realize that an earnest is a first instalment of the whole, a guarantee that the rest will follow, and it is a pledge in that sense. But there is another difference also between a pledge and an earnest. If you have given a pledge to cover a transaction, when you actually make the payment your pledge is returned to you. The terms 'pledge' or 'guarantee', or 'pawn' mean the same thing. You leave your deposit, but when the time comes and you make your payment, your deposit or your pledge is returned to you. But that does not happen in the case of an earnest. The reason is that an earnest is a part or portion of the whole, and therefore it is not returned to you when the remainder is paid.

Take a simple illustration. Imagine that you owed someone a pound. You may give a pledge for that; for instance, you may give a book as a pledge. Then when you pay your debt you are given back your book. But if instead of giving a book as a pledge you gave an earnest, a shilling let us say, then when you come to settle up with the man from whom you borrowed, you do not get your shilling back, and then give him a pound, you simply add nineteen shillings. This is so because your earnest was actually a part of the whole. So if we are to derive the full benefit from the Apostle's teaching here we must hold on to that idea.

One of the defects of some of the popular modern translations of Scripture is that they have missed this point completely. The translation found in the Revised Standard Version, for instance, is not only weak but totally inadequate. It translates thus: 'which is the guarantee of our inheritance until we acquire possession of

GOD'S ULTIMATE PURPOSE

it.' That, of course, is true; it is a guarantee; but the word used by Paul has a much fuller content. That prompts me to say that we should be careful in our use of these modern translations. Strict accuracy in language is not everything. A bias may come in, and it is interesting to note how men who may be experts in the knowledge of words, when one of two or three words may be used, often choose a word that is quite accurate but which lacks the fulness of meaning supplied by one of the other words. The theological standpoint of translators is important as well as their technical skill. We have already encountered several instances in this section of the Epistle to the Ephesians where the translators of the Revised Standard Version seem almost to delight in using the feebler word when they might have used the greater and the higher. 'Guarantee' here is a weaker word than 'earnest'.

An 'earnest' then is something which is given us 'on account'. The word 'until' brings this out yet more clearly – 'Who is the earnest of our inheritance until . . .' Until what? 'until the redemption of the purchased possession.' Note again how the Revised Standard Version states it: 'which is the guarantee of our inheritance until we acquire possession of it.' That, again, is legitimate, is possible; but their emphasis is on *we acquire*. The Authorized Version says: 'until the redemption of the purchased possession.' The word 'redemption' is omitted in the Revised Standard Version. The English Revised Version is slightly different from the Authorized and translates thus: 'which is an earnest of our inheritance unto the redemption.' It has kept the word 'redemption' and also the word 'earnest'. It continues: 'the earnest of our inheritance, unto the redemption of God's own possession.' Now 'God' is not mentioned in the Authorized Version. The reference to God is not actually found in the original; the revisers were interpreting at that point, as their use of italics shows.

With respect to the word 'redemption' we find that it is in the Greek, in the original; that is what makes its omission by the R.S.V. translators so significant. It is clear that 'the final completion of God's plan' is the meaning which it carries here. We find the same meaning in the First Epistle to the Corinthians, chapter 1 verse 30, where the Apostle says: 'Who of God is made unto us wisdom, and righteousness, and sanctification, and redemption.'

[304]

There are some who think of 'redemption', only in terms of the forgiveness of sins; but in sundry passages it has a wider scope. Sometimes it means 'forgiveness'; but the context will generally make the meaning plain. Obviously, as used in 1 Corinthians 1:30, 'redemption' means the 'final consummation', the end, God's complete purpose fulfilled in our entire emancipation and deliverance.

As we have seen earlier, the word which the Apostle used is a very particular and technical term. 'Redemption' means deliverance by means of the payment of a ransom price, and in the Christian sense it means the ransom price of the blood of Christ that has been paid for our final redemption and deliverance. So the Apostle is saying here that the blessing brought to us by the Holy Spirit, and the sealing in particular, is an instalment given to us until we receive in all its fulness what Christ has purchased for us by His own precious blood. The word 'acquire' of the R.S.V. introduces an idea which is alien to the Apostle's emphasis.

In considering the reading in the Revised Version – 'Which is the earnest of our inheritance unto the redemption of God's own possession' – we are confronted by two possibilities. We can look at the words either from God's standpoint or from the human standpoint. It is God's plan to gather out a people – the fulness of the Gentiles, the fulness of the Jews. He is doing so, for we read: 'known unto God are all his works' (Acts 15:18), 'the foundation of God standeth sure, having this seal, The Lord knoweth them that are his' (2 Timothy 2:19). God has His perfect plan for redeeming a given number of souls, and 'redemption', from the Godward aspect, refers to the time when all these have been safely gathered in. They are God's possession. 'The Lord's portion is his people' (Deuteronomy 32:9). Clearly, the translators of the Revised Version took that view of the matter. It is undoubtedly the view which the Apostle himself puts forward in verse 18 in this chapter. He prays that the eyes of our understanding may be enlightened, 'that we may know what is the hope of his calling, and what is the riches of the glory of his inheritance in the saints'. There we have a picture of the saints as God's inheritance, as God's heritage. So this is a legitimate view of this phrase.

Nevertheless it seems to me that the Authorized Version is

better in this instance. The way to decide the issue is not in terms of linguistics alone, but also in terms of the context and of doctrine. The Apostle at this point is concerned to give comfort and consolation and assurance to his readers, so I suggest that he is looking at this matter from the human standpoint rather than from God's side. He is saying that God has given us an instalment of our inheritance until we receive the whole. The translation of the Authorized Version falls naturally and comfortably into the entire context. Alternatively, it makes little difference, because the day when we shall have entered fully into our inheritance is the day when all God's possession in His people will also be complete.

We can now turn to the message, to the doctrine conveyed by this term 'earnest'. The first question is as to the difference between the sealing and the earnest. The seal is that which assures me that I am an inheritor; it gives me an assurance with regard to my relationship to the inheritance. The earnest is that which gives me an assurance with regard to the thing itself; it gives me the enjoyment of an actual portion of it and therefore increases my assurance that I shall receive all ultimately. There is an obvious difference between the two.

The Apostle's teaching, then, is that the Holy Ghost has been given to me, and that He, by bearing witness with my spirit, has assured me that I am a child of God. God has said to me, 'Thou art my son', and given full proof through the sealing that He is peculiarly interested in me in Christ; but He has also given me this earnest of my inheritance.

Let us look first at the earnest as a pledge. The best way of looking at the Holy Spirit as the pledge of my inheritance is to look at the matter in the way in which the Apostle expounds it in certain of the verses in the eighth chapter of his Epistle to the Romans. Take, for instance, the eleventh verse: 'But if the Spirit of him that raised up Jesus from the dead dwell in you, he that raised up Christ from the dead shall also quicken your mortal bodies by his Spirit that dwelleth in you.' Take note of the Apostle's argument in the context of this verse. He explains how in spirit we are already redeemed, dead to the law, dead to sin;

we are 'in Christ', we are risen with Him. But sin remains in our mortal body and we are at times discouraged because of the fight against it. The Apostle's comfort and encouragement to us is found in the verse just quoted. The fact that the Spirit dwells in us is an earnest, a pledge of what will yet happen to us completely an dperfectly. There is a day coming when our very bodies will be entirely delivered from sin, the guarantee of His blessing being the presence of the Spirit within our bodies. Because the Spirit is in me I know that my body is destined to be delivered finally from sin's presence.

We find the same idea in the twenty-third verse of this same eighth chapter where, after referring to creation, Paul says: 'Not only they (the whole creation) but ourselves also, which have the firstfruits of the Spirit, even we ourselves groan within ourselves, waiting for the adoption, to wit, the redemption of our body.' The presence of the Spirit within us is a guarantee of 'the adoption, the redemption of our body' which is to come, in spite of all the groaning of which we may be very conscious at the present time.

The same idea is found in the Second Epistle of Paul to the Corinthians, chapter 5, verses 1–5: 'We know that if our earthly house of this tabernacle were dissolved, we have a building of God, a house not made with hands, eternal in the heavens. For in this [the body] we groan, earnestly desiring to be clothed upon with our house which is from heaven: if so be that being clothed we shall not be found naked. For we that are in this tabernacle do groan, being burdened' – sin in the body, sin in the flesh, the law of the members – 'not for that we would be unclothed, but clothed upon, that mortality might be swallowed up of life. Now he that hath wrought us for the selfsame thing is God, who also hath given unto us the earnest of the Spirit'. The Spirit within me is an earnest, is a guarantee that although I am groaning now I shall be delivered and clothed with that house which is from heaven, truly 'a building of God'.

We now turn to look at the other aspect of the subject. The Holy Spirit within us is not only a pledge, He is also an instalment of our inheritance. The Apostle conveys this through the term 'firstfruits'. It is a reference to an ancient custom among farming communities. At the time of harvest the farmer went out and reaped a certain amount of his crop. He then took it home and, having turned it into flour, said to his wife, 'Bake this so that we can taste a sample of what is to come'. He had not yet gathered in the whole of the harvest but only a portion, the firstfruits. Having sown the seed in the Spring, and having waited through the months of summer, at last the harvest has arrived, and he is anxious to try a little of it. The Spirit and His work within us, especially the sealing, is the firstfruits of the great harvest that awaits us. Or we can think of it as a 'foretaste'. The 'firstfruits' was a specimen, and as we partake of it, we have a foretaste of what is to come, something to whet our appetite, something which gives enjoyment and ravishes our hearts.

In other words the Apostle's teaching is that the Holy Spirit within us gives us what we as Christians should be enjoying – a foretaste of heaven! Our coming together in public worship should be a foretaste of heaven. As we meet to consider these things, and to talk about them, and to discuss them, we are having a foretaste of heaven. Public worship should be a gathering of the firstfruits, a sampling of what is to be our lot in heaven. These New Testament Epistles constantly urge us to look forward to the enjoyment of heaven. We know little of what that means, and we are told but little about it in the Scriptures, but we can safely say that the two chief blessings in heaven will be to see our blessed Lord and Saviour, and to become like Him. 'Blessed are the pure in heart, for they shall see God' (Matthew 5:8). 'Beloved, now are we the sons of God, and it doth not yet appear what we shall be; but we know that, when he shall appear, we shall be like him, for we shall see him as he is' (1 John 3: 2). To see our blessed Lord and Saviour face to face, to see God; this is beyond our comprehension, and we cannot grasp it because it is so glorious. But in heaven we shall see God, and look into the face of our blessed Saviour who died for us. All we have at present, even our highest experiences, are the firstfruits; they are only the foretaste of bliss.

What the Apostle emphasizes is that we should be enjoying the firstfruits and the foretaste now: 'we ourselves who have the firstfruits of the Spirit' (Romans 8:23). And elsewhere he gives us some idea as to what that means. In the Second Epistle to the Corinthians, chapter 3, verses 17 and 18, he writes: 'Now the Lord is that Spirit, and where the Spirit of the Lord is, there is liberty. But we all, with open face beholding as in a glass the glory of the Lord, are changed into the same image from glory to glory, even as by the Spirit of the Lord.' That is to happen now! We do not see Him yet face to face, but we do see Him with open face as in a glass, as in a mirror. It is but a reflection which we see now but by the Spirit we are seeing a reflection of the glory of the Lord.

Paul says much the same thing in his First Epistle to the Corinthians, chapter 13, verse 12, where we read: 'But now we see through a glass darkly, but then face to face. Now I know in part, but then shall I know even as also I am known.' Now we see 'through a glass darkly', we see a 'riddle in an enigma', as some-one has translated it. It is not clear as yet; we are seeing the real glory itself, but only as in a glass darkly. The face of the mirror is not sufficiently polished to catch the full glory; there are elements of distortion and indistinctness; but *then* 'face to face'! But thank God that what I do see now is a part of the eternal glory; it is an instalment, it is the firstfruits, it is a foretaste, it is an earnest. It is not only a guarantee, it is a part of the thing itself. I am entering into the glory in a measure even now. Such is the Apostle's teaching. It begins here imperfectly and only in small portions; nevertheless it is real, a part of the glory itself, as much as I can stand and bear while I am still in the flesh.

The second aspect is that we become like our Lord, and share His life. To be like Him means perfection, absolute perfection, without spot, without blemish, without wrinkle or any such thing. Jude in the striking benediction at the end of his Epistle says, 'Now unto him that is able to keep you from falling and to present you faultless before the presence of his glory with exceeding joy . . .'. We are given some idea of it in the description given in the Book of Revelation: 'But the fearful, and unbelieving, and the abominable, and murderers, and whoremongers, and sorcerers,and idolaters, and all liars, shall have their part in the lake which burneth with fire and brimstone: which is the second death' (21:8). They will not be in heaven, but outside. In the same chapter we read further: 'There shall in no wise enter into it [the holy city] anything that defileth, neither whatsoever worketh abomination, or maketh a lie: but they which are written in the Lamb's book of life' (v. 27). Again, in the twenty-second chapter of the same Book, the last chapter of the Bible, we read: 'He that is unjust let him be unjust still, and he that is filthy let him be filthy still' (v. 11). That is hell – outside heaven! 'And he that is righteous let him be righteous still, and he that is holy let him be holy still.' That is heaven! Take also verses 14 and 15: 'Blessed are they that do his commandments, that they may have right to the tree of life and may enter in through the gates into the city. For without are dogs, and sorcerers, and whoremongers, and murderers, and idolaters, and whosoever loveth and maketh a lie.' 'Nought that defileth' shall enter in: it is utter, absolute purity. That is what we shall enjoy when we shall see Him as He is, and shall have been made like Him. But we are promised a foretaste of even that also in this life and world, for the Holy Spirit is the earnest of our inheritance. We are to know something about the joy of holiness, and a hatred of sin, and to abominate the world and all its ways, all its desires, and all it represents. We should learn to hate sin as Christ hated it, and to enjoy holiness and purity and righteousness. Do you know what it is to enjoy holiness, to feel that His commandments 'are not grievous', to delight in the law of the Lord, to love it because it is what it is? We are to have the foretaste of such a state.

Furthermore, love is a great characteristic of heaven. When we shall see Him we shall love Him altogether; but we are to begin to love Him here. Paul prays for the Ephesians in his third chapter, that 'being strengthened with might by his Spirit in the inner man', they may begin to know something of the 'breadth and the length and the depth and the height, and to know the love of Christ which passeth knowledge, that (they) might be filled with all the fulness of God'. Do you love God? In heaven you will love Him absolutely. Do you begin to love Him here? We are meant to do so; and if we have the firstfruits we shall do so: to know His love to us, to love Him, and to love one another. In heaven we shall all love one another; but that is to begin here. If we have the firstfruits of the Spirit in us we shall begin to love one another because we belong to Christ.

The same applies to joy. The joy of heaven is unmixed. This is described in the closing chapters of the Book of Revelation: 'And God shall wipe away all tears from their eyes, and there shall be no more death, neither sorrow, nor crying, neither shall there be any more pain, for the former things are passed away' (21:4). Unmixed joy! But that again is to begin here. 'The kingdom of God is not meat and drink, but righteousness and peace and joy in the Holy Ghost' (Romans 14:17). 'Whom having not seen ye love; in whom though now ye see him not, yet believing, ye rejoice with joy unspeakable and full of glory' (1 Peter: 1:8) – now! If the Holy Ghost is in us we shall know something about this joy. That is why the Apostle repeatedly appeals to the Philippians, 'Rejoice in the Lord alway, and again I say, Rejoice' (4:4). We are also to know something of 'the peace of God that passeth all understanding'. Heaven is perfect peace and bliss, and we are to know something about it here. Whatever circumstances we may find ourselves in, we may be at peace – whether we are abased or abounding, in want, in need, or full and in abundance, we should always be enjoying this perfect peace of God.

Receive, then, the doctrine conveyed by the term 'earnest'. Through the Holy Spirit within us as an earnest we are to begin enjoying heaven even here. 'Celestial fruits on earthly ground from faith and hope may grow.'

> *Children of the heavenly King,*
> *As ye journey, sweetly sing . . .*
> *We are travelling home to God*
> *In the way the fathers trod;*
> *They are happy now, and we*
> *Soon their happiness shall see.*

We do not see it all, but God in His infinite grace and kindness and compassion has given us a foretaste. Are we enjoying it? Do you know Him? Are you seeing Him with an open face as in a glass? Has His glory ever been revealed to you? Do you know something of *His* love, and do *you* love Him? Do you know the joy of holiness and of purity and of sanctification, and are you enjoying 'the peace of God which passeth all understanding'? 'Who is the earnest of our inheritance, until the redemption of the purchased possession.'

27
Tests of Christian Profession

'Wherefore I also, after I heard of your faith in the
Lord Jesus, and love unto all the saints, cease not to
give thanks for you, making mention of you in my
prayers.'

Ephesians 1:15–16

We have completed our study of the great statement which began
at verse 3 and went on without interruption to the end of verse 14.
It is one of the mightiest statements of the Christian faith which
is found anywhere in the Scripture, if indeed it is not actually the
mightiest of all. Having completed his statement, the Apostle
now turns, as it were, to these Ephesians to whom he is writing,
and also the other churches, to apply what he has just been saying.

We must never forget that this is a pastoral letter, and that its
purpose was thoroughly practical. The Apostle must not be
thought of as a theologian who sits down to write a theological
disquisition; his object was to help Christians, to strengthen them
and to encourage them in their daily Christian living. This is the
apostolic way of doing so; the Apostles believed that the best way
to help Christians is to teach them the great doctrines of the Faith
and then to apply the doctrine to them.

The Apostle, therefore, at this point, seems to suggest that
thus far he and his readers have been looking at Christianity in its
essence. He has been rejoicing in the fact that it is for Gentiles as
well as for Jews, the two being sharers together in Christ and in
the firstfruits of the great harvest which is to come. He is
particularly concerned that the Ephesian believers to whom he is
writing should realize that they are partakers in these blessings;
and so he begins his new section with an emphatic 'wherefore', a
word that acts as the link between what has gone before and what
is to follow. Because all that he has been describing is true of the
Christians at Ephesus he tells them that he prays for them con-

stantly and without failing in his prayers – 'Wherefore I also, after I heard of your faith in the Lord Jesus, and love unto all the saints, cease not to give thanks for you, making mention of you in my prayers'.

Then the Apostle proceeds to indicate the exact nature of his prayer. Observe that, as should always be the case with Christian prayer, there are two aspects to his praying. First of all, he 'ceases not' to give thanks for them. He thanks God for the fact that they are in this Christian life at all; for the fact that they have been made fellow-heirs and co-inheritors with the Jews in the great glorious kingdom of God that is coming. They have been sealed, they have the earnest of the Spirit, they are looking forward to the time of 'the redemption of the purchased possession'. His thanksgiving is significant because it is an essential part of the Christian life. No man can truly be a Christian without rejoicing that others also have become Christian. Nothing should gladden the heart of the believer more than to know that others also are in a like position and enjoying the same blessings. So the Apostle offers up his constant praise and thanksgiving to God; and then, and only then, he begins to offer his petitions, which are found from verse 17 to the end of the chapter.

It is good that we should keep in our minds the general structure of the chapter. The Apostle starts with the doctrinal statement which we have studied. Next he thanks God that the Ephesians are involved in all the blessings he has named, and are partakers of them. Then, because of that, he is praying to God constantly for them, and asking that their understanding of the faith may increase and develop, and that they may experience it more and more. Thereby he gives us an excellent summary of what our Christian life should be. We should be entering more deeply into an understanding and an experimental experience of the great and glorious things which the Apostle has already been describing.

As we turn to this last section of the chapter we find that the Apostle starts by thanking God for the Ephesian Christians. But how does he know that they are Christians? He tells us that he has heard certain things about them: 'Wherefore I also, after I

heard of your faith in the Lord Jesus and love unto all the saints
. . .' Some have felt that there is a problem raised by the Apostle's
use of the word 'heard', because we read in the Book of the Acts,
chapter 19, that it was Paul himself who first took the Gospel to
Ephesus and preached it to its citizens, and that those who
believed did so very largely as the result of his ministry. The
apparent contradiction can be solved by pointing out that what
Paul has heard is not only that they entered into the Christian life
but that they were continuing in it. They were still exercising
their faith; it had not been some passing emotion which had come
and gone; they had gone on believing, they had continued as
Christians. Having heard this news, Paul thanks God for it. Not
only so, there were probably large numbers who had entered the
church since Paul had been at Ephesus, and he has heard about
these further converts. And if, as we suggested earlier, this is
probably a circular letter which included churches which the
Apostle had never visited, then we can understand why he says
that he has 'heard' of their faith. Plainly he has reasons for knowing
that the people to whom he is writing are continuing in the
Christian life.

But what exactly has Paul heard about these Christians? What
is it that gives the Apostle this definite assurance concerning
them?, what is it that he has in mind when, on his knees in the
presence of God, he thanks God for them. This is important for
the reason that it supplies us with tests which we can apply to
ourselves. How do we know we are Christians? How can others
know that we are Christians? What are our grounds for thanking
God that we are Christians, and for thanking God for other
Christians. The mere fact that a man may say that he is a Christian
does not prove that he is a Christian. The history of the Church
throughout the ages proves that that is perhaps one of the greatest
fallacies into which we can ever fall. Sometimes people who have
called themselves Christians have been the greatest enemies of the
Christian faith. The mere fact that we think we are Christians is
not enough; the fact that other people may say that we are
Christians is not enough. There must be some test. If we are to
have real and solid assurance, then we must have some valid tests
to apply; and fortunately for us the Apostle provides them for
us here.

[314]

There are many such tests provided for the Christian in the New Testament. The First Epistle of John was undoubtedly written with the specific purpose that we might be able to test ourselves to know whether we are in the faith. The Apostle Paul exhorts the Corinthians, saying: 'Examine yourselves whether ye be in the faith; prove your own selves' (2 Corinthians 13:5). And there are many other similar exhortations in the New Testament Epistles. But here the Apostle reduces all tests to two. We can be quite sure that when he does so they can be regarded as what we may call acid tests. We need not trouble to apply all the various tests to ourselves; all we need do is to apply the two tests which are suggested here by this man of God. If we pass these two tests we can be happy about ourselves. You can go through the others at your leisure, but if you would bring them all to a focus, here are the tests to apply. Whatever else may be true of us is irrelevant if we fail to pass these two tests. I say so on the authority of the Apostle. He gives us the grounds of his certainty and his assurance with regard to these people: and we note that they are two tests that are found everywhere in the New Testament. One refers mainly to our belief; the other mainly to our practice. Once more we have faith and works; they go together and must never be separated. They are indissoluble; and there is no value in having the one without the other.

This is a constant theme throughout the New Testament. Take, for instance, chapter 13 of the First Epistle to the Corinthians, where the Apostle says that it is useless for a man to say that he has faith, or that he can speak with the tongues of men or of angels, or that he has certain unusual gifts, if he is lacking in love. The Epistle of James says likewise that 'faith without works is dead' (2:20). Without works that so-called faith is nothing but an intellectual belief. The proof of true faith is that it shows itself in action. Here, the Apostle confronts us with these two things together – 'Wherefore I also, after I heard of your faith in the Lord Jesus, and love unto all the saints . . .' Of all the many things that the Apostle had heard about the Ephesians, and the various tests that can be applied, he says these two things assure him that they are true Christians, these two things enable him to thank God for them without any difficulty.

The first fact concerning them is their 'faith in the Lord Jesus', or as it might be translated, 'the faith that is among you in the Lord Jesus'. This refers to their personal, individual faith in the Lord Jesus. This is, of course, the most vital thing of all; this is what we may call the differentia of the Christian faith. This is the central, vital, acid test. We must not put our manner of living in the first position, we must not put conduct and behaviour in the first position. There are many very good people, very moral people, very benevolent people in the world who are not Christians. Many do not even claim to be; indeed they may be violent opponents of the Christian faith. But as regards life and living they are good people. Clearly, therefore, this is not the point at which we begin.

We must also indicate that it is not a man's noble ideas or his high idealism that matter; a vague, general, benevolent, idealistic view does not mean that a man is a Christian. This needs to be emphasized at the present time because of the confusion that exists concerning it. You can scarcely read an obituary notice about a great man in the papers without coming across this confusion. The kind of remark that is often made about some man who has died is that he was not a Christian but he was a great man, an able man, a man who did much good, and who had many noble ideas with respect to life; then, as if to sum it up, they add: 'We may not be able to say that he was a formal Christian, but . . .' What they mean is that though he did not say that he was a Christian, and was not a member of a Christian church, and did not subscribe to the Christian Creeds, he was nevertheless a Christian. No man could have lived such a wonderful life without being a Christian. In other words, a man's life, or a man's ideas, or a man's nobility of character, or his concern about the uplift of the race, or the improvement of life in general, determine whether he is a Christian. The peculiar characteristic of these days is this utter confusion about first principles and primary definitions; and, alas, this is true not only in general but even in the Evangelical section of the Christian Church. The landmarks are becoming less and less distinct, and the cry today is, 'Do not worry about definitions. If a man claims to be a Christian, he is a Christian, so let us work together'.

But we must go even further. We are not even to start by asking whether a man believes in God. That is not the acid test, for there are many people in the world who believe in God who are not Christians. The Jews, who put to death the Son of God, believed in God. Orthodox Jews today who may be strongly opposed to Christianity believe in God. Mohammedans and others are believers in God. So the Apostle emphasizes, 'your faith in the Lord Jesus'. He Himself, this blessed Person, has to be at the centre. This test includes all the other tests. If a man believes in the Lord Jesus he must of necessity believe in God, and his general ideas must be right. This is an all-inclusive test. So the Apostle is not so much concerned about other tests, but comes at once to the centre. He seems to have acted on the principle which is frequently employed in the realm of chemistry. A chemist who is trying to identify a substance has a number of tests which can be applied, but if he is in a hurry he does not trouble to go through all the various possible tests, he immediately applies the acid test. In the realm of Christianity the acid test is the Lord Jesus Christ Himself, so the Apostle says, 'your faith in the Lord Jesus'.

A Christian is a man in whose life and in whose whole outlook the Lord Jesus Christ is at the centre. He sees everything in Him. He starts with Him, he ends with Him. Jesus Christ has become the controlling factor everywhere. There are many religious people and many religious movements today which are very active and zealous and gain their so-called converts, but often Jesus Christ is not mentioned by them. They talk about 'Coming to God' and 'Listening to God' and so on without Jesus Christ being mentioned. That by definition is not Christianity, however good they may seem to be, and however religious they may be. The Christian is a man who sees and finds everything in His Lord and Saviour Jesus Christ.

Let us see how the Apostle in many places in his writings emphasizes this truth. In his Epistle to the Philippians he warns his readers against certain Judaisers, who went the round of the churches saying, 'Yes, it is right to believe in Jesus Christ but you must be circumcised as well,' you must become a Jew in addition, as it were. The Apostle answers that teaching with this striking asseveration, 'We are the circumcision, which worship God in the spirit, and rejoice in Christ Jesus, and have no confidence in the flesh' (3:3). To have faith in the Lord Jesus means that we see everything in Him, that He is our all and in all. If a man tells me that he has faith in the Lord Jesus he tells me that he has no faith in himself, that he has come to see that all his righteousness is but as refuse, filthy rags, useless, worthless. He has no confidence in the flesh, no confidence in himself; he relies entirely and utterly on the Lord Jesus Christ and His work on his behalf. To have faith in the Lord Jesus means that you trust Him utterly, entirely and absolutely. It means that you believe that He came into this world to save you and that it is He Himself who saves you.

I emphasize this for the reason that there are some people who seem to think that to have faith in the Lord Jesus means that you believe that He came into the world to tell you that God loves you and that God forgives your sins. But as I understand the New Testament, that is not faith in the Lord Jesus. Such people teach that the Cross is just a great declaration of the fact that God is ready to forgive you, that He is even ready to forgive the Cross itself. But if that is so, then the Lord Jesus is not the Saviour; He simply announces that God forgives and that salvation is possible. The New Testament, however, tells us that the Lord Jesus is Himself the Saviour, that He came into the world in order to save us. It is He, and what He has done on our behalf, that constitute the means of our salvation. That is what 'faith in the Lord Jesus' means. In other words it means that if He had not come there would be no salvation. But according to the other teaching, God would still forgive, and all the Lord Jesus does is to tell us that God forgives, and to give us this message in a very poignant and moving manner. They say that He does so by the display of love on the Cross when He forgave the people who put Him to death, and thereby announced God's love. But that is not what the New Testament means by saying that He is our Saviour. It asserts that 'In him we have redemption through his blood, the forgiveness of sins'. Faith in the Lord Jesus means, then, that I cast my entire hope upon Him and what He has done on my behalf; it means that I have no confidence in my own life, in my own acts, nor in those of anyone else; that I realize that I am a hopeless and a lost sinner, and that I am saved only because of 'Jesus' blood and righteousness'. A hymn by Count Zinzendorf, translated from the German by John Wesley, states it perfectly –

Jesus, Thy blood and righteousness
My beauty are, my glorious dress;
Midst flaming worlds in these arrayed,
With joy shall I lift up my head.

It is in this dress that I shall stand boldly in the great day that is coming. Faith in the Lord Jesus means that I have no interest in anything else, and have no confidence anywhere else but in Him and His blood and in His righteousness which is given to me.

But I must call attention to the way in which the Apostle states this matter. Observe that he says 'faith in the *Lord* Jesus'. We must always pay attention to the Apostle's every term. He was writing under the inspiration of the Holy Spirit, and so he never does anything haphazardly or accidentally. When he varies his expressions and his terms he has very good reason for doing so. We have seen already that he has used this Name some fifteen times in this chapter. He has been referring to Him as 'Christ Jesus', as 'Jesus Christ', as 'the Lord Jesus Christ' and so on; but here he deliberately says 'faith in the Lord Jesus'. Not faith in Jesus Christ, not faith in the Lord Jesus Christ, not faith in Jesus, but 'faith in the Lord Jesus'. In verse 17 we have the expression 'the God of our Lord Jesus Christ' – the full term; but here 'The Lord Jesus'. The explanation must be that, as he is applying the acid test, he uses the bare essentials, the minimum. He is not concerned about the fulness immediately. His immediate object is to call attention to the Person. His point is that the Saviour is One of whom I can say at one and the same time that He is the Lord, and also Jesus. He is God, He is man. The term brings us face to face with that essential truth. It is an all-inclusive expression; between 'Lord' and 'Jesus' everything is included.

Lord and *Jesus* are the two poles, the extremes which include everything. The Christian's Saviour is the Lord of glory, the Substance of the eternal Substance, the second Person in the blessed Holy Trinity, the eternal Son; yet Jesus also. 'Thou shalt call his name Jesus' (Matthew 1:21). This Lord is the Babe in His utter helplessness, the One who came down so low, the Man, the One who went to the Cross, the One who was buried, the One who rose again. All is included there in 'Lord Jesus'.

We have already marvelled several times at these staggering

truths in the first fourteen verses, but it is more necessary than ever today to repeat them constantly. He alone is a Christian who believes that Jesus of Nazareth is the eternal Son of God. A Christian believes in the Incarnation, in the Virgin Birth, and the miracle involved in that Birth; he believes in the eternal generation of the Son; he ascribes to Him no lesser term than this – The Lord! Elsewhere we find the Apostle referring to Him as 'our great God and Saviour'. Such is the One in whom alone our faith is fixed.

The Apostle, in making this same point in the First Epistle to the Corinthians says in its twelfth chapter: 'No man can say that Jesus is the Lord but by the Holy Spirit' (v. 3). The natural man does not believe this; the princes of this world did not recognize Him, 'for had they known (him) they would not have crucified the Lord of glory' (1 Corinthians 2:8). They thought He was a man only, a carpenter, Jesus; they did not realize that He was the Lord. In this expression, 'Lord Jesus', we have the 'mystery of godliness', namely, that 'God was manifest in the flesh', together with all that followed the birth at Bethlehem. Hence the Apostle uses these terms; he is extremely anxious to focus attention on the Person as such.

Of course, if a person believes this he will have no difficulty in believing in the miracles wrought by the Lord Jesus. When God is on earth in the flesh he expects the supernatural and the miraculous; and so he does not stumble at the Gospel accounts of miracles and try to explain them away psychologically. The Lord Jesus is the One in whom my faith is reposed. I cannot save myself, no man can save me; but the Lord Jesus can. Such is the faith of the Christian; and nothing less can satisfy him. God alone can save him, God in the flesh, the Lord Jesus. To believe in the Lord Jesus tells me why He came, and explains what He has done. When I look at such a Person and consider why He came, there is only one answer: 'When the fulness of the time was come, God sent forth his Son, made of a woman, made under the law, to redeem them that were under the law' (Galatians 4:4–5). He lived like a man, and was 'tempted in all points like as we are, yet without sin' (Hebrews 4:15). He is truly Jesus, the Man, and He was spared nothing in that respect. He came to give obedience to the law of God and He did so. He came to take the punishment meted out by the law upon sin, and He has done so. Jesus is the Crucified One; He was the Lord who was crucified. The Son of God, God the Son, has died for me and for my sins. It is all included here, in this Epistle to the Ephesians.

Finally, we must emphasize that you cannot separate the Lord and Jesus. The Person is one and indivisible. He is always the Lord. There is no such thing as 'coming to Jesus'. In one sense, a man cannot even come to Christ. He can only come to the Lord Jesus. If this doctrine is true a man cannot accept Him as Saviour only, and then perhaps later decide to accept Him as Lord, for He is always the Lord. The One who died for our sins is the Lord. And He died for our sins because sin is under the wrath of God; it is transgression against the law, it is enmity against God, so it must be punished. If I say that I need a Saviour it is because I need a Saviour from sin, including deliverance from the power of sin and everything connected with sin. If I have a true conception of sin I cannot only ask to be forgiven. I must desire to be delivered from its power and pollution as well. We cannot believe in 'Jesus' and leave out 'the Lord'. We believe in one indivisible Person. In Him there are two natures in one Person; and when we believe in Him we believe in Him as the Lord of glory and the Lord of our life. When we believe in Him we believe that He died for our sins, that He has bought us, purchased us, ransomed us. When we believe that, we give ourselves to Him. We do not 'come to Jesus', and we do not believe in Jesus: we come to the Lord Jesus, we believe in Him as He is.

The Apostle is always careful about this matter. For instance, we find it written in his Epistle to the Colossians: 'As ye have therefore received Christ Jesus the Lord, so walk ye in him' (2:6). We cannot receive Him as anything but the Lord, and therefore the Lord of our life. Have you this faith in the Lord Jesus? Do you rest your faith in Him alone as the One who died to atone for your transgressions? Do you say:

> *On Christ, the solid Rock, I stand,*
> *All other ground is sinking sand.*

Are you utterly committed to Him? Is your faith entirely, altogether, exclusively in Him, the God-Man, the Lord Jesus?

We turn now to the second aspect which is, 'and love unto all the saints'. The one follows the other as the night the day. As I have already said, this is the argument of the First Epistle of John. Indeed it is the argument found in all parts of the New Testament. The Apostle Peter, having reminded the people to whom he was writing his First Epistle that they had purified their souls in obeying the truth through the Spirit unto unfeigned love of the brethren, proceeds immediately to say: 'See that ye love one another with a pure heart fervently' (1:22). By nature we all hate one another, as the Apostle reminds us. 'For we ourselves also were sometimes foolish, disobedient, deceived, serving divers lusts and pleasures, living in malice and envy, hateful, and hating one another' (Titus 3:3) – man in his unredeemed, natural state! But Paul has heard that the Christians in Ephesus have love unto all the brethren; so he knows that something must have happened to them.

Further, the natural man, the man who is not a Christian, the man who is not born again, has no interest in Christian people. He generally dislikes them because he finds them to be dull and uninteresting, and 'narrow-minded'. These are his terms about Christians, and he certainly would not choose to spend a number of hours in the presence of such a person. He feels that there is no affinity, no community of interest. It follows therefore that when it can be said of a man that he loves the saints, you can be sure that the man has been given a new nature, he has been born again. This is something which is quite inevitable. Like attracts like: 'Birds of a feather flock together.' 'Blood is thicker than water.' We are ready to forgive things in people related to us which we would not forgive in others, because we are of the same blood as they are; we belong together and there is this community of interest. So when we find ourselves beginning to have such feelings about Christian people, about the saints, we have a proof that we must be one of them. There is a community of interest, and we feel that we belong to the same family. This is the unvarying truth about the Christian. Paul had heard that these Ephesians loved all the saints; they liked to be with them, they liked to spend time with them; they were people they liked above all others.

I have sometimes thanked God for this test when I have been assaulted by Satan, when he seemed to have pressed me hard by his accusations and driven me almost into a corner. At such times I have been glad to be able to fall back on this argument and say: 'Well, whatever I am, I would rather spend my time in the company of the humblest Christian than with the greatest in the land who is not a Christian.' The devil has no answer to this; it is a final proof of salvation. Or to state the matter in a different way; it is a proof that the Holy Spirit is in us. We cannot love truly unless the Holy Spirit is resident within us. It is He who produces love, and especially love of all the saints. So if we love the saints it is a proof that the Holy Spirit is in us. The Apostle has been referring to the Holy Spirit as a 'seal' and an 'earnest' and as the One who dwells within us; and love of the brethren, of the saints, is a proof of it. The Apostle John in the third chapter of his First Epistle says: 'This is his commandment, that we should believe on the name of his Son Jesus Christ, and love one another' (v.23).

Again, we can assert that if we love all the saints it is a proof of the fact that we love God also. It works in the following manner. I love them because they are in the same relationship to God as I am; these are the people who have been chosen and separated out of the world, who have been translated from the kingdom of darkness into the kingdom of God's dear Son. These people and I are walking together through this world of sin in the direction of heaven and I am going to spend my eternity with them. We are all facing such a glorious prospect together because of the amazing love of God. I do not deserve it, they do not deserve it; let us therefore join together in praising God. If I love them I must love God, for He has made them what they are, and made me what I am; so together we can ascribe the glory to Him. Paul had no need to give all the details, he states the one thing that covers them all. If you love the brethren, if you love the saints, it guarantees all these other things. It is an all-inclusive test.

Note that the Apostle says that he has heard of their 'love unto *all* the saints'. They not only love those whom they happen to like; but all the saints. Not only the clever ones, not only the learned ones, not only the pleasant ones, not only those who belong to a particular social stratum – no, *all* the saints. A Christian is a man who has a new test for everyone and everything. When he meets a person for the first time he does not look at his clothing, he does not look at his general external appearance. That is the carnal way of judging people. He does not ask himself, Where has he come from, what school has he attended, what is his bank balance? Those are no longer his questions or his tests. He is interested in one thing only now. Is he a child of God, is he my brother in Christ? Are we related?

A good story is told in connection with Philip Henry, the father of Matthew Henry the Commentator. He and a certain young lady had fallen in love with each other. She belonged to a 'higher' circle of society than he did, but the young lady had become a Christian, and therefore social standing no longer counted with her or constituted any kind of obstacle to their marriage. Her parents, however, were not pleased, and expostulating with her they said, 'This man Philip Henry, where has he come from?', to which she gave the immortal reply, 'I don't know where he has come from, but I know where he is going'. We love the saints because we know where they are going. They and we are marching together to Zion. We belong to the same Father, to the same household, to the same family; we are going to the same home and we know it. Some of us are very difficult, and very trying, and very unworthy; but, thank God, because we are God's children we are travelling together towards our heavenly home; and we know that the day will come when all our faults and blemishes and spots and wrinkles will disappear and we shall all be glorified and perfected together, enjoying the same glorious eternity.

Those are the two acid tests of any profession of Christianity that we can apply to one another. Let us remember the order in which the Apostle places them. He does not put 'love to all the saints' before 'faith in the Lord Jesus'. This, however, is being done today on a large scale. We are told 'not to bother about definitions', that theology does not matter, that what a man believes is irrelevant, that we must love all who claim to be Christians. But that is not the Apostolic order. The Apostle Paul was never interested in vague sentimentality. 'Faith in the Lord Jesus' must be first; then, and only then, but definitely then, 'love unto all the saints'. And no man is a saint unless he has faith in the Lord Jesus. Place them in the right order, keep them in the right order, and then insist upon both. The first commandment to the Christian is not that we should love one another but that we should believe in the Lord Jesus. We are told about the early disciples that they 'continued steadfastly in the apostles' doctrine and fellowship and breaking of bread and prayers'. Today the fellowship is put first, and the doctrine is almost regarded as a hindrance and an obstacle. For this reason the church is in her present parlous condition. She has departed from the Apostolic order – faith in the Lord Jesus first, doctrine first; and then 'love towards all saints'.

28

'The Father of Glory'

'Wherefore I also, after I heard of your faith in the
Lord Jesus, and love unto all the saints, cease not to
give thanks for you, making mention of you in my
prayers; that the God of our Lord Jesus Christ, the
Father of glory, may give unto you the spirit of
wisdom and revelation in the knowledge of him.'

Ephesians 1:15–17

Here the Apostle tells the Ephesian Christians that he is praying
for them, that he ceases not to give thanks for them, making
mention of them in his prayers to God. We have already remarked
on the fact that his prayer is divided, as prayer always should be,
into thanksgiving, which includes general adoration and worship,
and then petition. We now come to consider how the Apostle
offers his petitions to God. We have here a great object lesson in
this respect. There is perhaps no aspect of our Christian life that
so frequently raises problems in people's minds as prayer. And
it is right that such should be the case, because prayer is, after all,
the highest activity of the human soul.

Every preacher will, I am sure, agree that preaching is com-
paratively simple as compared with praying, because when one is
preaching one is speaking to men, but when a man prays he is
speaking to God. Many find it difficult to concentrate, others to
know how to speak and how to form their petitions, and so on.
The moment you take prayer seriously you begin to learn its
profound character. Of course, those who 'say their prayers'
mechanically are not aware of any difficulties; all seems so simple.
They simply repeat the Lord's Prayer and offer up a few petitions
and they imagine that they have prayed. But such a person has
not started praying. The moment you begin to face what really
happens in prayer you find inevitably that it is the profoundest
activity in which you have ever engaged. How little we have

[326]

prayed, how little we know about prayer! It is not surprising that the disciples of our Lord turned to Him one day and said, 'Lord, teach us to pray as John also taught his disciples' (Luke 11:1). But they were probably not only thinking at that moment of John and his disciples, they had been watching their Lord Himself and the way He repeatedly withdrew for prayer. I do not hesitate to assert that unless you have ever felt something of what those disciples felt, and offered that petition, it is certain that you have never prayed in your life. If you have never been aware of difficulties it is because you have never realized what prayer involves.

As we face this whole question of prayer, therefore, we can do nothing better than watch some of the great models and examples which we have in the Scriptures in such abundance. Among such examples, surely, there is none greater than the Apostle Paul himself. Let us watch him as he prays. Fortunately not only here in this chapter, but in other places also, he tells us how he prays, and something of what it means to him. Let us look at him and observe everything he says, let us watch his every word.

How easy it is to read a statement such as the one we are considering and assume that it is but a number of words without much significance. Fortunately the Apostle takes the trouble to tell us exactly what he prays and why he does so pray; and if we succeed in grasping the essence of his teaching it will make all manuals on the subject of prayer quite unnecessary. Some are interested in the question of posture; should we kneel? should we stand? should we prostrate ourselves? The manuals on prayer generally deal with such questions, and also with the amount of time to be spent in prayer, the order and the arrangement of our petitions, and so forth. I grant that in a limited way there is a place for such things; but we find, when we read the literature on the question of prayer, and the lives of the saints, that such an approach tends to characterize what we may describe as the Catholic view of worship. On the other hand, the Protestant and, surely, the more spiritual view, pays much less attention to such details, for when we are right at the centre, and concerned with the fundamental principles, these other things tend to look after themselves.

The first thing we observe is that the Apostle prays to God the Father. He does not pray to the Lord Jesus Christ; he does not pray to the Holy Spirit. We must not pay too much attention to this matter, although it has often engaged the attention of theologians and expositors, and rightly so. It is certainly a subject on which we cannot speak with any finality, for it is a great mystery. Our Lord Himself taught that life eternal is to 'know the only true God, and Jesus Christ, whom he has sent' (John 17:3). It is possible for the Christian to have fellowship with the Father and with His Son, Jesus Christ, and not only by the Holy Spirit but also with the Holy Spirit, as John Owen and others have taught. Nevertheless it is interesting to observe that the Bible, speaking generally, teaches us to address our prayers to God the Father.

I pause to make this point for one reason only, namely, that I have sometimes gained the impression that many Christians seem to think that the hallmark of spirituality is to pray to the Lord Jesus Christ. But when we turn to the Scriptures we discover that that is not really so, and that, as here, prayers are normally offered to the Father. The Lord Jesus Christ is the Mediator, not the end; He is the One who brings us to the Father. We go to the Father by Him; He is the great High Priest; He is our representative. Normally we do not pray to Him, but to the Father, in the name of the Lord Jesus Christ, through the Lord Jesus Christ, relying upon the Lord Jesus Christ. As the Apostle Peter reminds us, all He has done is designed to bring us to God, not to Himself. We must not attach too much importance to this, yet it is important that we should observe it, because there is an enemy at hand who is always ready to mislead us; and to persuade us to put false emphasis in certain matters.

I have sometimes thought that perhaps the greatest danger confronting evangelicals at the present time is (and I speak with reverence) so to emphasize the Person of the Son as to forget the Father. We fail to realize that the Son came to glorify the Father and to bring us to Him. In this respect we are often misled by the hymns, in many of which prayers are offered to the Lord Jesus Christ, and to the Holy Spirit. A profitable exercise is to compare the hymn-books and the Scriptures at this point. The Apostle Paul, quite specifically as we find here and everywhere else in this

Epistle and in other Epistles, offers his prayer to God the Father.

The second matter which we observe is the way in which the Apostle prays to the Father. Let us pay close attention to his terms and ask ourselves why he said certain things, and expresses his thoughts in the way he does. The best way of profiting from reading the Scriptures is to ask questions of the Scriptures, to talk to the Scriptures, to take every phrase carefully and ask, 'Why did he say this, why that? The first thing we observe is that the Apostle pauses to remind himself of certain things. He is writing to Ephesian Christians and he has been reminding them of the riches of God's grace, and of his rejoicing in the fact that they have experienced it. On their behalf he desires to thank God, but before doing so he pauses to remind himself of what he is going to do. In particular he reminds himself of the One to whom he is going to speak. This is a most vital point in connection with prayer, indeed I am ready to assert that this is the key to the whole question of prayer. I go further and suggest that difficulties with respect to praying all ultimately arise because we fail to do what the Apostle invariably did. He does not get on his knees, or stand – or whatever posture he adopts – and begin to speak immediately. He stops, he pauses, he recollects, he meditates, he talks to himself first, and reminds himself of what he is about to do. He reminds himself of the One to whom he is going to speak. Were we all to do the same we should begin to pray truly, perhaps for the first time.

We all tend to be creatures of extremes; we tend to oscillate from one extreme to the other; and so there are two common excesses in connection with prayer. The one is to take the liturgical view of prayer which concentrates attention upon the beauty of worship, the beauty of language and phrases, the beauty of words and diction, the balance and perfection of forms and arrangements and ceremonies. This applies to the Catholic type of worship, whether Roman or Orthodox or Anglican. It can be very beautiful; but surely, speaking generally, it tends to be remote; there is such emphasis upon the beauty and the greatness and the august that somehow you feel that God is far away in the distance, and there is a sense of unreality about it. It may be well-nigh perfect from the aesthetic or artistic standpoint, but it does not suggest a living act of worship.

[329]

The danger that arises is that many of us, in reacting against the liturgical type of worship rush to the other extreme and regard praying as just a series of telegraphic petitions, with no adoration or worship or praise. Indeed some seem to think that this is a sign of great spirituality. They feel that they are so familiar with God and so sure of their standing before Him that they can rush into His presence and offer a sentence or two of petition, and finish. But surely both the extremes are wrong; and we find in the model and the example provided by the great Apostle that he invariably combines what is good and right in both the extreme methods. The two elements are always present, and he invariably places them in the right order. No man knew better how to pray than this Apostle; and there has been no man who has had a greater abundance of answers to his prayers. He prays with confidence, with boldness of access, and assurance; and yet the other element of worship and adoration was always there and always came first.

We must all feel guilty as we examine ourselves in the light of the Apostle's teaching and methods. Do we stop to think, to recollect, and to remind ourselves of what we are actually doing when we pray. I, personally, am ready to admit that I often fail in this respect. One day recently I wanted to thank God in a certain matter; but at the time I also had business in hand which needed urgent attention. I was on the point of offering up a hurried word of thanksgiving to God in order that I might turn to the urgent task; but realizing what was happening I suddenly said to myself: 'That is not the way to thank God, Do you realize whom you are about to thank?' Everything must be laid aside when you are turning to Him; everything, everyone, all things, however urgent. What are they compared with Him? Stop! Pause! Wait! Recollect! Realize what you are doing.

So let us listen to the Apostle as he reminds himself of certain things concerning God before he utters a word. He prays, he says, to 'the God of our Lord Jesus Christ'. Why does he begin his words about prayer in this manner? Why does he not say 'I am going to pray', and describe his petition? The answer is that he deliberately says he is not praying to an unknown God. He is not, as a certain poem puts it, 'thanking whatever gods there be for his unconquerable soul'. No! he is going into the presence of

God Who is known to him, the God who has made Himself known, the God who has revealed Himself to Paul in no uncertain way.

In the Old Testament we find that the Psalmist and others prayed to 'the God of Abraham and of Isaac and of Jacob'. It is difficult for us to realize what such a phrase meant to an Old Testament saint. He had seen something of the power and the majesty of God in a thunderstorm or a pestilence, or in the conquering of some enemy. God had manifested His power and given the Jews some conception of His greatness. Their tendency was to be afraid to approach near to God. But then they remembered that this God was the God of Abraham, the God of Isaac, the God of Jacob, the God of their fathers, the God of Israel. And this caused them to feel that they were praying to a God whom they knew.

This is an essential part of Old Testament teaching. The godly Israelite knew God his Maker as a covenant God and a covenant-keeping God. When he went in fear and trembling to the God of Abraham, Isaac and Jacob, what he was really saying in effect was, 'O God, I come realizing that Thou hast revealed Thyself to my fathers, that Thou hast said certain things, that Thou hast made a covenant with my people, the people to whom I am privileged to belong, and therefore with me'. God had made a covenant with Abraham that in his seed 'all nations should be blessed' and that He would bless his seed in particular. He had pledged Himself, He had sworn with an oath, He had confirmed it with an oath. 'To Abraham and to his seed were the promises made' (Galatians 3:16), and these people belonged to that seed, so they went to God in the confidence and strength of His promise: 'the God of our fathers', 'The God of Abraham, and the fear of Isaac' (Genesis 31:42), 'The God of Jacob', the God of Peniel. They went with confidence to Him, knowing Him in that way in which He had revealed Himself.

The Apostle, however, does not pray to 'the God of Abraham, of Isaac and of Jacob'; he prays to 'the God of our Lord Jesus Christ'; and he does so because there is a new covenant. God has now made a covenant with man in the Person of our Lord and Saviour Jesus Christ. This is the 'Covenant of grace', the 'Covenant of Redemption' appearing in a new form. It is the same Covenant

[331]

in essence as the old one, but now it is in the Person of the Son, the Second Adam, the new Man. The representative of the human race is the Lord Jesus Christ, and God has covenanted with Him for His people. So when Paul reminds himself that he is praying to 'the God of our Lord Jesus Christ' he reminds himself that he is praying to the God of our salvation, he is praying to the God who has originated and brought to pass all the things we have been considering from verse 3 to verse 14 in our chapter. He is praying to the God who has, before the foundation of the world, chosen and elected us and planned His glorious purpose in Christ for our final complete salvation. What a difference it makes to prayer when you begin in that manner! You no longer go to God uncertainly, or with doubts and queries as to whether He is going to receive you; you remember and realize that you are praying because He has done something to you, and drawn you to Himself in and through 'our Lord Jesus Christ'. You realize that you are approaching 'the God of peace that brought again from the dead our Lord Jesus, that great Shepherd of the sheep, through the blood of the everlasting covenant' (Hebrews 13:20).

However, Paul goes even further, for his words remind us that God is actually the God of the Lord Jesus Christ Himself. Do we realize what that means? In eternity God the Father was not the God of God the Son, although the relationship of the Father and Son existed eternally. But when the Lord Jesus Christ came to earth and took on Him 'the likeness of man', 'the likeness of sinful flesh', He now approached the Father as a man, and so God became His God. Thus He was able to speak of 'my God and your God; my Father and your Father' (John 20:17). The God whom I am approaching, says Paul in effect, is the God of Jesus my Lord, is the God of the Lord Jesus Christ Himself. In the four Gospels we read that the Lord Jesus Christ sometimes 'arose a great while before day' and went up into a mountain to pray. And I, says the Apostle, am praying to the same God to whom He prayed.

The Lord Jesus relied on God for everything; it was God who sustained Him. He said 'The words I speak, I speak not of myself' (John 14:10). The Father had given Him both the words and also the works that accompanied them. Nothing is so obvious about our Lord's life as His utter reliance upon God the

Father. He received strength and power, indeed all the sustenance He needed, from Him. So Paul says that he is praying to the God of our Lord Jesus Christ, the God who sustained Him, the God who never forsook Him. Even the terrible moment of the cry of dereliction on the Cross was immediately followed by 'Into thy hands I commend my spirit' (Luke 23:46). It was God who raised Him from the dead, who did not forsake Him in hell or 'leave his soul to see corruption'. This is the God to whom I am praying, says Paul, 'the God of our Lord Jesus Christ'. But even beyond that, He is the God in whose presence the Lord Jesus Christ is at this moment, the God in whose presence He is our Advocate and Intercessor. He is seated at the right hand of the Father, 'ever living to make intercession for us'. In the light of all this we can go with assurance to 'the God of our Lord Jesus Christ'.

We can sum it up by saying that our God is the God who cannot be thought of truly apart from the Lord Jesus Christ, because we cannot know God without Him. 'No man hath seen God at any time: the only begotten Son which is in the bosom of the Father, he hath declared him' (John 1:18). It is on the basis of that declaration that I go to God, the God who has been revealed by Christ; He is the One who brings me to Him, He is the One who died in order that I might have this access. I enter into His presence in one way only, as the author of the Epistle to the Hebrews says: 'Having, therefore, brethren, boldness to enter into the holiest by the blood of Jesus . . .' (Hebrews 10:19). I am only admitted into the presence of God by the life and death and resurrection of the Lord Jesus. I approach the God who sent His Son to save me and who has treasured up in Him all His treasures of wisdom and of grace. The riches of grace which I enjoy come to me from the God of our Lord Jesus Christ. In other words I am approaching the God who has promised me all these things in His own Son; has pledged Himself to them in His Son; has covenanted with the Son. Jehovah is the covenant-giving and the covenant-keeping God, and He will never break His word. And He has told me these things in His Son – no longer in prophets, no longer in parts, or in types, but in His Son. (Hebrews 1:1-3). Hence the Apostle says in the third chapter of this Epistle, 'In whom we have boldness and access with con-

[333]

fidence by the faith of him' (v. 12). Whenever we pray to God we should always remind ourselves of these things. We should approach God with full assurance of faith, and full assurance of hope, because of the Lord Jesus Christ; and we should never fail to stop and to recollect this, and to remind ourselves of it all, as the Apostle invariably does, before we begin to speak in prayer.

But the Apostle adds even more, he describes the God of our Lord Jesus Christ as 'the Father of glory'. This addition has troubled the commentators. Some have tried to explain it by saying that it means, and should read, 'the God of glory, the Father of our Lord Jesus Christ'. But that is to do violence to language. The two phrases are separate and distinct, as we have them in the Authorized Version.

Let me attempt to expound these words with fear and trembling. Who am I to speak on such words? As we approach them it is good for us to remember the words spoken to Moses at the burning bush: 'Take off thy shoes from off thy feet, for the place whereon thou standest is holy ground' (Exodus 3:5). 'The Father of glory!' There can be no doubt but that this means, partly, that God is the source and embodiment in and of Himself of all glory. There are many such phrases in Scripture. We read of God in the twelfth chapter of the Epistle to the Hebrews as 'the Father of spirits' (v. 9). We read of Him in the Epistle of James as 'the Father of lights, with whom is no variableness, neither shadow of turning' (1:17). In the Book of the prophet Isaiah God is described as 'The eternal Father' or 'Father of eternity' (9:6). So 'the Father of glory' means the source, the fount of all glory. As to 'glory' what can we say? Words fail us utterly. Glory is God. Glory is the summation of all the excellences and perfections and attributes of the Lord God Almighty Himself. That is why He is referred to at times in the Scriptures as 'the glory'. The ultimate characteristic of God is glory. He is that in and of Himself. His essence is glorious. It is unutterable, absolute perfection. So we can but stand in amazement before this expression, 'the Father of glory'.

When Stephen was on trial and addressing the Sanhedrin, we are told in the report of his speech, in the seventh chapter of Acts, that he reminded them of the history of the children of Israel, and said, 'The God of glory appeared to our father Abraham' (v. 2). The God of glory! The glorious God! He was reminding them that God's glory is ineffable and indescribable. He 'dwelleth in the light which is unapproachable', 'Whom no man hath seen, nor can see'. And this is the One whom you and I approach in prayer.

Moreover, everything God does is a manifestation of His glory. We recall how Paul ended his description of the plan of salvation in the words 'unto the praise of his glory', in verse 14. Everything God does is a manifestation of His glory. Paul says in the Epistle to the Romans that Christ was raised from the dead 'by the glory of the Father' (6:4). His every act is a manifestation of His glory. 'The heavens declare the glory of God' (Psalm 19:1). Do you see the glory of God in the sun and moon and the stars, in the firmament, in flowers, in the whole of creation? They all declare the glory of God. Everything He does is glorious, perfect in its beauty and in every other respect. I speak with reverence when I say that the greatest thing the Lord Jesus Christ did was to manifest the glory of God. In His high priestly prayer as recorded in the seventeenth chapter of John's Gospel He says so Himself in various ways. And when He describes His second coming the words He uses are, 'For the Son of man shall come in the glory of his Father with his angels' (Matthew 16:27). Everything He did was designed to glorify His Father. God, and the glory of God, are the end, the terminus of salvation.

But Paul's expression can also be read legitimately as 'the glorious Father'. It is a Hebraism, a form of expression frequently found in the Hebrew language. Take as an example of this Paul's statement that he has been given the privilege of preaching the 'glorious gospel of the blessed God' (1 Timothy 1:11). I am quoting the phrase as it appears in the Authorized Version. But a better translation would be, 'The gospel of the glory of the blessed God' – not 'the glorious gospel', but 'the gospel of the glory'. So in the case of 'the Father of glory' we can read, 'the glorious Father'. In that case it means that God the Father is not only glorious, and the source of all glory, and the summation of all glory in Himself, He is also prepared to manifest and to impart that glory. He is a Father, and as a Father He gives, He generates, He passes on glory. God does not keep His glory to Himself, if I may so express it; He manifests it, He imparts it. He did so with the Son, and so we find our Lord saying in the seventeenth chapter of John's Gospel: Father, I pray that thou wouldest give me the glory I had with thee before the foundation of the world (17:5). He had laid aside that glory for the purpose of the Incarnation, and now He asks that He may have it again. And the Father gave it to Him. There is also His prayer recorded in the twelfth chapter of John's Gospel, 'Father, glorify thy Name' (John 12:28).

The Apostle Peter writes, 'Who by him do believe in God, that raised him up from the dead and gave him glory, that your faith and hope might be in God' (1 Peter 1:21). The Father glorified the Son while He was here on earth. He gave Him power to perform miracles, He gave Him words to speak, He enabled Him to raise the dead; He glorified Him in His death, He glorified Him in the resurrection. He is the glorious Father, the Father who gives His glory to the Son. This is a thought which staggers us because of its immensity, but it is true to say that, because He gives His glory to the Son, He is ready to give it also to us. We are in the Son because He is *our* Lord Jesus Christ. He is the Head, as Paul says at the end of our chapter, and we are members of His body. So the glory that is in Him becomes ours; and we go to the Father who is giving us this glory. We wait upon Him, we desire to know more of His glory. Paul is about to pray that these Ephesians may have 'the spirit of wisdom and of revelation' in the knowledge of this glory, so that, the eyes of their understanding being opened, they may see this glory and receive it fully. God is our Father, and He will manifest His glory to us.

I end by quoting again from what our Lord is reported as saying in the seventeenth chapter of John's Gospel: 'Father, I will that they also, whom thou hast given me, may be with me where I am, that they may behold my glory' (v. 24). When we go in prayer into the presence of God we should do so expecting some revelation of this glory. 'We all with open face beholding as in a glass the glory of the Lord are changed into the same image, from glory to glory' (2 Corinthians 3:18). The process of our glorification has already started; it will eventually be perfected, and we shall be glorified even in our bodies as well as in our spirits. We shall stand in the presence of the Father of glory and see Him.

Let us never again attempt prayer without reminding ourselves that we are going to speak to 'the Father of glory'. We need not be terrified; we must go with reverence and godly fear because of His glorious character; but at the same time we can go with confidence and assurance, because He is the God of *our* Lord Jesus Christ, and in Him and through Him *our* Father. So we pray, 'Our Father, who art in heaven, hallowed be thy name'. And if we start in that way we cannot go wrong.

29
The Christian's Knowledge of God

'Wherefore I also, after I heard of your faith in the
Lord Jesus, and love unto all the saints, cease not to
give thanks for you, making mention of you in my
prayers; that the God of our Lord Jesus Christ, the
Father of glory, may give unto you the spirit of
wisdom and revelation in the knowledge of him.'

Ephesians 1:15-17

We now turn to the petition which the Apostle actually offered
as it is recorded in the seventeenth verse: 'That the God of our
Lord Jesus Christ, the Father of the glory, may give unto you the
spirit of wisdom and revelation in the knowledge of him.' The
petition continues until the end of the chapter, but it can be
divided into two main sections. There is first of all a general
petition, and then Paul turns to certain particular matters. So we
start by looking at the general petition. Clearly this is very
important and must come first because it controls all that follows.

This petition is most remarkable, especially in view of what the
Apostle has already told us about these Ephesian Christians. They
have believed in the Lord Jesus Christ and placed their trust in
Him: 'In whom ye also trusted after that ye heard the word of
truth, the gospel of your salvation.' They have committed themselves to Him; but, even more, they have been 'sealed with the
Holy Spirit of promise', and he knows that they have, through
the Holy Spirit likewise, 'an earnest of the inheritance' which
they are destined to receive. Yet even so, we find here that Paul
still is not fully satisfied with their condition. We might have
thought that there was no need to pray for people who had
experienced such great blessings. But the Apostle prays, and is
urgent in his prayer; he does not cease to pray for them, and he
offers special petitions for them. And what he does for the
Ephesians he does for all the other Christians to whom he writes

[338]

his letters. He prays for all who have become Christian, for all whom he himself has established as churches. He had a great pastoral heart and felt a deep concern for them. He prays for them because so much more is open to them; and he desires them to know more and more of the endless riches of God's grace.

Conversion is not the end, it is merely the beginning; it is only the first step. It is comparable to birth. A child's birth is not the end, it is the beginning of its life; and regeneration and conversion is its spiritual counterpart. It is because he knows this, and is aware of the tremendous possibilities that lie ahead of these people, that the Apostle is praying for them. There are possibilities ahead for them in every conceivable respect, and as one who had grown so much in grace, as one who had scaled the heights of the spiritual life, the Apostle is anxious that they should catch a glimpse of the glorious views which he himself was enjoying from the mountain tops of that life, the panorama that was stretching out before him, and the new heights that kept appearing. He says concerning himself, to the church at Philippi even towards the end of his life: 'Not that I have yet apprehended' (3:13); and adds, 'Forgetting those things which are behind, I press forward'. God forbid that any should stop or stay only at the beginning with the mere first principles of the Gospel of Christ.

The apostolic prayers are most important because in them we are given clear pictures of the Christian life in its height and its depth, its length and its breadth; in them we see something of the glory of the life into which we have been brought by God's amazing grace and love.

One test of our position in the Christian life is whether the Apostle's actual petition comes to us as a surprise. I say this, because the popular teaching for many years has been that the Christian life can be divided up into two sections. First, we are told, people need to be saved; they need to be delivered from the guilt and punishment of sin. That is the business of evangelism. They agree that that is only the beginning and that there is a second step. The remaining step which such a person must take, they say, is to be delivered from the power and the tyranny and the thraldom of sin. Or, to use other terminology, they say that our first need is justification, and then all that remains is sanctification. So the convert must now be introduced to the doctrine of sanctification. All we need pray for such people, therefore, is that they may be sanctified.

All this, of course, is true, but what I am concerned to emphasize is that this is not what the Apostle prays for the Ephesians. He prays that God may give them 'the spirit of wisdom and revelation in the knowledge of him'. The significance of this for us is that most of our troubles in the Christian life arise from the fact that our ideas are so man-centred, so subjective. We start with man and his needs instead of starting with God. Man needs forgiveness, and then deliverance from sin in order that he may not be unhappy in a life of failure. We become obsessed with man and his needs and what can be done for man. But the Apostle's approach is entirely different. Our view of salvation must never be man-centred; it must always be God-centred. This is the particular characteristic of the Apostle's teaching. We have seen that he starts in verse 3 with 'Blessed be the God and Father of our Lord Jesus Christ'. So when he comes to his petition for these Ephesians, it is not so much for their sanctification, or their happiness, or their joy, but that they may have 'the spirit of wisdom and revelation in the knowledge of God'. This is what he introduces first.

This is nothing exceptional on the part of the Apostle. His prayer for the Philippian Christians is that their love may grow, and that they may increase in knowledge and in spiritual understanding. In the Epistle to the Colossians his petition is still the same. The Apostle's chief concern for his converts always was that they might come to know God. He does not think primarily in terms of subjective states and conditions, but about their total relationship to Almighty God. There is a grave danger of our forgetting this and of developing a false emphasis. We must always follow the apostolic pattern and put things in the right order. Later in this Epistle the Apostle has much to say about sanctification; but he does not start with that theme. He has much to say about happiness and joy, but he does not start with that either. He starts where we should always start, namely, with our need to know more and more about God.

So the first petition is that the Ephesians might have this 'spirit of wisdom and revelation in the knowledge of him'.

[340]

In considering what this means, the first thing necessary is that we should be clear as to the reference in the word *Him*, as mentioned here. There are some who think that it is a reference to the Lord Jesus Christ. But regarding that as quite wrong, I suggest that it is clearly a reference to God the Father. Surely the whole context indicates this; for the Apostle goes on at once to indicate that the first strand in that knowledge is that we should know 'what is the hope of his calling'. That surely settles the question for, as we have already seen, it is God the Father who calls us and chooses us and predestinates us. The same applies to 'the riches of the glory of his inheritance in the saints, and the exceeding greatness of his power to us-ward'. These clauses clearly refer to God the Father. 'His power to us-ward who believe', which the Apostle desires us to know, is, he tells us, 'according to the working of his mighty power which he wrought in Christ', which can only be a reference to God the Father. So the knowledge which the Apostle desires us to have is primarily and essentially a knowledge of God, the eternal Father.

Of course, as the Apostle makes quite plain in this Epistle, and as the New Testament makes plain everywhere, this knowledge is only possible to us in and through the Lord Jesus Christ. So there is a sense in which we cannot separate them. The knowledge we are to have, as our Lord Himself says in His high priestly prayer, is a knowledge of the Father and the Son. 'This is life eternal, that they might know thee, the only true God, and Jesus Christ whom thou hast sent' (John 17:3). The Apostle in his Second Epistle to the Corinthians writes: 'God, who commanded the light to shine out of darkness, hath shined in our hearts, to give the light of the knowledge of the glory of God in the face of Jesus Christ' (4:6). It is the knowledge of the glory of God, this Father of glory to whom he is praying, that we need, and it is to be found 'in the face of Jesus Christ'. 'No man hath seen God at any time; the only begotten Son which is in the bosom of the Father, he hath declared him' (John 1:18). This knowledge is mediated, and is only possible for us in and through our blessed Saviour; but the knowledge ultimately is the knowledge of God Himself.

We are here face to face with the highest reaches of our Christian faith and life, and as we come to look at it, we can but say, 'Who is sufficient for these things?' The knowledge of God

[341]

is what the Apostle prayed for all these young Christians at Ephesus. It is the prayer needed by all Christians always and at all times. Our supreme need is to know God. As our Lord said in His high priestly prayer: 'O righteous Father, the world hath not known thee, but I have known thee, and these have known that thou hast sent me' (John 17:25).

The term 'knowledge' is a very strong, a very powerful term. It does not convey the sense of a casual, cursory acquaintance. It does not mean a superficial knowledge. There is such knowledge, of course, but the Apostle's term conveys the ideas of accurate and exact knowledge, certain knowledge, and also an experimental knowledge. It is profound knowledge. He could not have used a stronger term; it means the fullest knowledge that we can think of. His prayer for these people is that they should come to such a knowledge of God. Here they were still on earth, and many of them probably slaves, as was not unusual in those early centuries. They were ordinary people, perhaps ignorant, uneducated and illiterate; but that does not make any difference. What he prays is that they may come to this full knowledge, this full-orbed knowledge, this accurate, precise, exact, experimental knowledge of the One whom he has just described as not only 'the God of our Lord Jesus Christ' but the ineffable 'Father of glory'.

As we come to analyse this concept we must start by emphasizing negatively, that the Apostle is not praying that we may have an intellectual or theoretical knowledge of God only. There is such a knowledge, and it is most important. God has revealed Himself in order that we might know Him in that sense. He has done so in nature, He has done so in history, He does so in providence. But beyond that, He has done so in the giving of the Ten Commandments and the Moral Law, in order that they might instruct people as to the nature of the being and the character of God. Man's troubles are always due to his ignorance of God. So God has given us this general knowledge of Himself. But that is not the kind of knowledge which the Apostle has in mind here. It is vital that we should know something about the attributes of God. In the period in the religious life of this country known as the age of the Puritans, we find that a large number of great Puritan preachers constantly expounded the attributes of God – His eternity, His omnipresence, His omnipotence, and so on. Such preaching is very important, but it is what can be described as theoretical or intellectual, notional or propositional knowledge. Now while the Apostle certainly includes that kind of knowledge in his prayer, he goes beyond it.

To state it in other words, when Paul writes here about our coming to a knowledge of God, he means more than that we should know a number of things about God. There is a very good reason for this, as James explains in his Epistle when he says, 'The devils also believe, and tremble' (James 2:19). The devils have that kind of knowledge of God. They are not ignorant concerning the greatness and the might and the majesty of God. They believe in God in that sense, but that knowledge of God is not saving knowledge because it leads to nothing more than trembling. So we must emphasize that the knowledge which the Apostle has in mind does not stop at knowing certain things which are true about God. We need to know such things; we need to know that He is the 'Creator of the ends of the earth', that He is 'the Judge of all the earth', that He is almighty and everlasting. It is our ignorance of such truths concerning God that accounts for so much superficiality and glibness in our Christian life. There is 'no fear of God before their eyes' is still true of many. We are not 'godly' men and women as our fathers once were. Let us heed the words of the Apostle.

Again, Paul is not referring only to knowledge of the blessings which God gives. He is going to deal with such blessings later on as we shall see in his three-fold petition, namely, that the Ephesians may know in particular what is the hope of God's calling, what the riches of the glory of His inheritance in the saints, and what the exceeding greatness of His power to us-ward who believe. But he has not come to these yet, and is still praying in a more general sense. What we have here is quite staggering and astounding. He is concerned that we should have an immediate knowledge of God, a real fellowship with God. To use the current theological expression, he is concerned that we should have an 'encounter' with God. He means a knowledge of God which is personal and intimate. Whatever views we may hold of certain modern tendencies in theological teaching, we must at least agree that this returning emphasis on the idea of a divine-human encounter, a meeting with God, this 'existential moment' when I know that God is there and I here, the 'Thou-I' and 'I-Thou' relationship, is good. The knowledge Paul has in mind is not mere theory, mere notion; not something abstract or academic; it is personal, immediate, a real meeting. He is praying about the true knowledge of God.

It is almost impossible to put this truth into words, but it means that God should be real to us, and that we should be conscious of Him and conscious of His presence. I make no apology for asking whether you have ever known this? Is God real to you? When you get on your knees and pray, do you know that God is there, do you realize His presence? It is this that the Apostle has in mind; he desires that we should come to know and to realize something of the glory of God. Hence he has emphasized that he is praying to 'the God of our Lord Jesus Christ, the Father of glory'. Have you ever felt and sensed something of the glory of God? Have you known anything of what Jacob felt when he said, 'Surely the Lord is in this place . . .' and 'How dreadful is this place! this is none other but the house of God, and this is the gate of heaven'? (Genesis 28:16–17). It means that we know and realize something of the love of God as well as the glory of God. The glory fills us with a sense of awe and 'godly fear', but the love reassures us.

I stress again that this is not only a general belief in the love of God; it means that we begin to know something of, and experience directly and personally, God's love. To 'know' a person means something beyond casual acquaintance. We tend to say thoughtlessly 'I know So-and-so', when what we really mean is that 'I was once introduced to him and spoke a few words to him' or 'I am acquainted with him'. But that is not really to know a person. The term 'knowledge', as used here by the Apostle and in other parts of Scripture, means an intimate knowledge. This is clear when it is used of God's knowledge of us. God says of the children of Israel through the prophet Amos, 'You only have I known of all the families of the earth' (3:3). Obviously that does not mean that God was not aware of the existence of the others, for God knows all nations. *Known* in this connection means known in a particular, immediate, personal, special sense; it means that He had taken a special interest in them. So the Apostle was praying that these Ephesians might know the love of God to themselves personally, and might also feel that love.

This means having fellowship with God in a true and in a real sense. Such is the meaning of the statement we have already quoted: 'This is life eternal, that they might know thee, the only true God, and Jesus Christ whom thou hast sent' (John 17:3). The Jews knew about Him; they had been trained in the law and knew their Scriptures; but that is not sufficient; 'life eternal' means to 'know God' and to 'know Jesus Christ'. We find the Apostle John expressing this same desire for the Christians to whom he wrote his first Epistle and whom he calls his 'little children'. He says 'I write to you that your joy may be full' (1:4). He explains also how this may come about, saying, 'I am writing these things in order that you may have fellowship with us'. But fellowship with the Apostles is not all, so he adds, 'and truly our fellowship is with the Father and with his Son Jesus Christ'. Fellowship means communion, intimacy, partnership, a sharing of the same life. That is the connotation of this great word 'knowledge'.

If it be asked how we may know that we have this knowledge, the answer is, that anyone who knows anything about this matter, feels a sense of privilege, a sense of wonder, a sense of praise and of glory. To come to such a knowledge of God is what Christianity really means. Certain illustrations and examples from Scripture will help to explain the matter. This is what Job meant when he said, 'Oh, that I knew where I might find him!' (23:3). He had not lost his theoretical knowledge of God; he had not ceased to know about the attributes of God and about the works of God. That is not what Job was seeking. He had experienced fellowship and communion with God, but for the time being he had lost it. What he was seeking was the Person Himself, the direct contact with God. This becomes quite clear later when the Lord manifested and revealed Himself to him, and Job said: 'I have heard of thee by the hearing of the ear, but now mine eye seeth thee' (42:5). The contrast is between the 'hearing of the ear' and the 'But now . . .'. Thinking about God in general had led Job to much speaking and arguing, but when he feels the presence of God he puts his hand upon his mouth, and repents in dust and ashes (40:4; 42:6).

Moses expresses the same idea on many occasions. God had

given him the great and important task of leading the children of Israel to Canaan, and he, the meekest of men, conscious of his own inadequacy, says 'If thy presence go not with me, carry us not up hence'. But Moses was not satisfied even when God promised that, and rising with great daring he turned to God and said, 'I beseech thee, show me thy glory' (Exodus 33: 12–21). Have you ever felt that desire? The Apostle is praying that these Ephesians may begin to hunger and thirst for it, may realize that all that has happened to them has been designed to the end that they may see and know the glory of God, this Father of glory.

'Show me thy glory'. The Psalmist expresses the same idea in the forty-second Psalm; 'As the hart panteth after the water brooks, so panteth my soul after thee, O God. My soul thirsteth for God, for the living God' (vv. 1–2). He was not thinking of the God of theology, as it were, the God of the textbook, the God of propositions, but of 'the living God', the personal God. His soul was thirsting for Him; he was panting after that knowledge 'as the hart panteth after the water brooks'. This is a direct knowledge of God, not indirect; not a knowledge about, but immediate personal knowledge. It is the kind of experience Isaiah speaks about in the sixth chapter of his prophecy, when he says: 'I saw the Lord sitting upon a throne, high and lifted up, and his train filled the temple.' The house was filled with smoke, and the posts of the door moved. It was a glimpse of the glory of God. Seeing it he says: 'I am a man of unclean lips': 'Woe is me'. He has been in the presence of the glory, he has sensed it, he has felt it (vv. 1–8). This is true knowledge of God.

Our blessed Lord Himself taught the same truth; for instance, we find in the eleventh chapter of Matthew's Gospel: 'All things are delivered unto me of my Father, and no man knoweth the Son but the Father, neither knoweth any man the Father save the Son and he to whomsoever the Son will reveal him' (v. 27). Our Lord has come to give us salvation, which means ultimately that we know God. He states this again when He says: 'If a man love me he will keep my words, and my Father will love him, and we will come unto him and make our abode with him' (John 14:23). That is true Christianity, 'The life of God in the soul of man', as Henry Scougal termed it in his famous book; the Father and the Son coming and making their abode within us. Or let us turn again to Christ's high priestly prayer. He prays 'that the world may know that thou hast sent me, and hast loved them as thou hast loved me' (John 17:23). Such is the knowledge that Paul desires for these Ephesian Christians.

The Apostle also prays that the Ephesian Christians may have 'the spirit of wisdom and revelation', that they may come to such a knowledge of God. This is something beyond believing, beyond trusting, even beyond being sealed with the Spirit. The difference is that in the sealing with the Spirit we are given to know that we are His; the Holy Spirit 'bears witness with our spirit that we are the children of God' (Romans 8:16). It is God saying to us, 'Thou art my son, my child'. Is there anything beyond that? Yes; to know God Himself! That is the summit, the 'summum bonum'. It is wonderful to know that I belong to God; it is an infinitely greater privilege and blessing to know God Himself. Such is the knowledge which the Apostle desires for these Ephesian Christians.

This, too, is a knowledge which is meant for all Christians. The danger of certain types of 'soul culture' arises at this point. The Roman Catholic Church, and all Catholic teaching, does not hesitate to deny what I have asserted. It divides Christians into two groups, the 'religious' and the 'laity'. The 'religious' are those who become specialists in the religious life – the mystics, the saints, the people who forsake the world and segregate themselves from society and give themselves only to prayer, to meditation, to mortification of the body and contemplation. These, and these alone, according to Catholic teaching, can attain to this knowledge of God. A man engaged in business or in the ordinary affairs of life, an ordinary Christian, cannot attain to such a knowledge. But according to the teaching of the Scripture, this is grievous heresy. God forbid that any of us should succumb to it! We need go no further than this very prayer of the Apostle for the Ephesians to refute it. He is offering this prayer for all the members of the church at Ephesus. He is not praying for apostles, for elders, or for some exceptional Christians called 'saints'. He is praying for them all, that they all may have this 'spirit of wisdom and revelation in the knowledge of him'.

The fulfilment of this prayer is the peculiar promise of the new covenant. Through the prophet Jeremiah God gave the promise of a new covenant which He would make, as recorded in the thirty-first chapter of Jeremiah's prophecy. That promise is quoted twice in the Epistle to the Hebrews, in chapters 8 and 10. The promise, the prediction of what will happen under the new covenant when Christ would have done His work of salvation, runs: 'And they shall not teach every man his neighbour, and every man his brother, saying, Know the Lord: for all shall know me, from the least to the greatest' (Hebrews 8:11). Its characteristic is, 'All shall know me'. In the quotation from the prophet Joel, made by the Apostle Peter in his sermon on the day of Pentecost, we find also the following: 'And it shall come to pass in the last days, saith God, I will pour out of my Spirit upon all flesh: and your sons and your daughters shall prophesy, and your young men shall see visions, and your old men shall dream dreams: And on my servants and on my handmaidens I will pour out in those days of my Spirit; and they shall prophesy' (Acts 2: 17–18). Note the expressions, 'I will pour forth my Spirit upon *all* flesh'; 'they *all* shall know me, from the least unto the greatest'.

This knowledge is open to all. Thank God, the history of the Church throughout the centuries confirms this. This is not a matter of intellectual understanding, it does not depend upon circumstances and conditions. Two things only control this, namely, the realization that it is possible, and then the desire for it. 'Blessed are they that do hunger and thirst after righteousness, for they shall be filled'; 'Blessed are the pure in heart, for they shall see God' (Matthew 5:6, 8).

Do you know God? I am not asking whether you believe things about Him; but have you met Him? Have you known yourself for certain in His presence? Does He speak to you, and do you know that you speak to Him? '*The Practice of the Presence of God*' by Brother Lawrence tells us that this is possible in the kitchen while you are washing the dishes, and performing the most menial tasks. It matters not where you are as long as you know that this is possible, that Christ died to make it possible. He died 'to bring us to God', and to this knowledge. Is your fellowship 'with the Father and with his Son Jesus Christ'? O that we might know God! Begin to cry with Job, 'Oh that I knew where I might find him', and you will soon find yourself desiring, hungering to know Him. The most vital question to ask about all who claim to be Christian is this: Have they a soul thirst for God? Do they long for this? Is there something about them that tells you that they are always waiting for His next manifestation of Himself? Is their life centred on Him? Can they say with Paul that they forget everything in the past? Do they press forward more and more that they might know Him, and that the knowledge might increase, until eventually beyond death and the grave they may bask eternally in 'the sunshine of His face'? 'That I might know him!'

30

Wisdom and Revelation

'Wherefore I also, after I heard of your faith in the
Lord Jesus, and love unto all the saints, cease not to
give thanks for you, making mention of you in my
prayers: that the God of our Lord Jesus Christ, the
Father of glory, may give unto you the spirit of
wisdom and revelation in the knowledge of him.'

Ephesians 1:15–17

The great question that now arises for us is: How can a man
come to know God? Job put that question once and for ever
when he asked, 'Can a man by searching find out God?'(11:7).
The answer to that question is given in the verse which gives the
content of the Apostle's prayer. We need 'the spirit of wisdom
and revelation'; that is the secret! We must be careful to observe
that the Apostle is not praying here that these Ephesians might
have a general spirit of wisdom; he is not praying that they may
become wise men, or that their actions and activities may be
characterized by wisdom. That type of wisdom is excellent, and
we should all attempt to become wise in that sense. But Paul is
not praying that all their conduct in life and all their relationships
may be governed by this kind of wisdom and understanding. He
was praying rather that they might have in abundance the Holy
Spirit Himself, who is the only agency whereby we can ever have
spiritual wisdom and understanding. In other words I agree with
those who say that the word *spirit* here should be spelt with a
capital S and not with a small one. You will find in many places in
the Scripture, in the Authorized Version and in sundry other
translations, that though the reference is clearly to the Holy
Spirit, the small 's' is used instead of the capital S. This can
generally be decided in terms of the context; and in this particular
instance the prayer and the petition is surely that they might have
in abundance the Holy Spirit, the Spirit who gives wisdom and

[350]

brings wisdom, the Spirit who alone can reveal things to us. In other words the Apostle is once more emphasizing the peculiar work of the Holy Spirit.

This reminds us again of the way in which the Apostle shows us that the work of salvation is divided up among the Three Persons in the blessed Holy Trinity. Nothing is more 'amazing', to use Isaac Watts' term, than the fact that the Three Persons in the blessed Holy Trinity are involved together in rescuing us and redeeming us out of 'this present evil world' and fitting us for eternal glory. From verse 13 Paul has been reminding us that the peculiar, special work of the Holy Spirit is to seal us and to be our 'earnest' until the redemption of the purchased possession. Now he reminds us of another work of the Spirit, without which we can never know salvation at all. That is to say, it is the peculiar work of the Holy Spirit to apply to us the redemption that was planned by the Father and worked out and achieved by the Son.

Nothing finally proclaims so clearly whether a man has a right view of himself as a sinner and a right view of salvation, as his awareness of his need of, and his active constant dependence upon, the power of the Holy Ghost. A man's attitude towards the biblical teaching concerning the Holy Ghost proclaims clearly whether he holds right views on the doctrine of Man, the doctrine of Sin, the doctrine of the Lord Jesus Christ, the doctrine of Redemption – indeed the whole of the Christian doctrine of Redemption. This is so because there is no doctrine which shows us quite so clearly our utter and complete helplessness and hopelessness as this particular teaching concerning the work of the Holy Spirit in the application of redemption to us.

The end, the goal, is to bring us to know God. God made man; He made him in His own image and likeness and man was meant to live a life in correspondence with God, to be in fellowship with God. Man's creation was an expression of God's love. God as love gives Himself, His love goes out; and man was made to be the recipient of that love and to respond to it. But sin came in and separated man from God; it alienated him, it broke off the communication. Man became a fugitive and a wanderer; he became a stranger to God and did not 'know' God any longer. The whole end and object of redemption is to bring man back into that knowledge. The Bible's teaching is that the Holy Spirit alone can bring us back to that knowledge of God and His ways. Hence the Apostle prays, 'That the God of our Lord Jesus Christ, the Father of glory, may give unto you the Spirit of wisdom and revelation in the knowledge of him'. He prays that the Holy Spirit may do it because He alone can do it. Let us proceed to establish this foundational truth.

First of all I suggest that this is a simple fact. Man by nature does not know God. I make that as an asseveration, as something which really needs no demonstration. We can prove the matter by asking two simple questions: Do you *know* God? Does any man by nature *know* God? The Bible from cover to cover gives the answer that man does not, and our own experiences confirm that answer and substantiate it completely. This explains why people find prayer so difficult. If you cannot pray for an hour, why cannot you? You can talk to neighbours and friends for an hour easily, nay, for hours. Why then is it difficult to speak to God for an hour? There is only one answer; it is because we do not *know* Him. We do not know Him sufficiently, and we are not conscious that we are in His presence. This is a simple fact.

But we must go further and say that man, left to himself, by all his endeavours can never come to a knowledge of God. By searching, by natural ability, by relying on their own wisdom and understanding, men can never find God. This is the absolute proposition laid down by the Apostle Paul in his First Epistle to the Corinthians in the memorable statement, 'The world by wisdom knew not God' (1:21). This attempt to discover God has been the great quest of mankind from the very beginning. The Greek philosophers had attempted it. There is in man an innate sense of consciousness that there is a God; every man has it. The so-called atheist has it and is simply trying to argue against it, trying to buttress up something he does not want to believe in his mind, but which something within him keeps on asserting. Archaeological research has shown that the most primitive tribes in the world all have within them a sense of a Supreme God, a supreme Being at the back of everything. It is universal in mankind. So man has been trying to satisfy this sense of longing, this awareness that he has; and he has generally done so with his

mind. Everything we try to discover in this life is done by means
of our minds. Scientific discovery is the result of the use of the
mind. You put up your hypothesis or supposition or theory; and
then you test it by your experiments. In the mundane realm, this
procedure is perfectly right and often adequate. Now that is
human wisdom; it is man's method. He delves into the mysteries,
he does his research work, he seeks and continues searching; he
uses his powers, especially his mental ability. But the fact is that
in the attempt to know God and, to find God, such effort and
endeavour proves futile: 'The world by wisdom knew not
God.'

I agree with those who teach that God determined the particular
hour when He would send His Son into the world in such a
manner that Greek philosophy should have been given its oppor-
tunity, and should have done its utmost, to bring mankind to this
knowledge of God and should have completely failed to do so.
This is a sheer fact of history. God allowed the Greek philosophers
to have their day before He sent His Son into this world. He
arranged all that first in order that this great assertion might be
made, that 'The world by wisdom knew not God'. It proved in a
most positive manner that man at the height of his ability is as
helpless as a little child when faced by the knowledge imparted to
the Ephesian believers by the Spirit. This is so for the reasons
which the Apostle proceeds to give in the second chapter of his
First Epistle to the Corinthians.

The best commentary on this seventeenth verse in the first
chapter of the Epistle to the Ephesians is that second chapter of
the First Epistle to the Corinthians. There, the Apostle elaborates
in a chapter what he puts here in a phrase. Man does not know
God and in and of himself can never arrive at the knowledge of
God because that knowledge is 'a hidden wisdom' (1 Corinthians
2:7). It is concerned about 'the deep things of God', the abyss of
God's everlasting character, the immensity of God's eternal being
and His ways which are 'past finding out'. Man's mind is too
small, too limited to plumb such depths. I am not insulting man,
but simply saying that God is infinitely great and infinitely above
us and beyond us, and man's mind is too small to grasp such
'infinities and immensities', as Thomas Carlyle termed them.

But that is not the only difficulty, and in a sense it is not the main one. The real trouble lies in the fact that 'God is a Spirit, and they that worship him must worship him in spirit and in truth' (John 4:24). All truth concerning God is spiritual in its character, and as the natural man encounters the light of the eternal world, his boasted ability is made to appear to be even ridiculous, the result being that we are all brought to the same level. Nothing is more glorious and encouraging about the Christian message and the Christian way of salvation than the fact that human divisions and distinctions are quite irrelevant. It is the only sphere in which this is true. In regard to the things of God, natural ability, or lack of ability, is quite immaterial. Thank God that this is so. If it were otherwise, those who are intelligent and born with intellect would have a great advantage over others; furthermore, there would be no point in sending missionaries out to parts of the world where people have never yet received any education at all; indeed, the missionary enterprise would be impossible. If men must have strength of mind and learning and understanding and the ability to exercise and use their faculties before they can become Christian, then it would be ridiculous to preach the gospel to ignorant and illiterate people. Moreover, it is a fact that while many men of great intellect do not believe the gospel, it is possible for a man in Central Africa who has never had a day's education, to believe it and to enter into an apprehension of it. The explanation is that this knowledge is spiritual in character; it is a knowledge of God who is 'Spirit', and who can only be known in a spiritual manner.

It is a basic truth that man, as the result of sin, is no longer spiritual; he has become carnal or, to use Paul's term, he has become a 'natural' man (1 Corinthians 2:14). All knowledge, according to the Apostle's argument in 1 Corinthians, chapter 2, demands certain affinities or a certain correspondence. He says: 'What man knoweth the things of a man, save the spirit of man that is in him?' (v. 11); in other words, one man understands another because they are both men and they have the same spirit, in a natural sense. You must be musical to understand music, you must have a certain poetic faculty if poetry is going to speak to you. You cannot arrive at knowledge in these realms unless there is some kind of basic correspondence. You may be a genius, but if you lack the poetic feeling poetry will be nonsense to you. In every realm and department of thought and knowledge there must be some aptitude, something that responds to, and corresponds with, the object you are anxious to know. Because of this requirement, man in this matter of knowledge of God is completely helpless and hopeless. It does not matter how great his mind may be, or his understanding, man by nature is no longer spiritual; he is 'carnal', 'sold under sin'. The spiritual faculty with which he was originally created has become atrophied, and can no longer be exercised. Whatever man may do, however much he may try to raise himself up and to stimulate his mind, he cannot produce the necessary faculty and affinity to arrive at a knowledge of God. These things, says the Apostle in another phrase, 'are spiritually discerned' (v. 14). Without a spiritual faculty you cannot discern them. Hence the things of God are foolishness to the natural man and he does not see anything in them. He lacks this essential capacity or faculty.

We must start therefore by seeing quite clearly that apart from the Holy Spirit man can never arrive at this knowledge of God. It is the peculiar function of the Holy Spirit to bring us to this knowledge. This cuts right across all our normal human way of looking at truth and at knowledge. It is entirely different. Our Lord has stated this once and for ever in the words, 'Except ye be converted and become as little children, ye shall in no wise enter into the kingdom of heaven' (Matthew 18:3). That is a universal truth. Whoever a man may be, whatever his ability or his culture or his learning, he has to come down and become as a little child; he has to realize his utter helplessness, his complete bankruptcy. Above all he has to admit his complete failure to know God in spite of his intellectual powers. If he fails or refuses to do so, he will never have this knowledge. It was to Nicodemus, a master in Israel, a man of intellect and learning, that our Lord said, 'Marvel not that I said unto thee, Ye must be born again' (John 3:7). In this realm man cannot proceed from where he is, he must go back to another beginning; he must make a completely fresh start. 'Ye must be born again', because this is an entirely different realm. It is the realm of the Spirit, and no man can walk into this in his own strength and ability. We all have to enter into this kingdom in the same way. There are not many ways of entering it; there is but one, and it is the way of repentance, involving complete admission of failure and utter bankruptcy. Without the Holy Spirit know-ledge of God is impossible: and He has been sent in order to give us this knowledge.

The Apostle proceeds to tell us that the Spirit gives us this knowledge in two main ways. First, He gives us the necessary wisdom: 'That the God of our Lord Jesus Christ, the Father of glory, may give unto you the Spirit of *wisdom*.' *Wisdom*, as used here, does not mean a general spirit of wisdom. It means 'know-ledge'. In the Bible generally the word *wisdom* stands for know-ledge, as, for example, in the Book of Proverbs: 'The fear of the Lord is the beginning of wisdom' (9:10). It does not mean what we normally mean by wisdom, namely, the result or consequence of knowledge. We can state it thus, that what the Apostle is praying for the Ephesians is that they may have that knowledge which makes us wise unto salvation. 'Wisdom' stands for knowledge, information, understanding.

This wisdom or knowledge was what the Greeks sought; they were 'natural scientists' in this sense. They felt that there was so much to learn, so much of which they were ignorant; so they set out to amass knowledge. This present generation to which we belong is typically Greek in its outlook. It delights in Encyclo-paedias, it desires to know something about everything. It asks itself questions, and reads books, because it thinks that that is the way to make a perfect world and to live the right kind of life. Man claims that he wants knowledge. To that demand the Bible says: If you want knowledge, if you want wisdom, if you want true understanding, there is only one place in which you can find it; here it is! According to the Bible, wisdom starts with 'the fear of the Lord'. It is only found by waiting upon Him, and looking to Him for the knowledge we need. The Holy Spirit helps us to obtain this knowledge by giving us the faculty which is essential to an understanding of the biblical message.

The great question is: What do I really need to know in order to live as I should in this world? Is it best for me to start on a course of reading history, the long story of mankind, and to say, 'Well now, where did men in the past go wrong, where did they make their mistakes? If I can but discover that, then I shall know what to avoid and what not to do'. Many think that that is the way. Others disagree and say, 'No! all you need is to look into yourself, to become a psychologist and to analyse your own mind and your motives'. It is for this reason that psychology has had a great vogue in this present century. The whole theory has been that what we need is a particular knowledge of ourselves; so we have delved into ourselves and analysed our so-called unconscious mind, we have recorded our dreams and analysed them, and we have allowed psycho-analysts to examine us while we were lying passively on their couches in a state of 'free association'. This, we think, is the way to arrive at true knowledge and understanding.

But the Bible says No! to all that, and assures us that the knowledge which we need is of a very different order; it is a knowledge to which the Holy Spirit alone can bring us. It is a knowledge of God Himself. We must start with this knowledge of God, the Author and the Creator of all things. Before I begin to analyse myself or to allow others to do so, I should have asked the question: What am I, where have I come from, how can I possibly explain my very being? Such questions drive me back to God. I see nature and creation, it all suggests God to me. But I cannot find Him there. I find there the marks of His fingers but I want *Him*. How can I find *Him*? 'Oh, that I knew where I might find *him*' (Job 23:3). That is the question! I look at history, I look at providence, I look into myself, I look everywhere and yet I cannot find Him. Where can I find God? There is only one solution: I must wait upon God; and God must tell me about Himself. That is revelation; and it is the function of the Holy Spirit to give us this revelation.

It is only thus that we shall discover the truth about God, about God's character, about God's being, about God Himself, God as God. We have seen that the greatest philosopher cannot arrive at Him, but thank God, God has been pleased to tell us about Himself. He has given us the wisdom, the knowledge, we need about Himself and His gracious purposes. Where can you find out about the plan of redemption apart from this revelation? How can man ever know that God has a heart of love and that He looks upon man in sin with a piteous eye? How could man have found that out? He could not have done so; he failed to do so, despite all the philosophical heights attained by Greek thinkers. God has had to reveal it; the knowledge and the wisdom are given by Him through the Holy Spirit alone.

Let me illustrate: take the Lord Jesus Christ. As a natural man you look at Him and you may say: 'A remarkable phenomenon! It is astonishing that a carpenter who never had any intellectual training in the schools as a Pharisee, nor as a philosopher, could have uttered those incomparable pearls of wisdom. An amazing phenomenon!' Try to understand Him, try to analyse Him – you cannot. You may try to do so by saying with the biologists that He is a kind of 'sport' which has been thrown up inexplicably by one of the odd tricks of nature, that He does not conform to the rules of the gradual development and evolution of mankind. You can look at the Lord Jesus Christ with all your human wisdom at its very acme, and not begin to understand Him. But when you submit to the revelation, you are given the knowledge that, in a measure, enables you to understand Him. There are two natures in that Person. He is Jesus the Nazarene, He is the carpenter, the son of Mary; but more, He is the everlasting Son of God! Two natures, one Person! You are given a fact; and also an explanation of the fact. But such wisdom is only to be obtained by the Holy Spirit.

By looking at Jesus and analysing Him you will never see Him and come to know Him, and the blessings He came to give, because your categories are not big enough. I quote again the Apostle Paul's words in 1 Corinthians 2:7–8: 'We speak the wisdom of God in a mystery . . . which none of the princes of this world knew, for had they known it they would not have crucified the Lord of glory.' They did not know that He was 'the Lord of glory'; they only saw the human frame, the man only. They could not see the other, they could not arrive at a true knowledge of Him, try as they might. This knowledge is given by the Holy Spirit – 'God hath revealed (it) unto us by his Spirit, for the Spirit searcheth all things, yea, the deep things of God' (1 Corinthians 2:10). He opens our eyes to the mystery of the Incarnation, of the two natures in one Person – unmixed, unconfused, and yet but One Person. He then leads us to see the way of salvation.

Go with your natural mind at its highest and look at the cross on Calvary's hill. What do you see there? The best you can possibly see is the death of a martyr, the death of a pure soul, the death of an honest person who rather than recant or withdraw His teaching preferred to suffer death. A natural man, with the human mind and ability at their highest, can see nothing more than that in the cross. He cannot see the 'love so amazing, so divine'. That 'wondrous' and glorious truth is only seen by eyes that have been enlightened by the Holy Spirit. The Holy Spirit alone can enable us to understand that 'God hath laid upon him the iniquity of us all' (Isaiah 53:6). The world laughs at that and ridicules it. Of course it does, says Paul, for 'the natural man understandeth not the things of the Spirit of God'. He cannot do so because 'they are spiritually discerned'. The natural man does not begin to understand it; he does not know himself, he does not know sin, he does not know the love of God, so how can he understand? The Holy Spirit alone can give this knowledge, and He does so. Even the disciples did not understand Calvary and its purpose until after the resurrection, in spite of the fact that they had spent three years looking into the eyes of the Son of God and listening to His every word. They could not take it in, they could not understand. You must have this illumination given by the Holy Spirit, and this knowledge imparted, before you can see it. God reveals the truth concerning Himself; had He not done so we would be left in utter darkness. Hence Paul prays that Ephesian believers may have the Spirit of wisdom, the Spirit that gives the wisdom, the knowledge.

This knowledge was given at first through the apostles and prophets. Hence Paul says at the end of chapter 2 that the Christian Church is built upon 'the foundation of the apostles and prophets' (v. 20). Truth came through them and their preaching and teaching. But soon it was given in another form in what we call the New Testament, in the Gospels, the Book of Acts, the Epistles and the Book of Revelation. This knowledge had already been given in partial form through the Old Testament. The writers of the books that constitute the Old Testament were not simply expressing their own ideas about life. According to the Apostle Peter in his Second Epistle, chapter one, 'Prophecy is not of any private interpretation'. He means that the prophecies were not simply men's interpretation of life, men's personal view of the world and what is happening in it. Not that, he says, but rather, 'holy men of God spake as they were moved [inspired, carried along] by the Holy Ghost' (vv. 20–21). It was the Holy Ghost who gave them what they saw, and guided them in writing it: 'All Scripture is given by inspiration of God, and is profitable for doctrine and for reproof' says the Apostle Paul likewise (2 Timothy 3:16). The Scriptures are not the result of man's seeking, but of God's revelation and inspiration. The Spirit of wisdom operates now through this Word of God found in the Bible and brings us to this knowledge.

The Apostle also speaks of 'the Spirit of *revelation*'. This obviously implies, that we need fresh knowledge or understanding, as we have already seen. It has already been given and therefore we must reject the teachings of individuals or churches who claim to have received fresh revelation over and above what we have in the Scriptures. Speaking generally, that is a claim put forward by the Roman Catholic Church. She claims to have received further revelation either through oral tradition handed down by the apostles or as the result of her own interpretation of the Scriptures. There are individuals who make the same claim. But that is not what is meant by 'revelation', as used here by the Apostle, for he has already dealt with that under 'wisdom'. 'Revelation' here is to be understood in the following way. Man's capacity to understand spiritual truth as the result of sin and the fall has been so greatly marred, that even when you put this wisdom that God has given us through the Holy Spirit before his eyes he cannot see it or comprehend it. The extent of man's fall is so great and extensive that no man by the exercise of his own will or understanding can ever save himself or become a Christian. I have repeatedly stressed the argument of 1 Corinthians 2:14 about the natural man. How, then, can any man ever come to understand these things? The answer is: 'We have the mind of Christ' (1 Corinthians 2:16). Man needs the Holy Spirit to make this revelation clear to him. The Holy Spirit has already inspired and guided holy men to put this knowledge in written form, but before we can 'see' it and receive it something further is necessary; the Spirit must operate also upon us. He must open our eyes to see what there is before us. This needs no demonstration. The Apostle Paul tells us in his Second Epistle to the Corinthians, chapter 3, that the majority of the Jews were in a very sad state; their minds were blinded, and there was a veil over their eyes. They read their Old Testament Scriptures every Sabbath but they could not discern the meaning. They were reading the Word of God but they could not understand it. 'If our gospel be hid', says Paul in the fourth chapter of that same Epistle, 'it is hid to them that are lost, in whom the god of this world hath blinded the minds of them which believe not, lest the light of the glorious gospel of Christ, who is the image of God, should shine unto them'.

This truth is illustrated perfectly in a story about William Pitt the Younger, and his friend William Wilberforce. William Wilberforce, the pioneer in the movement for the abolition of slavery, was a fine Christian man who had been converted at the age of twenty-six by reading a book by Philip Doddridge called *The Rise and Progress of Religion in the Soul*. He was an active Christian. He was also a member of Parliament and a friend of William Pitt the Younger whom he had known since their university days. Pitt, like so many statesmen, was a formal Christian and went on special occasions to church but really had no understanding of spiritual things. They were great friends and Wilberforce was troubled and anxious about the soul of William Pitt. He prayed for him, and he was specially anxious for him to go with him to hear a London preacher named Richard Cecil, a spiritually-minded man who preached spiritual messages. Wilberforce used to listen to him regularly and he revelled in the doctrine preached. He often asked Pitt to accompany him but Pitt always had some excuse or other. But at last Pitt promised to go, and one day they went together to listen to Richard Cecil. Wilberforce felt that he had never heard Richard Cecil expound God's truth in a more wonderful Spirit-filled manner. His heart was ravished by the truth, it was heaven to him. He could not help wondering as to what was happening to his friend. Eventually the service ended and they went out together. Almost before they had left the building William Pitt turned to Wilberforce and said, 'You know, Wilberforce, I did my very best to concentrate with the whole of my power upon what that man was saying, but I have not the slightest idea as to what he has been talking about.'

That is a true story, and how true of so many still! From the standpoint of sheer ability William Pitt was a greater man than William Wilberforce. He had a very great mind and intellect; but the truth of God as expounded by Richard Cecil meant absolutely nothing to him, for his eyes had not been opened by the Spirit. The truth meant everything to Wilberforce; it meant nothing to Pitt. Pitt had not received 'the Spirit of revelation'.

Paul prays that the Ephesian Christians might have 'the spirit of wisdom and revelation'. They were already Christians, but they were only at the beginning, were babes in Christ. There was so much that they had not seen as yet. One of the most thrilling experiences which a Christian gets is to go through his Bible year after year and to find suddenly as he reads a passage that he has often read before, something which stands out and speaks to him in a most amazing manner. He had been blind to it before. That is what makes preaching year after year possible. The Holy Spirit gives to preachers fresh revelations of truth. They had always been there, but the preacher is led to see them in a progressive manner by this 'spirit of revelation'. Without this spirit of revelation the preacher would fail and become bankrupt of ideas. I am more dependent upon Him than I have ever been. The truth is so great, and my mind is so small; but the Spirit of revelation gives us understanding.

We have been considering one of the most important doctrines of the Christian faith. The Protestant Reformers used to tell their hearers that there is a double action of the Holy Spirit. There is the 'Testimonium Spiritus Externus' – the Spirit that is in the Word, as it were, the Spirit that inspired the men who produced the Word. That is essential. But it is not enough. Before I know that this is God's Word and God's truth, before I can read the Bible and discover health and food for my soul, something additional is necessary – the 'Testimonium Spiritus Internus'. The Spirit in the Word; the Spirit in the reader! And without the Spirit in him no man will be able to understand the meaning of the Word. The two operations are absolutely essential.

In other words we have seen that the Apostle prays for the Ephesian believers that the God of our Lord Jesus Christ, the Father of glory, may give them 'the Spirit of wisdom (Testimonium Spiritus Externus) and 'the Spirit of revelation', the ability to see it and to receive it and revel in it and to enjoy it (Testimonium Spiritus Internus). What a perfect provision for damned, blind, helpless, wretched sinners! All the truth I need to know and the ability to receive it and to apprehend it! And all given freely through the Holy Spirit of God! What a perfect salvation! 'All I need, in Thee to find.'

> *Glory be to God the Father,*
> *Glory be to God the Son,*
> *Glory be to God the Spirit –*
> *Great Jehovah, Three in One!*
> *Glory, glory*
> *While eternal ages run!*

31
'The Hope of his Calling'

'The eyes of your understanding being enlightened;
that ye may know what is the hope of his calling.'

Ephesians 1:18

Having considered what we have described as the general, the all-inclusive petition which the Apostle Paul offered for the Ephesians, we come now to the particulars. This is invariably the Apostle's method; you first state the whole, and then come to the parts. We find that he is concerned that they should understand three things in particular. Each one is introduced by the word 'what'. He prays that they may know *'what* is the hope of his calling', *'what* the riches of the glory of his inheritance in the saints', and *'what* is the exceeding greatness of his power to us-ward who believe'.

But the Apostle cannot begin to deal with these particulars without again reminding us of a vital principle. He prays: 'the eyes of your understanding being enlightened; that ye may know' these three things. We may feel at first glance that he has already said as much as this in saying that we need 'the Spirit of wisdom and revelation'. But this is not an instance of tautology; the Apostle is not repeating himself. He is in effect saying to them: I have told you that the supreme thing, the central thing, is to know God Himself; but I want you to know these subsidiary things also, these particulars; and yet again I must tell you and remind you that you can only receive them to the extent that your understanding is enlightened by the Holy Spirit. The Authorized Version uses the word understanding at this point, but some of the other versions read, 'the eyes of your *heart* being enlightened'. The variation depends upon which of the original manuscripts the translator adopts as the best. But in any case there is no contradiction. In the Bible the 'understanding' and the 'heart' are often identified. The heart in biblical usage not only means the emotions; it also means the centre of personality, the source of our being and of our activity. The Apostle is therefore praying that in a total sense – not merely in an intellectual manner, or in an academical, theoretical way – we may come to know these things. He is praying that with our whole being we may come to know these truths and to respond to them.

The best way to understand this prayer is to realize once more, that the Apostle is contrasting the condition of the natural and the spiritual man. Later, in chapter 4, he will show us what we all are by nature, and demonstrate our need to have the eyes of our understanding enlightened. He says: 'This I say therefore, and testify in the Lord, that ye henceforth walk not as other Gentiles walk, in the vanity of their mind, having the understanding darkened, being alienated from the life of God through the ignorance that is in them, because of the blindness of their heart: who being past feeling have given themselves over unto lasciviousness, to work all uncleanness with greediness' (vv. 17–19). The operative phrase here is, 'Having the understanding darkened', the consequence being that they are 'alienated from the life of God' and 'ignorant' and are 'walking in the vanity of their mind'. This means that what we all need is not a new faculty, for we all have the faculty of mind and understanding in a natural sense. The tragic thing about man is not so much that he has lost a faculty, but that as the result of sin and the Fall he cannot use and exercise his faculties properly. The Apostle in speaking about pagans, the unbelieving Gentiles, says that their understanding is 'darkened'. They have an understanding but it is 'darkened'.

Let us take a simple illustration. There are certain people who have become blind, who cannot even see light. Their trouble is not that they have lost an eye; they still have the organ. The trouble may be that there is something wrong with the lens of their eye. But that does not mean that the lens has disappeared, but that a film has developed over it, an opacity which is called a cataract. The lens is there as it was when they could see quite normally, but because this opacity has developed they cannot see. The eye has become 'darkened', a veil has come over it, so that it can no longer receive the light that is coming from the outside. The state of man's mind by nature and 'in sin' is comparable to the defective eye. The blind person does not need a new eye; what he needs is that the opacity, the veil, the mist that has developed in his lens should be removed. The moment that occurs he will be able to appreciate the light and see things as he did before. Now that is the condition of man in sin; he has a natural understanding, he has the faculty, the ability, but he cannot use it in spiritual matters. It is blinded, it is darkened, this veil has come upon it, the shutter has fallen; and though the glorious light of God's revelation is there shining before him in the Scriptures, and indeed even in nature, he cannot see it. Therefore it is necessary that this 'eye of our understanding' should be enlightened, that the opacity, the veil, should be taken away in order that the spiritual eye may be able to function as it did in man's original creation.

My illustration helps as far as it goes. But we must add a further truth which is taught in the Scriptures, namely, that man's trouble is not only that his understanding has become darkened, but because of that, he also needs power. It is as if the eye, because of its not being used, becomes atrophied; the very optic nerve itself, as it were, has lost its power. So man needs a dual operation; he needs the removal of the opacity, and also the restoration of power and strength to his spiritual optic nerve.

The Holy Spirit supplies both these needs, and He alone does so. We have seen that great men of the world, when confronted by spiritual truth, can see nothing. There is no purpose or point in taking a blind man to look at a most beautiful bit of scenery; he just cannot see it. He may even deny that there is any such scenery. The trouble is that he cannot see it. It is there! 'The eyes of our understanding' must be enlightened before we can appreciate spiritual truth.

We must be careful to remember also that this is a prayer which Paul offers for *Christian* people. He is praying here for those who are already 'in Christ Jesus', who are fellow-heirs with the saints, and who have been sealed with the Holy Spirit. From this fact we deduce the following principles. First, that as long as we are in this life and in this world we shall always need the enlightening work of the Holy Spirit. We shall never be in a position in which we no longer have such a need. As long as we are here, and encompassed by infirmities, and in a world of sin, and indeed have a principle of sin still remaining in us, we shall need this enlightening operation of the Holy Spirit. Surely we all know that by experience. However much we may have learnt, however great our understanding of the Scriptures may be, if we begin to backslide in our daily life and living we shall find that the Word no longer speaks to us as it did. This is an invariable law. We can never take a spiritual holiday. We can never go on living on a reserve which we have accumulated. As it was with the manna in the wilderness, so spiritual understanding has to be collected freshly day by day. Unless we realize our dependence upon the Holy Spirit the Word will not speak to us. If we read the Word of God without praying for enlightenment, we shall probably get very little out of it. We must never depart from this consciousness of our dependence upon the Spirit's power and enlightenment. The 'anointing', the 'unction from the Holy One', of which the Apostle John speaks is needed constantly and increasingly (1 John 2:20, 27).

The second principle which we deduce is that spiritual knowledge is obviously progressive. Paul thanks God that the Ephesians knew much already; and yet he desires them to increase in knowledge; indeed he keeps repeating his petitions. In the great prayer in the third chapter of this Epistle he prays very much for the same thing. We are but little children paddling at the very edge of a great and mighty ocean of truth; and nothing is quite so tragic as the type of Christian who gives the impression that he has 'arrived'. That is generally the result of thinking of the Christian life solely in terms of the experience of forgiveness, sanctification, and so on. This leaves a man thinking that he has 'arrived', that he has finished, that he has all! But such an idea is entirely contrary to the New Testament teaching, where the picture is rather that of a progressive growth and development, and an ever-increasing understanding.

Scripture tells us that we start as babes in Christ. Then we begin to grow and to garner knowledge; and this goes on and increases. Sometimes we may think foolishly that we know everything, and then suddenly something quite new opens before our gaze. We continue to learn; we proceed 'from glory to glory', 'forgetting the things that are behind' we press forward as Paul did, always anxious to learn more and to know more. Such is the normal Christian life.

This, therefore, seems to me to be a very good test of our whole Christian position. Is our spiritual knowledge greater today than it was a year ago? Looking back across let us say ten years in the Christian life, can you say that your spiritual knowledge is greater than it was? I am not asking whether you have a greater knowledge of the letter of the Scripture, as you may have an increasing knowledge of Shakespeare; I am not asking if you have memorized a large number of biblical verses. I am asking whether your spiritual knowledge and understanding have grown? Is your grasp of truth more profound? Do you really feel that you are being led ever onwards, as it were from chamber to chamber in a great mansion, and discovering fresh treasures of wisdom and knowledge? That is the test. Paul prayed that the Ephesians might ever have an increasingly greater spiritual knowledge and understanding of the truth.

The third principle we deduce is that we should be constantly praying for this enlightening of the eyes of our understanding. This again can be stated in the form of a question. Do we day by day pray to God, the God of our Lord Jesus Christ, the Father of glory, to enlighten the eyes of our understanding? It should be our constant daily prayer. We should always preface our reading of the Word by praying for this enlightenment. The constant desire of our lives should be that we might 'grow in grace and in the knowledge of the Lord'. The trouble with so many of us is that we have never awakened to this realization. We seem to think that we have 'arrived', that we 'know'. We know more than those liberal theologians, those modernists, and people who are not Christians; so we seem to think that we have encompassed the whole of Christian knowledge. The fact is that we are but tyros, we are babes, we are merely at the very beginning. We must press on unto perfection. Are we interested in Christian doctrine? Do we really see the importance of it, or do we find it rather boring and dull? Do we always seek some excitement, something to entertain us? Do we realize that, having been

saved and called and placed in Christ, what God desires is that
we should grow in our understanding of truth and of doctrine,
that we should become more concerned about this than about
anything else, that the 'eyes of our understanding', our comprehension, may be enlightened to that end.

Bearing that in mind – and how vitally important it is! – we come
to the first of the three things the Apostle would have these
Ephesians know, namely, 'what is the hope of his calling'. There
has been considerable dispute as to the meaning of the word
'hope' in this statement. Some have said that it means the things
for which we hope. But this cannot be right, for it is these things
that Paul deals with in his second petition concerning knowing
the 'riches of the glory of his inheritance in the saints'. Sometimes
'hope' means that in the Scripture, but not here. Surely the Apostle
is referring to our hope in and of itself. He means our realization
that we have been called to these things and for these things. In
other words it refers once more to assurance of salvation.

The next word that faces us is 'calling' – 'that ye may know
what is the hope of his calling'. This word introduces us at once
to a great theological question and principle, a great matter of
doctrine. Let us test ourselves once more. I have been emphasizing
that nothing is more important than that the eyes of our understanding should be enlightened. Have your 'eyes' been so
enlightened that, as a Christian, let us say, of a number of years'
standing, you understand this term 'calling'? We are meant to
understand it. But what is this 'calling' to which the Apostle
refers? You have probably read this Epistle to the Ephesians
many times, but do you know the meaning of this term? Here, we
have a great New Testament term, a term which unfortunately we
hear very infrequently at the present time, but which formerly
counted for very much, especially among evangelical people.

The fathers used to teach, and rightly, that there are two calls
or 'callings' in Scripture. There is a general call and there is a
particular call. For instance, we read in the seventeenth chapter
of the Book of the Acts, that the Apostle Paul while preaching to
the Athenians said, 'But the times of this ignorance God winked
at, but now commandeth all men everywhere to repent'. That is

the general call. The gospel of Jesus Christ issues a general call to all mankind to repent and believe the gospel. The gospel is to be preached to all creatures everywhere throughout the world; and they are all to be 'called' to repent and believe. Obviously the Apostle cannot be referring to that usage at this point because this is not a general letter to the world but a special letter to Christian people. He is offering this special prayer for those who have already believed in the Lord Jesus Christ. This is therefore a reference to another type of call which is found in the Scriptures.

There is a special call, or, to use the actual term the fathers used, there is an 'effectual call'. The general call of God is not always effectual. Many people will find themselves in hell eventually who have heard the general call. There are men who are living in sin and gloating in it who can tell you exactly what the gospel says. They can describe what the call to repentance means, and what the offer of the gospel means. They have a general intellectual knowledge of it. They have heard the general call, but they have not responded to it; it has not been 'effectual' in their cases. But there is a type of call or calling which is effectual. This is what the Apostle states so clearly in the eighth chapter of his Epistle to the Romans in these words: 'We know that all things work together for good to them that love God, to them who are the called according to his purpose'. The 'called' in that instance cannot relate to the general call because those who have heard it and have not responded do not 'love God', and have not 'been called according to his purpose.' The 'called' to whom the Apostle is referring there and to whom alone the great promise applies, he defines further when he goes on to say: 'For whom he did foreknow, he also did predestinate to be conformed to the image of his Son, that he might be the firstborn among many brethren. Moreover whom he did predestinate, them he also called: and whom he called, them he also justified' (Romans 8: 28–31). This refers to a special calling. The people who have been called in that sense have been justified and, furthermore, they have been glorified; but that is not true of the man of the world who has received the general call to repent and to believe.

So what we have in Ephesians 1:18 is not a general call, it is the effectual or special call. We can state it in the following way.

God, through the gospel and by the Holy Spirit, sends out this general call to the whole world, but He calls certain people in particular, and no man is a Christian unless he is called in this special sense. 'The called' are the Christians; the Christians are 'the called'. They are people in whom the Word of God has been made effective; it has come to them in power, it has come as a command which they find to be irresistible, and they readily respond to it with the whole of their being. The Apostle's petition is that they might know the *hope* of this calling. 'You have been called', he says elsewhere, 'with a heavenly calling'. In another place he says 'that Christians have been called with a holy calling'. What he desires us to know is the hope of this calling, the assurance of it, the certainty of it. Have you got assurance of your salvation? To use the words of Peter, have you made 'your calling and election sure'? That is the secret of a happy Christian life. The enemy is there, the devil attacks with his suggested doubts and uncertainties; sin troubles us and makes us think that perhaps we have never been Christians at all. Are you certain of the hope of your calling?

This is of the very essence of the Protestant and the Evangelical position. Roman Catholics dislike the doctrine of assurance of salvation, and denounce it. They do not want us to have personal certainty; our assurance must lie in the Church to which we commit ourselves. Not only so, but we have to go through purgatory they say, before we arrive at the promised rest. Everything is uncertain; and all depends upon the Church, and the prayers of the Church for us, and the lighting of candles and the payment of money for indulgences, and the work of supererogation of the saints. The whole Roman position is uncertain and precarious. But the essence of Protestantism, as Martin Luther discovered to his great and eternal joy, is that the individual Christian may know his salvation as certain; he may defy all devils and hell and Satan himself; the Christian knows the Christ whom he has believed; his hope is sure; his calling and election are sure.

Assurance and certainty should be the possession of all Christians. Denial of this is not confined to the Roman Catholics. Certain modern schools of theology also reject it. The Barthian school of thought which, in its rejection of the old Liberalism, appears to resemble the evangelical position, is nevertheless radically different, and particularly for this reason, that it dislikes assurance. It teaches that a Christian can never be sure. But according to the prayer of the Apostle a Christian should know the hope of his calling, he should be absolutely certain of it.

The first step in the attaining of this assurance is that the eyes of our understanding be enlightened. We have also seen that part of the answer is found in the whole doctrine of the sealing of the Spirit, the purpose of which, as we saw when considering verse 13, is to bring us to this assurance. But that is not all, otherwise the Apostle would not be praying in this manner for the Ephesian believers. He would simply have said, I thank God that you have your assurance; you have been sealed with the Spirit, and you need nothing more. But what he says in effect is this: I know that you have been sealed with the Spirit, but I still pray that the eyes of your understanding may be enlightened, and that you may know what is the hope of your calling – His calling of you.

The distinction seems to be as follows: the sealing of the Spirit, as we saw, is mainly subjective, it is something which happens in the realm of experience and which in a sense cannot be stated in words; it is the Spirit bearing witness with my spirit, directly, that I am a child of God. But thank God, it is not the only ground of assurance, for if we are to rely only upon our subjective consciousness we may find ourselves one day in a state of great doubt. You may have had the sealing with the Spirit, and yet, as the result of falling into sin, or by reason of circumstances, illness or some feebleness in your flesh, the devil may so bombard you as to shake your confidence. He is like a roaring lion, as the Apostle Peter reminds us, and he may come and attack with such power that your whole universe is shaken, and you may be tempted to say, 'What I had must have been a false experience, I must have been deluding myself'. If you rely only on the subjective you may find yourself in a state of great misery. Hence the Apostle is greatly concerned that we may know further grounds of assurance and have a further basis of certainty for our whole position. He is referring now to something objective, and the eyes of our understanding must be enlightened to receive this.

It is something that comes through the mind and then works through our whole being. It is not theoretical, but it starts with the mind; it is essentially a matter of understanding. Our understanding is no longer darkened, we have become alive to spiritual truth; and our assurance and certainty is grounded in that understanding.

The first ingredient, the first essential in this assurance, this hope, is that we should come to a deeper and a greater knowledge of the God who has called us. Notice that the Apostle is very careful to say, 'that ye may know what is the hope of *his* calling'. To have a sure hope, to have a deep certainty, we must seek a deeper knowledge of the God who has called us. Nothing can give me greater hope and assurance than my knowledge of the character of God. 'I dare not trust the sweetest frame', as the hymn reminds us, because frames are so changeable, but I can rely upon Him always. God is eternal, God is immutable, God is everlasting; God never changes His purpose. There is no greater comfort or consolation than this. God never starts a work without finishing it. You and I are constantly guilty of doing so. We become excited and enthusiastic and keen about certain projects, and others looking on are amazed at us and our enthusiasm and energy and efforts, and are made to feel that they have done nothing. But, far too often, in six months' time the picture is entirely different. We have lost heart and interest and have become slack and formal Christians again. But that is never true of God. God is everlastingly the same, He is 'the Father of lights with whom is no variableness, neither shadow of turning' (James 1:17). There is no greater comfort or ground of assurance than that. For it is this unchanging eternal God who has called me; and as another hymn reminds us:

> *Things future, nor things that are now,*
> *Not all things below nor above,*
> *Can make Him His purpose forego,*
> *Or sever my soul from His love.*

Then too we must realize that our whole position rests upon God's covenant. The eyes of our understanding must be enlightened before we can know anything about God's covenant. God made a covenant – a covenant of redemption, a covenant of salvation – with His own Son before the foundation of the world. And because it is His covenant, it is an everlasting covenant. God is Jehovah, the covenant-keeping God; the One who says, 'I am what I am'. God has given 'a people' to His Son whom He is to redeem. The Son has entered into the covenant promising to do so. The Lord Jesus Christ is the Head of a new humanity, He is our representative, He is our Federal Head, and we are represented by Him. The covenant between the Father and the Son is an everlasting covenant. This covenant has been revealed and repeated to men. The promise of redemption was given to Adam, to Abraham, repeated again to Moses, then to David, and taught constantly in the writings of the prophets whom God raised up and sent to the children of Israel. The more we understand the truth about God's covenant of redemption the greater will be our assurance.

Again, we have the great truth taught in the sixth chapter of the Epistle to the Hebrews in verses 13–20. God has even taken an oath in order to help us. He need not have done so, but He did so to Abraham. He 'confirmed' His promise with an oath. He 'swore by himself'. There was no one greater by whom He could swear, so God has 'sworn by himself' that His purpose will not change. He has underwritten it, He has pledged it, He has made it absolutely certain and inviolable. The oath of God! Have you studied that in the Word? Have you spent time in meditating upon it? The author of the Epistle to the Hebrews suggests that those Hebrew Christians who had been very diligent in 'ministering unto the saints' and in other practical matters, had been negligent in this respect, so he exhorts them to show 'the same diligence to the full assurance of hope unto the end' (Hebrews 6:11). Go back to the covenant, study the oath of God, realize its relevance to you, be enlightened about this matter. This is the way to make your hope sure.

Then think of the power of God. I but mention this for the moment because the Apostle will deal with it in particular in his third petition here. But we can be certain of this, that nothing can prevent God's purpose, nothing can withstand God's plan. It is absolutely certain because the power of Almighty God is behind it.

We must also realize that the 'call' of God is one part of His plan. While it has many parts, God sees that plan as a whole, and therefore if we are in the plan at all, the ultimate end is absolutely certain for us. The logic of that statement is demonstrated by Paul in the eighth chapter of Romans, verses 29–31: 'For whom he did foreknow, he also did predestinate to be conformed to the image of his Son, that he might be the firstborn among many brethren. Moreover whom he did predestinate, them he also called: and whom he called, them he also justified: and whom he justified, them he also glorified'. He next asks, 'What shall we then say to these things?', and then answers his own question: 'If God be for us, who can be against us?' The logic is inexorable; it is the basis of our certainty concerning this blessed hope. In other words, if I have been called 'effectually' I am certain to reach the glorious end. If I am called in the mind of God, I am already 'glorified'. It is as certain as that! When God starts a work He always finishes it. 'He who hath begun a good work in you will perform it until the day of Jesus Christ' (Philippians 1:6). Nothing can stop it. The covenant is one, the plan is one; if one link is present, all the other links will and must follow. 'No-one shall pluck them out of my hand', says our Lord (John 10:28). Are you clear about this? Do you go frequently to that eighth chapter of the Epistle to the Romans, and read it and pray over it and say, 'This is true of me; I have been called, therefore I am justified, therefore I am glorified, in Christ'. Do you answer the devil when he attacks you, by quoting these Scriptures? That is what our Lord did when tempted by the devil. He had this understanding, and He answered the devil from the Scriptures. This is part of what is meant by having the eyes of our understanding enlightened.

Finally, we need to understand the doctrine underlying what has already happened to us. One of the greatest and most practical grounds of assurance is the doctrine of the new birth, or of regeneration. If I am born of God, of the Spirit, I cannot fall away; it is impossible. There is no such thing as 'falling from grace'. It is utterly inconceivable and impossible that the eternal God should implant in us a seed of eternal life and then allow anything to destroy it. The idea that we can be born again one day, then sin and lose our eternal life, and then be born again, and thus oscillate between the two positions, is based on an utter ignorance of the doctrine of regeneration. Those who subscribe to it need to have the eyes of their understanding enlightened. According to the biblical teaching, if I am a Christian at all I am 'in Christ', I am united to Christ, I am joined to Christ. As I was 'in Adam' so I am now 'in Christ'. I am bound to Him by indissoluble links. The moment we understand this doctrine our hope will be certain and sure. You cannot be in and out of Christ; you cannot be 'in Christ' one day and out of Christ the next; if you are 'in Christ', you can never be out of Christ again. You are either in to all eternity or out to all eternity. We must grasp and know this doctrine of our blessed, mystical union with Christ. He is the Head, as Paul is going to elaborate at the end of this chapter, and we are the body; we are 'in him' and belong to Him and are joined to Him.

I ask again, Do these things mean everything to you? That is the test of our spirituality, the test of our growth in grace.

Let me apply my test by asking whether we can honestly say, and with confidence –

> *My hope is built on nothing less*
> *Than Jesus' blood and righteousness;*
> *I dare not trust the sweetest frame,*
> *But wholly lean on Jesus' Name.*
> *On Christ, the solid Rock, I stand;*
> *All other ground is sinking sand.*

And can you continue to recite that hymn even when the clouds are black and everything seems to be against you, and say –

> *When darkness veils His lovely face,*
> *I rest on His unchanging grace;*
> *In every high and stormy gale*
> *My anchor holds within the veil.*

But above all, can you go and join the hymn-writer in his final stanza? –

> *His oath, His cov'nant, and His blood,*
> *Support me in the 'whelming flood:*
> *When all around my soul gives way,*
> *He then is all my hope and stay.*
> *On Christ, the solid Rock, I stand;*
> *All other ground is sinking sand.*

'The Hope of his Calling'

Do you know 'the hope of his calling'? Have you made 'your calling and election sure'? Are you resting upon 'His oath, His cov'nant, and His blood', His unchangeableness, whether you see Him or not, whether you feel Him or not? Are you able to rest upon the truth concerning Him which, in His grace, He has revealed to us in His Word by the Holy Spirit, and which He enables us to grasp and to apprehend by enlightening the eyes of our understanding? Seek it! You are meant to rejoice, you are meant to have a steadfast hope that nothing can shake. You can have it in this way.

32
'The Riches of the Glory of His Inheritance in the Saints'

'The eyes of your understanding being enlightened;
that ye may know what is the hope of his calling,
and what the riches of the glory of his inheritance
in the saints.'

Ephesians 1:18

We now come to look at the latter half of this statement – 'and what the riches of the glory of his inheritance in the saints'. This is the second of the three particular petitions which the Apostle offers for the Ephesian Christians, and like the first it is introduced by the word 'what'. We must bear in mind as we look at it that this, like the first petition, can only be understood by those who have 'the eyes of their understanding enlightened'. Likewise it is covered by the general prayer that they might have the Spirit of wisdom and of revelation. Without this we shall not be able to see these things.

There are two main views with respect to this second petition. There are some who maintain that it refers to God's own inheritance, that it means God's own inheritance in the saints. The Old Testament statement that 'the Lord's portion is his people' lends some colour to that view of the matter (Deuteronomy 32:9), and there are phrases in the New Testament which mean very much the same thing. The Apostle Peter in his First Epistle says of Christians: 'Ye are a chosen generation, a royal priesthood, a holy nation, a peculiar people' (2:9). The expression 'peculiar people', as found in the Authorized Version, really means 'a people for God's own possession'. So there are those who say that what is meant here in Ephesians is the sum total of God's people when they shall all have been finally gathered in. God is calling out a people unto Himself from this present evil world; He is calling out people from among the Jews and the Gentiles. A day will

[378]

come when the 'fulness of the Gentiles' shall have been gathered in, and when 'all Israel' likewise shall have been saved. That will constitute the totality of God's people. Such expositors claim that the Apostle in this expression is looking forward to that day, and praying that these Ephesians, and all of us as Christians, may come to know the exceeding greatness of God's own inheritance in the saints, in His own people. In other words the petition is, that we may have some dim conception of the magnitude of this glorious company of the redeemed to which we belong and amongst whom we shall spend our eternity. That is certainly one possible explanation.

The other view is that the Apostle is praying that the eyes of our understanding may be enlightened in order that we may come to know the character of the inheritance to which we are going, the inheritance which God is preparing for us. This is the same idea as that expressed by Paul in his First Epistle to the Corinthians: 'Eye hath not seen, nor ear heard, neither have entered into the heart of man, the things which God hath prepared for them that love him' (1 Corinthians 2:9). The Apostle is praying that we may come to see more and more of what lies ahead for us, and that we may have more frequent glimpses of it. He does not wish it to be something remote and strange to us. His desire is that we may not only look at our title deeds and specifications, but that by faith we may have an occasional glimpse of the inheritance itself, and stand as it were with Moses on the top of Mount Nebo and look into the promised land of our inheritance.

Both explanations are possible and it is impossible for us to say dogmatically or categorically that one is right and the other wrong. It is a matter of personal preference, and for myself I do not hesitate to take the second view, as we took it when expounding verses 11 and 13. I do so for the reason that I am not happy with the idea of God having an inheritance. Everything belongs to God; the whole universe is God's. So it seems to me to be inappropriate to use the expression 'God's inheritance' in that sense. On the other hand, nothing can be more appropriate than to look at it from the other standpoint which also fits in with the argument of this first chapter. Paul says that we have not only believed, but that we have been 'sealed with that Holy Spirit of promise, which is the earnest of *our* inheritance until the redemption of the purchased possession'. The possession has been purchased for us by the blood of Christ; we are already heirs but we are still left in this world. But God gives us the earnest of the Spirit, He gives us a foretaste, until we enter into this purchased possession, our final redemption. Thus the term 'inheritance' in this eighteenth verse points in the same direction.

From the practical standpoint it makes but little difference which of the two explanations we adopt, for in both cases it is a prayer that we may come to know something of that glorious state to which we are going, and for which God is preparing us, when with all the redeemed we shall be safely gathered in and shall enjoy to all eternity the benefits of this great salvation.

Having thus defined the exact meaning of the prayer let me ask another question: Why should we consider this? indeed is it right that we should do so? The question arises because this whole idea and emphasis is disliked at the present time. There are many people today who say: 'That is typical of your Christianity. Here we are in this troubled modern world with all that we have experienced in this twentieth century with its two horrible wars, with the discord and the turmoil and the uncertainty, and the dread possibility of another world war, and all the possibilities of the use of atomic power, and yet you urge us to spend time in trying to glimpse into eternity and life after death. You should be urging people to do their utmost to try to stop the manufacture of armaments, and to protest against the manufacture of the atomic bombs. Why do you not address appeals to the governments of the world and stir up the whole Christian Church to put an end to these distresses? Your "pie-in-the-sky" is not only useless; it means that you are abandoning your duty. You are remote from life, you are turning your backs upon the difficulties. Is it not time that the Church entered into political life and tried to make a better world?'

Such is the argument. Christianity, it says, is the dope of the people, some kind of 'sob stuff' to make people feel happier for the moment, to give them a comfortable feeling by persuading them to turn their backs upon reality and to dwell in imagination and fantasy on some supposed Elysium. The modern man dislikes this idea of looking into the unseen and the eternal, this other-worldly emphasis, this very thing for which the Apostle is praying here.

The opposition to what I am preaching is not confined to the world outside, or to Communists. Many in the Church hold the same view. There are certain hymns which tell us that we should not be animated by the fear of hell or by a desire for reward and glory; we must be altruistic and believe in Christianity for its own sake. That view began to be popular towards the end of the last century, and there have been many expressions of it in this present century. The story is constantly repeated of an old woman in a country of the Middle East who was found one day walking along carrying two buckets. In one of the buckets she had fire, and in the other water. A man stopped her and asked her what she was doing with those two buckets. She replied that she was carrying the fire in order to burn heaven and the water in order to drown hell. That is regarded as excellent. There are still many who object to the prominence we give to the preaching of personal salvation. They say that we must not think about ourselves and our own problems; we should be interested in the state of society and in the social conditions. The curse of evangelicalism, they say, has always been that it is so personal and self-centred and narrow and selfish.

In reply we need go no further than our text. The Apostle Paul prays in a manner that gives the lie direct to all such talk. He prays that we may know 'what is the hope of his calling and the riches of the glory of his inheritance in the saints'. But quite apart from the Apostle's own words, there is nothing more fatuous as a criticism of this other-worldly view that is commended in the Scripture than the particular argument which I have just outlined. History alone, in and of itself, proves this beyond any doubt whatsoever. The greatest benefactors that this world has ever known, the men who have brought the greatest good to this world, have been the men who have emphasized most of all the importance of 'seeing the unseen'. One has but to read the eleventh chapter of the Epistle to the Hebrews to find proof of this. There we have a list, or a gallery as it were, of the greatest benefactors this world has ever known; that is why they stand out in history. And they are all people, we are told, who fixed their eyes not so much on this world as on the next. That does not mean that they ignored this world. They were not monks or anchorites living in monasteries or deserts; they did not subscribe to the false, ascetic Roman Catholic teaching which has so bedevilled this whole question. The alternative to the popular view which is being advocated today is not monasticism. The 'heroes of the faith' of Hebrews chapter 11 started with the unseen world, and then in the light of that, they applied themselves to the present world.

But this is not only true of great people in the Scriptures, it has been true throughout history. For instance, hospitals were started by saints. It has always been men who have a true view of man and of life in the light of eternity, who always have been most concerned about human suffering. The man who takes a 'this-worldly' view is generally a man who lives to himself and has little concern about his neighbour. Spiritual men have generally introduced the greatest reforms. Hospitals, education and culture, factory acts and suchlike things have come through the efforts of saintly people, generally evangelical people who have been concerned about knowing 'the riches of the glory of God's inheritance in the saints'. This is true of the more evangelical Roman Catholic saints as well as Protestant saints, but it has been particularly true of the latter. No man was more concerned about decent, proper living in this world than John Calvin. The story of that man and how he reformed the life of Geneva, has inspired many others who have borrowed his ideas, and this has been the greatest motive power in the history of democracy.

This is seen in England in the story of the Puritans who laid the foundation of the greatness of this country. The Puritans, led politically by that great man Oliver Cromwell, were all men who lived in the light of the unseen. No man was more aware of the unseen than Oliver Cromwell, or more desired to have the eyes of his understanding enlightened that he might know the hope of God's calling and the riches of this glory than he. He was a man with a markedly other-worldly view, but that did not mean that he neglected this world; he was a great reformer, a great benefactor of the common people, and so were all his coadjutors.

If you read the history of the eighteenth and nineteenth centuries you will find a similar pattern. It is granted even by secular historians that the Evangelical Awakening of the eighteenth century undoubtedly saved this country from a revolution similar to the French Revolution; and it did so, because the leaders of that revival, having seen the true meaning of life in the light of eternity, then tried to improve life as it is lived in this world. In other words it is out of spiritual revivals that the greatest secular improvements have always come.

To come nearer our own times, it is a simple fact of history that Trade Unions came into being largely as the result of the activities of men who had been saved by this gospel, and who began to see that working men should not live as animals in drunkenness and in vice and in ignorance. This is often put popularly by saying that Trade Unionism owes more to Methodism than to Marx. The things of which men boast and talk so much today have come from the minds and the lives of men who have realized the importance of the next world and of life in eternity. Indeed I do not hesitate to aver that it is when men forget the next world that things go wrong in this world. It sounds so practical to say that we should concentrate on politics and social affairs; but if we do so without knowing about the next world, if we do not put our activities into the context of eternity, we shall always find that this world will degenerate.

For the past thirty or forty years the emphasis has been on this world, and preaching about heaven and glory has been unpopular. But look at this world as it is today; see what is happening in it and to it. When men forget the next world and concentrate only on this present life, this world becomes a kind of living hell, with confusion and lawlessness and immorality and vice rampant. It is only men who have a complete view of life who really know how to live in this world. The only man who really respects life in this world is the man who knows that this world is only the ante-chamber to the next world. It is only the man who knows himself to be a child of God, and who knows that this world is God's world, who is really concerned about decency in this world. So if you would live a full and a rewarding life in this world you must start by realizing that the highroad to such a life is to consider the world to which we are going, to meditate on 'the riches of the glory of his inheritance in the saints'.

It was necessary that we should spend time in answering that foolish fatuous argument. But, positively, why should we look at these things? Why should I trouble to know something about 'the riches of the glory of his inheritance in the saints'? One sufficient answer is the comfort it brings. It is in the light of this that the Apostle Paul is able to work out his great argument in the Epistle to the Romans, chapter 8. He says: 'For I reckon that the sufferings of this present time are not worthy to be compared with the glory that shall be revealed in us' (v. 18). That is the conclusion of the argument. The Roman Christians were having a hard and a difficult time, and the Apostle has no comfort to give them but in these words. He admits that things were bad and trying. Christianity is always realistic; it never pretends that there is nothing wrong, or advocates putting on a cheery smile and saying that all is well. Rather does it say with the Apostle in verses 19–23 in that same eighth chapter: 'even we ourselves, that have the firstfruits of the Spirit, groan within ourselves.' The Christian is not a simpleton who puts on a fatuous grin and pretends that there is nothing wrong; so that he never has any troubles and sings perpetually, 'and now I am happy all the day'. That is the position, not of Christianity, but of a false psychology. The Christian above all men knows what a terrible world this is; but he also knows that he is but 'waiting for the adoption, to wit, the redemption of our body' (Romans 8:23). This is what enables him to utter the asseveration of verse 18. The Apostle says the same thing to the Corinthians in his Second Epistle to them: 'Our light affliction, which is but for a moment, worketh for us a far more exceeding and eternal weight of glory' (4:17). It is the 'far more exceeding and eternal weight of glory' that gives us the comfort, and therefore the encouragement and the stimulus to go on in the fight in this world. Is there anything more encouraging, is there anything more stimulating?

Observe the Apostle as he works out the argument in the fifteenth chapter of his First Epistle to the Corinthians. He argues that if there is no resurrection from the dead, and if this life is the only life, and death is the end of the story, then the only conclusion to draw is, 'Let us eat and drink for tomorrow we die' (v. 32). If there is no other life, why have I troubled to fight with beasts at Ephesus? (v. 32), and so on. There is nothing that so encourages us to Christian living, there is no greater stimulus to continue in it, than to know something about 'the riches of his inheritance in the saints'. The more I know of them the more I shall be encouraged to forsake sin, and to mortify the flesh, and to prepare myself for that which God has awaiting me. It is the greatest incentive to holiness and to holy living; there is nothing comparable to it. 'He that hath this hope in him purifieth himself, even as he is pure', as the Apostle John says (1 John 3:3). The lack of true scriptural holiness today is surely due to the fact that we do not spend sufficient time in meditating upon the glory that awaits us. The world is too much with us, and we tend to think of salvation too much in terms of present experience rather than in the light of the glory which awaits us. This contemplation of the glory is the high road to holiness.

But there is an argument which settles this matter once and for ever. It is what we are told about our blessed Lord Himself. The author of the Epistle to the Hebrews states it thus in his twelfth chapter: 'Looking unto Jesus, the author and finisher of our faith' (v. 2). That is what we are to do. We have a race to run. It requires us to 'lay aside every weight, and the sin that doth so easily beset us, looking unto Jesus, the author and finisher of our faith'. But the author is careful to add: 'Who for the joy that was set before him' – in the light of the joy that was set before Him, because of the joy that was set before Him – 'endured the cross, despising the shame'. That was the truth concerning our blessed Lord and Saviour Jesus Christ when in this world. He did not disdain keeping His eye upon 'the recompense of the reward'. Because He was looking to the joy of the glory that awaited Him, He went through it all, even the cruel death on the cross; it helped Him to go through. And in the seventeenth chapter of John's Gospel, as we have seen earlier, He prays that He may have again that glory which He shared with the Father before the foundation of the world.

To object to the Apostle's petition which desires that we may come to know these things, is not only unspiritual, it is entirely unscriptural also. The Apostle actually states this in the form of a commandment in his Epistle to the Colossians: 'Set your affection on things above, not on things on the earth' (Colossians 3:2). The comparison is that of setting the needle of a compass. We are to set our affections, to keep them trained upon, and steadfastly gazing upon 'the things which are above, not on things which are on the earth'.

Let us therefore get rid of the false spirituality which prides itself on being unusually pure because it is not interested in heaven and hell. Not to be interested in heaven and hell is to be unlike the Lord Jesus Christ; it is to be unlike all the apostles; it is to be unlike the greatest saints, the best people this world has ever known. How much time do you spend in thinking about heaven? How often do you set your gaze there? Have the eyes of your understanding been so enlightened that you know these things? I do not hesitate to assert that the more spiritual we are, the more we shall think about heaven. The nearer we are to Christ the more we shall meditate upon the glory which He has prepared for us. This is an invariable and infallible test of true spirituality.

That brings me to my last point, and I ask, What are these things which we are to know? The Holy Spirit alone can make them clear to us. Most of us have to agree with Richard Baxter when he says, 'My knowledge of that life is small, the eye of faith is dim'. After all, how little do we know about these things! There are many who are in trouble about this matter. As a pastor, I have often been asked this question: 'Why do we not know more about heaven and the life to which we are going? Why are we not told more about it?' I give a very simple answer to that question. It is that the glory is so marvellous, so wonderful, so perfect, that our human language is incapable of conveying a true idea of it to us. The glory is such that were an attempt to be made to describe it, because sin has so debased the coinage of our language we should have unworthy conceptions of it. To attempt to describe it would be to detract from it. Therefore God in His mercy has not told us much about it. But let us concentrate on what we are told.

The Apostle speaks of 'the riches of the glory' – he piles superlative on top of superlative. There is nothing greater than glory, yet he talks about the riches of the glory. That gives us some conception of this transcendent glory which is beyond the reach even of our imagination. All we can be told is that it is the 'riches of his glory'. So do not be troubled about that! Heaven is infinitely more wonderful than you or I can ever imagine it to be. It is entirely beyond the reach of all our categories; but we are told certain things. The central part of the glory is that we shall be with Him. 'Let not your heart be troubled: ye believe in God, believe also in me.' . . . 'I go to prepare a place for you. And if I go and prepare a place for you, I will come again, and receive you unto myself; that where I am, there ye may be also' (John 14:1-3). That is enough – to be with Him! This is also Paul's view of death. He was no longer worried about death, because death to him meant 'to be with Christ, which is far better'.

Then too, our Lord, in His high priestly prayer, prays a very special petition to His Father: 'Father, I will that they also, whom thou hast given me, be with me where I am; that they may behold my glory, which thou hast given me: for thou lovedst me before the foundation of the world' (John 17:24). His greatest prayer for us is that we may see Him as He is, and in His glory. There is nothing beyond that! So John again in his First Epistle writes: 'It doth not yet appear what we shall be, but we know that, when he shall appear, we shall be like him, for we shall see him as he is' (1 John 3:2). When we arrive in this glory our very bodies will have been changed. 'He will change this body of our humiliation, that it may be fashioned like unto his glorious body', the body of his own glorification (Philippians 3:21). We shall be perfect and entire, 'without spot or wrinkle or any such thing'. We know that!

The Apostle Paul on the road to Damascus was given a glimpse of this glory. It is not surprising, therefore, that he writes to the Ephesians about 'the riches of the glory', because there, on the road to Damascus, he saw the face of the risen Lord; and it was so resplendent and glorious that he was blinded by the sight. The light was above the brightness of the sun at noonday, and it was a manifestation of the glory of the Lord. Paul never forgot it. How could he forget it? But he also tells us of an occasion in his life some fourteen years before he wrote about it, when he was lifted up into the third heaven, 'caught up into paradise'. While he was there, he heard 'unspeakable words which it is not lawful for a man to utter' (2 Corinthians 12:3-4). It was a foretaste of this glory, and of heaven. He never forgot that also. It is not surprising, therefore, that he speaks of 'a far more exceeding and eternal weight of glory'.

Then in the twenty-first chapter of the Book of Revelation the glory is all described in symbolical language. The heavenly city was 'pure gold, like unto clear glass' (v. 18). There was no temple there, because God Himself is there. There was no sun, no moon; there were no stars, because the Lamb in the midst was the city's light. The 'face of Jesus Christ' illuminates and irradiates all. We shall dwell in His glorious presence.

That is something of what Paul means by 'the eyes of your understanding being enlightened; that ye may know what is the riches of the glory of his inheritance in the saints'. It is to the heavenly city that you and I are going. The Apostle Peter in his own manner expresses it in these words: 'Blessed be the God and Father of our Lord Jesus Christ, which according to his abundant mercy hath begotten us again unto a lively hope by the resurrection of Jesus Christ from the dead; to an inheritance incorruptible and undefiled, and that fadeth not away, reserved in heaven for you' (1 Peter 1:3-5). Note what he says about it. It is 'incorruptible'. There is nothing sinful there, nothing unworthy. 'Incorruptible, and undefiled, and that fadeth not away.' We cannot conceive of it; we are accustomed to a world of sin, and to death and decay. How beautiful flowers are! but look at them tomorrow or the following day. You throw them out into the dustbin. There is decay and pollution in everything in this world. The same applies to our physical frames. We are subject to illness, old age, and so on. But not there – 'incorruptible and undefiled, and that fadeth not away'! There will be no sorrow there, no tears, no sin, no separation, nothing that makes us unhappy and depresses us. 'The riches of the glory of his inheritance'!

But this is only for 'the saints'. 'Naught that defileth' enters the holy city; outside are whoremongers and adulterers and idolaters and liars, and all that are abominable. What I have been trying to describe is only for the saints. The Lord Jesus Christ speaks similarly in Matthew 25: 'Come, ye blessed of my Father, inherit the kingdom prepared for you from the foundation of the world' (v. 34). It has been prepared only for 'the saints'; for those who have loved His little ones, and have visited them in prison and given them food and clothing, and so on. The Kingdom has been prepared for them, and for them only, before the foundation of the world. Paul says that he was commanded to call people from 'darkness unto light, and from the power of Satan unto God, that they might receive the forgiveness of sins, and inheritance among them which are sanctified by faith which is in me (Christ)' (Acts 26:18).

It comes to this: while we are in this life and in this world, a great process of separation and sifting is taking place. God lays His hand upon, and apprehends, those who are to go to this glory, this inheritance; they are 'called saints'. The saints are those who have been separated and set apart for God by the Holy Spirit. As a result they have believed the gospel of salvation in Jesus Christ and Him crucified. They trust in Him and in His perfect work, and in that alone. We are all of us at this moment either saints, or else we are sinners. This glory of which we have been speaking is only for the saints. It is for them; and no one and nothing can rob them of it. 'Neither death, nor life, nor angels, nor principalities, nor powers, nor things present, nor things to come, nor height, nor depth, nor any other creature, shall be able to separate us from the love of God, which is in Christ Jesus our Lord' (Romans 8:38–39).

If you are a saint, if you are one of God's people, you are going to this glory of which I have been speaking, and nothing can prevent that from happening. Do you know that you are a saint? Are you certain that you are one of God's people? Make certain of it. Then, having made certain of it, dwell upon it, apply your mind to it, read the Scriptures, delve into them, commit them to memory, repeat them to yourself daily. Say to yourself, 'That is what I am destined for, that is the inheritance which has been prepared for me, that is how I am going to spend my eternity'. How much of our time do we spend in doing so? Let us pray for ourselves what the Apostle prayed for the Ephesians. Let us pray God by His Spirit 'to enlighten the eyes of our understanding' that these things may become real to us, so that we shall not spend all our time in thinking about this world, and this passing life, but rather about that which is coming for certain, and which is so glorious. 'The riches of the glory of his inheritance in the saints.'

'Set your affection', your heart's desire, upon Him and upon the things which He has prepared for them that love Him. 'The crowning day is coming by and by.' There is a glory awaiting us which 'eye hath not seen nor ear heard', which has not even entered into the heart of man to conceive. Let us get to know these things; let us look upon them; let us live in the light of them. And then, as men who have seen them, let us live our life in this world to the maximum, telling others about this glorious God and what He does for all who trust in Him, and helping as best we can to 'go about doing good' in this passing world of time, even as our blessed Lord did when He was here.

33
'The Exceeding Greatness of His Power'

'And what is the exceeding greatness of his power to us-ward who believe, according to the working of his mighty power, which he wrought in Christ, when he raised him from the dead, and set him at his own right hand in the heavenly places, far above all principality, and power, and might, and dominion, and every name that is named, not only in this world, but also in that which is to come: and hath put all things under his feet, and gave him to be the head over all things to the church, which is his body, the fulness of him that filleth all in all.'

Ephesians 1:19–23

We have now reached the Apostle's third particular petition for the Ephesian Christians, and we find that, as with the previous two, it is introduced by the word *what*. Once more we must be careful in our interpretation. The Scofield Bible, so-called, introduces these three petitions with the following general heading: 'The prayer for knowledge and power.' By so doing it suggests that the Apostle is praying two things for these Ephesians: first that they may have certain knowledge, and then that they may have power. I suggest that that is a wrong interpretation and a rather serious one. The Apostle, here, is not so much praying that the Ephesians may be given power, as that they may know the power of God that is already working in them. Clearly, the two things are entirely different, as is shown by the entire context. The object of this section of the Epistle, as we have seen repeatedly, is to give assurance and certainty in order that true Christians may have confidence; so here it seems quite clear that the Apostle is emphasizing the power of God in the saints rather than the power which God gives to the saints.

This immediately raises a fundamental problem of theology and doctrine; indeed it raises two possible views of Christian salvation. It is interesting to observe that differing views of salvation are generally determined by this question of power. One view is that salvation is the result of something I do, plus the power that is given to me by God. I, plus the power of God! It is granted that I cannot achieve salvation without the power or the help that God gives me, but this conception of salvation is that God aids me and God enables me to arrive at it. The other view is that salvation is the result of God's power at work – in me and through me, and this is the view which we must take of this particular passage.

At this point the Revised Standard Version is helpful. Instead of saying, 'What is the exceeding greatness of His power to us-ward (or toward us) who believe', it says, 'what is the immeasurable greatness of His power in us who believe'. The Apostle is emphasizing the power of God in us. It is of course true to say that God gives us strength and power; and we need that power constantly; and in its place and setting that needs to be taught: but here the grand object which the Apostle has in mind is to make the Ephesians see and realize, and us with them, the greatness of God's power in us, what He is doing in us. The result would be that our fears would vanish, and we would have a new confidence and assurance with respect to our salvation. Indeed this is ultimately the final ground of assurance both objective and subjective – the former leading to the latter.

It is fascinating to observe the way in which the Apostle handles his material, and works out his argument. He has made clear to us the nature of the call itself and how it is founded on the character of God. Then he has given us a glimpse into that transcendent glory for which we are destined. And now he emphasizes the power of God working in us. The logic in the sequence of these three petitions seems to me to be as follows. With his great pastoral heart the Apostle is concerned about these Ephesians. He knows that they have believed, that they have trusted in the Lord Jesus, and that they have been sealed by the Holy Spirit; nevertheless he is praying for them without ceasing, and praying that they may advance into the depths of understanding and knowledge and comprehension of the Christian life and its possibilities. So he has offered the first two petitions, and this third petition becomes quite inevitable.

It is inevitable because no man can have any conception at all of that inheritance, that glory, to which we are going, without immediately becoming conscious of certain things. The very greatness of the glory on the one hand, and our state and condition in sin on the other, tend to create doubts within us. We hear or read the descriptions of these unseen and eternal things – 'the far more exceeding and eternal weight of glory' to which we are going – and having looked at them we tend to turn and say to ourselves, But surely all that is not really possible for me! Surely I am not fit for such glory, and I never can be! We contrast ourselves, and what we know ourselves to be, with the brightness of God's glory. We turn to the twenty-first chapter of the Book of Revelation and read of the Lamb in the midst, and of all the glory, and that outside are the dogs (22:15) and all that is evil, and we say, But surely this is impossible for us, this is too wonderful, it is too glorious! Such in all probability is our immediate reaction. Or we may say to ourselves, How can I ever fit myself for such glory? If I spent the rest of my life in nothing else but culturing and nurturing my spiritual being, would I ever be fit?

It is such feelings that have led men to become monks, to segregate themselves from the world, and to give themselves to holy meditation and prayer and fasting. Such thoughts are almost inevitable to anyone who takes these things seriously. And then I begin to think of my waywardness, my weakness and my selfishness and proneness to sin. I say to myself: 'It is one thing when in the house of God and listening to these things to feel how wonderful they are, and to look forward to them, and to determine to do something about them; but then I know that I have often had such thoughts and feelings, yet have failed to carry them out. I have deliberately determined and decided to seek these things with the whole of my being; but I am so wayward and unreliable. I cannot trust myself, my feelings, my moods and states, my resolutions. Such is the kind of creature I am; and you confront me with that glory, that inheritance, that purity, that ineffable perfection! It is impossible.'

I then go on to consider my frail body, with seeds of decay in it;

I know it to be subject to illnesses; and I find it almost impossible to believe or even to imagine myself enjoying a state of glory. And then, added to all this, there is life as we know it in this world, with its changing circumstances; there is the world and its influence upon us , friends and others enticing us and attracting us to sin; there is our preoccupation with worldly things, business and affairs, and the need to make a living so as to maintain ourselves and our families! All these things, the pressures of life and of circumstances, conspire together to make it impossible for me to find time for preparation for this glory.

Finally, at the back of all this, we know that we are confronted by a mighty adversary, a most subtle foe, the devil, 'as a roaring lion roaming about seeking whom he may devour', confronting us at every corner, 'the accuser of the brethren' who knows about our every weakness and who in his subtlety is ever enticing, attracting and luring us into sin and failure and indolence. Furthermore we realize that between us and that glory there lies the fact of death, that awful spectre, 'the last enemy', and the power of death and the grave. We cannot enter into the promised glory without passing through death; and we know that many a saint has trembled as he has thought of the dissolution of the body, the passing through the 'valley of the shadow of death', and the crossing of the last river.

These are the thoughts that crowd into our minds, and they come especially to those who see most clearly 'the riches of the glory of his inheritance in the saints'. It is because of this that I pay my little tribute to the greatness of the Apostle's pastoral heart and to the working of his majestic mind. He leads us on from step to step. He knows that if we have grasped the meaning of the other two things for which he has prayed, we shall urgently need this further petition. He deals with all our problems and difficulties. So he prays also that we may know 'the exceeding greatness of his power toward us who believe, according to the working of his mighty power, which he wrought in Christ, when he raised him from the dead, and set him at his own right hand in the heavenly places'. Should you have felt that I have been lingering too long in the vestibule, as it were, of this text, my answer is that the mere vestibule is more marvellous than the greatest palaces of man. We are about to enter one of the

[394]

sublimest chambers of the palace where the 'exceeding riches' of God's grace are stored. The Apostle is ready to tell us about the exceeding greatness of the power which God is exercising in believers.

I say that he is ready to deal with it, but then the transcendent glory of his thoughts seems to lead him away from his immediate object and purpose of helping us, right up into the eternal glory; but it is only an apparent digression for he returns to us in the first verse of the second chapter. His theme is the greatness of God's power toward us, or in us, that believe. In describing that power he mentions the raising of the Lord Jesus Christ from the dead, and the setting of Him in the highest position of power. He tells us how He has been made the Head of the Church. Thus we are given, as it were, the whole doctrine of the Church in a nutshell. But having done that Paul comes back to his predominant theme in the first verse of the Epistle's second chapter.

His theme can be divided into two main sections: firstly, the greatness of the power in and of itself; secondly, how we may be certain and sure that this great power is working in us.

We can approach the first section most conveniently, perhaps, in the form of a number of propositions. The first is that Christian salvation is a demonstration of the power of God in us. I am increasingly convinced that the ultimate trouble with those of us who spend so much of our Christian lives in 'the shallows and miseries' of doubt and uncertainty and hesitancy, is that they have never really laid hold of this first great fundamental principle. Our starting point must always be, 'I am what I am by the grace of God', and by the power of God. A Christian is the result of the operation of God, nothing less, nothing else. No man can make himself a Christian; God alone makes Christians. That is the real meaning of this third petition.

But let us consider several supporting statements elsewhere in the Scripture. 'I am not ashamed of the gospel of Christ', says the Apostle in his Epistle to the Romans. His reason for saying so is that 'it is the power of God unto salvation to everyone that believeth' (Romans 1:16). Again, he says, 'We preach Christ crucified', because he is assured that Christ is 'the power of God and the wisdom of God' (1 Corinthians 1:24). In Paul's eyes preaching is of no value unless it is in 'demonstration of the Spirit and of power'! 'Our gospel came unto you not in word only, but also in power, and in the Holy Ghost, and in much assurance' (1 Thessalonians 1:5). Christians, he tells us, are God's workmanship (Ephesians 2:10).This truth is fundamental to an understanding of the Christian position. Again, in writing to the Philippians, he says: 'He which hath begun a good work in you will perform it until the day of Jesus Christ' (Philippians 1:6). Again, in the same Epistle we find: 'God worketh in you both to will and to do of his good pleasure' (2:13). Referring to his own preaching the Apostle says: 'Whereunto I also labour, striving according to his working, which worketh in me mightily' (Colossians 1:29).

But perhaps no expression of what it is that makes us Christian brings out this idea so clearly as Paul's statement that a Christian is a 'new creation' (2 Corinthians 5:17). He is nothing less than that. He is not merely a member of a church, he is not merely a good man, he is not merely a man who has made a decision. A person can do all that and still not be a Christian. A Christian is one who has been created anew; and there is only One who can create, namely, God. It takes the power of God to make a Christian. What unworthy views we often have of Christianity and of being Christian! We think so much in terms of ourselves, and what we do, and what we have decided, and what we have taken up, and what we propose to do. We certainly have much to do, but the entire teaching of the New Testament emphasizes above all else that we can do nothing until God has first done something in us. 'You hath he quickened, who were dead in trespasses and sins (Ephesians 2:1). We are all spiritually dead by nature, and no man can do anything until he has been quickened, raised, given life, and created anew. According to the New Testament no category is adequate to describe what we are in Christ save this conception of the re-birth, regeneration; and no man can give birth to himself. The power of God is the beginning and the end of salvation; all is of Him and His power.

The second principle reminds us of the greatness of God's power. In describing it the Apostle piles superlative on superlative, for human language is totally inadequate for the task. He prays that the Ephesians may know what is the 'exceeding greatness'; not the greatness only but the *exceeding* greatness. The word used by the Apostle might equally well be translated 'surpassing'. God's power not only surpasses our power of expression, it surpasses our power of comprehension! Take all the dictionaries of the world, exhaust all the vocabularies, and when you have added them all together you have still not begun to describe the greatness of God's power. The Apostle uses the best terms available, the 'surpassing' greatness, the 'exceeding' greatness, but they are not sufficiently specific for him. He adds to them by saying, 'According to the working of his mighty power'.

We must analyse this new phrase, for it is one of the greatest that even Paul ever used. We must know 'the exceeding greatness of his power to us-ward who believe, according to the working of his mighty power'. A better word than 'working' would be 'energy'. *Energy* is a much stronger word because it gives the impression of something which is efficacious. It is not mere static or potential power; energy is power that has been liberated, and is actually working. It is kinetic power, manifested power, the energy working itself out and permeating everything. Then take this second word *mighty* which stands for 'strength', and strength in a very special manner. Paul's word suggests a strength which overcomes, which prevails, which conquers, a strength which coming up against resistance overcomes it. It is the kind of strength which can 'make low' every high mountain, it can 'exalt' every valley; there is nothing that can stand before it. The Apostle is describing this power of God as 'the energy of the strength' of God to whom nothing is impossible.

The third term which appears in the Authorized Version as 'power' really stands for 'might'; the might of God, God's own essential might and inherent power. Once more we must indicate that the Apostle is not using words in a haphazard manner but that there is a definite gradation in the use of them. He first speaks of energy, a power in action; and then says that it comes from a force which is irresistible, which in turn comes from the ocean of God's might, the eternity of God's illimitable power.

A similar description of God's power is given by Isaiah in the fortieth chapter of his prophecy. He expresses it by asking a series of questions: To whom can we liken God?, with whom can we compare Him? And having said that all comparisons are useless, he proceeds to say: 'He sitteth upon the circle of the earth' (v. 22). He contrasts God with idols, he contrasts Him with political and governmental powers, with princes and governors, and men of wisdom; but all that is as nothing compared with God's power. No one is able to advise Him or give Him anything; He is everything in and of Himself; He is everlasting in might and strength and power.

The Apostle Paul is asserting that this eternal might and strength of God's power is exerting itself in us and overcoming all obstacles and resistances. To state it in different language, we can say that the Apostle is telling these Ephesian Christians that he is praying that they might know 'the efficacy of the force of his strength'; or that they might know 'the energy of the might of his strength' towards them. But all language is totally inadequate to convey this truth. The making of a Christian is the result of the manifestation of the might of God exerting itself. Have you realized that that is true of you? Do you realize that you are what you are because this eternal, illimitable might of God has been working energetically in you? that it is still doing so, and will continue to do so?

When we talk about 'the energy of the strength of the might' of God's power our minds boggle and reel at the stupendous magnificence and the majesty of it all. So the Apostle proceeds to help us with an illustration of it. The energy of the strength of God's might has already been manifested in an objective manner in the resurrection of the Lord Jesus Christ from the dead: 'which he wrought in Christ when he raised him from the dead and set him at his own right hand in the heavenly places, far above all principality and power', and so on. We may well ask at this point, Why does the Apostle choose this particular illustration? Why does he show forth the might of God by the resurrection of Christ, rather than by the Creation. The Creation was a notable manifestation of the power of God, for He had but to say 'Let there be light', and 'there was light' (Genesis 1:3). His mere fiat, His Word, was enough; and He made everything out of nothing. Or why did the Apostle not use the comparison of God's power and might as exercised in providence? All these spinning orbs in the heavens are maintained and sustained by God's power;

everything is ordered by Him. The world would collapse if God by His providential power ceased to sustain it and keep it going. All things work, and work together, because God has so made them. And He did not merely make them and then leave them; He is still energizing them. The power of God is manifested in providence and in the whole ordering of the life of the world. Or why did Paul not refer to the might of God as manifested in some of the great judgments of history? Has there been anything more signal as a manifestation of God's power than the Flood, when the very windows of heaven were opened and the mountains were all covered with water? Or why did he not use the destruction of Sodom and Gomorrah, or the mighty miracles in connection with the exodus of the children of Israel from Egypt to Canaan – the dividing of the Red Sea, the dividing of Jordan? Why does He not choose one of these or other similar events, but instead, the raising of the Lord Jesus from the dead?

The Apostle chooses Christ's resurrection, I believe, because it is an objective demonstration of the power of God. He chooses it also because it is such a perfect analogy of what happens to us spiritually. It also helps to introduce the doctrine of our mystical union with Christ, and to show that when Christ was raised, we were raised with Him, and are seated with Him even now in the heavenly places (2:6). But beyond all that, I believe that he chose it because it is the proof, beyond every other proof, of the fact that every obstacle and hindrance and enemy set in our path shall be overcome. The raising of the Lord Jesus Christ from the dead is proof positive and absolute, that even the 'last enemy' has been conquered and defeated.

The Apostle Peter in the first sermon delivered under the auspices of the Christian Church on the day of Pentecost at Jerusalem says: 'Whom God hath raised up, having loosed the pains of death, because it was not possible that he should be holden of it' (Acts 2:24). We have to realize that in addition to all our own weakness and sinfulness and waywardness, our last enemy is death. We fail to realize the greatness of God's power in us because we have never quite realized the power of death. The Bible bears constant witness to the power of death. Death overcomes all men; no man can escape it, however powerful he may be. As the Apostle says in his Epistle to the Romans: 'death has passed upon all men' (5:12). It is not surprising that the Old Testament writers refer so frequently to it and its terrible power. They trembled and feared as they thought of this power that was there waiting to receive them. Death and the grave were for all.

Furthermore, the power of death and of Hades is the power exercised by Satan himself. That is why the author of the Epistle to the Hebrews glories in the fact that our Lord Jesus Christ came and lived and died in order that 'he might destroy him that had the power of death, that is, the devil, and deliver them who through fear of death were all their lifetime subject to bondage' (Hebrews 2:14-15).

So the Apostle is reminding us that, by raising the Lord Jesus Christ from death and the grave, God has given us this public demonstration and manifestation that the last enemy has been conquered. 'The last enemy that shall be destroyed is death'; but Christ has already conquered death. 'The sting of death is sin, and the strength of sin is the law. But thanks be unto God who giveth us the victory through our Lord Jesus Christ' (1 Corinthians 15:26, 56-57). Death, hell and Satan have been conquered, and we can say triumphantly, 'O death, where is thy sting? O grave, where is thy victory?' (1 Corinthians 15:55).

There is but one conclusion to draw from this. Whatever may be true of our experience, whatever may be true of the world and its darkness, whatever may be true of the seeds of decay and of illness and of death that are in our bodies, and howsoever great is the power of the last enemy, we can be certain and confident of this, that nothing can prevent the carrying out of God's purpose with respect to us. There is no power that can withstand Him; there is no might or influence that can match Him, there is no possible antagonist that can equal Him. The mightiest foes, the devil, death and hell have already been vanquished, and the resurrection of Christ is the proof of it.

We thus have positive proof that there is nothing 'too hard for the Lord', and that 'with God nothing shall be impossible'. So if when we think of the glory and the perfection and the marvel and the wonder of what is awaiting us, and then feel that we are so unworthy and so weak that we have no hope of enjoying it, here is the answer. The God who is working in us will keep us while still here, and make us fit for the future indescribable glory.

It is He who is doing so, not we ourselves. 'With Him nothing is impossible', nothing can finally resist Him. So we must say with Paul; 'I am persuaded, that neither death, nor life, nor angels, nor principalities, nor powers, nor things present, nor things to come, nor height, nor depth, nor any other creature, shall be able to separate us from the love of God, which is in Christ Jesus our Lord' (Romans 8: 38–39), and then sing with Augustus Toplady,

> *The work which His goodness began*
> *The arm of His strength will complete;*
> *His promise is Yea and Amen,*
> *And never was forfeited yet.*
> *Things future, nor things that are now,*
> *Not all things below or above,*
> *Can make Him His purpose forego,*
> *Or sever my soul from His love.*

Do you realize the exceeding greatness of His power in you? Do you realize the energy of the strength of His might that is already working in you? And do you realize that because it has begun it will continue, and continue until you will find yourself 'faultless and blameless, without spot or wrinkle or any such thing' in the presence of God in the glory?

34
'Power to us-ward who Believe'

'And what is the exceeding greatness of his power
to us-ward who believe, according to the working
of his mighty power, which he wrought in Christ,
when he raised him from the dead, and set him at
his own right hand in the heavenly places.'

Ephesians 1:19–20

As we continue our study of this third petition I would remind
you again that it is most important that we should realize that the
Apostle is praying here, not that the Ephesians may have more
power, but that they may come to know the greatness of the
power of God that is already working in them.

First of all, let us be clear in our minds as to what exactly the
Apostle wants us to realize and to experience of this exceeding
great power of God in us. There are those who say that what the
Apostle had in his mind was simply our future resurrection, and
that he was concerned about nothing else. They maintain that he
was more or less saying to them: Very well, I have established the
fact that you are heirs of God, and I have given you a glimpse of
the inheritance to which you are going, and now I want you to
know that not even death itself can rob you of that, because God's
power will enable Him to raise you from the dead, even as He
raised His own Son from the dead. They maintain that that is all,
and that it is exclusively a reference to our resurrection at the last
day and our entry into the eternal glory. But is that so? He
includes that, of course, but I maintain that he is referring not
only to the climactic event at the 'final consummation' but also to
the whole of the Christian life from beginning to end.

There are several ways in which we can establish our contention. In the first place it would seem rather odd, or incongruous,
that the Apostle should be praying with such urgency that the
Ephesians might be confident of the power of God only with
regard to their final resurrection. That does not seem to be a very

appropriate thing to do for people whom he is anxious to encourage in the present. This is substantiated by his use of the expression which in the Authorized Version is translated 'according to' – 'and what is the exceeding greatness of his power to us-ward who believe *according to* the working of his mighty power which he wrought in Christ when he raised him from the dead'. The significance of those two words 'according to' is the key to our interpretation. Do they refer to the 'believing' that has just preceded them, or has Paul, as it were, paused while writing 'to us-ward who believe' and before going on to say, 'according to his mighty power which he wrought in Christ'? What is the meaning of 'according to'? The answer to that question as given in the authoritative Grimm-Thayer Lexicon is that 'according to' really means 'in consequence of' or 'by virtue of', or 'through' or 'on account of', 'from', 'owing to'. Those are the words which they suggest as a better translation than 'according to'. So we might read thus: 'what is the exceeding greatness of his power in us who believe, *in consequence of* [in virtue of] the working of his mighty power, the energy of the strength of his might.' In other words the Apostle is giving an account of how we come to believe. We believe in virtue of His power, we believe in consequence of His power, we believe 'through', 'on account of', 'owing to' His power.

Lest someone might think that we are relying solely upon a lexicon, let me adduce some parallel statements and passages where the same word is used in exactly the same way. Several are to be found in this first chapter of the Epistle, beginning in the fifth verse where we read: 'Having predestinated us unto the adoption of children by Jesus Christ to himself, according to the good pleasure of his will.' That clearly means 'as a consequence of the good pleasure of his own will'. And again in verse 7: 'In whom we have redemption through his blood, the forgiveness of sins, according to the riches of his grace', that is, 'in virtue of', as 'the result of', 'in consequence of' the riches of his grace. Again in verse 9 we find: 'Having made known unto us the mystery of his will, according to his good pleasure which he hath purposed in himself.' In each case the meaning is, 'as the result of', 'in consequence of', 'by virtue of'. The same meaning is found in verse 11: 'In whom also we have obtained an inheritance, being predestinated according to the purpose of him who worketh all things after the counsel of his own will.'

This is such a crucial matter that I do not apologize for seeking further examples and illustrations. Take chapter 3, verse 7 of this Epistle. The Apostle, in referring to the gospel of Christ, says: 'Whereof I was made a minister, according to the gift of the grace of God given unto me by the effectual working of his power.' The Apostle was made a minister 'by virtue of', 'as a consequence of', the gift of the grace of God. That is what produced it, was the cause of it. But take verse 10 in that same chapter where Paul says: 'To the intent that now unto the principalities and powers in heavenly places might be known by the church the manifold wisdom of God, according to the eternal purpose which he purposed in Christ Jesus our Lord.' Then in verse 16 he prays: 'That God would grant you, according to the riches of his grace . . .' Then in verse 20: 'Now unto him that is able to do exceeding abundantly above all that we ask or think, according to the power that worketh in us.' It clearly means 'by virtue of', 'in consequence of'; and it can carry no other meaning there. The same word is used in exactly the same way in all these instances. Take one more further example in the Epistle to the Philippians where the Apostle says: 'For I know that this shall turn to my salvation through your prayer, and the supply of the Spirit of Jesus Christ, according to my earnest expectation and my hope . . .' (1:19).

Perhaps the most striking example of all is that which is found at the end of the third chapter of that same Epistle to the Philippians where Paul says: 'For our conversation is in heaven; from whence also we look for the Saviour, the Lord Jesus Christ: who shall change our vile body, that it may be fashioned like unto his glorious body, according to the working whereby he is able even to subdue all things unto himself.' In that instance 'according to' does not tell us much, but if we read it as 'by virtue of' the working, 'as the result of the working', then the meaning opens out perfectly. Further examples are found in Philippians 4:19; in the first chapter of Colossians, verses 11 and 29; in the Second Epistle to the Thessalonians chapter 1, verse 12; and chapter 2, verse 9; also in 2 Timothy 1:8, Titus 1:3, Hebrews 2:4, 1 Peter 1:3 and 2 Peter 3:15.

I have adduced all this evidence in order to establish this matter beyond any question. The Apostle is dealing here with the Christian life from beginning to end, and saying that we should know the exceeding greatness of God's power to us, from the moment we believe in the Lord Jesus Christ. Our very believing is the result of this power of God. The whole of the Christian life, and not only our resurrection at the end, is the result of God's power in us. We are not Christians at all and cannot be Christians apart from this mighty working of the power of God.

But, of course we need not have based our exposition upon the meaning of words and upon grammar only, for the very passage we are studying makes the meaning quite plain. We have already indicated that the Apostle continues with this same theme into his second chapter. He interrupts himself because, in illustrating this power in terms of God raising our Lord from the dead, he digressed for a moment; but he returns to his theme in chapter 2, verse 1, in these words: 'And you hath he quickened, who were dead in trespasses and sins; wherein in time past ye walked.' Later, in verse 4, he says: 'But God, who is rich in mercy, for his great love wherewith he loved us, even when we were dead in sins, hath quickened us together with Christ.' That is an obvious reference to the manifestation of God's power, So, clearly, the Apostle is not referring to the resurrection that is to come, but to the spiritual resurrection that has already taken place in us. He is talking about us as believers, and we are believers because this power of God has already worked in us in that manner. So from every standpoint – from that of grammar and of language and of context, and everything else – the Apostle is clearly concerned here that we may know the exceeding greatness of this power from the very beginning to the very end of our Christian lives.

But the question now arises as to whether we all live in the light of this truth. I ask the question for the reason that most of us tend to betray what we really believe about these matters in our common talk. There is a very simple way of showing and proving whether we realize this or not. If we really 'know' what the Apostle is praying for, then we will always give the impression that we are surprised at the fact that we are Christians at all! This

will show itself in our praise and in our thanksgiving. It will do
so as a sense of 'wonder, love and praise' and astonishment, and
in our ascribing everything to God and claiming nothing for
ourselves. We shall satisfy the Apostle's requirement when he
says, '. . . he that glorieth, let him glory in the Lord' (1 Corinthians
1:31).

Do we realize that our very believing the Gospel is by virtue of
the power of God that worketh in us? I keep on asking the
question because there is a strong tendency to talk in a superficial
manner about 'believing', as if it were an easy thing which any
man can do if he feels disposed to it. How lightly and glibly many
talk about believing in the Lord Jesus Christ, or about believing
the gospel! There is much talk about our need of power after we
have become Christian, but how rarely does one hear anything
about the need of power before we become Christian! There is
much emphasis on believing and 'decision'; and it is suggested
that anyone who wants to become a Christian can easily accomplish it.

It seems to me that there are two main explanations of this
superficial, indeed false, view of believing. The first is that it is
due to an appalling failure on our part to realize the consequences
of sin and of the Fall of man. We fail to understand the devastating
effect that the fall of Adam has had upon the entire human race.
The second is our failure to realize what is involved in the 'new
birth', or 'regeneration'; we fail to realize the greatness of the
change that is described in those terms, and what is included in
them, and why regeneration is ever necessary. These are the cause
of all glib use of the word 'believe', and the tendency to say that
the natural man is able to believe, but that as a believer he needs
much power.

There is no excuse for this because the biblical teaching concerning the natural man should have kept us from such error.
Such teaching is found in the Old Testament as well as in the
New Testament. 'Can the Ethiopian change his skin, or the
leopard his spots?' (Jeremiah 13:23) That alone should have been
sufficient to prove the point. Then there are the statements which
we have quoted several times because of their cruciality, in
chapters 1 and 2 of Paul's First Epistle to the Corinthians, and
especially verse 14 in chapter 2: 'The natural man receiveth not

the things of the Spirit of God: for they are foolishness unto him: neither can he know them, because they are spiritually discerned.'

The Apostle's teaching is that the fact that anyone at all believes the gospel is a great miracle which can only be explained adequately in terms of the surpassing greatness of the power of God; that it takes the energy of the strength of God's might to bring anyone to believe the Christian gospel and to accept the Christian faith. We believe by virtue of this tremendous power.

To make this still more plain and clear, let us look at some of the things which have to be overcome before any one of us can become a believer. I am not referring to a glib intellectual assent to a number of propositions, but to a true and living faith. Paul equates believing with being born again, as does the Apostle John in his First Epistle. The true believer is a man who is 'born again', not a man who may say 'Yes' today and 'Nay' tomorrow. Why should this power of God be necessary before any man can believe in that true sense? The answer is found by considering some of the effects of the Fall and of sin upon the human race.

Consider in the following way what the Fall has done to the mind of man. Here is a man 'born in sin, and shapen in iniquity', born 'a child of wrath even as others', in a world where the gospel is preached by the Christian Church. What is the relationship of the message to the man? Scripture tells us that his 'understanding is darkened', that his mind is in a state of darkness as the result of sin. This does not merely mean that he is ignorant. He is ignorant, of course, and he does not know the gospel message. But he is not only ignorant in that respect, there is something much worse. Even though you may put the gospel before him, he cannot see it. 'If our gospel be hid, it is hid to them that are lost; in whom the god of this world hath blinded the minds of them that believe not' (2 Corinthians 4:3-4). 'There is a veil over their hearts' (2 Corinthians 3:15), says the Apostle about the unbelieving Jews. That is why Paul has already been praying that the Ephesians might have 'the Spirit of wisdom and revelation in the knowledge of him. Merely to put the gospel before a man is not enough, something must be done in the man. The Spirit is in the Word; but the Spirit must be in the man also, and without this he cannot see the truth. These things 'are spiritually discerned' says Paul to the Corinthians (1 Corinthians 2:14). When man fell, not only was he separated from God, his spiritual faculty itself was paralysed. His mind is dark and dim, his whole understanding is darkened, he lacks the ability and the capacity.

But that is not the end of the story as regards man's mind. He lives in a world where false views are taught and recommended by great names. Such views are loudly advertised; and he as a man of the world, and a child of his age, is entirely prejudiced in their favour. The truth of God is ridiculed, criticized, derided and dismissed. All the prejudice of the life of the world round and about him is against the gospel; and this has a tremendous effect upon the man. We all know of the tendency of the average person to believe what he reads in newspapers, and especially when they give the views of leading people such as philosophers and scientists with respect to the Bible. All this greatly influences the man's mind and his thinking as he is confronted by the gospel. Yet we are given the impression that to believe the gospel is a very simple matter!

But there is something much worse even than this. Consider the state of the natural man's heart. The first thing the Bible tells us about man's heart is that, as the result of the Fall, man is proud. The Apostle Paul constantly uses the word 'boasting', which is often translated as 'glorying' in the Authorized Version. 'God forbid that I should glory' means 'God forbid that I should boast'. There is nothing so characteristic of fallen man as his boasting, his glorying, his pride, and especially his pride of intellect! That is the last citadel. This is not surprising because man's mind is his crowning gift. It is what separates him most of all from the animals – his mind, his reason, his capacity to think and to look objectively at himself. We have the authority of our Lord Himself for saying that the most difficult persons to convince of the truth are the 'wise and the prudent'. He says: 'I thank Thee, O Father, Lord of heaven and earth, because thou hast hid these things from the wise and prudent, and hast revealed them unto babes. Even so, Father: for so it seemed good in thy sight' (Matthew 11:25–26). It is He, again, who says: 'Except ye be converted, and become as little children, ye shall in no wise enter into the kingdom of heaven' (Matthew 18:3). This demand for childlikeness results from pride of intellect. The natural man always has a feeling that to become a Christian means to become a

fool, that the Christian has 'gone soft', has become an emotional-
ist, and has jettisoned his mind and reason and logic. The idea is
that if you still believe this 'old old story' you are not abreast of
the times, you are not a reader, you are not a thinker, you are not
cultured. This attitude works on man's pride, especially his pride
of intellect and of understanding. He does not intend to be
regarded as a fool! He wants to be abreast of the times, and always
'up-to-date'.

We are also told that fallen man's heart is 'hardened'. This
means that man is not only in a state of sin but that he also
delights in it and glories in it. As the Apostle says in Romans 1:32,
'not only do (they) the same (terrible sins), but have pleasure in
them that do them'. But more, 'The wrath of God is revealed from
heaven against all ungodliness and unrighteousness of men, who
hold down the truth in unrighteousness', says the Apostle in
Romans 1:18. They deliberately hold truth down because their
hearts are hardened. If they come under a certain amount of
conviction they try to stifle it and stamp on it, and argue against it.
They even invent arguments against it, they will put up camou-
flage and all kinds of resistance. They resist the force of truth with
might and main.

In the seventeenth chapter of the prophecy of Jeremiah we read
in verse 9: 'The heart is deceitful above all things and desperately
wicked.' This means that man in sin is always fooling himself, and
in a sense he cannot help doing so, because his very heart is
deceitful, twisted and perverted; there is a mechanism in it which
turns man against his own better judgment at times. This explains
the process of rationalizing our sins, and our ability to explain
them away to our own satisfaction. It also explains our efforts to
persuade ourselves that we are better than we really are, and that
if we do a certain amount of good it will somehow balance the
evil we have done. The 'deceitfulness' of the heart makes a person
think that God can be bought by an offering, as the Jews imagined
in the time of Jeremiah. How deceitful, how utterly dishonest are
our hearts! We all 'put on appearances' and know that we are
doing so; and yet we do it.

But according to Jeremiah the heart is not only 'deceitful above
all things', it is also 'desperately wicked'! That statement is true of
the most respectable person that has ever been born; it is true of

persons who may be highly religious. There is an evil principle within us which delights in sin. 'This is the condemnation, that light is come into the world, and men loved darkness rather than light, because their deeds were evil' (John 3:19). Men rejoice in iniquity, they write about it, joke about it, talk to one another about it. They boast about their evil doings, they love them, they gloat over them because their hearts are 'desperately wicked'. Such is a part of the description of the natural unregenerate heart and of man in sin as the result of the Fall. It is to such a person that the Gospel comes with its message about holiness and light and the truth about God. It calls upon him to forsake the world and its sin and to follow Christ 'who knew no sin, neither was guile found in his mouth'. Easy to believe? We can but repeat the stanza in the well-known hymn of Thomas Binney:

> O how can I, whose native sphere
> Is dark, whose mind is dim,
> Before the Ineffable appear,
> And on my naked spirit bear
> The uncreated beam?

But that, alas, is not all. The heart of man, according to the Scriptures, is, as the result of the Fall and of sin, even guilty of hating God. The natural, sinful mind is not content with an intellectual detachment which does not believe the Bible and rejects the revelation about God; it hates God. 'The carnal (natural) mind is enmity against God, and is not subject to the law of God, neither indeed can be' (Romans 8:7). There can be no question about the truth of that assertion. We are all alienated from the life of God, says Paul in the fourth chapter of this Epistle to the Ephesians; and this is so because God is so utterly and entirely different from what we are, and from what we like.

So the position of man in sin is that his spiritual faculty is darkened. His mind is darkened and covered with a veil of sin and unbelief; he is mastered by the mind and the way of the world; his heart is desperately wicked and deceitful, hardened, proud, implacable; but above all he harbours an active hatred of God, a deep-seated enmity against God. How obvious this is in this modern world! How ready men are to believe any theory that claims to explain away the act of Creation; they accept avidly a

mere theory such as that of evolution, which is becoming increasingly discredited on scientific and philosophical grounds.
They do so because all such teaching is against God. This natural
hatred and enmity of man in sin against the Lord God Almighty
is seen not only in the newspapers but even in learned works.
Man is doing his utmost to get rid of God and to explain the
cosmos without Him. He has been doing so, and especially during
the past hundred years, with all his powers.

At the same time man's will is paralysed. There is a defect
even in man's will. Sin has affected the whole of man. Our failure
to appreciate the power of God in our very act of believing is due
to our failure to realize the devastating effect of the Fall. It
marred and defaced God's image in us, with the inevitable
consequences that our minds and wills became defiled.

In the light of all this is it still possible for you to say that fallen
man can easily believe the gospel if he decides to do so? Is such a
person capable of believing it? Surely there is only one answer to
the question; it is contained in the words, 'What is the exceeding
greatness of his power to us-ward who believe by virtue of his
mighty power working in us?' To bring one soul to believe in
God and in Christ demands 'the exceeding greatness of the
strength of God's eternal might'; and without it we are utterly
and completely helpless. 'By the grace of God (and by that alone)
I am what I am' (1 Corinthians 15:10). Why do I believe this
gospel? why am I not today as are so many millions in the world?
Why am I interested in the Bible?, why do I believe it? There is
but one answer. It is by the grace of God, who worketh in me
mightily. He began the work, He will continue with it, He will
finish it; and I shall stand before Him perfect, entire, complete,
and cast my crown before Him, 'lost in wonder, love and praise'.

35
His Power from Beginning to End

'And what is the exceeding greatness of his power
to us-ward who believe, according to the working
of his mighty power, which he wrought in Christ,
when he raised him from the dead, and set him at
his own right hand in the heavenly places.'

Ephesians 1:19

The most urgent practical question for every Christian is this:
Are we aware of the fact that the almighty power of God is
working in us? Do we realize that we are what we are solely and
entirely by the grace and the power of God? Do we realize in our
own personal lives and experiences that it is this exceeding great
power of God that accounts for everything in the Christian life?
I press these questions again because I am convinced that the
main trouble with most of us is our failure to realize the greatness
of the salvation into which we have been brought, and which we
enjoy together. One cannot read the New Testament, and
especially that most lyrical book which we call the Book of the
Acts of the Apostles, and also the Epistles, and notice their
terminology, without realizing that there was a joyful, indeed a
thrilling quality about the first Christians, the New Testament
Christians. This is seen very clearly in the Epistle to the
Philippians which in a sense is a great refrain on the theme of
rejoicing: 'Rejoice in the Lord alway, and again I say, Rejoice'
(4:4).
   Rejoicing is the theme of the whole of the New Testament. The
Christian is meant to be a rejoicing person. And yet, if we are
honest, we have to admit that far too often we give the impression not so much of rejoicing as of depression. We give the
impression that to become a Christian means to carry a great
load upon the shoulders and to have endless cares, worries and
anxieties. Indeed the world caricatures the Christian in that way

because of what we are all too frequently. To 'scorn delights, and live laborious days' is far too often the idea of what the Christian life means and is. This is undoubtedly due to the fact that we have somehow not realized the greatness of our salvation. We do not realize the greatness of what has happened to us; or the greatness of what is happening to us, the process through which we are going even now. And we do not realize the greatness of the perfection to which we are going and for which we are being prepared.

This leads not only to a failure to rejoice but also to an absence of a sense of wonder. One cannot read these Epistles of Paul without feeling constantly that he was amazed at himself. Take a notable statement of his in the Epistle to the Galatians: 'I live, yet not I . . .' (2:20). Paul cannot understand himself; he has become an enigma and a problem to himself. This astonishment at himself is due to his realization of the tremendous thing that God has been doing in him. We should all be likewise amazed at ourselves, and we should stand and look at ourselves and say, 'Is it possible? is it really true of me? Yet not I, but Christ liveth in me'. That is one of the best tests of our profession as Christians.

It is because this element is missing in us that – to borrow the Apostle's language – we do not 'stand out as luminaries, as lights in the world, in the midst of this crooked and perverse generation' (Philippians 2:15). Somehow or another we do not grasp the idea of this mighty working of God in salvation. Far too often we think of it solely in terms of forgiveness. We think of the Christian life as just a matter of knowing that we are forgiven, and then our living the Christian life as best we can. We miss the drama, the grandness and the greatness of it all, and especially this power which the Apostle is anxious for the Ephesians to know. We conceive of the Christian life in terms which do not postulate as an absolute necessity 'the exceeding greatness of the power' of Almighty God. But such is the Christian life.

We seem to miss this conception even when we consider our Lord Himself. We fail to realize the greatness of what happened when He, the Son of God, came on earth. Do we habitually think of that event in terms of the second chapter of the Epistle to the Philippians verses 5–9: 'Let this mind be in you, which was also in Christ Jesus: who, being in the form of God, thought it not robbery to be equal with God: but made himself of no reputation and took upon him the form of a servant, and was made in the likeness of men: and being found in fashion as a man, he humbled himself, and became obedient unto death, even the death of the cross. Wherefore God also hath highly exalted him, and given him a name which is above every name'? That is the measure of salvation and of the power that was involved in Him and His work. We seem to forget that when He died upon the Cross He offered Himself, as we are told in the Epistle to the Hebrews, 'through the eternal Spirit'. We have become so familiar with the facts about the Cross and the death of the Lord that we seem to lose the sense of power that was involved there. And when we come to the resurrection of the Lord Jesus Christ, do we realize that it was the greatest manifestation of the energy of the strength of God's might that the world has ever known. According to the Scriptures nothing but the almighty power of God could have raised Him again from the dead, and exalted Him to the high position where He is at this moment at the right hand of God. We forget that He was 'declared to be the Son of God *with power* by the resurrection from the dead'. We seem to miss this idea of power everywhere in the Christian life. It is a miracle that there is a single Christian in the world or ever has been. By nature not one of us would or could believe the gospel; nothing but the power of God can make us believers.

But it is also by this selfsame power that we continue in the Christian life. It takes the same power which enabled us to believe to enable us to continue at all in the Christian life. We would not be able to stand for a single hour in the Christian life were it not for this power of God that is working in us. This is true in spite of the fact that we have a new principle of life in us, and a new mind and a new outlook. And when we think of the perfection for which we are destined, it should be obvious that apart from this power of God our situation would be utterly hopeless if we had nothing but our own strength and power.

There is no difficulty in showing that what the Apostle teaches here in this Epistle is abundantly confirmed by other statements

[414]

in the Scripture. We do this because this is a matter which is vital to our enjoyment of the Christian life. If we do not know this power, sooner or later we shall be depressed and unhappy, and begin to wonder whether we are Christians at all; and then begin to wonder whether we can continue and ever arrive in the glory. The devil would soon discourage us utterly.

In the third chapter of this Epistle the Apostle says: 'Now unto him that is able to do exceeding abundantly above all that we ask or think, according to the power that worketh in us . . .' (v. 20). Or take a statement in his Second Epistle to the Corinthians. He has been telling these Corinthians in chapter 5: 'For we know that if our earthly house of this tabernacle were dissolved, we have a building of God, an house not made with hands, eternal in the heavens' (v.1). If we should die or if we should be killed, all is well; we know that! Then he proceeds to say: 'He that hath wrought us for the selfsame thing is God' (v. 5). We have been wrought, we have been made, we have been fashioned, we have been formed by God, by the power of God, for this destiny. That is our hope, the thing on which we rest, the basis of our assurance.

Then there is the statement in Paul's Epistle to the Philippians: 'Work out your own salvation with fear and trembling, for it is God that worketh in you both to will and to do of his good pleasure' (Philippians 2:13). In the third chapter of the same Epistle the Apostle tells us that his greatest desire was, 'that I might know him, and the power of his resurrection' (v. 10). He desired to know more and more this same power of God that was manifested in the resurrection of Christ. That self-same power is now working in believers. The Apostle Paul, who had made such strides and advances in the Christian faith, desires to know above everything else the power of His Lord's resurrection. He says, 'not that I have already attained'; but he desires to attain. So he forgets the things that have gone, his initial conversion, his first experience, and presses forward for 'the prize of the high calling of God in Christ Jesus'. That is his prayer for himself and for all other believers.

Again, there is the striking statement of all this in the last chapter of the Epistle to the Hebrews: 'Now the God of peace, that brought again from the dead our Lord Jesus, that great shepherd of the sheep, through the blood of the everlasting covenant, make you perfect in every good work to do his will, working in you that which is well pleasing in his sight' (13:20–21). The One whom he desires to work in those Hebrew Christians is 'the God of peace, that brought again from the dead our Lord Jesus'. It is an exact repetition of what we have here in Ephesians chapter 1, verse 20. He alone can 'make us perfect in every good work'.

But we take a further example from the Apostle Peter. Peter says that as Christians we have been brought again to a lively (living) hope 'by the resurrection of Jesus Christ from the dead, unto an inheritance incorruptible and undefiled, and that fadeth not away, reserved in heaven for you, who are kept by the power of God through faith unto salvation ready to be revealed in the last time' (1 Peter 1:3–5). We are kept by the power of God; and apart from that we could not stand. Peter again in his Second Epistle writes: 'According as his divine power hath given us all things that pertain unto life and godliness' (1:3). His 'divine power' has given them.

The Apostle John in the same manner, writing as an old man at the end of his life, to encourage Christians whom he was leaving behind in this cruel world, and who were somewhat shaken by false teaching, and false living and practices, says: 'Greater is he that is in you, than he that is in the world' (1 John 4:4). It is God's power alone that can hold us, and sustain us until we arrive in the glory.

Then too we can turn to the benediction at the end of the Epistle of Jude: 'Now unto him that is able to keep you from falling, and to present you faultless before the presence of his glory with exceeding joy . . .' And He is not only able to keep us from falling, but He is actually doing so.

But above all, let us turn to the words of our blessed Lord Himself. Under the very shadow of the cross He prays to His Father, and His prayer is this: 'And now I am no more in the world, but these are in the world, and I come to thee. Holy Father, keep through thine own name those whom thou hast given me, that they may be one, even as we are one' (John 17:11). He says: 'I pray not that thou shouldest take them out of the world, but that thou shouldest keep them from the evil one'. His eternal heart of love thinks of this little band of believers whom

He is about to leave in this evil, sinful world, and His petition is:
'Father, keep them', for if the Father does not keep them they are
lost.

Why is this power essential? Why is it so important that we
should know this exceeding great power that is working in us?
There are two main answers, one negative and the other positive.
Firstly, I must know and realize this power because of the power
of the forces that are set against us. The Christian in this life and
world is like his Lord before him; and there are certain things he
has to face. He has to wage a constant warfare against the mind
and the outlook of the world. I fear that many of us are not
aware of the subtle power of worldliness – everything for which
the world stands. Again let me quote the Apostle John: 'Love
not the world, neither the things that are in the world – the lust of
the flesh, and the lust of the eyes, and the pride of life' (1 John 2:
15 and 16).

Nothing is so dangerous to the soul, because of its subtlety, as
the worldliness which meets us at every turn. You start with it in
your newspapers in the morning. They do not confine themselves
to important international or national news, matters of urgency
and of crisis, or threat of war, but constantly in their news and
views they suggest lust and desire and everything that is opposed
to the commandments of God. The same pernicious influence is
found in an endless succession of books and films in a most
seductive and attractive form. Then there is what the Apostle
describes as 'the pride of life', all that is represented by so-called
'society life', pride of ancestry and class, and the external pomp
and show. It is so pleasing, and so enticing to the natural man and
so many nice people participate in it. This is surely the biggest
fight the Christian Church has to wage at this present hour. There
has been a lowering of moral standards everywhere. We have
travelled very far from the days of Puritanism. The line between
the Church and the world is almost invisible, and the people of
God no longer stand out in their uniqueness as they once did.
The New Testament is full of warnings about this subtle,
tremendous power of the world, which would drag us away from
the Christ in whom we believe, which would make us deny Him

[417]

in practice and reduce us to a state described in the words, 'Having a form of godliness, but denying the power thereof' (2 Timothy 3:5).

But we not only have to fight the world but also the flesh. The 'flesh' does not always mean gross sin; it can appear in the form of lethargy and laziness. How easy it is to feel that we are not quite fit physically or intellectually to read the Bible. You feel a prompting to read the Bible, but you say, 'I am rather tired, I have had a heavy day in the office, my mind is not quite up to it, and it is not right to read the Scriptures when you are not at your best; so I will read the newspaper now; later on I will read the Scriptures when I am feeling refreshed and better'. The result is that you go to bed without having read the Scriptures. We have to wage a constant battle against lethargy and laziness, and the equally subtle temptation to procrastination. These are the instruments used by the devil to hinder our progress.

Then there is the fight against physical conditions such as ill health. If you read the lives of the saints you will find that the men who have accomplished most in this world have often been men who have had a great fight with some physical weakness or illness. Count up the number of volumes under the name of John Calvin, for instance. All these Commentaries on the Scriptures, and the other works, were produced by a man who was a martyr throughout his life to asthma and to chronic indigestion, and who died at the age of 55. But we tend to make an excuse of physical weakness. All this shows that, were it not for the power of God, we would never accomplish anything, we would not stand for a moment, we would be undone.

Consider next the force of habits. You have entered upon the Christian life knowing about and experiencing regeneration. You have rejoiced in the statement that 'old things are passed away; behold, all things are become new'. But the Christian convert soon discovers that these things do not mean exactly what he thought they did. It is his understanding that is at fault, encouraged perhaps by a superficial evangelism. He begins to find that there are certain long-standing habits within him which are very difficult to break. Habits tend to persist and the old nature is not annihilated. It is still there and has to be dealt with. We are commanded 'to mortify the deeds of the body' (Romans 8:12).

All evil habits do not suddenly fall away out of your life. God in His grace may, and often does remove some of them, but He leaves others. The force of habit is a terrible power, so great that there is nothing but the power of God that can keep us and preserve us against it. Though we have a new mind, and a new outlook, and desire to live the new life, certain habits tend to hinder us. It is the power of God alone that can enable us to conquer them.

Then there is the devil. I sometimes think that our failure to realize the exceeding greatness of God's power in us is due to the fact that we have never realized the power of the devil. How little do we talk about him; and yet in the New Testament his activities are constantly emphasized! If we but realized something of the power of the devil we would be praying this prayer that Paul offered for the Ephesians, that 'the eyes may be opened to the greatness of God's power' in us. The Bible teaches that the devil's power is second only to that of God. The power of the devil is made terribly clear in the story of Adam and Eve. They were both perfect. Man was made in the image and likeness of God; he was in communion with God, he spoke to God, he knew God. Moreover he was in Paradise – a perfect environment. He had never sinned, and there was nothing within him to drag him down – no lust, no corruption. He had been given an original righteousness; he stood upright and was indeed a reflection of God. And yet he fell; and he did so because of the power and the subtlety of the devil. Yet many Christians regard the devil almost as a creature of fun, and may even deny his existence. Hence they do not realize their need of this power of God. Adam, the perfect man, was defeated and brought down by this powerful foe. Jude tells us in his Epistle that the power of the devil is so great that even the archangel Michael, when he contended with him about the body of Moses, 'durst not bring a railing accusation against him, but said, The Lord rebuke thee' (v. 9). The archangel was aware of the power of the devil. The Apostle Peter writes: 'Your adversary the devil, as a roaring lion, walketh about, seeking whom he may devour' (1 Peter 5:8). Are we conscious of this, as the Apostle Paul was, and as he reminds us in the twelfth verse of the sixth chapter of this Ephesian Epistle, 'We wrestle not against flesh and blood, but against principalities, against powers,

against the rulers of the darkness of this world, against spiritual
wickedness in high places'? Because of these things we need to be
enlightened with respect to the power of God working in us.
Nothing else can enable us to stand against the wiles of the devil.

So far we have been looking at our problem negatively. The
positive side is that we are called upon to keep the commandments
of God. Christ calls us to keep His commandments. We are
meant to honour the Ten Commandments and the Moral Law of
God – 'That the righteousness of the law might be fulfilled in us,
who walk not after the flesh but after the Spirit' (Romans 8:4). We
are called to obey that Moral Law of God; we are called to live
according to the teaching of the Sermon on the Mount; we are
called to take up the cross and to follow Christ in 'the narrow
way', and to live as He lived. Such is our calling. 'Be ye perfect,
even as your Father which is in heaven is perfect.' Chapter 13 of
Paul's First Epistle to the Corinthians is also a picture of what we
are meant to be. We are not simply meant to believe that our sins
are forgiven and then seek a little power from God to live a good
life.

It is when we realize the nature of our high calling that we
begin to understand the seventh chapter of the Epistle to the
Romans: 'To will is present with me, but how to perform that
which is good I know not; for the evil which I would not, that I
do; but the good that I would I do not. O wretched man that I
am' (vv. 18, 24). It is only then we find ourselves singing from
the heart, and not merely with our lips, the hymn of Augustus
Toplady –

> Not the labours of my hands
>   Can fulfil Thy law's demands;
> Could my zeal no respite know,
>   Could my tears for ever flow,
> All for sin could not atone;
>   Thou must save, and Thou alone.

We must understand clearly what the Apostle is praying for the
Ephesians. It is not that they may realize their need of power and
then ask God for it; he prays that they may realize that this power

is in them. The view of the Christian which depicts him as a man who may have lived for years without this power of God, and who suddenly comes to a realization of his need and asks for it, and obtains it, is unscriptural. You cannot be a Christian even for a moment if the power of God does not sustain you.

Let me suggest a parallel. Many people seem to think of the natural creation in these terms. They believe that God created the world at the beginning, and then (to use the old illustration), as a watchmaker with a watch, having made the world He wound it up and then allowed it to go on functioning. But that is not true. According to the Bible's teaching God who made this world is also sustaining it every moment. If God withdrew His power from the world it would collapse immediately; it is the Spirit of God that gives life and being and sustenance, to all things. It is precisely the same in the new creation. It is a complete fallacy to think that God creates a man anew, and then leaves him to himself; and that that man forty or some fifty years later may perhaps realize his need of power and ask for it. He could not have stood for a moment were it not for this power of God which is in him. It is our realization of this that varies; but from the moment God puts His hand upon a man and brings him to the new birth and new life, He continues to exert this power in him.

The way in which His power works in us is stated in Paul's words to the Philippians when he says, 'It is God that worketh in you both to will and to do' (Philippians 2:13). The power of God manifests itself and works in us through the written Word and through the Holy Spirit. He works in my personality, affects my will, and creates desires and longings within me. Suddenly I am aware of a desire to read the Word, or a desire to pray to God. It is the result of the working of God the Holy Spirit generating a prayer, or stimulating me to some other activity. He is constantly stimulating my will and giving me power to act. As Isaac Watts reminds us, 'His power subdues our sins'. He is working in us constantly; His Spirit 'breathes upon the Word' and enlightens our understanding, which in turn moves our hearts and stimulates our wills.

What we need to realize is that God is working, and that sometimes when we do not know it, He is working. Moreover if we ignore His promptings and urgings and leadings, we may suddenly find ourselves being chastised by God. Then we awaken to the fact that we have forgotten Him and our need of His strength and power; and we turn to Him again and begin to pray for forgiveness and strength. That is another aspect of God's working in us. 'It is a fearful thing to fall into the hands of the living God' (Hebrews 10:31). If you are children, says the author of the Epistle to the Hebrews, be prepared for chastisement. If you have the life of God in you, if He has started 'a good work' in you, He will not give it up, He will bring it to perfection. If you will not be led by Him, you will be driven; if you refuse to be enticed and attracted, you will be chastised. God wills our perfecting, and He will stop at nothing less. The work will go on, the power of God will continue to be exercised in us until we are faultless; until we all together have become 'a glorious church, not having spot or wrinkle or any such thing'. He wills that we should be holy and without blemish in His presence.

Is there anything more important for us than to know all this? We are in the hands of God, and He is working in us. He has given us the power to believe, He is working in us now, fashioning us, moulding us, bringing us to perfection. We cannot escape it, we are in His hands and He will go on with the work. Blessed be His name!

Oh that we might know this more and more, and realize the high privilege of our calling, the marvel, the miracle of this new life which is all from God, and which is all by God. My comfort, my consolation, my strength, my assurance, is to know that God is working in me; and that He will never cease to work in me until I stand before Him in glory.

36
'The Church which is His Body'

'And hath put all things under his feet, and gave him to be the head over all things to the church, which is his body, the fulness of him that filleth all in all.'

Ephesians 1:22–23

Having looked at the power of God in general we now come to this further statement concerning it. If you read this passage hurriedly you might well come to the conclusion that from verse 20 to the end of the chapter is a digression. The Apostle is praying that we may know the exceeding greatness of God's power to us-ward who believe, but he seems to be carried away from his theme in describing that power. He says that it is the power which God exercised when He raised Christ from the dead. He then proceeds to describe the position of the Lord Jesus Christ risen from the dead, His exaltation and His power and His relationship to the Church. He seems temporarily to have left his theme, only to return to it in the first verse of the next chapter. But actually, of course, that is not the case. There is a sense in which these verses are a slight digression, but if we examine them closely we shall find that Paul is still dealing with the essential matter he has in hand. He wants us to realize the greatness of the power that is working in us, and to know exactly how it works. That, I suggest, is the matter with which he deals in the last two verses of this chapter. And he does so in terms of the concept, the doctrine, of the Church, as 'the body of Christ'.

Here we are facing one of the great New Testament doctrines – the doctrine of the Christian Church. There is no figure which is used so frequently in order to give us some idea of the doctrine of the Church as this picture or metaphor of the Church as 'the body' of Christ. The Apostle uses it in his Epistles to the Romans and to the Corinthians very explicitly, and by suggestion in other Epistles also. It is not surprising that the Apostle should have prayed so earnestly that we might have the 'Spirit of wisdom and revelation'; nor is it surprising that he repeats the petition and says that we need to have 'the eyes of our understanding enlightened', for this is undoubtedly one of the highest and most sublime doctrines, and therefore one of the most difficult to understand. The Apostle himself in the fifth chapter of this Epistle to the Ephesians refers to this doctrine as a 'great mystery', and a mystery by definition is something that cannot easily be understood. It is only as we are enlightened by the Holy Spirit that we can understand it at all.

The difficult nature of the doctrine, however, must not be made an excuse for not considering it. Many are guilty of this fault and say that they have neither the time nor the ability to study it. But let it be pointed out that these New Testament Epistles were written to men and women like ourselves; indeed they were written to people who lacked most of our advantages. It seems clear that the majority of the members of the Early Church were slaves who had had no kind of education in the modern sense. When the Apostle wrote this letter to them he meant them to read it and to understand it; he meant them to grapple with it. He knew that they could not do so by their natural powers alone, but he knew too that any man who is enlightened by the Holy Spirit is not only anxious to understand, but can understand and realize that it is his duty to do so. There is nothing more discouraging about the modern Church, nothing more culpable, than her failure to grapple with these great New Testament truths. There is much talk today about simplicity, some people saying that 'they cannot be bothered with doctrine'. There is also much emphasis upon singing; but the church is not a place where people are to be entertained, or where people come to sit and listen either to singing or to the accounts of other people's experiences, coupled with a brief, light, comfortable message. If we are to become grown men, if we are to rise to the height of our 'high calling in Christ Jesus', and to be virile Christians in this tragic modern world, then we must face these great and glorious doctrines, and so exercise our minds, our understandings, and all our senses, that we begin to have some dim conception of ourselves in this great setting and context of the body of Christ.

[424]

Let us then begin to consider what the Apostle has to say about the Church. It is clear that the Apostle himself knew the difficulty of conveying this truth. Hence he varies his comparisons and metaphors. The commonest of all his pictures, I repeat, is that of the Church as the body of Christ. But it is not the only picture. We find in the second chapter that he compares the Church to a building. Jesus Christ Himself he says, is 'the chief corner stone' and the apostles and prophets are the foundation. But he also compares the Church to a household, to a family. Believers are members of the 'household of God'. He also compares it to a great empire. Being a prisoner in Rome it naturally seems to have occurred to him that the Christian Church is in many respects like the Roman Empire. There is the great central seat of authority, but she has her people scattered throughout the world, and various officers who govern the Empire. Later in chapter 5 he compares the Church to a bride and says that the relationship between Christ and the Church is similar to that between a bridegroom and his bride. We recall also how our Lord Himself in the fifteenth chapter of John's Gospel compares the Church to a vine and its branches.

All these pictures are designed to enable us to have some understanding of our relationship to the Lord Jesus Christ, and especially in the two verses to which we are now devoting attention, that we may understand how the mighty power that is in Him comes into us, and enables us to live the Christian life and reach assurance that we are going to enjoy the 'purchased possession'. Such is the context of our verses. So we are not to consider the doctrine of the Church in a theoretical or academic or abstract manner. We are interested in it, as we must be in this context, in order that we may see how this 'exceeding great power of God', how 'the energy of the strength of God's might', actually operates in us.

The way to realize the truth about this power, the Apostle tells us, is to realize our relationship to the Lord Jesus Christ; and we can best do so through the picture of the Church as His body. Certain principles emerge at the outset. The first is – and it is a principle common to all the illustrations and metaphors – that we are 'joined' to Christ, that we are 'united' to Christ. Equally clearly the analogy emphasizes that we are united and joined to Christ, not in a mechanical or loose manner, but in an organic and vital manner, in a most subtle manner. This belongs, of course, to the very essence of this doctrine. Consider it in terms of a human body. From one standpoint a body is a collection of a number of parts – fingers, toes, arms, legs, and so on. But the essential truth about the body is that it is not a number of loose parts which are somehow or other attached or joined to one another. The marvel of the body is that all the parts are really one, that they are in an organic, essential and vital unity. To put the point crudely, my fingers are not joined to the palm of my hand loosely, they are not simply tied on; it is a living connection, it is a vital connection, there is a sense in which you cannot tell me exactly where the palm ends and the fingers begin. They are parts one of another; the connection is intimate and organic and vital and living. This is the first essential principle which we must lay hold of if we are truly to grasp the doctrine of the Church. All the pictures and analogies suggest it; but it is particularly clear in this analogy of the body.

We must not press it too far, but it seems to me that we are entitled to say that, as the various parts of my body are developed out of an original cell from which we all begin, in that sense every one of us is truly a member of the Christian Church, and is truly born again, is an off-shoot of Christ, a development out of Christ. We have come out of Him; we are not merely loosely attached to Him. This is vital to the idea of the Church. In his First Epistle to the Corinthians the Apostle tells us that it happens thus: 'For we are all baptized by one Spirit into one body' (12:13). It is a spiritual unity, it is a mystical unity; and it is therefore something which is indissoluble, for it is vital and organic.

Certain subsidiary truths emerge from this. Patently it is a unity which we ourselves cannot bring into being. We are back again at this fundamental principle that all is the result of the action of the power of God. It is the work of the Holy Spirit alone which makes us Christians. To state it in another form, we see that this relationship of the believer to Christ is not something spasmodic; it is not something which may exist today and not exist tomorrow. It is not something which depends upon our concentration or faithfulness. As it is the work of the Spirit, and done by Him in His own way; it is permanent. You cannot pass in and out of the body of Christ. There is no such thing as 'falling from grace' in a final sense. You may backslide, you may be excommunicated from the visible Church; but if you are in the body of Christ, you are in the body of Christ, and you will remain in the body of Christ. The union is organic, vital, spiritual.

The second principle which is particularly emphasized by the Apostle here is that the Lord Jesus Christ is the Head of the Church. He says that God 'hath put all things under his feet, and gave him to be the head over all things to the church which is his body, the fulness of him that filleth all in all'. This is notoriously a difficult statement to expound, and there are many different views with regard to its exact interpretation. Let us start with considerations of which we can be quite certain. Paul says that the Lord Jesus Christ is 'the head of the church', 'the head of the body'. He is not thinking primarily here of authority or government. Of course, it is true that Christ as Head of the Church is the sole authority, and we must recognize no other. There is no head of the Church save the Lord Jesus Christ; and it is of the essence of the reformed position that we assert this truth. We recognize no human being as the Head of the Church; Christ alone is the King and the Head of the Church.

But that is not what the Apostle is emphasizing at this point; he is concerned to say that Christ as the Head of the Church is the source and the centre of the life of the Church. This is made quite clear by the analogy of the body. In the body the head is the source and the centre of power. The body derives its vital energy from the head. Nothing provides a greater proof of the divine inspiration of the Scriptures than the way in which the Apostle Paul and others were led to use this analogy. They did not possess the knowledge we now have of anatomy and physiology; but the analogy is quite perfect in such terms. There is not a part of the body which is not controlled by nerves and the nervous system. The life in every muscle and in every part is conveyed to it by nervous energy and power. And all the nerves ultimately can be traced back to the brain, which is in the head. It is the centre and the source which controls all the nervous energy of the whole body and of every separate part and particle of the system. When the Apostle says that Christ is the Head of the Church he means that He is the Head of the Church in that sense. We have no life apart

[427]

from Him; all the energy and power come from Him. To state it negatively, we can say that we have no independent life as Christians. He is the Vine, we are the branches; branches would never have existed without a vine. All comes from Him. The Apostle John says: 'Of his fulness have all we received, and grace for grace' (John 1:16). The life of the whole body and every individual part comes from the head, and that is what is particularly meant by saying that Christ is the Head of the Church.

Another obvious deduction is, that the same life is found in every single part and portion of the body; and that it is this which gives unity to the body. A man's body is a single unity because of this intimate connection, because of this inter-relationship. No part of the body has an independent existence; all parts are bound together and are made sensitive to one another because of this principle of organic unity. At a time such as this when there is so much talk about the unity of the Church and of a World Church, let us remember that unity conceived of in terms of a mere joining of external organizations is completely unscriptural. To amalgamate a number of denominations cannot produce spiritual unity. There have been many attempts to do so but they have never actually succeeded and never will succeed. But whether they succeed or not in terms of organization, they cannot succeed spiritually. It is the Holy Spirit that makes and constitutes the unity; it is the common life and energy that makes us one. It is this essential living quality in the nervous system, and in the blood which flows through the whole human body, that accounts for the unity of the body. Precisely the same principle obtains in the life of the Christian Church. That a number of people should meet together in a conference and agree to say that for the sake of unity they will no longer emphasize the Virgin Birth, or the Substitutionary theory of the Atonement, or a belief in miracles, or various other doctrines, cannot produce the unity of which the Apostle speaks. The only unity is a unity in the Spirit, a unity which is made by the Spirit, and dictated by the Spirit, and sustained and maintained by the Spirit. And as He is the Spirit of truth, and has revealed that truth as we have it in the New Testament, unity must result from an accepting of that truth, and cannot be produced by any common denominator framed by subtle ecclesiastics.

[428]

Our third deduction is drawn from the statement, 'the church which is his body, the fulness of him that filleth all in all'. These words tell us that Christ fills the body with His own life. We are told in the Scriptures that in the Lord Jesus Christ dwells 'all the fulness of the Godhead bodily' (Colossians 2:9), and here we are told that in the same way, and by the same analogy, the fulness of the Son is in the Church which is His body.

Once more the analogy of the human body is helpful. There is a sense in which every part of my body is full of my life and of me. My life and being are in every part of my body; indeed, the moment I cease to be, every individual member of my body will die. If you sever the main nerve, or the blood supply, for instance, to a finger, it will soon cease to be a part of my body. The whole of my life is in every single part. Such is the astounding statement made here about the Christian Church, and about ourselves as members of the Christian Church. His 'fulness' is in her, in us. The whole life of the vine is in the branch. It is all there, in a sense, while in another sense, of course, it is not all there. But in this organic, vital sense it is all there. So, as Christian people, we must realize that however much we may be conscious of our weakness, and of the strength of sin within us and without, and of the world and the flesh and the devil – we must realize that all the attributes and powers and graces of the Lord Jesus Christ are in us as members of His body. All His life is in us; we are made 'partakers of the divine nature' (2 Peter 1:4). He is the source of all power in us who are the members of His body. He gives us the energy which is necessary for us to play our individual parts.

The body is one, and yet it consists of a number of individual members or parts. As Paul says in 1 Corinthians: 'Ye are the body of Christ, and members in particular' (12:27). In the human body, as he points out, the hand has one function and the foot has another; the nose and eyes and the ears and the various parts of the body all have their individual parts to play. There are 'comely parts' and 'less comely parts', but they are all essential and they all work together to the one common end of the proper functioning of the whole body. But what we have chiefly to remember is that, as members of the mystical body of Christ, and having our individual parts to play, the energy and the power we exercise all comes from Him. He Himself made this quite clear when He said:

'Apart from me ye can do nothing.' We may be very active and busy; but that is not of necessity doing His work. The Apostle Paul warns preachers in particular in the third chapter of his First Epistle to the Corinthians that some people, in putting up a building, use 'wood, hay and stubble' (v. 12). It may have all the appearance of a good building, but when it comes to be tested by fire, it will be entirely burned and destroyed. The work that is of value, the work that lasts, is the work that He, and He alone, enables us to do in His way and using the materials He provides. Without Him we can do nothing; but with Him all things are possible. So we may say with Paul, 'I can do all things through Christ which strengtheneth me' (Philippians 4:13).

All this is implicit in the idea that the Lord Jesus Christ is the Head of the Church; and so as we contemplate life and all its difficulties, and as we are tempted by Satan to feel that all is impossible, and that we cannot go on because we are so weak and the difficulties so baffling, we must remind ourselves of this truth and say: I am a very small and unimportant member, but I am a member of the body of Christ; I am 'in him', and therefore, whatever may be true of me personally, the life of the Head is in me, I am related to that nerve centre, I am in touch with Him, His vital energy is in me. The Apostle prays that the Ephesians, and we with them, may come to understand this. He wants us to have 'the eyes of our understanding enlightened' that we may know 'the exceeding greatness of his power to us-ward that believe'. So we must not think of Christ as some kind of great power-house to which we can occasionally be connected, and sometimes not connected, as if by a switch. We are always 'in him', we are members of His body, He is the Head and we are His members and there is this vital, indissoluble connection between us. As our eyes are opened to this truth we can take fresh courage, and take up our task again and say: In Christ I cannot fail, I must not fail, He will not allow me to fail.

I almost hesitate to mention the next great principle which is taught here in the phrase, 'The church, which is his body, the fulness of him that filleth all in all'. We have just seen that one interpretation of '. . . the fulness of him that filleth all in all' is that His fulness is in the Church, His body. However, I agree with those who say that it also means that there is a sense in which we as the Church are His fulness. But let us be clear as to what this means. The Lord Jesus Christ as the eternal Son of God is eternally self-sufficient and independent and has no need of us. But when we think of the Lord Jesus Christ as the Mediator, as the God-Man, as the One who has come to achieve redemption and to present His people to His Father, then in that sense He is joined to the body and needs it. A head alone is not complete. A head needs a body, and you cannot think of a head without a body. So the body and the head are one in this mystical sense. As such we Christian people are a part of 'the fulness' of the Lord Jesus Christ.

This is the amazing New Testament conception of the Church, and since the Lord Jesus Christ ascended and returned to heaven, this body of His, the Church, is being perfected. Think of a new-born babe. In a sense the child is perfect; but it can grow and develop, and it will attain to a certain maturity. The same is true of the Christian Church. From the Ascension to the Second Advent the body of Christ has been growing and developing; and there is a day coming when she will be complete and perfect. Then the 'fulness' of the Gentiles will have come in, and the fulness of Israel will also have been saved. Then the body will be complete and entire and will have attained its fulness. So I must learn to think of myself, humble unworthy insignificant Christian as I am, as someone who is essential and vital to the 'fulness' of the mystical body of Christ. What an idea! To the extent to which we grasp this idea we shall receive strength not to sin. It will enable us to see sin in a new light. A member of this mystical body continuing in sin? Impossible! There is no way which leads so directly to holiness and sanctification as the understanding of this New Testament doctrine of the Church as the body of Christ. We are a part of 'his fulness', of His mystical completeness as the Mediator, as the One given to the Church by God to be its Head.

But let us proceed to certain conclusions. One of the most glorious is that in view of the fact that the Church is the body of Christ, and that He is the Head, we are entitled to say that what is true of Him is true of us. The clearest exposition of this is found

in the fifth and sixth chapters of Paul's Epistle to the Romans. As
we were all 'in Adam', so all we who believe in Him are now 'in
Christ'. Adam sinned and we all sinned with him. We were all in
Adam as it were, in the loins of Adam, and when he acted he
acted for us all as our head and representative. We are responsible
for Adam's sin; that is, original sin. But we must look at the other
side. We are now 'in Christ'; He is the Head of the body of which
we are the parts. Whatever the Head does the whole body does
also. So we have been 'crucified with Christ'. When He was
crucified I was crucified; my old man, the man I was in Adam,
was crucified. I, the man that was born in sin, have died with
Christ. In that sense I am as dead as He was. I am 'dead to sin',
I am 'dead to the law'. I have finished with both. Crucified with
Him, dead with Him, buried with Him! But, glorious fact, the
thing the Apostle emphasizes is that I am also risen with Him.
Even as the power of God raised Christ from the dead, He also
raised me with Him. The Apostle argues in the Epistle to the
Colossians: 'If ye then be risen with Christ . . . set your affection
on things above, not on things on the earth' (3:1). In Romans 6:11
he states it thus: 'Reckon ye also yourselves to be dead indeed
unto sin, but alive unto God.'

All this follows inevitably from the truth concerning the Church
as the body of Christ. In the second chapter of this Epistle to the
Ephesians the Apostle actually tells us that we are already 'seated
in the heavenly places' with the Lord Jesus Christ – 'Even when
we were dead in sins he hath quickened us together with Christ
(by grace ye are saved), and hath raised us up together and made
us sit together in the heavenly places in Christ Jesus' (vv. 5–6).
We are there already because of our mystical union with Him.
Because He is the Head, and we are the body, what is true of Him
is true of us. Do you believe this truth? Are you living in the
holy consciousness of it? Is this to you the most exhilarating
thought you have ever met? It is true. This is not mere theory,
it is fact. We are already 'in Christ' in all these respects. We have
finished with the law that condemns. We have finished with the
death that finally leads to perdition, the 'second death' so-called.
We have no relationship to it because we are in Christ, risen with
Him, and seated in the heavenly places with Him.

That brings us to a final thought. Many Christians are often perplexed and in difficulty with regard to the exact relationship of the Lord's working in us and our working. They are confused about the doctrine of 'abiding in Christ', and it has generally been represented as something entirely passive, and in terms of 'Let go and let God'. I suggest that this analogy, this metaphor of the Church as the body of Christ, should save us from such confusion and enable us to see the relationship between His working and our working. Paul's statement in the second chapter of his Epistle to the Philippians states it clearly: 'Work out your own salvation with fear and trembling, for it is God that worketh in you both to will and to do' (v. 13). This cannot possibly mean, that if we want to have victory in our life we must cease to work; the mistake we make is that we do too much, we are too active. We must do nothing but look to the Lord, He will do it for us! Such is the theory! But Paul issues a specific command telling us that we must work, and must do so 'with fear and trembling'. He also adds: 'For (because) it is God that worketh in you both to will and to do.'

How can we reconcile the two statements? Let us return to the illustration of the human body. Think of a muscle, or a group of muscles in a man's arm. In every muscle there is life and power, supplied, as we have already seen, by the nerve that goes to it. It comes originally from a centre in the brain from which the nerve which goes to that muscle derives its power and strength. The muscle is not isolated, it cannot do anything in and of itself; but it is alive because it is receiving energy and life from the brain through the nerve. In its normal state it is relaxed and flabby. In that state it can achieve little, if anything; it cannot enable you to lift weights, for instance. Before that muscle or group of muscles can be of value or help to us they must be exercised and developed. If we fail to exercise and develop them and simply wait for some sudden great accession of power, we shall be sadly disappointed. To develop a muscle we must exercise it. And the more we exercise the muscle, the greater will be the energy and the power supplied to it. These two things work together at the same time. We must not say that it is all from the brain, or that it is all in the muscle; the muscle makes use of the power that it receives from the brain through the nerve. The brain acts through the developed muscle.

[433]

This illustrates a vital truth about our Christian life and warfare, about our development, about our growth in holiness and in sanctification. The two extreme schools of thought are patently quite wrong in their teachings and conclusions. Those who maintain that believers do everything in the Christian life are wrong; and those who say that believers have nothing to do but just 'look to Christ' and 'wait for Him to do it' are equally wrong. Because the Church is the body of Christ, and every single part and portion is vitally connected to Him as the life of all, every Christian has this power in him. But we must exercise the power; and as we exercise the power, we shall inevitably receive more power. If therefore you are conscious of failure and constant defeat, do not pray only that you may have strength and power; 'resist the devil' and 'mortify your members which are on the earth'. Do not expect the Lord Jesus Christ to take your lusts and passions out of you; do not expect Him to do all for you while you simply 'abide' in Him. Exercise the power that is in you. As a Christian the life of Christ is in you; realize this, and begin to use it and to exercise it. Make use of your spiritual muscles, mortify the members of your body which have been used as instruments of sin; do all you can with all your might; and as you are doing so, increased power and energy will flow into you.

What is true of the physiology of the body is equally true spiritually. The way to receive more power is to use and exercise the power you have. As a Christian you are not lifeless, you are connected to the Head. The spiritual nervous power is there in Him. You say, 'My muscles are flabby', and I reply, 'Exercise them'. Similarly do not wait for a sudden blessing of sanctification, do all you can, and the blessing will come. You will be conscious of greater power, and the Lord will reveal Himself to you in the power and the wonder of His might.

Let us never forget that 'the energy of the strength of God's power' is in us because of our relationship to the Lord Jesus Christ who is the Head of the body, of which we are parts. There is no excuse for sin, there is no excuse for failure; the energy is there, and I must use it, I must exercise my faculties, and I shall then find that there is infinitely more energy available. I shall go on 'from strength to strength', 'from glory to glory', until eventually I, with all other Christians, attain unto that perfect man, unto the measure of the stature of the fulness of Christ. May God, by the Holy Spirit so enlighten 'the eyes of our understanding' that we may know that we are members of His body!

37
The Final Consummation

'And what is the exceeding greatness of his power to us-ward who believe, according to the working of his mighty power, which he wrought in Christ, when he raised him from the dead, and set him at his own right hand in the heavenly places, far above all principality and power, and might, and dominion, and every name that is named, not only in this world, but also in that which is to come: and hath put all things under his feet, and gave him to be the head over all things to the church, which is his body, the fulness of him that filleth all in all.'

Ephesians 1:19–23

We bring to a conclusion our study of the message of this noble and moving statement, and indeed this chapter, which is in many ways the greatest which the Apostle Paul ever wrote. He prays without ceasing that these Ephesians might know the 'exceeding great power of God, the energy of the strength of God's might' which is working in them. He prays thus urgently because there is nothing which is so strengthening to faith, nothing which so enables us to continue in the Christian life and warfare, as a realization of these things.

The way to enjoy a rich experience in the Christian life, as I understand the New Testament, is to grasp the New Testament teaching, the New Testament truth. In other words, the way to a rich subjective experience is, in the first instance, a clearer objective understanding of truth. People who neglect doctrine rarely have great experiences. The high road to experience is truth, and to concentrate on experience alone is generally to live a Christian life which is 'bound in shallows and in miseries'.

The Apostle Paul's final word is that we are to know the exceeding greatness of God's power towards us as believers. We must realize that the energy we need comes to us from and through Christ the Head of the body, and that all the aids we need are in Christ, and that God has placed them in Him and treasured them up in Him. Above all else, therefore, we must know the truth concerning Him. So we find that the Apostle closes on the note of the glory and the pre-eminence of Christ. We have already seen how the Apostle keeps on repeating the blessed Name as he leads us through the chapter. He starts with Him. What is Paul? He is 'an apostle of Jesus Christ'. Then he proceeds to, 'Blessed be the God and Father of our Lord Jesus Christ'. How he rejoiced in and gloried in the Name that is above every other name! May we learn to do the same as we proceed to consider what the Apostle tells us.

Let us first look at the actual description. The Apostle tells us that if we are to understand this power which is working in us we must see it as it is illustrated in what God has done in Christ, in the power 'which he wrought in Christ, when he raised him from the dead'. What a display of power that was! When all the forces of evil and of hell, when death and the grave were trying to hold Him, He was raised by the mighty power of God. Death could not hold Him, the grave could not retain Him. 'He burst asunder the bands of death.' He rose triumphant over the grave. But it did not stop at that! The Apostle says not only that God 'raised him from the dead' but also that He 'set him at his own right hand in the heavenly places'. And our blessed Lord is there at this moment. To be set at a host's right hand in any function is always a mark of honour, and sometimes a mark of authority. This is so at a dinner, or banquet or any important civic or social occasion. And this is the place of honour given to the Lord Jesus Christ by His Father. 'The highest place which heaven affords is His, and His by right.' The right hand is always the place of authority, and the Apostle assures us that God has raised His Son from the dead and has placed Him in a position of authority. We have a similar statement, parallel to this, in the second chapter of the Epistle to the Philippians: 'Wherefore God also hath highly exalted him, and given him a name that is above every name' (Philippians 2:9). No higher position, no greater honour could have been given to our Lord Jesus Christ.

[437]

But still the Apostle has not finished. He continues with his description of the glory and honour given to the Son. God has 'set him at his own right hand in the heavenlies, far above all principality and power and dominion and every name that is named, not only in this world but also in that which is to come'. The learned commentators, as is their way, when they come to this passage, spend much time in trying to work out to whom these terms 'power' and 'principality' and 'dominion' refer. Was the Apostle thinking of evil angels or of good angels? That is the question which they discuss. What is surely quite clear is that Christ has been placed in a position of authority and honour which is above all powers. There are evil powers which have exercised dominion in this world – 'We wrestle not against flesh and blood, but against principalities, against powers, against the rulers of the darkness of this world, against spiritual wickedness in the heavenlies' (Ephesians 6:12). The world is as it is today because of these principalities and powers, these unseen spiritual forces. But the Son of God is far above them all. He is greater than they in might and dignity and majesty and position.

But I maintain that the Apostle refers not only to such powers but also to the good angels, the blessed angels. He has been set above them all. A perfect description of this is found in the first chapter of the Epistle to the Hebrews, where the author describes something of the greatness of the angels and their power, and then ends by saying that, after all, they are but 'ministering spirits' (v. 14). They are not equal to the Son; they lack His uniqueness. God has not said to any of them, 'Thou art my Son, this day have I begotten thee' (Hebrews 1:5). Such language is reserved only for His own Son. I suggest, therefore, that the Apostle is telling us that the Son of God, our Lord Jesus Christ, is elevated and exalted even above the archangels Gabriel and Michael, the special servants of God. He is above them all, He is at God's right hand, sharing the throne with His Father, far above all principality and might and dominion and power. Such is the measure of the power of God as displayed in the Lord Jesus Christ. The Father not only raised Him from death and the grave but He has elevated Him and placed Him in the place of supreme honour and authority at His own right hand.

But Paul adds to this again, and says: 'He has put all things under his feet.' Every thing is in subjection to the Lord Jesus Christ. He is master over every one of them. Or to look at it more positively: 'and gave him to be the head over all things.' God has made His Son the Controller of all things, including the material universe. He 'wings an angel, guides a sparrow'. When God made the world He did not make it, as some have taught, as a watchmaker makes a watch, and winds it up and leaves it. The universe is sustained actively by God, and He has handed that authority over to the Son. He is the Controller, the Head over all things. He controls 'the stars in their courses', the ocean in its movement, the wind and the rain, the hurricane and the storm, the sunshine, everything. All life is in His hands, He is 'the head over all things'.

But this applies not only to the material universe, but also to the moral universe and the spiritual universe. God has made Him the Head of all; He has given Him this dignity. The Creator of the Universe, the Artificer, the Controller of the cosmos, has given to the Son to be in control of everything everywhere.

It is most important that we should realize certain related truths, in particular with respect to this description of the glory of Christ. First, we must realize that Christ's honours are already His. There are many who are so anxious to emphasize the glory of the coming visible manifestation of the kingdom and reign of Christ that they become guilty, though unconsciously so, of detracting from what is already true of Him. They spend so much time in looking to the future that they forget the present, and completely underestimate the present position of the Lord and His people. Their attitude is that we have nothing to do but to wait for the coming glory and live as best we can in the present in the light of that hope. We have already emphasized the glory that is coming, the blessed hope on which we should 'set our affection'; but we must not do so at the expense of failing to realize what is true at this moment. God has already done these things in Christ. He has raised Him from the dead, He has set Him at His own right hand in the heavenly places far above other powers, He has put all things under His feet, and He has given Him to be the Head over all things. It is because we so often forget this, that we are so fearful and alarmed and terrified, and begin to harbour fears that the kingdom of Christ is perhaps going to be defeated in this world. We are like Uzzah the man who put his hand upon the ark of God to steady it on a certain cart long, long ago! (2 Samuel 6:6-8). The Lord Jesus Christ Himself has already given the answer to all such fears and forebodings by saying, 'All power is given unto me in heaven and in earth' (Matthew 28:18). It had already been given to Him when He gave His commission to His disciples to go out to preach and to disciple the nations. He claimed that He had that authority and power and that He would be with them to the end of the age. He had the power then, and He has it at this moment. He is controlling history. It was 'a Lamb as it had been slain' that was alone strong enough to take the book sealed with seven seals, which John saw in his vision, and tear off the seals and open the scroll of history (Revelation 5: 1-6). The Lord Jesus Christ is the Lord of history; He is already the Lord of history. He is not outside history; history is not working itself out apart from Him; He controls it at this moment. It is in His hands and He is unfolding it. Paul tells the Corinthians: 'For he must reign until he hath put all enemies under his feet' (1 Corinthians 15:25). Do not allow thoughts about the coming visible manifestation of the kingdom to rob you of the realization of the fact that the Lord Jesus Christ is reigning *now*. He is glorified, the crown is upon His brow; He is the King at this moment. He will come in visible manner; but He is King now, as certainly as He will be then. May 'the eyes of our understanding be enlightened' that we may know this.

The author of the Epistle to the Hebrews gives expression to this glorious truth in these words: 'Thou hast put all things in subjection under his feet. For in that he put all in subjection under him, he left nothing that is not put under him. But now we see not yet all things put under him. But we see Jesus, who was made a little lower than the angels for the suffering of death, crowned with glory and honour' (2:8-9).

This glory and honour have been given to Him, because of what He did while here on earth. In the second chapter of the Epistle to the Philippians this is made very clear by the Apostle's use of the word *Wherefore* in verse 9. It is because Christ counted it not robbery to be equal with God, but emptied Himself and came down and humbled Himself, even to the death of the Cross, that 'God hath also highly exalted him'. It is because He so

[440]

humbled and abased Himself and suffered so much to redeem us, and rescue us, that God has set Him at His own right hand.

But let me repeat that the most precious aspect of this statement is that all this honour and dignity has been given to Him as the Mediator, as the God-Man. He is at the right hand of God not only as the eternal Son. As the eternal Son He was there before the foundation of the world, He was there from eternity. He was one with the Father, co-equal, co-eternal. He always shared the glory with the Father. But here we read that God has raised Him and exalted Him to His throne. The two statements are reconciled by the fact that the Apostle is writing about Christ here as the Son of Man, as the God-Man. Think again of Paul's words to the Philippians: 'Wherefore God also hath highly exalted him, and given him a name which is above every name, that at the name of Jesus every knee should bow' (2:9–10). He does not say, at the name of the Lord, but 'at the name of Jesus'. It is as 'Jesus', as 'the Son of Man', that He has been exalted. This means that human nature has been raised to that surpassing height of glory.

The Apostle's purpose here, as we have continued to emphasize, is a very practical one. His Epistle is not a theoretical disquisition. He is anxious to help the Christians, and he tells them that they must realize that the power which is in them is to be measured by the fact that God has taken human nature in Jesus and has raised it in Him and with Him to the right hand of God; and it is there now with all authority and power. What a staggering thought! The One who is at the right hand of God, far above all principality and power and might and dominion, the One under whose feet all things are in subjection, and to whom all power and authority have been given, is the One who once was a Babe, lying helplessly in a manger in Bethlehem! He is the little boy aged twelve who was found arguing with the doctors of the law in the temple. He is the carpenter of Nazareth. He is the young man who began to preach at the age of thirty. He is the One who knew what it was to be weak and tired and who once sat down by the side of a well about mid-day because He was weary and not able to accompany His disciples when they went to buy provisions. He is the One who slept from sheer fatigue in a boat. He is the One who was crucified through weakness, and apparently defeated by cruel men and their machinations. It is He, Jesus, who has thus been raised! This is the way to measure the exceeding greatness of God's power. When He became man, when He took our human nature, He was made like unto His brethren. He became subject to temptation, subject to the frailties of our flesh; and in Him that human nature has now been raised to the heights and is at God's right hand. Such is the measure of the power of God.

And He is at the Father's side,
The Man of Love, the Crucified.

Again, we must emphasize that God has given all this power and honour and dignity to Him for the Church. How is it that we Christian people can remain so silent? why is it that we are not 'lost in wonder, love and praise'? 'God has raised him from the dead, and has set him at his own right hand . . . and has put all things under his feet, and has made him to be head over all things to the church.' It means 'for the sake of the church', that He might exercise His authority and power in the interests of the Church, in order that He might finally redeem His people and present them faultless to God. Not for His own sake alone, not only that He might participate in the full glory of His Father again, not only that He might exercise this great power over the cosmos and enjoy it; but for our sakes, 'for the church which is his body'!

What does this mean to us and for us? We can answer in a number of simple statements. Because of the doctrine of the Church as the body of Christ, because I am in Him and a member of His mystical body – I am almost afraid to say it, but it is the truth! – what is true of Him is true of me, and is true of all of us who are Christians. God has given it all to Him for the sake of 'the church which is his body, the fulness of him that filleth all in all'.

O! the privilege of being a Christian. O! the honour of being a Christian! We see great people in the world vying with one another for some mark or title of honour, for some high position, or to be near some notable personality. They are prepared to pay great sums of money for such honour and to make great sacrifices for it. Yet all Christians, whoever they are, and however unimportant they may be in the world, because they are 'in Christ', are, without exception, sharing our Lord's exalted position in glory. This is actually true of us now, as the Apostle tells us in his second chapter – 'And hath raised us up together and made us sit together in heavenly places in Christ Jesus' (v. 6). You cannot separate the head from the body, or the trunk from the body, so what is true of the head is true of the whole body. Just as our Head is in glory, so His body is there – mystically, spiritually!

The Apostle is not content that the Ephesians should grasp that this is true of them positionally while yet in this world; it is yet to be true of them absolutely and in fact. This is shown clearly in the Epistle to the Hebrews, where Christians are described as 'heirs of salvation' (1:14). The writer then continues: 'For unto the angels hath he not put in subjection the world to come, of which we speak' (2:5). The heirs of that realm are not the angels, but those who are God's children, which is demonstrated by a quotation from the eighth Psalm: 'What is man, that thou art mindful of him? and the son of man that thou visitest him? Thou madest him a little lower than the angels; thou crownedst him with glory and honour, and didst set him over the works of thy hands: thou hast put all things in subjection under his feet. For in that he put all in subjection under him, he left nothing that is not put under him. But now we see not yet all things put under him' (2:7–8)'. It is not yet true of man that 'all things are put under him', but it will be! We are told that because we can say with certainty, 'But we see Jesus . . . crowned with glory and honour' (verse 9), and because we are 'in him', this dignity is yet to be true of us.

In a similar way Paul in his First Epistle to the Corinthians says: 'Know ye not that the saints shall judge the world . . . and angels?' (chapter 6; 2–3). Our Lord Himself has said that just as His Father has given Him to share His throne with Him, so we as overcomers, also, are to share Christ's throne with Christ (Revelation 3:21). We shall be 'lords of creation' in the full sense. We shall reign with Christ. We shall share His supremacy. As we are members of His body, nothing can prevent this from happening.

But even in the present our position is wonderful. The Apostle again in that First Epistle to the Corinthians, after rebuking his readers for boasting of Paul, Apollos, Cephas, or any other name, writes: 'All things are yours; whether Paul, or Apollos, or Cephas, or the world, or life, or death, or things present, or things to come, all are yours, and ye are Christ's; and Christ is God's' (3:21–23). And this is true of us also because of our relationship to Christ.

We must say a word also about the safety of our position. 'Ye fearful saints, fresh courage take,' says a hymn. Another hymn supplies the grounds on which that exhortation can be made:

> *Commit thou all thy griefs*
> *And ways into His hands,*
> *To His sure truth and tender care,*
> *Who heaven and earth commands:*
> *Who points the clouds their course,*
> *Whom winds and seas obey;*
> *He shall direct thy wandering feet,*
> *He shall prepare thy way.*

When you feel your weakness and ineptitude, and as you are conscious of the forces that are set against you, remember that He, the Head of the body to which you belong, is at the right hand of God, that all authority and power is in His hands, controlling the universe and the cosmos, that He is Head over all things. He can direct everything, the wind and the storm, the rain and the sunshine; He can order all things, and is doing so – for you!

That, in turn, leads me to say a word about the mystery of our position. 'If you say', says someone, 'that all this is true, and that I am related to Christ in that way, why is it that I ever have to suffer, why is it that I am ever taken ill, why is it that calamities ever visit me, why is it that my crops are ever ruined by storms? Why should anyone dear to me die, why is it that I am not enjoying a perfect life without any problems?' The answer is supplied by the mystery of our position in Him. We do not understand it fully, but we know that our trials are a part of the process of our sanctification. 'Whom the Lord loveth he chasteneth' (Hebrews 12:6). It is not that He is unable to prevent these things from happening; He chooses not to do so; it would be bad

[444]

for us were He to do so. Because of the effects of sin and its operations within us, He has to chastise us; He knows what is best for us. There are times when we need the sunshine, there are times when we benefit by the storm. The Psalmist can say: 'Before I was afflicted I went astray', 'It is good for me that I have been afflicted' (Psalm 119:67, 71).

Many a Christian looking back across life has thanked God for a loss, for illness, for sorrow; these troubles helped in the nurture of his soul and his spiritual development. God knows best what is good for us; His heart is love, and we are in His hands. What we must always remember is that nothing can happen to us apart from Him, and that 'all things work together for good to them that love God'. God is concerned about our holiness, about our ultimate eternal happiness; and He orders all things for our good. Let us rest in His love and in the power of His might.

In the light of this elevated doctrine, our final position is certain and sure. The final security and perseverance of the saints is beyond doubt because we are members of Christ's body, and He is at the right hand of God in the place of absolute authority and might and dominion. Nothing can be more certain than this: 'He must reign till he hath put all enemies under his feet' (1 Corinthians 15:25). Nothing can thwart Him for He is the Master of all. He defeated the devil while He was here on earth; He routed him upon the cross. The devil is under control, and he will be cast into the lake of final perdition. As certainly as the Lord Jesus Christ rose from the grave, we shall rise from the grave. And we shall rise without corruption; we shall be faultless and blameless. The fact that the Head has risen is a guarantee that the body must rise. We have already risen spiritually; we shall soon rise physically, materially, bodily. Nothing can prevent this. With Paul we can say 'I am persuaded, that neither death nor life, nor angels, nor principalities, nor powers, nor things present, nor things to come, nor height, nor depth, nor any other creature, shall be able to separate us from the love of God, which is in Christ Jesus our Lord' (Romans 8:38–39). He is above all created powers, far above them all. He is the Head of the universe, and I belong to Him. Neither devil nor hell, nor force, nor might, can ever pluck me out of His hands. In Him we are safe, we are secure; our final destiny is assured and certain.

Christian people, do you know these things? Do you live in the light of them and in the strength of them? Do you now understand why Paul prayed for these Ephesians, and all others who were to receive this circular letter, with such constancy and persistence? He prays that 'the eyes of their understanding may be enlightened'. He desires that they should know 'the hope of their calling', that they might be sure of it. They must also know something of 'the exceeding riches of God's grace' and of His 'inheritance in the saints'. Have you tasted the firstfruits? Have you enjoyed the foretaste? Are you disappointed because I have said so little about politics or social conditions or modern art and drama and culture? Do you think only of this 'present evil world', or do you know something about the next? Have you had glimpses of the world to come, and have you longed for more? Have you tasted of the harvest that is coming? Has it ravished your heart and stimulated your appetite? Are these things real to you? Feeble defeated saint, do you know that all this power of God is in you? It is there because you are 'in Christ' and His life is flowing into you. Realize it. Believe it. Trust to it. Act upon it. And it will come to you with still greater force. Let us offer the Apostle's prayer for ourselves: 'the eyes of your understanding being enlightened, that ye may know what is the hope of his calling, and what the riches of the glory of his inheritance in the saints, and what is the exceeding greatness of his power to us-ward who believe, according to the working of his mighty power which he wrought in Christ when he raised him from the dead, and set him at his own right hand in the heavenlies, far above all principality and power and might and dominion, and every name that is named, not only in this world but also in that which is to come; and hath put all things under his feet, and gave him to be the head over all things to the church, which is his body, the fulness of him that filleth all in all.' May God by His Spirit open our eyes to these things, that we may realize the greatness of our inheritance, and dwell upon it until we can say confidently with the Apostle: 'Our light affliction, which is but for a moment, worketh for us a far more exceeding and eternal weight of glory' (2 Corinthians 4:17).

> *Here in the body pent,*
> *Absent from Him I roam,*
> *Yet nightly pitch my moving tent*
> *A day's march nearer home.*

'To be with Christ . . . is far better!'